T0206360

Lecture Notes in Computer Science 14562

The series Lecture Notes in Computer Science (LNCS), including its subseries Lecture Notes in Artificial Intelligence (LNAI) and Lecture Notes in Bioinformatics (LNBI), has established itself as a medium for the publication of new developments in computer science and information technology research, teaching, and education.

LNCS enjoys close cooperation with the computer science R & D community, the series counts many renowned academics among its volume editors and paper authors, and collaborates with prestigious societies. Its mission is to serve this international community by providing an invaluable service, mainly focused on the publication of conference and workshop proceedings and postproceedings. LNCS commenced publication in 1973.

Hwajeong Seo · Suhri Kim
Editors

Information Security and Cryptology – ICISC 2023

26th International Conference
on Information Security and Cryptology, ICISC 2023
Seoul, South Korea, November 29 – December 1, 2023
Revised Selected Papers, Part II

 Springer

Editors
Hwajeong Seo 🆔
Hansung University
Seoul, Korea (Republic of)

Suhri Kim 🆔
Sungshin Women's University
Seoul, Korea (Republic of)

ISSN 0302-9743   ISSN 1611-3349 (electronic)
Lecture Notes in Computer Science
ISBN 978-981-97-1237-3   ISBN 978-981-97-1238-0 (eBook)
https://doi.org/10.1007/978-981-97-1238-0

This Springer imprint is published by the registered company Springer Nature Singapore Pte Ltd.
The registered company address is: 152 Beach Road, #21-01/04 Gateway East, Singapore 189721, Singapore

Paper in this product is recyclable.

Preface

The 26th International Conference on Information Security and Cryptology (ICISC 2023) was held from November 29 – December 1, 2023. This year's conference was hosted by the KIISC (Korea Institute of Information Security and Cryptology).

The aim of this conference is to provide an international forum for the latest results of research, development, and applications within the field of information security and cryptology. This year, we received 78 submissions and were able to accept 31 papers at the conference. The challenging review and selection processes were successfully conducted by program committee (PC) members and external reviewers via the EasyChair review system. For transparency, it is worth noting that each paper underwent a double-blind review by at least three PC members. For the LNCS post-proceeding, the authors of selected papers had a few weeks to prepare their final versions, based on the comments received from the reviewers.

The conference featured three invited talks, given by Rei Ueno, Tung Chou, and Anubhab Baksi. We thank the invited speakers for their kind acceptances and stimulating presentations. We would like to thank all authors who have submitted their papers to ICISC 2023, as well as all PC members. It is a truly wonderful experience to work with such talented and hardworking researchers. We also appreciate the external reviewers for assisting the PC members. Finally, we would like to thank all attendees for their active participation and the organizing members who successfully managed this conference. We look forward to seeing you again at next year's ICISC.

November 2023   Hwajeong Seo
                                                                             Suhri Kim

Organization

General Chair

Yoojae Won   Chungnam National University, South Korea

Organizing Chairs

Young-Ho Park	Sejong Cyber University, South Korea
Junbeom Hur	Korea University, South Korea

Organizing Committee

Daewan Han	National Security Research Institute, South Korea
Hyun-O Kwon	Korea Internet & Security Agency, South Korea
Jeong Nyeo Kim	Electronics and Telecommunications Research Institute, South Korea
Jungsuk Song	Korea Institute of Science and Technology Information, South Korea
Kihyo Nam	UMLogics, South Korea
Jonghwan Park	Sangmyung University, South Korea
Jongsung Kim	Kookmin University, South Korea
Youngjoo Shin	Korea University, South Korea
Dongyoung Koo	Hansung University, South Korea
Changhee Hahn	Seoul National University of Science and Technology, South Korea
Hyunsoo Kwon	Inha University, South Korea

Program Chairs

HwaJeong Seo	Hansung University, South Korea
Suhri Kim	Sungshin Women's University, South Korea

Program Committee

Wenling Wu	Institute of Software Chinese Academy of Sciences, China
Zhenfu Cao	East China Normal University, China
Swee-Huay Heng	Multimedia University, Malaysia
Taehwan Park	National Security Research Institute, South Korea
Toshihiro Yamauchi	Okayama University, Japan
Jiqiang Lu	Beihang University, China
Joonsang Baek	University of Wollongong, Australia
Katsuyuki Okeya	Hitachi High-Tech Corporation, Japan
Keita Emura	Kanazawa University, Japan
Bimal Roy	Indian Statistical Institute, India
Dongseong Kim	University of Queensland, Australia
Donghoon Chang	IIIT-Delhi, India
Hung-Min Sun	National Tsing Hua University, Taiwan
Iraklis Leontiadis	Inpher, USA
Baodong Qin	Xi'an University of Posts and Telecommunications, China
Xinyi Huang	Fujian Normal University, China
Sherman S. M. Chow	Chinese University of Hong Kong, China
Daniel Slamanig	Universität der Bundeswehr München, Germany
Reza Azarderakhsh	Florida Atlantic University, USA
Ben Lee Wai Kong	Gachon University, South Korea
Anubhab Baksi	Nanyang Technological University, Singapore
Olivier Sanders	Orange Labs, France
Kwangsu Lee	Sejong University, South Korea
Munkyu Lee	Inha University, South Korea
Jooyoung Lee	KAIST, South Korea
SeogChung Seo	Kookmin University, South Korea
Jaehong Seo	Hanyang University, South Korea
Jihye Kim	Kookmin University, South Korea
Jongsung Kim	Kookmin University, South Korea
Aaram Yun	Ewha Woman's University, South Korea
Taekyoung Youn	Dankook University, South Korea
Jungyeon Hwang	Sungshin Women's University, South Korea
Minhye Seo	Duksung Women's University, South Korea
Dohyun Kim	Catholic University of Pusan, South Korea
Seongmin Kim	Sungshin Women's University, South Korea
Haehyun Cho	Soongsil University, South Korea
Myungseo Park	Kangnam University, South Korea
Dongyoung Koo	Hansung University, South Korea

Hyojin Jo	Soongsil University, South Korea
Wonsuk Choi	Korea University, South Korea
Daehee Jang	Kyunghee University, South Korea
Yeonjoon Lee	Hanyang University, South Korea
Jonghwan Park	Sangmyung University, South Korea
Seungkwang Lee	Dankook University, South Korea
Yongwoo Lee	Inha University, South Korea
Konwoo Kwon	Hongik University, South Korea
Youngjoo Shin	Korea University, South Korea
Ilgu Lee	Sungshin Women's University, South Korea
Joohee Lee	Sungshin Women's University, South Korea
Joonwoo Lee	Chungang University, South Korea
Dongyoung Roh	National Security Research Institute, South Korea
Changmin Lee	Korea Institute for Advanced Study, South Korea
Heeseok Kim	Korea University, South Korea
Seunghyun Park	Hansung University, South Korea
Kiwoong Park	Sejong University, South Korea
Sokjoon Lee	Gachon University, South Korea
Byoungjin Seok	Seoul National University of Science and Technology, South Korea
Taejin Lee	Hoseo University, South Korea
Donghyun Kwon	Pusan National University, South Korea
Kyunbaek Kim	Chonnam National University, South Korea
Dooho Choi	Korea University, South Korea
Seongkwang Kim	Samsung SDS, South Korea
Jihoon Kwon	Samsung SDS, South Korea
Seunghyun Seo	Hanyang University, South Korea
Namsu Chang	Sejong Cyber University, South Korea

Contents – Part II

Korean Post Quantum Cryptography

Contents – Part I

Signature Schemes

Cyber Security

A Comparative Analysis of Rust-Based SGX Frameworks: Implications for Building SGX Applications

Heekyung Shin[1], Jiwon Ock[1], Hyeon No[1], and Seongmin Kim[2](✉)

[1] Sungshin Women's University, Seoul, Korea
{220224009,220224011,220224007}@sungshin.ac.kr
[2] Department of Future Convergence Technology Engineering,
Sungshin Women's University, Seoul, Korea
sm.kim@sungshin.ac.kr

Abstract. The widespread adoption of Intel Software Guard Extensions (SGX) technology has garnered significant attention, primarily owing to its robust hardware-based data-in-use protection. To alleviate the complexities of SGX application development, an approach involving the incorporation of a Library Operating System (LibOS) within an enclave has gained prominence. This strategy enables SGX utilization without necessitating extensive modifications to legacy code. However, this approach increases the potential attack surface and may be susceptible to memory corruption vulnerabilities. To address this challenge, the trend of leveraging Rust programming language offering memory safety guarantees for implementing system components has prompted the development of Rust-based SGX frameworks. But still, a gap exists in providing guidelines or systematic analyses to aid developers in selecting a suitable Rust-based SGX framework, considering factors like implementation cost and runtime overhead. This study undertakes a comprehensive comparative analysis of three representative SGX frameworks implemented with Rust: Rust SGX SDK, Occlum, and Fortanix EDP. Our analysis encompasses an exploration of their internal implementations, focusing on their impact on both performance and security. Additionally, we quantify the engineering effort required for migrating legacy Rust applications and evaluate the supplementary overhead incurred when subjecting these frameworks to CPU and memory-intensive workloads. By conducting this analysis, we aim to provide valuable guidance to developers seeking to choose a Rust-based SGX framework that aligns with their application's specific purpose and workload characteristics.

Keywords: Trusted Execution Environment · Intel SGX · Rust

This work was supported by the Sungshin Women's University Research Grant of H20210012.

1 Introduction

The commercialization of Intel Software Guard Extensions (SGX) technology [12] has garnered substantial industrial and academic attention. In particular, Intel SGX technology plays a pivotal role in evolving the confidential computing paradigm [28]. This interest is primarily driven by its robust hardware-based data-in-use protection and its inherent practicality, notably its compatibility with the x86 architecture ensuring native speed [6]. By leveraging SGX to legacy applications, it is possible to guarantee the confidentiality and integrity of cloud-based TEE service. In fact, leading cloud service providers (CSPs) have begun offering public cloud instances supporting SGX functionalities. These ground-breaking solutions, known as confidential VMs, include commercial products like Amazon Nitro Enclaves [3] and Azure Confidential Computing [26]. Such innovation has expedited the widespread adoption of confidential computing across diverse domains, such as safeguarding AI/ML models [13,21], protecting digital assets [22], and securing key management services [10,35].

Basically, there are two primary approaches for implementing the SGX program: 1) porting an application based on SGX SDK [1] and 2) running unmodified applications on top of frameworks that support SGX compatibility [6]. In particular, the adoption of a Library Operating System (LibOS) within the enclave has emerged as a viable strategy to facilitate the utilization of SGX without necessitating modifications to legacy code [5,6,27,33]. The LibOS-based strategy offers distinct advantages when porting legacy applications into the SGX environment. Developers are relieved from the complexities of segregating security-sensitive components from the original code-base and re-implementing system call wrappers for enclave transitions. However, it is important to note that this design choice expands the potential attack surface, given that the entire LibOS codebase is loaded and executed within an SGX enclave. SGX does not guarantee the memory safety of the enclave, which means that memory corruption vulnerabilities inherent in traditional code written in languages like C or C++ (e.g., Heartbleed [7]) can still be effective even when executed within the security boundary provided by SGX CPU [20,29]. Therefore, an additional instrumentation or protection mechanism is required to achieve robustness over memory vulnerabilities.

Simultaneously, the rise of the Rust programming language has equipped developers with a potent instrument for constructing robust and secure applications. Rust delegates memory safety checking (e.g., rust pointer always references valid memory) to the Rust compiler. In contrast to low-level codes implemented in C or C++ that are prone to subtle memory bugs, Rust guarantees memory safety by rejecting the compilation of them by introducing features, such as ownership and lifetime elision rules [24]. Furthermore, Rust is fast and memory-efficient as its runtime does not require a garbage collector to reclaim memory space, making it well-suited for the development of performance-critical services. This appeal leads to the adoption of Rust in state-of-the-art system software, including container runtimes [2], microkernels [19], and storage systems [17].

Such a trend has also spurred the development of the SGX framework tailored for Rust utilization. The state-of-the-art LibOS-based SGX frameworks have extended support for the execution of Rust applications [27,33]. Besides, several studies [8,31,34] utilize Rust programming language [24] as the foundation for building SGX frameworks. Such design choice enables developers to reduce runtime overhead (e.g., garbage collection), thereby drawing attention to the potential of leveraging Rust in SGX framework development. Nevertheless, a notable gap persists in the absence of comprehensive guidelines or systemic analyses that can aid developers in selecting the most suitable Rust-based SGX framework for their applications. Such guidelines would encompass considerations related to implementation cost and runtime overhead, crucial factors when deciding to execute existing applications or develop new Rust applications in the SGX environment.

This study conducts a comparative study on existing Rust-based SGX frameworks to provide implications for newly implementing or porting legacy security-sensitive Rust applications. For this, we conduct an in-depth analysis between three cutting-edge Rust-based SGX frameworks: Rust SGX SDK, Occlum, and Fortanix EDP. First, we explore the internal implementation details of each framework relevant to the application performance and security. Then, we quantify the engineering effort required to deploy legacy Rust applications atop these frameworks, providing insights into the ease of transition. Finally, we evaluate the additional overhead incurred by each framework, subjecting them to CPU-intensive and memory-intensive workloads to gauge their performance implications. We believe our analysis provides guidance for developers to select an appropriate Rust-based SGX framework when implementing an SGX application according to its purpose and workload characteristics.

2 Background

2.1 Intel SGX and LibOS-Based SGX Framework

Intel SGX is a secure processor architecture to ensure trustworthiness of application to protect sensitive and valuable information. It offers an isolated protection domain in memory called an *enclave*, which is only decrypted within the CPU package when executing it as an enclave mode. This ensures that even system administrators or other software running on the host cannot access the sensitive data in the enclave. To help developers implement SGX applications, Intel provides the SGX Software Development Kit (SDK). The SDK offers essential libraries and toolchains for tasks such as enclave signing and debugging [25]. It simplifies the process of creating secure enclaves and managing their execution. For building an SGX application using SDK, a developer needs to separate an application codebase into two parts, an enclave region and an untrusted region. In addition, the transition interface between them must be defined by a developer in the Enclave Definition Language (EDL). This interface specifies the secure functions ECALLs for entering an enclave mode and functions OCALLs that can be invoked to switch execution to the untrusted region. Additionally, EDLs detail how data should be transferred in and out of the enclave, specifying data structures and communication mechanisms. Note that OCALLs are typically used for handling system calls, as SGX does not allow executing syscall instructions in an enclave mode.

LibOS-based SGX focuses on using a Library OS that provides operating system functionality in the form of a library to act as an interface between applications and hardware. It runs entirely within an enclave, and to port an application into an enclave, the application binary needs to be loaded and executed along with the libraries it relies on. One of the key advantages of LibOS-based SGX is the simplification of the enclave interface. This minimizes the number of system calls that occur within the enclave, ensuring that the code running within the enclave does not require system calls that involve crossing between user and kernel domains. LibOS also plays a crucial role in implementing and managing necessary operating system functionalities within the enclave when executed in user space. This allows enclaves to handle privileged operations that would typically require execution in processor supervisor mode, maintaining security isolation while performing necessary tasks. Operations represented as system calls, particularly those related to file system operations, can be straightforwardly implemented within LibOS by modifying data structures related to the file system implementation. These system calls do not impact the security of other application programs and do not require execution by privileged system software [30]. Frameworks such as Gramine [33], SGX-LKL [27], and Haven [6], which implement LibOS-based SGX, offer the advantage of enhancing portability by freeing applications from dependence on a specific operating system.

2.2   Rust Programming Language

Rust is a newly introduced programming language developed by Mozilla Research that guarantees safety on the memory side with cost-free abstraction [24]. Rust delegates memory safety checking (e.g., rust pointer always references valid memory) to the Rust compiler. In contrast to low-level codes implemented in C or C++ prone to subtle memory bugs, Rust guarantees memory safety by rejecting their compilation by introducing features, such as ownership and lifetime elision rules [24]. Such design choice enables developers to minimize a runtime overhead (e.g., garbage collection), which in turn introduces the attention to utilizing Rust for implementing system software [24]. Rust introduces a unique *ownership* system central to its memory safety guarantees [16]. The ownership system enforces strict rules about how memory is allocated and deallocated, ensuring that memory is managed safely without the risk of common bugs like null pointer dereferences, data races, and memory leaks. Rust also incorporates *lifetime*, which are annotations that specify the scope or duration for which references are valid [16]. It prevents references from outliving the data they point to or being used after the data has been deallocated.

3   Characteristics Analysis of Frameworks

To take advantage of Rust mentioned above (e.g., guaranteeing in-enclave memory safety), recent studies utilize Rust when implementing an SGX framework

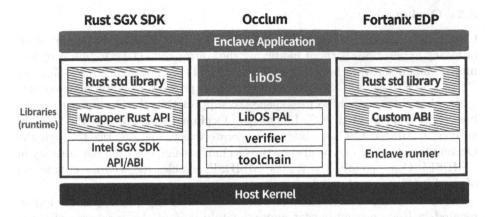

Fig. 1. Rust-based SGX Framework Overview. (The red boxes indicate regions that are isolated and protected by the enclave application, while the black dashed boxes are regions that are written in Rust). (Color figure online)

itself and enable developers to execute Rust applications on SGX environment [8,31,34]. In particular, we provide an overview of three existing frameworks that facilitate the development of SGX applications in Rust: *Rust SGX SDK, Occlum,* and *Fortanix EDP*. As depicted in Fig. 1, these frameworks each exhibit a distinct system architecture. It is worth noting that Occlum exclusively employs a LibOS-based approach, while both Rust SGX SDK and Fortanix EDP offer a custom interface to interact with the host OS for system operations.

3.1 Fortanix EDP

Enclave development platform (EDP) [8], developed by Fortanix, offers a distinct advantage in generating and running enclave from scratch with Rust code, eliminating the dependency on the Intel SGX SDK [8]. Notably, Fortanix EDP introduces its own unique API and ABI while ensuring binary-level compatibility for Rust applications. Specifically, EDP's `usercall` interface is designed not to expose existing enclave interface attack surfaces. It achieves this by incorporating elements that handle memory allocation in user space and data copying from user memory within the context of a Rust-type system. This approach effectively safeguards against direct memory access, preemptively mitigating time-of-check time-of-use (TOCTOU) attacks. It's worth noting that the `usercall` interface establishes a connection to the syscall interface through an enclave. Within the untrusted region, an enclave runner takes on the responsibility of managing enclave loading and serves as an intermediary layer bridging the gap between `usercall` requests originating from the enclave and the syscall interface required for external interactions. While EDP enables the utilization of much of Rust's standard library for application implementation, it intentionally imposes restrictions on specific functionalities, such as multi-processing support and file system operations, for security reasons.

3.2   Occlum

Occlum is a memory-safe multi-process LibOS for Intel SGX to enable execution of legacy applications without modifying the source code [31]. Occlum proposes multi-domain software fault isolation (MMDSFI) by leveraging Intel Memory Protection Extensions (MPX) technology [14] to preserve isolation between processes that share a single address space. To support this, the Occlum framework has newly implemented SGX LibOS, the Occlum toolchain, and the Occlum verifier. Untrusted C/C++ code can generate executable binaries through the Occlum toolchain and be verified by the Occlum verifier, ensuring the integrity of MMDSFI. Consequently, the verified MMDSFI enables the secure construction of the LibOS within the enclave.

LibOS based on Intel SGX SDK and Rust SGX SDK is predominantly implemented in Rust, accounting for approximately 90% of the codebase, with the remainder implemented in C. This supports the execution of enclaves in both C and Rust, providing protection for enclave programs against potential memory vulnerabilities. Furthermore, to protect LibOS from unsafe entities, a shim layer called occlum-PAL is provided to the application, offering APIs. This isolation mechanism is crucial for security as it prevents one process from interfering with or accessing the memory of another with strict boundary checking. By securely sharing the enclave's single address space with Occlum's SFI-isolated processes (SIPs) which is a unit of application domain, it supports multi-tasking efficiently. For example, compared to other SGX frameworks that utilize LibOS with supporting multi-tasking [5,6,33], startup time is 1000 times faster and IPC (inter-process communication) is up to 3 times faster [31].

3.3   Rust SGX SDK (Teaclave SGX SDK)

The Rust SGX SDK, developed by Baidu, offers a secure platform for executing Rust-based applications within SGX environments [34]. This SDK introduces a wrapper Rust API that layers Rust functionalities on top of the SGX SDKs, originally implemented in C and C++. Through this layered approach, it establishes a secure connection between the Intel SGX SDK code and the trusted application. Notably, as a dependency on the Intel SGX SDK, it places trust exclusively in the software operating within an enclave while maintaining untrusted towards the rest of the system. The SDK doesn't provide its own Application Binary Interface (ABI) but instead adheres to the same ABI as the vanilla Intel SGX SDK. This strategic choice ensures seamless compatibility between the Rust SGX SDK and the Intel SGX environment. Consequently, any updates or alterations within the SGX ecosystem can be swiftly accommodated without the risk of breaking compatibility.

4   Qualitative Aspects Affecting Application Performance

In this section, we conduct in-depth analysis by systemically exploring the internal design of each framework and categorize three key indicators related to application performance: Memory boundary check, Enclave transition, and additional runtime overhead. Table 1 summarizes our analysis result.

Table 1. Estimating framework performance impact overhead based on framework analysis

	Memory boundary check	Enclave Transition	Runtime Overhead	Memory Safety
Occlum	MMDSFI	PAL API	Enclave SIP	Enclave SIP
Incubator Teaclave SGX SDK	Runtime (Enclave-runner)	Legacy ECALL/OCALL	Rust Wrapper API	Rust Wrapper API
Fortanix EDP	Sanitizable function	Usercall (Custom)	Own ABI	Own API and ABI

4.1 Memory Boundary Check

To avoid overhead caused by unnecessary bound checking, Rust SGX SDK provides a `Sanitizable` function to check the raw byte array and verify that memory represents a valid object when binding an application. For the case of Fortanix EDP, the `enclave-runner` runtime checks before entering an enclave to ensure processor state sanitation, similar to Rust SGX SDK. Finally, Occlum utilizes SFI (Software Fault Isolation), a software instrumentation technique that sandboxes untrusted domains within a single address space to reduce the enclave size in a multi-tasking environment. However, Occlum performs boundary checking for every memory access to ensure that it does not deviate from the domain boundary, which becomes a runtime overhead.

4.2 Enclave Transition (ECALL/OCALL)

Rust SGX SDK follows the design choice made by Intel SGX SDK for implementing enclave transition wrapper, ECALL (enclave call) and OCALL (out-call)[1]. To make legacy ECALLs and OCALLs implemented in C compatible with Rust application code, Rust SGX SDK provides wrapper routines by leveraging Rust's unsafe keyword, which explicitly translates the boundary between C code and Rust code for foreign function interface (FFI). During the conversion, sanity checking is performed, resulting in runtime overhead. Fortanix EDP, on the other hand, defines the `usercall` interface written in Rust, instead of writing ECALL and OCALL for enclave transition. Because they use their own call process, which is not optimized for SGX, each interaction related to the enclave would generate transition overhead using the `usercall` interface [34]. Similarly, Occlum inserts a trampoline code with a byte that identifies the domain ID in MMDSFI to securely implement untrusted binaries generated by the toolchain in LibOS. In other words, entry into the LibOS within the Enclave can only occur using

---

[1] Note that ECALLs are used for to enter the enclave and OCALLs are used to switch an execution flow to untrusted region, respectively.

this trampoline code. Furthermore, to exit outside the LibOS, one must verify the predefined domain ID once again before being allowed to escape. Therefore, from the user's perspective in Occlum, there is no need to write an EDL file. Instead, users can utilize the pre-defined `occlum build` command to build the enclave image and the `occlum run` command to use the enclave entry point. Within the Occlum framework, the run command is passed to the PAL API Layer to enter the enclave. The process of passing through the PAL Layer to enter the enclave can involve transition overhead [33].

4.3   Runtime Overhead (Miscellaneous)

The Rust SGX SDK raises an additional overhead due to the dependency on Intel SGX SDK by calling a different directory SGX instruction with the Rust layer, rather than directly executing the assembly code. On the other hand, Fortanix EDP uses its own ABI, called `fortanix-sgx-abi` [9], implemented with a pure rust abstraction layer, so it is relatively overhead-free [15]. When assuming multi-tasking scenario, Occlum has an advantage compared to other frameworks, as it handles multiple process domains (SIPs) within a single enclave region. Such a design also saves the cost of inter-process communication (IPC) overhead between processes.

4.4   Memory Safety Guranteed by Each Framework

Both the Rust SGX SDK and Occlum have dependencies on the C language Intel SGX SDK layers, with the Rust SGX SDK utilizing a wrapper API implemented in Rust, and Occlum having 90%of its LibOS code written in Rust. When these frameworks have dependencies on the Intel SGX SDK, they remain susceptible to various vulnerabilities, including DoS attacks and side-channel attacks. In other words, Occlum and Rust SGX SDK may share similar security threats at the library level. However, Occlum can leverage enclave SIP to defend the enclave against attacks such as code injection and ROP attacks by providing isolation between processes that protect SIP from other SIPs and between processes that protect LibOS itself from any SIP and LibOS.

In contrast, Fortanix EDP distinguishes itself by defining its own API and ABI based on the Rust language, thereby enhancing security against vulnerabilities like side-channel attacks that are inherent in the Intel SGX SDK. Additionally, Fortanix EDP is designed in a way that similar to how a LibOS operates, does not expose the enclave interface surface to the user. Additionally, by limiting the number of usercall interfaces to fewer than 20, it reduces the attack surface. Furthermore, it allocates memory in user space and utilizes elements like `fortanix_sgx::usercalls::alloc` to prevent direct memory access, thereby proactively mitigating Time-of-Check-to-Time-of-use (TOCTOU) attack.

Rust SGX SDK introduces an extra layer of wrappers, which can lead to performance degradation. This may manifest as slower enclave execution and a higher demand for system resources. While Occlum provides isolation between SIPs, there can be overhead in terms of communication and data sharing between processes due to this isolation. Fortanix EDP makes changes to memory allocation and access methods to defend against TOCTOU attacks. However, these changes can result in additional overhead for memory management and internal enclave operations. Additionally, limiting the number of user call interfaces for security purposes can restrict the functionality and flexibility of enclaves. All three frameworks may require extra security and compliance checks during enclave execution and communication, which can slow down the overall execution speed.

5 Performance Evaluation

In this section, we describe our experimental setup and present the results of our experimental evaluations of application workloads on each framework. Based on the analysis Sect. 4, specified the following evaluation metrics: 1)Execution time measurement to evaluate the performance of the application according to the characteristics, 2) Enclave size measurement result to evaluate the enclave hardening and security. The results of the two performance evaluations are summarized in Table 2 and Table 3.

Experimental Setup. Our evaluation was assessed on Ubuntu 20.04. The SGX SDK for developing SGX applications utilized 2.18v. For the Rust language, we used rustc 1.66.0-nightly, which is compatible with all frameworks. Additionally, Occlum used glibc 2.31, as there are glibc versions compatible with running musl-based applications.

Application Benchmark. *Ring* is a library that exposes a Rust API, primarily utilized for performing CPU-intensive workloads related to encryption. It emphasizes the implementation, testing, and optimization of a core set of cryptographic operations exposed through an API that is both easy to use and resistant to misuse. Considering the computationally intensive nature of encryption and decryption processes, we intend to leverage this code to evaluate the CPU computational load of each framework.

HashMap in Rust is utilized for mapping and storing keys and values, offering swift search and insertion operations. However, this process entails the need for basic object implementations, an array of hash tables, and individual objects for each hash item, resulting in a memory-intensive workload with substantial RAM consumption. Moreover, this hash map not only provides a default hash function but also allows users to specify hash functions for custom data types. It permits custom hash behavior for specific data, enabling the implementation of optimal hashing strategies. Chaining is primarily employed for collision handling, and the size dynamically adjusts to automatically optimize memory usage when adding or removing data. We intend to employ this *HashMaps* to assess the memory computational load of each framework.

5.1   Performance Overhead

We evaluated the execution times of Ring, and Hashmap core logic within an Enclave, using a local environment as a baseline, without employing SGX Enclave.

Occlum performs processes by excluding the Occlum toolchain and Occlum verifier from the LibOS, instead delivering only verified MMDSFI to the LibOS. Accordingly, the necessary code (LibOS) is loaded inside the Enclave, minimizing time delays associated with context switching and exhibiting execution times similar to baseline environment. On the other hand, Fortanix EDP, which employs an intermediate Shim layer called `enclave-runner` to load the Enclave and handle logic processing, resulted in significantly higher program execution times. When a user invokes the enclave, the Enclave-runner inspects and sanitizes the code using the Enclave entry ABI, then loads and enters the enclave. Once inside the Enclave, after performing the logic between the `enclave-runner` and the Enclave, the enclave exit ABI is called to terminate the thread. Therefore, including these processes, Fortanix EDP had the longest execution times for application workloads.

Incubator Teaclave SGX SDK demonstrated the fastest execution times in the Hashmap and Ring workloads. This can be attributed to the use of a Rust wrapper optimized for the Intel SGX API, enabling faster execution even within the SGX environment, including Without SGX execution. Notably, the `sgx_tcrypto` used in the Ring workload called the crypto module implemented in C through unsafe calls, resulting in faster execution times. However, it did not guarantee Rust's memory safety. Therefore, Incubator Teaclave SGX SDK implements functions such as Rust's Lifetimes to ensure memory safety by automatically invoking `drop` functions when the lifespan of objects within `sgx_tcrypto` expires, securely releasing internal references to data in the C/C++ heap, without relying on unsafe calls.

In summary, the performance overhead shows that Incubator Teaclave SGX SDK, which uses SGX-optimized APIs, is the fastest, while Fortanix EDP, which utilizes the intermediate layer of enclave-runner, incurs the most significant performance overhead.

5.2   Enclave Size

Our goal is to evaluate the confidentiality of each framework by measuring the size of the TCB(Trusted Computing Base) that must be safeguarded within the enclave.

In the case of Occlum, we determine the enclave's size by assessing the size of the generated binary. For the Rust SGX SDK, the enclave size can be determined by examining the Enclave.so file generated during the compilation process. In the case of Fortanix EDP, the process involves converting binary files generated using Cargo into SGXS (SGX Stream) files, which adhere to the SGX enclave format. The measurement of enclave size in Fortanix EDP is based on the resulting SGXS file.

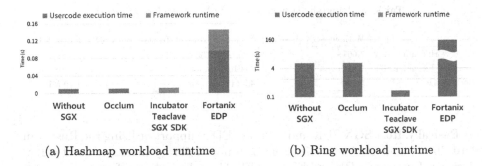

(a) Hashmap workload runtime   (b) Ring workload runtime

Fig. 2. Breakdown of benchmark execution time. (Figure (a) and Fig. (b) represent charts illustrating the overall runtime of the frameworks and the runtime within the SGX Enclave, respectively. In particular, in the Hashmap workload, the runtime attributed to memory access increases, rendering the framework runtime itself negligible in the representation).

The usercall API of Fortanix EDP is included within the enclave, yet it allows for the creation of the smallest possible enclave size. This is attributed to the intentional design choice of keeping the usercall API minimal, which is considered to be the reason for this outcome. The Rust SGX SDK follows the enclave design of the Intel SGX SDK but necessitates the inclusion of various Rust wrapper libraries depending on the nature of the workload. As a result, it can be observed that Fortanix EDP generates a relatively larger enclave size compared to the Rust SGX SDK.

As a result, Occlum's Enclave size is assessed as the largest among the frameworks. Occlum incorporates the entire LibOS within a single Enclave. Within the LibOS, there are components such as a binary loader for verifying whether the binary files are signed by the Occlum verifier or Occlum's encrypted file system to securely protect files, contributing to the larger Enclave size evaluation.

Table 2. Hashmap workload results for each framework

	Without SGX (baseline)	Occlum	Incubator Teaclave SGX SDK	Fortanix EDP
Framework runtime	0.011 s	0.011 s	0.012 s	0.146 s
Usercode Execution time	0.0084 s	0.0090 s	0.0004 s	0.0965 s
Enclave size	N/A	4.4 MB	1.4 MB	1.18 MB

6   Quantifying Engineering Effort

To assess the qualitative effort in development, we describe the engineering effort according to the characteristics of the framework and analyze the results for Lines of Code as a factor to evaluate.

Table 3. Ring(sha2) workload results for each framework

	Without SGX (baseline)	Occlum	Incubator Teaclave SGX SDK	Fortanix EDP
Framework runtime	7.661 s	7.863 s	0.225 s	149.037 s
Usercode Execution time	7.6584 s	7.8610 s	0.2130 s	148.9848 s
Enclave size	N/A	4.5 MB	1.6 MB	1.19 MB

Basically, Rust SGX SDK and Fortanix EDP support utilizing the Rust standard library, and Occlum utilizes the C standard library (musl_libc and glibc). However, Rust SGX SDK and Fortanix EDP have limitations of several functionalities (e.g., environment variable, timing, networking) due to security concerns. Therefore, development costs are incurred in that developers have to implement these functions themselves to use. In contrast, Occlum not only utilizes using easy-of-use command-line tools unique to Occlum but also provides several built-in toolchains and libraries to facilitate developer porting or development tasks. Yet, developers have the disadvantage of having to spend a lot of time learning about SGX SDK APIs, programming models, and systems. In addition, Fortanix EDP can implement the ability to handle memory isolation, usercalls, and SGX instruction sets by adding only std::os::fortanix_sgx proprietary modules compared to general Rust standard libraries, and relatively reduce programmer development costs. Fortanix EDP also has the advantage of not requiring much experience from developers because it does not require SGX background knowledge and does not require EDL files to separate trust areas.

Table 4. Hashmap Workload Lines of Code

		Rust Code	EDL File (ECALL/OCALL def)	Cargo.toml	Configuration File
Without SGX (baseline)		12	N/A	10	N/A
Incubator Teaclave SGX SDK	modified	2	N/A	8	N/A
	add	81	10	34	N/A
Occlum	add	0	N/A	0	17
Fortanix EDP	add	0	N/A	3	N/A

This evaluation is based on a Hashmap workload in a local environment without utilizing the SGX enclave as a reference. The results of the additional Lines of Code are summarized in Table 4 as follows. Rust's Cargo serves as a package manager for building and managing Rust applications. To build packages using Cargo, the creation of a Cargo.toml configuration file is required. Additionally, SGX also requires the Enclave.edl file with the context switch. This file defines ECALLs for entering the reserved Enclave and OCALLs for returning from the Enclave to the user space.

Rust SGX SDK provides a Rust wrapper for the Intel SGX SDK, originally written in C/C++. It uniquely distinguishes between the app and Enclave areas, necessitating the definition of the Enclave.edl file. As a result, in the main logic of the app layer, instead of using the pure Rust standard libraries, the developer employed the provided sgx_types and sgx_urts. It also, involved writing code for creating the Enclave, making function calls to enter the Enclave, executing code within the Enclave, and retrieving the results. Within the Enclave, the developer performed the Hashmap workload. Ultimately, this resulted in 2 lines being modified and an additional 81 lines of source code being written.

Occlum offers a user-friendly Occlum-cargo command to execute Rust applications, and it provides shell scripts and yaml files for this purpose. As a result, there was no need to modify or add significant code to the core logic of the Hashmap workload or the Cargo.toml file. However, there was a requirement to write 17 lines of source code for the shell scripts and yaml file.

In Fortanix EDP, a pure Rust language approach was utilized, along with a custom ABI/API, to ensure security by not exposing the Enclave interface to developers. This design choice allowed for the avoidance of writing an Enclave.edl file. The core logic of the Hashmap workload was leveraged without any modifications, thanks to the support of the Rust standard library. Instead of using a custom ABI/API, the Cargo.toml file was configured with a build target of x86_64-fortanix-unknown-sgx for building. As a result, only three lines of source code were added to the Cargo.toml file.

To minimize the developer's effort, it is evaluated as most suitable to utilize Fortanix EDP, which allows the development of applications using only the Rust language without requiring background knowledge of the SGX architecture.

7   Related Work

Gramine [18], previously known as Graphene, is a lightweight library operating system designed for Linux multi-process applications. This unique library OS facilitates the execution of existing applications within SGX enclaves without necessitating any modifications, except for the inclusion of an enclave manifest specifying security settings and configurations. Gramine uses this manifest to perform authenticity and integrity verification and subsequently leverages it to load the application along with its requisite dependencies.

SCONE [4] is a software platform designed for securely running container-based applications using SGX within Docker containers. It offers a secure C standard library interface that automatically encrypts and decrypts input/output (I/O) data, thereby minimizing the performance impact of thread synchronization and system calls during the enclave transition. In addition, SCONE supports user-level threading and asynchronous system calls to improve performance.

PANOPLY [32] represents a system designed to bridge the gap between the standard OS abstraction and the specific requirements of SGX for commercial Linux applications. Inspired by the principles of micro-kernels, PANOPLY has completely rethought the logic of the OS without trying to emulate it. It achieves this by intercepting calls to the glibc API, which allows the glibc library to reside outside the enclave's TCB. Consequently, even if the underlying OS encounters issues or malfunctions, PANOPLY ensures the application's integrity attributes remain intact, ensuring its continued proper functioning.

Among them, SCONE and PANOPLY employ thin "shim" layers that encapsulate API layers like system call tables. This architectural strategy serves the purpose of minimizing the code required within the enclave, thereby reducing both the interface's size and the potential attack surface between the enclave and the untrusted OS. Gramine, SCONE, and Panoply all represent solutions for enhancing the security of applications in container environments. They share the common characteristic of being developed in the C programming language, which means that they may not exhibit the same level of robust memory safety as the Rust-based SGX frameworks examined in this paper.

Several studies have aimed to streamline the engineering effort required for deploying applications in SGX environments, simplifying the process for developers. Glamdring [23] proposes automating the code partitioning process to utilize SGX. Once developers annotate security-sensitive data of the target application, Glamdring automatically splits the application into two sections: one for the trusted enclave and the other for the untrusted, non-enclave part. Through efficient code relocation, including the creation of SDK interface specifications and the relocation of resource-intensive features outside the enclave via runtime profiling, Glamdring minimizes the engineering effort involved.

Hasan et al. [11] conduct the comparison of the comparison between 'Port' and 'Shim' approaches for implementing SGX applications. The porting approach entails rewriting or modifying the application's code to align with the SGX environment. While it may be more complex, it typically offers superior performance. Conversely, the shimming approach involves the creation of an intermediary layer that acts as an adapter between the application and the new SGX environment. This approach requires fewer code changes due to the presence of SGX libraries but may introduce some performance overhead. The choice between 'Port' and 'Shim' hinges on various factors, including time constraints, available resources, and performance requirements, providing developers with flexibility in their approach.

Existing research on SGX-related studies for enhancing application security in container environments commonly share the characteristic of being developed in the C programming language. However, it is essential to note that, compared to the Rust-based frameworks analyzed in this paper, these solutions may not be as robust in terms of memory safety, owing to their development in C/C++. In contrast to the aforementioned studies, our studies focus on analyzing SGX frameworks that utilize the Rust programming language to enhance the security of user code and data from a memory safety perspective. Furthermore, we assess the performance of these three frameworks, each with distinct methods of supporting SGX, from the standpoint of developers. This assessment aims to provide guidelines that can promote the adoption of SGX.

8 Conclusion

This paper analyzes the implementation cost when developing Rust applications with existing Rust-based SGX frameworks. Through the comparative analysis over three frameworks, we confirm that Occlum has strength in performance, while developing Rust applications using Fortanix EDP is effective from the implementation cost perspective.

References

1. Intel Software Guard Extensions (Intel SGX) SDK. https://software.intel.com/content/www/us/en/develop/topics/software-guard-extensions/sdk.html. Accessed June 2021
2. Agache, A., et al.: Firecracker: lightweight virtualization for serverless applications. In: 17th USENIX symposium on networked systems design and implementation (NSDI 20), pp. 419–434 (2020)
3. Amazon: AWS Nitro Enclaves. https://aws.amazon.com/ec2/nitro/nitro-enclaves/
4. Arnautov, S., et al.: SCONE: secure Linux containers with intel SGX. In: 12th USENIX Symposium on Operating Systems Design and Implementation (OSDI 2016), pp. 689–703. USENIX Association, Savannah (2016). https://www.usenix.org/conference/osdi16/technical-sessions/presentation/arnautov
5. Arnautov, S., et al.: SCONE: secure Linux containers with intel SGX. In: SCONE: Secure Linux Containers with Intel SGX, OSDI 2016, pp. 689–703. USENIX Association, USA (2016)
6. Baumann, A., Peinado, M., Hunt, G.: Shielding applications from an untrusted cloud with haven. In: 11th USENIX Symposium on Operating Systems Design and Implementation (OSDI 2014), pp. 267–283. USENIX Association, Broomfield (2014). https://www.usenix.org/conference/osdi14/technical-sessions/presentation/baumann
7. Durumeric, Z., et al.: The matter of heartbleed. In: Proceedings of the IMC. ACM (2014)
8. Fortanix: Fortanix EDP. https://edp.fortanix.com/
9. Fortanix: Fortanix SGX ABI. https://edp.fortanix.com/docs/api/fortanix_sgx_abi/
10. Han, J., Yun, I., Kim, S., Kim, T., Son, S., Han, D.: Scalable and secure virtualization of HSM with ScaleTrust. IEEE/ACM Trans. Netw. (2022)
11. Hasan, A., Riley, R., Ponomarev, D.: Port or shim? Stress testing application performance on intel SGX. In: 2020 IEEE International Symposium on Workload Characterization (IISWC), pp. 123–133 (2020). https://doi.org/10.1109/IISWC50251.2020.00021
12. Hoekstra, M., Lal, R., Pappachan, P., Phegade, V., Del Cuvillo, J.: Using innovative instructions to create trustworthy software solutions. HASP@ ISCA 11(10.1145), pp. 2487726–2488370 (2013)
13. Hunt, T., Song, C., Shokri, R., Shmatikov, V., Witchel, E.: Chiron: privacy-preserving machine learning as a service. arXiv preprint arXiv:1803.05961 (2018)
14. Intel: Intel MPX. https://intel-mpx.github.io/
15. Jo Van Bulck, Fritz Alder, F.P.: A case for unified ABI shielding in intel SGX runtimes. In: A Case for Unified ABI Shielding in Intel SGX Runtimes, Systex 2022 (2022)

16. Jung, R., Jourdan, J.H., Krebbers, R., Dreyer, D.: RustBelt: securing the foundations of the rust programming language. Proc. ACM Program. Lang. **2**(POPL) (2017). https://doi.org/10.1145/3158154
17. Kulkarni, C., Moore, S., Naqvi, M., Zhang, T., Ricci, R., Stutsman, R.: Splinter: {bare-metal} extensions for {multi-tenant} {low-latency} storage. In: 13th USENIX Symposium on Operating Systems Design and Implementation (OSDI 2018), pp. 627–643 (2018)
18. Kuvaiskii, D., Kumar, G., Vij, M.: Computation offloading to hardware accelerators in Intel SGX and Gramine library OS (2022)
19. Lankes, S., Breitbart, J., Pickartz, S.: Exploring rust for unikernel development. In: Proceedings of the 10th Workshop on Programming Languages and Operating Systems, pp. 8–15 (2019)
20. Lee, J., et al.: Hacking in darkness: return-oriented programming against secure enclaves. In: 26th USENIX Security Symposium (USENIX Security 2017), pp. 523–539 (2017)
21. Lee, T., et al.: Occlumency: privacy-preserving remote deep-learning inference using SGX. In: The 25th Annual International Conference on Mobile Computing and Networking, pp. 1–17 (2019)
22. Liang, X., Shetty, S., Zhang, L., Kamhoua, C., Kwiat, K.: Man in the cloud (MITC) defender: SGX-based user credential protection for synchronization applications in cloud computing platform. In: 2017 IEEE 10th International Conference on Cloud Computing (CLOUD), pp. 302–309. IEEE (2017)
23. Lind, J., et al.: Glamdring: automatic application partitioning for intel SGX. In: 2017 USENIX Annual Technical Conference (USENIX ATC 2017), pp. 285–298. USENIX Association, Santa Clara (2017), https://www.usenix.org/conference/atc17/technical-sessions/presentation/lind
24. Matsakis, N.D., Klock, F.S.: The rust language. In: The Rust Language, HILT 2014, pp. 103–104. Association for Computing Machinery, New York (2014). https://doi.org/10.1145/2663171.2663188
25. McKeen, F.X., et al.: Innovative instructions and software model for isolated execution. In: HASP 2013 (2013)
26. Microsoft: Azure confidential computing. https://azure.microsoft.com/en-us/solutions/confidential-compute/
27. Priebe, C., et al.: SGX-LKL: securing the host OS interface for trusted execution. CoRR abs/1908.11143 (2019). http://arxiv.org/abs/1908.11143
28. Rashid, F.Y.: The rise of confidential computing: big tech companies are adopting a new security model to protect data while it's in use-[news]. IEEE Spectr. **57**(6), 8–9 (2020)
29. Schwarz, M., Weiser, S., Gruss, D.: Practical enclave malware with intel SGX. In: Perdisci, R., Maurice, C., Giacinto, G., Almgren, M. (eds.) DIMVA 2019. LNCS, vol. 11543, pp. 177–196. Springer, Cham (2019). https://doi.org/10.1007/978-3-030-22038-9_9
30. Shanker, K., Joseph, A., Ganapathy, V.: An evaluation of methods to port legacy code to SGX enclaves. In: Proceedings of the 28th ACM Joint Meeting on European Software Engineering Conference and Symposium on the Foundations of Software Engineering, pp. 1077–1088 (2020)
31. Shen, Y., et al.: Occlum: secure and efficient multitasking inside a single enclave of intel SGX. In: Proceedings of the Twenty-Fifth International Conference on Architectural Support for Programming Languages and Operating Systems. ACM (2020). https://doi.org/10.1145/3373376.3378469

32. Shinde, S., Le, D., Tople, S., Saxena, P.: PANOPLY: low-TCB Linux applications with SGX enclaves (2017). https://doi.org/10.14722/ndss.2017.23500
33. che Tsai, C., Porter, D.E., Vij, M.: Graphene-SGX: a practical library OS for unmodified applications on SGX. In: 2017 USENIX Annual Technical Conference (USENIX ATC 2017), pp. 645–658. USENIX Association, Santa Clara (2017). https://www.usenix.org/conference/atc17/technical-sessions/presentation/tsai
34. Wang, H., et al.: Towards memory safe enclave programming with rust-SGX. In: Proceedings of the 2019 ACM SIGSAC Conference on Computer and Communications Security, CCS 2019, pp. 2333–2350. Association for Computing Machinery, New York (2019). https://doi.org/10.1145/3319535.3354241
35. Wang, J., et al.: SvTPM: SGX-based virtual trusted platform modules for cloud computing. IEEE Trans. Cloud Comput. (2023)

BTFuzzer: A Profile-Based Fuzzing Framework for Bluetooth Protocols

Min Jang[1,2], Yuna Hwang[2], Yonghwi Kwon[3], and Hyoungshick Kim[1(✉)]

[1] Sungkyunkwan University, Suwon, South Korea
{min.jang,hyoung}@skku.edu
[2] Samsung Electronics, Suwon, South Korea
{min.s.jang,yuna.hwang}@samsung.com
[3] University of Maryland, College Park, MD, USA
yongkwon@umd.edu

Abstract. Bluetooth vulnerabilities have become increasingly popular in recent years due to, in part, the remote exploitability of Bluetooth. Unfortunately, in practice, security analysts often rely on manual analysis to identify these vulnerabilities, which is challenging. Specifically, testing various workloads while maintaining reliable Bluetooth connections between devices requires complicated network configuration settings. This paper introduces BTFuzzer, a profile-based fuzzing framework for Bluetooth devices. BTFuzzer eliminates the need for complex network configurations by feeding Bluetooth packets directly into the target device's Bluetooth library without going through the Over-The-Air (OTA) transmissions. BTFuzzer carefully crafts test inputs based on protocol profiles and specifications to maximize code coverage efficiently. Our evaluation results show that BTFuzzer is highly effective. In particular, the framework has identified two security bugs in the latest Android versions (i.e., 10 and later): CVE-2020-27024 and a publicly unknown information leak vulnerability. The first is an out-of-bounds read vulnerability (CVE-2020-27024). The second vulnerability allows attackers to connect to a victim's device and leak sensitive data without the user's awareness, as the adversary is not shown in the list of connected Bluetooth devices.

Keywords: Bluetooth · Protocol · Fuzzing · Memory Corruption · Remote Code Execution

1 Introduction

Recent Bluetooth vulnerabilities such as *BlueBorne* [16] have sparked interest in finding Bluetooth-related security bugs due to, in part, its broad impact across multiple platforms. For example, BlueBorne affects Bluetooth implementations across multiple platforms: Android, iOS, Windows, and Linux. As of September 2023, 720 CVEs have been registered as Bluetooth-related vulnerabilities [1], where they are remotely exploitable. For instance, CVE-2017-0781 is a vulnerability in the Android's BNEP service. It allows attackers to compromise Bluetooth devices [16,25] remotely. Due to Bluetooth vulnerabilities' high and broad

© The Author(s), under exclusive license to Springer Nature Singapore Pte Ltd. 2024
H. Seo and S. Kim (Eds.): ICISC 2023, LNCS 14562, pp. 20–38, 2024.
https://doi.org/10.1007/978-981-97-1238-0_2

security impact, security testing of the systems using Bluetooth is particularly important and critical.

Fuzzing is an automated testing approach that injects randomized inputs into a system under test to reveal vulnerabilities. For software testing, fuzzing has been successful over the years for various software systems, from OS kernels [6,7,15] to robotics systems [8–11]. However, unfortunately, fuzzing network protocols such as Bluetooth is still challenging. Specifically, the Bluetooth protocol is highly dependent on complex network configurations. Conducting various tests while preserving the same network configurations and states after each test requires non-trivial effort. In addition, practical challenges such as synchronization and delay of network communication further complicate the testing process. Worse, the root causes of many vulnerabilities stem from flaws in the Bluetooth chipset firmware rather than the software stack. Hence, various firmware implementations should be taken into consideration as well. Unfortunately, existing fuzzing approaches have difficulty thoroughly testing various layers of the system such as the Bluetooth protocol layer and the application layer. For example, many existing fuzzers generate test inputs targeting *device drivers*, which may not even reach the application layer, which may contains various potential vulnerabilities. In other words, existing techniques may underexplore a non-trivial amount of space for Bluetooth-related vulnerabilities.

This paper introduces BTFuzzer, a fuzzing framework that automatically identifies Bluetooth vulnerabilities. While there exist approaches for identifying Bluetooth security bugs [12,13], they suffer from various challenges such as (1) obtaining and maintaining complex network configurations during the test and (2) crafting complex test inputs that can penetrate various software layers without violating the constraints from device drivers, network protocol, and applications. Our approach, BTFuzzer, addresses these challenges by creating an interface to inject Bluetooth packets into the library directly. It maximizes code coverage by carefully crafting specific test inputs (e.g., Bluetooth packets) with respect to the protocol specifications such as Hand-Free Profile (HFP), Human Interface Device (HID), and Bluetooth Radio Frequency Communication (RFCOMM). The framework encompasses key components for comprehensive Bluetooth protocol fuzzing, including a packet generator, crash collector, and coverage analyzer.

To demonstrate the effectiveness of BTFuzzer, we conducted experiments on Android using open-source software. BTFuzzer found two previously unknown vulnerabilities that are exploitable in most Android devices: (1) An out-of-bounds read vulnerability (CVE-2020-27024 [24]), affecting systems running Android version 10 or later and (2) an information leak vulnerability that allows attackers to connect to a victim's device and leak data without the user's awareness as it is not visible in the list of connected Bluetooth devices.

Organization. The remainder of the paper is organized as follows: Sect. 2 provides background on Bluetooth and fuzzing. Section 3 introduces our proposed fuzzing framework. Section 4 presents our experimental results. Section 5 discusses related work. Section 6 concludes the paper.

2   Background

This section outlines the structure of Bluetooth that is essential for understanding BTFuzzer. We also provide an overview of the Bluetooth stack, Bluetooth profiles, and a generic fuzzing environment for Bluetooth protocols.

2.1   Bluetooth Components

Figure 1 illustrates a generic Bluetooth stack. Bluetooth packets move from the baseband to Logical Link Control and Adaptation Protocol (L2CAP) via the Host Controller Interface (HCI). L2CAP then routes these packets to the next appropriate stack for each channel. The HCI packet encapsulates data for the upper protocols and profiles, including L2CAP, and the path to the upper layer varies depending on the configuration of the HCI packet. If packets can be fed directly to the HCI, a security evaluation of the Bluetooth stack can be performed without the need for complex wireless configurations.

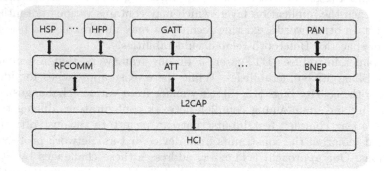

Fig. 1. Generic Bluetooth stack.

A Bluetooth profile is a protocol that aims to provide compatibility across various devices, allowing diverse Bluetooth devices to interact with each other. While the operation method may vary among devices, functions are implemented according to specific Bluetooth profiles, enabling communication between devices with different operating systems. Packet configurations differ for each profile and conform to the forms defined in their respective specifications [2]. Vulnerabilities may arise from improper profile implementations, making generating and transmitting packets tailored to each profile crucial for effective vulnerability discovery through fuzzing.

L2CAP operates based on the channel. A channel identifier (CID) [3] is the local name representing a logical channel endpoint on the device. When a Bluetooth device makes a connection, a channel is created and a CID is assigned. Communication with the device is possible through the assigned CID and channel. CID has a namespace designated according to its purpose. The CID namespace is 0x0000-0xFFFF. In the namespace, the null identifier (0x0000) is not used, and the identifiers from 0x0001 to 0x003F are reserved for a specific L2CAP function, which is called fixed channels. Therefore, when connected to a generic Bluetooth device, CIDs are allocated within the range of 0x0040-0xFFFF, which are called dynamically allocated channels.

L2CAP's upper layers support various protocols. Radio Frequency Communications (RFCOMM) replaces the traditional wired RS232 serial port and shares characteristics with the TCP protocol. Currently, The Headset Profile (HSP) and Handsfree Profile (HFP) are the popular profiles that use it. The Generic Attribute Profile (GATT), or often referred to as GATT/ATT, outlines how to exchange data between BLE devices using services and characteristics. It represents the highest-level implementation of the Attribute protocol (ATT). Each attribute has a 128-bit UUID and ATT-defined attributes determine characteristics and services. The Bluetooth Network Encapsulation Protocol (BNEP) enables the transmission of common networking protocols over Bluetooth and offers functionalities similar to Ethernet's. Running on BNEP, the Personal Area Networking Profile (PAN) specifies how two or more Bluetooth-enabled devices can form an ad-hoc network and access a remote network via a network access point.

2.2 Generic Fuzzing Environment for Bluetooth Protocols

The fuzz testing technique is widely employed to discover security vulnerabilities [4] automatically. A fuzzer can be specialized for a specific target (e.g., a particular protocol or class of applications) or designed for a generic purpose such as AFL. To conduct a successful vulnerability discovery, understanding the characteristics of various fuzzers and selecting the most suitable one based on the target and scope of the analysis is critical (Fig. 2).

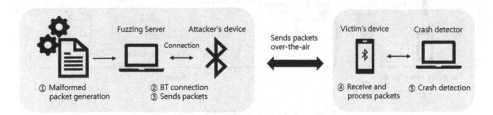

Fig. 2. Generic fuzzing environment for Bluetooth protocols.

Traditional Bluetooth fuzz testing requires two Bluetooth-capable devices: an attacker device that sends malformed packets and a victim device that processes the packets and potentially exposes vulnerabilities. The attacker device must maintain a state where it can send and receive packets. It must also implement a fuzzing engine with three functions: (1) Generating malformed packets (①), (2) Establishing a Bluetooth connection (②), and (3) Sending the malformed packets (③). The victim device must process packets (4) and detect crashes (⑤). Setting up this environment is time-consuming and complex, as it essentially requires constructing the entire system, including the network environment.

The Bluetooth software stack processes packets sent over-the-air (OTA) via the Bluetooth firmware on the target device. In OTA-based fuzzing, whether specific packets reach the Bluetooth software stack may depend on the firmware configuration of the Bluetooth chipset. This environment is more suited for Bluetooth firmware code analysis and has limitations for Bluetooth software stack vulnerability analysis.

BTFuzzer simplifies the fuzz testing process by directly transmitting packets to the victim device, bypassing the wireless environment. This approach allows quicker fuzz testing and eliminates the need for the packets to go through the Bluetooth firmware before reaching the software stack. BTFuzzer proposes an automated method to identify logical errors within the Bluetooth software stack.

3   Proposed System

In this section, we explain how to fuzz the Bluetooth stack using the proposed fuzzing framework, BTFuzzer.

3.1   Overview

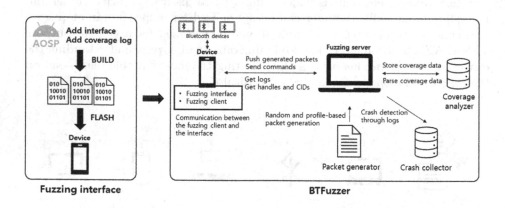

Fig. 3. Overview of BTFuzzer.

We propose a new fuzzing framework, BTFuzzer, which directly feeds packets into the target device, bypassing OTA. BTFuzzer generates packets and defines an interface for direct input into the device's HCI layer. Figure 3 provides an overview of the proposed system. This configuration allows direct access to the Bluetooth software stack for fuzz testing on profiles and protocols with independent specifications. We note that the framework is highly configurable, meaning that it can easily customized to support fuzz testing on diverse profiles and even other protocols of interest.

3.2 Fuzzing Interface

We create a specialized fuzzing interface to feed packets directly into the device. In particular, based on our analysis of the Android Open Source Project (AOSP) Bluetooth stack, we implement our fuzzing interface in `libbluetooth.so`.[1]

The `hci_initialize` function within `hci_layer_android.cc` initializes the HCI and creates (1) a fuzzing interface thread and (2) a socket for communication with the fuzzing client. This client then feeds commands and packets from the fuzzing server into the interface through the socket.

HCI Handles and L2CAP CIDs are essential for generating valid Bluetooth packets. The interface receives and processes predefined commands from the client to obtain these values. The currently connected Handles and CIDs are saved, and the gathered Handles and CIDs are used for packet creation. Additionally, HCI packets fed into the interface are categorized into four types for processing: COMMAND, ACL, SCO, and EVENT. Figure 4 illustrates the architecture of the fuzzing interface within the AOSP device.

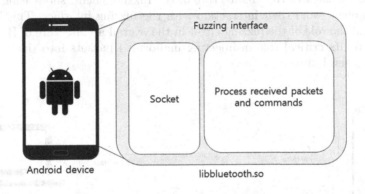

Fig. 4. Composition of fuzzing interface.

3.3 Fuzzing Server

The fuzzing server consists of the following three modules:

- **Packet generator:** This module creates a large corpus of malformed packets by randomly injecting errors into valid packets. This addresses performance degradation when feeding individual packets to the Android device via ADB. This ensures that the fuzzing process covers a wide range of possible inputs. The corpus is transferred to the Android device using the `adb push` command.
- **Crash collector:** This module collects crashes that occur during fuzzing.
- **Coverage analyzer:** This module analyzes the coverage of the Bluetooth software stack during fuzzing.

---

[1] The exact location of the implementation is '`AOSP\system\bt\hci\src\hci_layer_android.cc:hci_initialize()`.'.

HCI handles, and L2CAP CIDs are assigned when a Bluetooth device is connected. However, these values may change if the device is reconnected after a crash. This requires the packet generator to regenerate the packets. Additionally, the device's Bluetooth settings may change due to previous packets. To mitigate these issues, the fuzzing server initializes the Bluetooth stack before starting the fuzzing process. This ensures that HCI handles and L2CAP CIDs remain constant, allowing the use of pre-made packets even after a crash.

3.4 Fuzzing Client

The fuzzing client is specialized for interaction with the fuzzing interface, implemented in the `libbluetooth.so` library. This client is an executable file that establishes a connection to the fuzzing interface's socket. It reads from the corpus file located at a predefined path and sequentially sends packets into the Bluetooth stack via this socket. Essentially, the fuzzing client is responsible for sending malformed packets to the Android device for testing.

Figure 5 illustrates the architecture of the fuzzing client, showcasing its various components and their interaction with the fuzzing interface. This helps to understand the role of the fuzzing client in the overall architecture of BTFuzzer, highlighting its critical role in injecting malformed packets into the system to identify vulnerabilities.

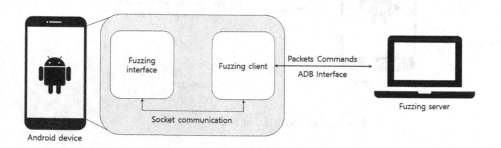

Fig. 5. Composition of the fuzzing client.

3.5 Packet Generator

This paper focuses on fuzzing three key Bluetooth protocols commonly used in smartphones: RFCOMM, HFP, and HID. These were selected because they are essential for core smartphone functions and have significant security implications.

- RFCOMM is a simple, reliable data stream to which other applications can connect as if they were serial ports. It is one of the foundational profiles used in most Bluetooth devices, meaning that it is an essential test subject.

– HFP is crucial for enabling smartphone call functionalities. Given that calling is a core function of smartphones and a profile used daily by many users, any vulnerabilities in HFP could have significant security implications, such as the potential for eavesdropping.

– HID is related to input devices such as keyboard and mouse. Vulnerabilities in HID could allow an attacker to remotely control the victim's device, making it critical for security analysis.

To generate test cases for these profiles, we have implemented two different types of packet generation techniques: mutation-based and profile-based.

First, the mutation-based packet generator takes existing valid Bluetooth packets and modifies them in various ways to create malformed packets. These malformed packets are then used to test how well the Bluetooth stack can handle unexpected or non-standard data.

Second, the profile-based packet generator creates packets according to the specifications of the target Bluetooth profiles (RFCOMM, HFP, and HID). By adhering closely to the specifications, we can test for vulnerabilities caused by wrong implementations of the protocols.

By combining the two different packet generation techniques, BTFuzzer aims to achieve a comprehensive set of test cases that can thoroughly evaluate the robustness and security of Bluetooth implementations in Android devices (Fig. 6).

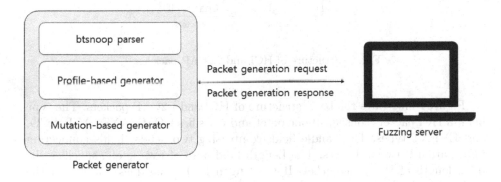

Fig. 6. Composition of the packet generator.

Mutation-Based Packet Generation. Mutation-based packet generation creates new packets through mutation, using packets transmitted and received between devices to enhance code coverage. Base packets are obtained from Android Bluetooth snoop logs [18]. Bluetooth HCI Snoop is specified in RFC 1761 [17]. A simple script was developed to parse these Snoop logs into a mutational hex format. Pyradamsa is used to mutate the parsed packets. A base packet is selected for mutation. A packet must be generated with a matching

HCI Handle and L2CAP CID to facilitate normal communication and data processing. In mutation-based generation, packets are created using two methods. The first method sequentially writes and mutates the entire set of recorded packets. The second method randomly selects a packet for mutation.

Profile-Based Packet Generation. Profile-based packet generation produces packets tailored for specific Bluetooth profiles and protocols. Target profiles and protocols were selected, and their specifications were analyzed. We examined the specifications for three items: HFP [19], HID [20], and RFCOMM [21]. Payloads for each item are generated using Python's random library. Like in mutation-based generation, the HCI and L2CAP portions, excluding the payload, utilize the allocated HCI Handle and L2CAP CID. Packets, including the generated payload, are generated with matching HCI and L2CAP lengths.

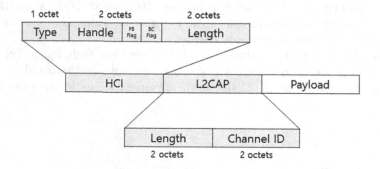

Fig. 7. Structure of HCI and L2CAP packets.

Figure 7 illustrates the basic structure of HCI and L2CAP packets. The type field in HCI packets consists of one octet and classifies COMMAND, ACL, SCO, and EVENT types. The handle field, comprising two octets, holds connection information between devices. The Length field, also of two octets, specifies the total length of the HCI packet. If the length field value does not match the packet length, Android Bluetooth HCI will immediately abort the connection. Therefore, it is crucial to calculate and set the correct length and handle values when generating a packet. Detailed specifications for HID, HFP, and RFCOMM, along with their implementation in BTFuzzer, are outlined below.

Figure 8 depicts the packet structure of HID. The Header field contains HID Header information in one octet. Only HANDSHAKE, HID_CONTROL, and DATA Message types are used for packet generation. These types facilitate data transmission from HID to the smartphone. The payload part consists of randomly generated data, varying in size from 0x00 to 0xFF.

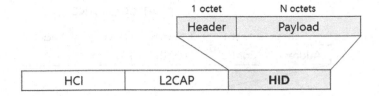

Fig. 8. Packet structure of HID.

Figure 9 shows the packet structure of RFCOMM. The Address field, consisting of one octet, contains the DLCI (Data Link Connection Identifier) or the connection information for RFCOMM. To transmit data correctly, this address value must be set accurately, which can be retrieved from Bluetooth logs. The Control field is one octet and includes frame type and poll/final bit information. Depending on the payload size, the Length field consists of one or two octets. If the payload size exceeds 127 bytes, two octets are used. The Payload field is filled with random values, and its size determines the Length field. Finally, the FCS field, comprised of one octet, is used for CRC (Cyclic Redundancy Check). It is calculated based on predefined CRC table values, Address, and Control fields.

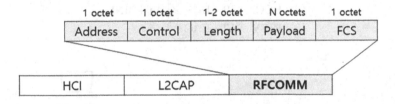

Fig. 9. Packet structure of RFCOMM.

Figure 10 presents the packet structure of HFP. The payload field is the only variable part based on AT Commands from the RFCOMM packet structure. We extracted a list of usable AT Commands from Android Bluetooth code and configured the system to randomly generate payloads for each AT Command.

3.6 Crash Collector

When a crash occurs during fuzzing, the crash collector gathers and stores relevant information. On Android devices, Signals 6 and 11 automatically generate tombstone files. The crash collector checks whether a tombstone file is created during fuzzing. If created, it collects the tombstone file from the Android device. The generated corpus, handle, and CID information are stored to facilitate crash reproduction. Figure 11 illustrates the components of the crash collector (Table 1).

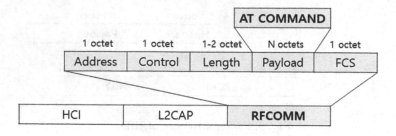

Fig. 10. Packet structure of HFP.

Table 1. List of AT Commands used for packet generation.

AT Command List		
AT+VGS	AT+VGM	AT+CCWA
AT+CHLD	AT+CHUP	AT+CIND
AT+CLIP	AT+CMER	AT+VTS
AT+BINP	AT+BLDN	AT+BVRA
AT+BRSF	AT+NREC	AT+CNUM
AT+BTRH	AT+CLCC	AT+COPS
AT+CMEE	AT+BIA	AT+CBC
AT+BCC	AT+BCS	AT+BIND
AT+BIEV	AT+BAC	

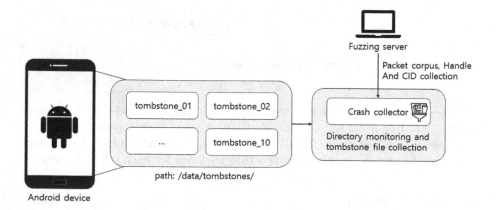

Fig. 11. Composition of the crash collector.

3.7 Coverage Analyzer

To measure the coverage of the code, the coverage analyzer inserts log codes into all AOSP Bluetooth stack files. To avoid duplicates, the log format is set as

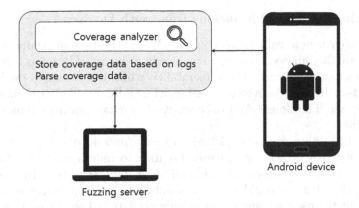

Fig. 12. Composition of the coverage analyzer.

`FUZZ_COVERAGE _FileName_Count`. For automated log insertion, we developed a Python script. Once log code insertion is complete, the number of logs added to each file and the total log count are recorded. By comparing the number of output logs during fuzzing with the total number of logs, we can assess the extent of code execution. Logs are inserted to identify most branching statements, allowing efficient code coverage measurement for `libbluetooth.so`. Figure 12 illustrates the structure of the coverage analyzer.

4   Evaluation

BTFuzzer was tested on a Pixel 3a device running Android 10. During the evaluation, it was paired with a Galaxy Watch, Galaxy Buds, a Bluetooth keyboard, and a Bluetooth mouse. Fuzzing was conducted after analyzing the packets obtained during basic interactions between the Pixel 3a and each Bluetooth device. After that, random packets were generated for fuzzing. The profiles evaluated were RFCOMM, HID, and HFP. To assess BTFuzzer's effectiveness, we applied it to the binary code before patching the vulnerability known as BlueFrag (CVE-2020-0022) [22,23], one of the most critical Android Bluetooth vulnerabilities of 2020.

BTFuzzer discovered two vulnerabilities that could affect most Android devices, including the latest version. One was reported to the Google Android Security Team and recognized as a new vulnerability under the identifier `A-182388143`. The other was reported as `A-182164132` but was marked as a duplicate of `A-162327732`, which has been assigned CVE-2020-27024 [24]. The BlueFrag vulnerability, for which the patch had been removed, was also detected.

The code coverage of BTFuzzer was assessed using the coverage analyzer. When delivering packets generated specifically for a particular profile, it was observed that the code coverage corresponding to that profile increased significantly. This observation validates the effectiveness of profile-based fuzz testing.

4.1   Hiding the List of Malicious Bluetooth Devices

We discovered a new vulnerability in the Bluetooth stack of Android devices. This vulnerability allows attackers to manipulate the list of Bluetooth-connected devices on a victim's device. The vulnerability, which is assigned to the identifier A-182388143. It was discovered by using RFCOMM profile-based fuzz testing with BTFuzzer. The Google Android Security Team has confirmed it as a security vulnerability.

The vulnerability can be exploited on most Android devices, including the latest version. An attacker could use this flaw to hide a malicious Bluetooth device connected to the user's device, making it undetectable to the user. Consequently, the attacker could access contacts and SMS messages or intercept calls without the user noticing the attacker's activities. The vulnerability can be exploited by sending just one malicious packet to the user's device.

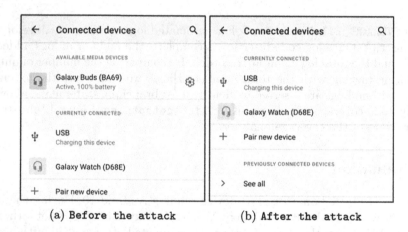

(a) **Before the attack**   (b) **After the attack**

Fig. 13. Result of the attack that exploited the A-182388143 vulnerability on Google Pixel 3a. The connected devices list is shown before (a) and after (b) the attack. Galaxy Buds are initially displayed in the connected list before the attack but not in the connected list after the attack. This is because the attacker was able to remove Galaxy Buds from the list by exploiting the vulnerability.

As shown in Fig. 13, we can see the Bluetooth device in the connected list before the attack is performed. However, after the attack is performed, the Bluetooth device is not visible in the connected device list even though the device can still maintain the connection with the victim device. This vulnerability was discovered while fuzzing RFCOMM. It was possible to trigger the vulnerability through a specific packet generated by BTFuzzer's Profile-based. This attack can hide the device by sending only one simple packet. We received a 2,000 USD reward from the Google Android Security Team for reporting this vulnerability. However, this vulnerability has not been patched yet and detailed information cannot be disclosed to prevent malicious exploitation.

4.2 Buffer Overflow Vulnerabilities

CVE-2020-0022. To demonstrate BTFuzzer's effectiveness, we conducted fuzzing tests on a binary containing the BlueFrag vulnerability, a significant Android Bluetooth vulnerability from 2020. Our goal is to evaluate whether BTFuzzer can find a known vulnerability effectively. Just less than 5 min, BTFuzzer detected the CVE-2020-0022 vulnerability. Figure 14 displays the crash log for this vulnerability, triggered by BTFuzzer.

```
pid: 7221, tid: 10924, name: bt_hci_thread  >>> com.android.bluetooth <<<
uid: 1002
signal 11 (SIGSEGV), code 2 (SEGV_ACCERR), fault addr 0x6ff73ffff0

backtrace:
    #00 memcpy+104
    #01 reassemble_and_dispatch(BT_HDR*) [clone .cfi]+948
```

Fig. 14. CVE-2020-0022 crash log.

A-182164132. The out-of-bounds vulnerability was discovered through the BTFuzzer, and the vulnerability was reported to A-182164132. However, it was already reported as a vulnerability with A-162327732. This vulnerability has been assigned CVE-2020-27024. CVE-2020-27024 is a vulnerability that can cause out-of-bounds read due to a missing boundary check in `smp_br_state_machine_event()` of `smp_br_main.cc`, Fig. 15 shows the CVE-2020-27024 vulnerability crash log triggered via BTFuzzer. The vulnerability (i.e., related to the missing boundary check) is mitigated through Bounds Sanitizer, which is supported from Android 10. However, it can be still exploited in the previous Android versions or customized/specialized Android systems forked from the previous Android versions. This vulnerability can be attacked when the connection handle is 0x02. Figure 16 shows packets that can reproduce CVE-2020-27024. Sending these two packets could trigger the CVE-2020-27024 vulnerability.

4.3 Coverage

Code coverage was measured using a log-based approach, in which 31,997 logs were instrumented into the Android Bluetooth-related code. Fuzzing was carried out for 24 h for each of the three methods used to generate packets: mutation-based, profile-based, and RFCOMM, HFP, and HID. The code coverage was then measured after each fuzzing run.

Figure 17 shows the change in code coverage over time during fuzzing. Figure 17(a) shows the total coverage for the 24 h, which reveals an initial rapid

```
pid: 3753, tid: 3802, name: bt_main_thread  >>> com.android.bluetooth <<<
uid: 1002
signal 6 (SIGABRT), code -1 (SI_QUEUE), fault addr --------
Abort message: 'ubsan: out-of-bounds'

backtrace:
    #00 abort+160
    #01 abort_with_message(char const*)+20
    #02 __ubsan_handle_out_of_bounds_minimal_abort+24
    #03 smp_br_state_machine_event(tSMP_CB*, unsigned char, tSMP_INT_DATA*)+1212
```

Fig. 15. CVE-2020-27024 crash log.

```
[Packet 1]
0202206900650006000befbb0057fe410e98007b22726573f3a0819e756c74223a22737563
63657373222c22726561736f6e223a302c226d73674964223a226d757369636f32d7175657565
6368616e6e6765642d696e64222c22636f756e74223a302c226c697374223a5b5d7dce249a

[Packet 2]
0202201500110007000bff1702000503c01af001c08007c07a86
```

Fig. 16. CVE-2020-27024 trigger packets.

increase followed by a slower growth rate. Figure 17(b) focuses on the first 10 min of this period, demonstrating a similar trend: an initial swift rise in coverage that eventually plateaus.

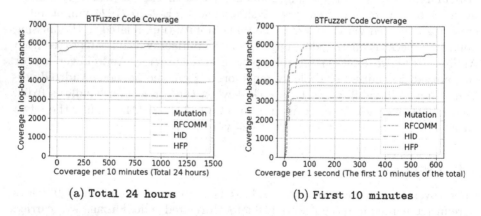

(a) **Total 24 hours**   (b) **First 10 minutes**

Fig. 17. Code coverage changes over time. (a) represents the 24-h coverage for mutation, RFCOMM, HID, and HFP methods. (b) represents the coverage changes during the first 10 min of the 24-h period.

Figure 18(a) and (b) present the coverage results of mutation-based and profile-based (HFP, RFCOMM, HID) fuzzing, respectively. Figure 18(a) illustrates the outcomes of profile-based fuzzing, where "Total" denotes the combined log results for HID, HFP, and RFCOMM, exceeding the individual log count for RFCOMM, the highest among them. Each method executed distinct code segments. Figure 18(b) contrasts mutation-based and profile-based fuzzing. Tests conducted on the same three types of Bluetooth devices (Galaxy Watch, Galaxy Buds, and a Bluetooth keyboard and mouse) showed that profile-based fuzzing achieved more code coverage than mutation-based fuzzing. Although profile-based fuzzing offers more code coverage, it requires understanding the profile and creating a packet structure code that aligns with the profile. Conversely, mutation-based fuzzing, while achieving less code coverage than profile-based fuzzing, allows fuzzing without profile comprehension. More importantly, each method executed different code segments, indicating that the two methods are complementary and could maximize fuzzing code coverage when combined.

Out of the 31,997 logs instrumented, 6,914 were recorded, representing approximately 21.6% of the total code coverage. Enhanced results are expected with further profile/protocol testing.

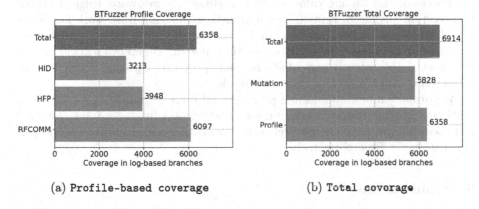

(a) **Profile-based coverage**   (b) **Total coverage**

Fig. 18. Coverage results for 31,997 instrumented logs. (a) represents the coverage of profile-based fuzzing, and (b) compares mutation-based and profile-based methods.

4.4 Summary of Evaluation Results

BTFuzzer is an effective tool for finding vulnerabilities in Android Bluetooth stacks. It found two vulnerabilities in the Pixel 3a, one of which was a new vulnerability that allowed attackers to hide a Bluetooth device in the list of Bluetooth-connected devices on a victim's device. BTFuzzer also detected the CVE-2020-0022 vulnerability, a significant Android Bluetooth vulnerability from 2020, in less than 5 min.

Our evaluation also shows that BTFuzzer's profile-based fuzzing is more effective than mutation-based fuzzing at achieving more code coverage. However, each approach targeted different code segments, meaning that they are complementary. We believe that combining both techniques could maximize fuzzing code coverage.

5   Related Work

Research on Bluetooth security is diverse, covering topics such as attacks via malicious devices, vulnerabilities in protocol implementations, and methodologies for vulnerability analysis, including active fuzzing studies.

One approach focuses on exploiting the Bluetooth function by taking control of Bluetooth communication authority. Xu et al. [5] describe an attack that leverages a device's inherent trust in an already-connected Bluetooth device. This research suggests that devices better manage Bluetooth function authority, pairing conditions, and the intent of paired devices. A more straightforward method of identifying vulnerabilities is to analyze Bluetooth protocol implementations. A notable example is BlueBorne [16], published by ARMIS Lab in 2017, which examined Bluetooth specifications and identified vulnerabilities and logical errors. However, auditing the code for the entire Bluetooth specification and its various profiles is challenging.

Another technique to consider is fuzzing. Mantz et al. [13] introduced a versatile framework for finding vulnerabilities in Bluetooth firmware. Ruge et al. [12] proposed an advanced, firmware emulation-based fuzzing framework for undisclosed Bluetooth implementations and firmware. However, these studies focus on chipset firmware-level security evaluation, not the Bluetooth software stack. Heinze et al. [14] recently suggested a fuzzing approach targeting specific L2CAP Channels in Apple's private Bluetooth stack.

We propose a new approach: a profile-based fuzzing framework for the Bluetooth stack. This framework facilitates creating and fuzzing packets for each Bluetooth profile, enabling comprehensive coverage of various protocols and profiles within the Bluetooth stack.

6   Conclusions

As Bluetooth technology becomes ubiquitous and its applications span multiple devices and functionalities, vulnerabilities in Bluetooth technology have become high-impact security risks. Despite ongoing research to enhance Bluetooth security, new vulnerabilities continue to be discovered and exploited, demanding a systematic approach to search for vulnerabilities effectively.

We introduce BTFuzzer, a scalable, profile-based fuzzing framework for Bluetooth devices. BTFuzzer implements in-device packet transmission, eliminating the need for complex environment setup. It generates packets according to specific Bluetooth profiles to maximize code coverage. BTFuzzer has identified a new vulnerability that allows an attacker's Bluetooth device to remain concealed while connected to a victim's device. Additionally, BTFuzzer has demonstrated its efficacy by detecting previously disclosed Bluetooth vulnerabilities.

BTFuzzer is a generic approach and not limited to Android. It is highly configurable, meaning that it can be easily configured to support other operating systems and protocols. Our preliminary results indicate that BTFuzzer is compatible with Linux Bluez, making it a viable tool for evaluating vulnerabilities in the Linux Bluetooth software stack. Further experimentation with the multitude of Bluetooth profiles will enhance code coverage and enable the discovery of additional vulnerabilities. We plan to expand our research to other operating systems, Bluetooth profiles, and other wireless technologies such as NFC, Wi-Fi, and Zigbee to improve wireless network security.

Acknowledgements. We thank our anonymous shepherd and reviewers for their valuable feedback and insights. Hyoungshick Kim is the corresponding author. This work was supported by Institute for Information & communication Technology Planning & Evaluation grant funded by the Korea government (No. 2018-0-00532, Development of High-Assurance (>=EAL6) Secure Microkernel (50%), No. 2022-0-00495 (30%), and No.2022-0-01199 (20%)).

References

1. MITRE. https://cve.mitre.org/cgi-bin/cvekey.cgi?keyword=bluetooth. Accessed 15 Sept 2023
2. Bluetooth Specifications. https://www.bluetooth.com/specifications/specs/. Accessed 15 Sept 2023
3. BLUETOOTH CORE SPECIFICATION Version 5.2, pp. 1026–1028. https://www.bluetooth.org/docman/handlers/DownloadDoc.ashx?doc_id=478726. Accessed 15 Sept 2023
4. Manès, V.J.M., et al.: The art, science, and engineering of fuzzing: a survey. IEEE Trans. Softw. Eng. **47**, 2312–2331 (2019)
5. Xu, F., Diao, W., Li, Z., Chen, J., Zhang, K.: BadBluetooth: breaking android security mechanisms via malicious bluetooth peripherals. In: Network and Distributed System Security Symposium (NDSS 2019) (2019)
6. Kim, S., Xu, M., Kashyap, S., Yoon, J., Xu, W., Kim, T.: Finding semantic bugs in file systems with an extensible fuzzing framework. In: ACM Symposium on Operating Systems Principles (SOSP 2019) (2019)
7. Schumilo, S., Aschermann, C., Gawlik, R., Schinzel, S., Holz, T.: kAFL: hardware-assisted feedback fuzzing for OS kernels. In: USENIX Security Symposium (USENIX Security 2017) (2017)
8. Kim, H., Ozmen, M.O., Bianchi, A., Berkay Celik, Z., Xu, D.: PGFUZZ: policy-guided fuzzing for robotic vehicles. In: Network and Distributed System Security Symposium (NDSS 2021) (2021)
9. Kim, T., et al.: RVFuzzer: Finding input validation bugs in robotic vehicles through control-guided testing. In: USENIX Security Symposium (USENIX Security 2019) (2019)
10. Kim, S., Kim, T.: RoboFuzz: fuzzing robotic systems over robot operating system (ROS) for finding correctness bugs. In: ACM Joint European Software Engineering Conference and Symposium on the Foundations of Software Engineering (ESEC/FSE 2022) (2022)
11. Jung, C., Ahad, A., Jeon, Y., Kwon, Y.: SWARMFLAWFINDER: discovering and exploiting logic flaws of swarm algorithms. In: IEEE Symposium on Security and Privacy (SP 2022) (2022)
12. Ruge, J., Classen, J., Gringoli, F., Hollick, M.: Frankenstein: advanced wireless fuzzing to exploit new bluetooth escalation targets. In: USENIX Security Symposium (USENIX Security 2020) (2020)

13. Mantz, D., Classen, J., Schulz, M., Hollick, M.: InternalBlue - bluetooth binary patching and experimentation framework. In: ACM International Conference on Mobile Systems, Applications, and Services (MobiSys 2019) (2019)
14. Heinze, D., Hollick, M., Classen, J.: ToothPicker: apple picking in the iOS bluetooth stack. In: USENIX Workshop on Offensive Technologies (WOOT 2020) (2020)
15. syzkaller. https://github.com/google/syzkaller. Accessed 15 Sept 2023
16. BlueBorne. https://www.armis.com/blueborne/. . Accessed 15 Sept 2023
17. RFC 1761. https://tools.ietf.org/html/rfc1761. Accessed 15 Sept 2023
18. Android Bluetooth Verifying and Debugging. https://source.android.com/devices/bluetooth/verifying_debugging#debugging-with-logs. Accessed 15 Sept 2023
19. Hands-Free Profile 1.8. https://www.bluetooth.com/specifications/specs/hands-free-profile-1-8/. Accessed 15 Sept 2023
20. Human Interface Device Profile 1.1.1. https://www.bluetooth.com/specifications/specs/human-interface-device-profile-1-1-1/. Accessed 15 Sept 2023
21. RFCOMM 1.2. https://www.bluetooth.com/specifications/specs/rfcomm-1-2/. Accessed 15 Sept 2023
22. BlueFrag. https://insinuator.net/2020/04/cve-2020-0022-an-android-8-0-9-0-bluetooth-zero-click-rce-bluefrag/. Accessed 15 Sept 2023
23. CVE-2020-0022. https://cve.mitre.org/cgi-bin/cvename.cgi?name=CVE-2020-0022. Accessed 15 Sept 2023
24. CVE-2020-27024. https://cve.mitre.org/cgi-bin/cvename.cgi?name=CVE-2020-27024. Accessed 15 Sept 2023
25. CVE-2017-0781. https://cve.mitre.org/cgi-bin/cvename.cgi?name=CVE-2017-0781. Accessed 15 Sept 2023

mdTLS: How to Make Middlebox-Aware TLS More Efficient?

Taehyun Ahn⬧, Jiwon Kwak⬧, and Seungjoo Kim(✉)⬧

School of Cybersecurity, Korea University, Seoul 02841, South Korea
{thyun_ahn,jwkwak4031,skim71}@korea.ac.kr

Abstract. Recently, many organizations have been installing middle-boxes in their networks in large numbers to provide various services to their customers. Although middleboxes have the advantage of not being dependent on specific hardware and being able to provide a variety of services, they can become a new attack target for hackers. Therefore, many researchers have proposed security-enchanced TLS protocols, but their results have some limitations. In this paper, we proposed a middlebox-delegated TLS (mdTLS) protocol that not only achieves the same security level but also requires relatively less computation compared to recent research results. mdTLS is a TLS protocol designed based on the proxy signature scheme, which requires about 39% less computation than middlebox-aware TLS (maTLS), which is the best in security and performance among existing research results. In order to substantiate the enhanced security of mdTLS, we conducted a formal verification using the Tamarin. Our verification demonstrates that mdTLS not only satisfies the security properties set forth by maTLS but also complies with the essential security properties required for proxy signature scheme (All of the formal models and lemmas are open to the public through the following url https://github.com/HackProof/mdTLS).

Keywords: maTLS · Middlebox · Proxy signature · Formal verification

1 Introduction

The advent of the COVID-19 pandemic has instigated substantial transformations in the business landscape. Notably, a significant proportion of enterprises have transitioned from conventional in-office working arrangements to facilitating remote work options for their workforce. Concurrently, the pandemic has spurred innovative shifts in operational methodologies, exemplified by the substitution of face-to-face business procedures, historically reliant on in-person meetings, with video conferencing solutions. As a result of these shifts, there has been a discernible escalation in network traffic, with notable statistics from the Telegraph indicating a remarkable 47% surge in internet traffic between 2019 and 2020 [28].

© The Author(s), under exclusive license to Springer Nature Singapore Pte Ltd. 2024
H. Seo and S. Kim (Eds.): ICISC 2023, LNCS 14562, pp. 39–59, 2024.
https://doi.org/10.1007/978-981-97-1238-0_3

Especially during the COVID-19 pandemic, the security of confidential information of various companies and individuals has been emphasized as most social activities, including business, are conducted remotely over the network. Among the most prominent and widely adopted technologies addressing network security concerns during this period is HTTPS (HyperText Transfer Protocol Secure) [36].

HTTPS represents a communication protocol that integrates the HTTP (HyperText Transfer Protocol) [13] to the TLS (Transport Layer Security) protocol [10], with the overarching objective of ensuring the confidentiality and integrity of data transmitted over networks. This protocol finds utility not only in desktops but extends its application domain to encompass a diverse array of embedded devices, including IoT (Internet of Things) devices. HTTPS offers several fundamental security attributes, including the following:

- *Encryption:* It serves as a pivotal mechanism within HTTPS, facilitating the obfuscation of sensitive information by encoding the data exchanged between communicating entities. Commonly employed encryption algorithms encompass symmetric key algorithms like Advanced Encryption Standard (AES) [19].
- *Authentication:* It constitutes an integral component of HTTPS, operating to ascertain the identity of entities by utilizing digital certificates.
- *Integrity:* It is another crucial facet of HTTPS, operating as a mechanism to detect unauthorized tampering or forgery of messages. Conventional algorithms used to maintain message integrity involve the implementation of Message Authentication Codes (MACs), such as the Secure Hash Algorithm (SHA) [9], to uphold the veracity and unaltered state of a network connection.

According to the Google transparency report, there has been a consistent increase in the loading speed of HTTPS pages in the chrome browser since 2014 [17]. Moreover, among the top 100 non-Google websites on the internet, which collectively constitute approximately 25% of global website traffic, 96 websites have embraced HTTPS, with 90 of them making HTTPS their default protocol. Additionally, according to Gartner's article [34], edge computing technology is anticipated to evolve into a core IT technology. This technology facilitates the secure communications of data collected through embedded systems deployed across various domains, relying on TLS protocols. Consequently, TLS communication is expected to assume an increasingly pivotal role. However, the robust encryption mechanisms employed by TLS to protect data can also be exploited by attackers to hide malware within network traffic, thereby evading detection by conventional security measures. In fact, according to research by Cisco and Sophos, TLS is vulnerable to detecting malicious traffic, and the number of such cases continues to increase [5, 14]. As a result, TLS cannot be considered a complete solution against cybersecurity threats.

For this reason, numerous organizations have deployed specialized middleboxes with distinct functionalities designed to enhance security for their clients, such as firewall and intrusion detection [39]. For instance, some companies have integrated Transport Layer Security Inspection (TLSI) [30] capabilities into middleboxes to identify and intercept malicious traffic attempting to infiltrate their internal networks. TLSI represents a technology devised to thwart unauthorized actions perpetrated by hackers on encrypted network traffic, and numerous entities, including industry giants such as Microsoft, are actively leveraging this technology [27].

However, according to a survey conducted in the United States, more than 70% of employees still believe that hackers can exploit middleboxes. Also, 50% of the respondents answered that their personal information could be infringed by exploiting vulnerabilities in the middleboxes [33]. Ironically, middleboxes, initially installed to fortify data security within TLS communications, have emerged as potential targets for cyberattacks. Consequently, safeguarding data transmitted over TLS communications necessitates a holistic approach considering network components, such as middleboxes, from the inception of communication channel construction. This approach goes beyond simply installing security-hardened components into an existing network.

As a consequence, numerous researchers have proposed a range of TLS extension protocols to enhance security during communication via the TLS protocol. However, prior research endeavors, driven primarily by a pursuit of security, have inadvertently encountered performance-related challenges. In this study, we will introduce the mdTLS protocol, which is meticulously designed based on the proxy signature scheme. The mdTLS is subject to comparative evaluation against maTLS [24], widely recognized as the most exemplary among prior researches in terms of both security and performance. First, we investigated the amount of arithmetic operations that must be performed for each designed protocol to compare the performance of the mdTLS and maTLS protocols. We then formally verified that the mdTLS satisfies not only the security properties verified in maTLS, but also three other security properties related to the proxy signature scheme. To ensure methodological consistency in our experimental setup, we employed the Tamarin [26,37,40], utilized in prior maTLS research, during the security analysis.

The remainder of the paper is organized as follows. First, we analyzed the strengths and weaknesses of related works (Sect. 2). Next, we introduced our mdTLS protocol (Sect. 3). After that, we compare the performance between maTLS and mdTLS (Sect. 4). In Sect. 5, we verified our protocol using Tamarin (Sect. 5). We showed that the performance can be further improved when the Schnorr digital signature is used in the protocol (Sect. 6). Finally, we present our concluding remarks (Sect. 7).

2 Related Works

Many researches have been conducted to improve TLS protocol. They are categorized into two types. One is the TLS-encryption extension-based approach. Their research is to improve the mechanism itself inside the protocol. The other one is the Trusted Execution Environment (TEE) based approach. Their research is to improve the protocol by using specific hardware.

2.1 TEE Based Approaches

A typical example of the Trusted Execution Environment (TEE) based approach is SGX-Box [18]. It utilized the remote attestation of Intel SGX. The server performs remote attestation to verify the integrity of the SGX-Box module in middleboxes. If remote attestation succeeds, they create a secure channel to prevent sensitive information from leaking between them. However, it is limited in that it is too dependent on its specific hardware (Intel SGX). Besides SGX-Box, there are many researches such as STYX [42], EndBox [16], and ShieldBox [41]. However, they also had the same limitations mentioned above.

2.2 TLS-Extension Based Approaches

A typical example of the TLS-extension approach is SplitTLS [20]. In SplitTLS, middleboxes act as servers and clients at the same time. This feature gives them too many privileges. It can cause some security incidents. For example, middleboxes such as CDN service providers could receive the private key to act as a server. It accidentally exposes the private key during the key-exchange phase. The worst thing is that when the middleboxes become compromised, malicious users (attackers) could abuse their privileges. Unlike SplitTLS, mcTLS [32] provides the least privilege to middleboxes. Middleboxes can read or write the TLS payload by obtaining MAC key pair from each endpoint. For example, they can only read the TLS packets when they get a unique key for reading. The advantage of mcTLS is that it does not force middleboxes to create or install further objects. Since the mcTLS uses only one key when creating a session, it is considered insecure. In the performance view, it has a limitation in that additional latency occurs when establishing the first connection. Furthermore, it does not follow TLS standards. David Naylor, who had proposed mcTLS, proposed an extended version of mcTLS called mbTLS [31]. mbTLS was created to improve compatibility with TLS standards. mbTLS establishes two types of sessions. One is the mbTLS session, and the other is the standard TLS session. If one of the endpoints does not use mbTLS, then traditional TLS sessions are activated. Overall, mbTLS offers improvements over mcTLS, which causes latency when adding a secondary session. maTLS [24] is another extended protocol to address security issues in SplitTLS. It treats middleboxes as equivalent entities to the server and includes them in the TLS session. As the server's certificate, middleboxes' certificates are issued by the Certificate Authority (CA), and by introducing the Middlebox Transparency (MT) log server, the middleboxes certificate contains a Signed Certificate Timestamp (SCT) [2,23]. This guarantees middleboxes' audition and improves the reliability of the middleboxes' certificates. Also, unlike SplitTLS, this procedure shows middleboxes can create their own official certificates without using custom root certificates or server certificates. However, these security elements entail performance issues. To make every session in each section, maTLS handshakes are essential between every entity. This is why maTLS's initial handshake takes more time than the original version of TLS.

3 mdTLS: Middlebox-Delegated TLS Protocol with Proxy Signature Scheme

In this section, we described the mdTLS protocol. At first, we defined the adversary model and security goals related to the mdTLS. After that, we described each phase in the protocol in detail.

3.1 Adversary Model

We considered the attacker's capability under the Dolev-Yao model [11]. Attackers can obtain and analyze messages in the network. Furthermore, they can get public keys. They aim to obtain certificates, perform an impersonation attack via forged certificates, and reveal private keys.

3.2 Security Goal

TLS currently provides the following properties in multi-party cases. Among them, we define "secure" for mdTLS by extending three security properties to cover the "delegation" concept.

Authentication: The notion of authentication was defined as that every entity must be able to verify whether they are talking to the "right person". This goal was divided into two sub-goals. First, each entity(client or server) can verify whether the other endpoint is operated by the expected middleboxes. It is called *entity authentication*. Second, If a session between two endpoints consists of an ordered set of middleboxes $MB_1 ... MB_{n-1}$, then any data received by MB_j must be a prefix of the data sent by MB_{j-1} or MB_{j+1}, where $1 < j < n-1$. It is called *data authentication*. We refined *entity authentication* into two security goals. First, the client ensures the delegated middleboxes by verifying the warrant in signature. It is called *verifiability*. Second, each middlebox can be identified as an appropriately delegated middlebox by checking its public key from the proxy signature. It is called *strong-identifiability*.

Secrecy: The notion of secrecy can be defined as that adversaries should learn nothing more from observing ciphertext in network connections. This goal is divided into two sub-goals. First, each mdTLS segment sent from entities should be encrypted with a strong ciphersuite. It is called *segment secrecy*. Second, each segment should have its own security parameters, such as a unique session key, to prevent the data from being reused. It is called *individual secrecy*.

Integrity: The notion of integrity means that only authorized or delegated entities can make or modify messages under their permissions. This goal is divided into two sub-goals. First, the entity can confirm which middleboxes have made each modification to the message. It is called *modification accountability*. Second, endpoints can determine the list and order of middleboxes that messages pass through. It is called *path integrity*. In mdTLS, we defined one security goal additionally. Delegated middleboxes can generate valid signatures. It means, in converse, undelegated entities cannot modify messages because they cannot generate and verify the signatures. Hence, it is called *strong-unforgeability*.

3.3   Overview of MdTLS Protocol

The mdTLS applies a proxy signature scheme based on the *partial delegation with warrant* [6,22,25] to improve performance while having the same security level as maTLS.

Proxy signature scheme [25] is a technique in which a proxy signer electronically signs on behalf of the original signer. When the original signer is temporarily absent, a proxy signer receives signature authority from the original signer and performs the proxy signing. This signing authority delegation technique can be used in various distributed systems, such as edge computing. There are four types of delegation in the proxy signature scheme: *full delegation, partial delegation, delegation by warrant,* and *partial delegation with warrant* [22,25].

- *Full delegation:* The proxy signer uses the original signer's private key to generate the proxy signature.
- *Partial delegation:* This method generates a proxy signing key using the private keys of both the original and the proxy signers. The advantage is that it can prevent the original signer from arbitrarily proxy signing, but there is no way to revoke or limit proxy signing authority.
- *Delegation by warrant:* This method uses a warrant that specifies the proxy delegation period and message space to limit proxy signing authority. It can compensate for the shortcomings of partial delegation, but performance in verification deteriorates because the verifier must additionally verify the warrant when verifying the proxy signature.
- *Partial delegation with warrant:* Kim et al. [22] first introduced this type of delegation. This method utilizes the advantages of both *partial delegation* and *delegation by warrant*. Proxy signing authority can be restricted or revoked through a warrant. Additionally, since this method only verifies the proxy signature, the verification efficiency can be improved.

The details of the mdTLS are shown in Fig. 1, 2. For reader's convenience, notation definitions are listed in Table 1. mdTLS is divided into 3 phases.

- *Generating certificates phase:* Before negotiation, server certificates are generated.
- *Handshake phase:* Negotiation between two endpoints on a network - such as a client and a server - to establish the details of their connection. During handshake, ECDH and ECDSA [21,29] are used in key exchange and digital signature, respectively.
- *Record phase:* Data communications are encrypted between the two entities.

The following statements below Table 1 are detailed sequences in which each entity establishes a secure communication channel based on the mdTLS.

Table 1. Notations in mdTLS

	Notation	Meaning
Entities	C	Client
	S	Server
	MB_i	i-th middlebox ($0 < i < n$)
	e_i	i-th entity (e_0: client, e_n: server)
ECDH	$(d_{e_i}^{ex}, Q_{e_i}^{ex})$	e_i's ECDH key pairs
ECDSA	p	A prime number
	E	An elliptic curve on $\mathbb{F}_p$
	q	A field size (prime number)
	G	A base point on E having prime order q
	d_{e_i}	A private key with $0 < de_i < q$
	Q_{e_i}	A public key with $d_{e_i} \cdot G$ on E
	H	Cryptographic hash function ($\{0,1\}^* \to \mathbb{F}_q$)
	$S^H(d_{e_i}, m)$	Sign message m with private key d_{e_i} using H
	$V^H(Q_{e_i}, m, \sigma)$	Verify signature σ generated by $S^H(d_{e_i}, m)$
Proxy-signature	$PS(skp, m)$	Proxy signing the message m with proxy signing key skp
	$PV(Q_{e_i}, m, \sigma_p)$	Proxy verification for proxy signature σ_p, with Q_{e_i}

Phase 0. Generating Certificates

1. Server sends Certificate Signing Request (CSR) to Certificate Authority (CA).
2. CA verifies CSR, creates pre-certificates, and submits to the Certificate Transparency (CT) log server to get SCTs [2].
3. After the CT log server adds pre-certificates to the logs, it returns SCTs to CA. Due to the Certificate Transparency policy [2,23], at least 2 SCTs from different CT log servers are required for certificates.
4. Using the X.509 v3 [7] extension, CA attaches SCTs to the certificate and issues the certificate to the server.

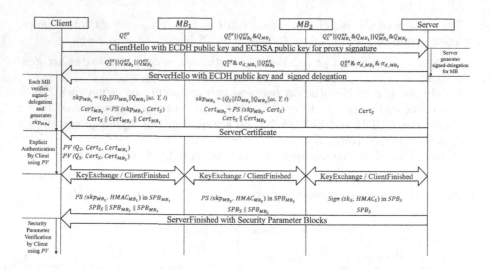

Fig. 1. Handshake phase of mdTLS

Phase 1. Handshake

1. Client generates ECDH key pair, and the public key Q_C^{ex} will be sent by ClientHello message.

2. Middleboxes attach their two types of keys to the ClientHello message. One is ECDH public key, $Q_{MB_i}^{ex}$, and the other is ECDSA public key, Q_{MB_i}, which will be used in the proxy signature scheme.

3. Server, the original signer, also creates its ECDH and ECDSA key pairs as middleboxes. When the server receives a ClientHello message, it operates the designation process to delegate middleboxes as proxy signers. Outputs of this process are called signed delegations $\sigma_{d\_MB_i}$. For delegation, the server has to sign the hash value of the delegation message. This message consists of Q_S, the identity of proxy signer ID_{MB_i}, Q_{MB_i}, and a warrant ω containing the message space and delegation period. In addition, 0 is prepended to represent that it is for the proxy signature scheme. $\sigma_{d\_MB_i}$ can be represented as (x_{Y_d}, s_d) according to ECDSA form. Signed delegations will be sent by ServerHello message with Q_S^{ex}.

   - $\sigma_{d\_MB_i} \leftarrow S^H(d_S, 0||Q_S||ID_{MB_i}||Q_{MB_i}||\omega)$
     - random value y_d ($0 < y_d < q$)
     - $Y_d \leftarrow y_d \cdot G$
     - $x_{Y_d} \leftarrow$ x-coordinate of Y_d
     - $c \leftarrow H(m_d)$ ($m_d = 0||Q_S||ID_{MB_i}||Q_{MB_i}||\omega$)
     - $s_d \leftarrow (c + d_S \cdot x_{Y_d}) \cdot y_d^{-1} \mod q$
     - $\therefore \sigma_{d\_MB_i} = (x_{Y_d}, s_d) =$ signed delegation

4. Middleboxes attach their own ECDH public key $Q_{MB_i}^{ex}$ to the ServerHello message. Then, middleboxes check whether signed delegations from the server are valid. If validation succeeds, middleboxes generate their proxy signing key skp_{MB_i}.

- $skp_{MB_i} \leftarrow (Q_S||ID_{MB_i}||Q_{MB_i}||\omega, x_{Y_d}, t)$
  - $c \leftarrow H(m_d)$ $(m_d = 0||Q_S||ID_{MB_i}||Q_{MB_i}||\omega)$
  - $r \leftarrow H(Q_S||ID_{MB_i}||Q_{MB_i}||\omega||c)$
  - $t \leftarrow r + d_{MB_i} \cdot H(Y_d||\omega) \bmod q$
    * $Y_d \leftarrow y_d \cdot G = s_d^{-1} \cdot (c + d_S \cdot x_{Y_d}) \cdot G$

5. Due to the **ServerCertificate** message, the server sends its certificate $Cert_S$ to the client and middleboxes. Middleboxes generate their own certificates $Cert_{MB_i}$ by proxy signing the received server's certificate. Then, their certificates are sent to the client by appending to the **ServerCertificate** message.
   - $PS(skp_{MB_i}, Cert_S)$ returns $Cert_{MB_i}$, which can be shown as below:
     - $(ID_{MB_i}, Q_{MB_i}, \omega, (x_{Y_d}, s_d), S^H(t, 0||Cert_S||Q_S||ID_{MB_i}||Q_{MB_i}||\omega||x_{Y_d}||s_d||r))$
       * $(x_{Y_p}, s_p) \leftarrow S^H(t, 0||Cert_S||Q_S||ID_{MB_i}||Q_{MB_i}||\omega||x_{Y_d}||s_d||r)$

6. The client, a verifier, verifies certificates to authenticate entities in TLS session. Unlike $Cert_S$, the client has to use proxy verification, PV, to verify $Cert_{MB_i}$, which requires the client to generate proxy public keys PKP_{MB_i} corresponding to each middleboxes. With PKP_{MB_i}, the client verifies $Cert_{MB_i}$.
   - $PV(Q_S, Cert_S, Cert_{MB_i})$
     - $Cert_{MB_i} \leftarrow (ID_{MB_i}, Q_{MB_i}, \omega, (x_{Y_d}, s_d), (x_{Y_p}, s_p))$
     - If $Cert_S \notin \omega$ then *return false*;
     - Else $PKP_{MB_i} \leftarrow r \cdot G + H(s_d^{-1} \cdot (c \cdot G + x_{Y_d} \cdot Q_S)||\omega) \cdot Q_{MB_i}$;
       * $c \leftarrow H(0||Q_S||ID_{MB_i}||Q_{MB_i}||\omega), r \leftarrow H(Q_S||ID_{MB_i}||Q_{MB_i}||\omega||c)$
     - $V^H(PKP_{MB_i}, 0||Cert_S||Q_S||ID_{MB_i}||Q_{MB_i}||\omega||x_{Y_d}||s_d||r, (x_{Y_p}, s_p))$

7. Server sends **ServerFinished** message with security parameter block (SPB). These blocks consist of signatures of $HMAC$. This $HMAC$ generates authentication code from security parameters such as ciphersuite and handshake messages. For middleboxes, they have to proxy sign their blocks with their generated skp_{MB_i}. For a client, it must verify middleboxes' signed blocks with its generated proxy public keys PKP_{MB_i}.

Phase 2. Record

- Modification log is attached to the message and helps to check whether a message is modified. Besides, endpoints can also check whether unauthorized entities modify messages without permission.

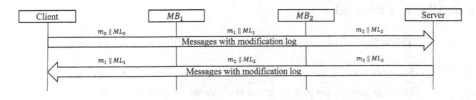

Fig. 2. Record phase of mdTLS

4   Performance Analysis for mdTLS

In this section, we analyzed the performance of the mdTLS by conducting a comparative analysis with maTLS, which we consider to be among the best of the existing TLS-extension protocols. Our performance analysis is focused on the number of computations in protocols. Both mdTLS and maTLS rely on ECDSA for the generation of security parameters. ECDSA, being based on the Elliptic Curve Discrete Logarithm Problem (ECDLP), involves a substantial number of point multiplication operations. These operations can significantly influence the performance of both protocols. Therefore, we conducted a performance analysis employing algorithms capable of measuring the number of point multiplication operations. It is important to note that this analysis is based on server-only authenticated TLS version 1.2 and assumes that 3 SCTs are created for each certificate through the Certificate Transparency policy [1–3, 23].

4.1   Preliminaries for Performance Analysis

To facilitate performance comparisons between two protocols that offer the same 128-bit security strength, we have set the elements within the protocols, as shown below [12].

- Types of elliptic curve: Secp256r1
- Private key size: 256 bits
- Hash size: 256 bits

4.2   Analyzing the Performance Between MaTLS and MdTLS

To measure the number of point multiplication operations, we employed the double-and-add algorithm, which averages 1 point doubling and 0.5 point additions per bit. Therefore, we considered an average of 1.5 point multiplication operations per bit. Following this, we divided the protocol into two segments and measured the number of point multiplication operations. The first segment corresponds to the generation and verification of certificates for utilization in the handshake phase. The number of computations for each protocol in this segment is detailed in Table 3 and 4 below. The second segment is where entities (server, client, middlebox) create and verify security parameters to be exchanged at the handshake phase. The number of computations for each protocol in this segment is detailed in Table 2 below (Fig. 3).

Table 2. Computational analysis for security parameter blocks

Descriptions	maTLS	mdTLS
Server generates security parameter blocks	384	384
Middlebox generates security parameter blocks	384N	384N
Client verifies blocks from the server	768	768
Client verifies blocks from the middleboxes	768N	768N

Table 3. Computational analysis for generating certificates

Descriptions	maTLS	mdTLS
- Server side		
Server generates keys and signature for CSR to CA	768	768
CA verifies CSR signature	768	768
CT log servers generate keys and signatures for 3 SCTs	2,304	2,304
CA generates keys and signs for server's certificate	768	768
- Middlebox side for maTLS		
Middleboxes generate keys and signature for CSR to CA	768N	–
CA verifies CSR signature	768N	–
MT log servers generate keys and signatures for 3 SCTs	2,304N	–
CA generates keys and signs for middleboxes' certificate	768N	–
- Middlebox side for mdTLS		
Each middlebox generates its keys	–	384N
Server generates signed delegations to assign proxy signers	–	384N
Middlebox verifies signed delegation and generate proxy signing key	–	768N
Middleboxes generate certificates with proxy signing key	–	384N

Table 4. Computational analysis for certificates verification

Descriptions	maTLS	mdTLS
Client verifies the signature and 3 SCTs in the server's certificate	3,072	3,072
Client verifies the middleboxes' certificates	3,072N	2,304N

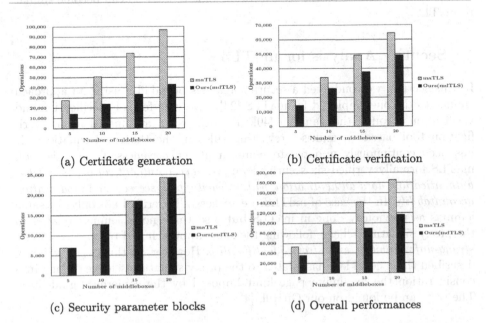

(a) Certificate generation

(b) Certificate verification

(c) Security parameter blocks

(d) Overall performances

Fig. 3. Performance of protocols when using ECDSA

We have implemented certain components essential for the functionality of mdTLS. We mainly implemented internal functions for computing data required during the handshake phase, such as key or signature generation and verification. We implemented and analyzed its performance within a virtual environment, specifically using docker container. The rest of our testbed in docker image is as follows:

- Ubuntu 22.04.3 LTS
- Intel(R) Core(TM) i5-10400 CPU @ 2.90 GHz
- 2GiB RAM

Table 5. Average execution time in implementation

Features	maTLS	mdTLS
ECDSA signing	1.4 ms	1.4 ms
ECDSA verification	2.5 ms	2.5 ms
Proxy signing	–	1.6 ms
Proxy verification	–	8.9 ms

Table 5 shows the time spent when signing and verifying the CSR files. Since the proxy signature scheme requires additional keys, the execution time of mdTLS is longer than maTLS. However, by reusing these keys when processing the security parameter block, the execution time of mdTLS can become similar to maTLS.

5   Security Analysis for mdTLS

In this section, we conducted a security analysis of mdTLS using an approach similar to the one employed for maTLS [24], involving formal specification and verification through the Tamarin [40]. Tamarin is an automated formal verification tool based on multiset rewriting rules in the theory of equations. It has been continuously updated to maintain its effectiveness. Using this tool, maTLS formally verified six security lemmas: *server authentication, middlebox authentication, data authentication, path integrity, path secrecy,* and *modification accountability*. In the case of mdTLS, we successfully verified not only the same lemmas as previously done in maTLS but also three novel lemmas related to the proxy signature scheme following the same approach and tools: *verifiability, strong-unforgeability,* and *strong-identifiability*. However, in this paper, we only described three novel lemmas related to the proxy signature scheme, taking into consideration the maximum page limit imposed by the conference guidelines. The rest can be found on our GitHub [4].

5.1　Experimental Setup

To analyze the security of the mdTLS, we established an experimental environment, as illustrated below. Our goal was to confirm that the formal model of mdTLS aligns with the security lemmas within our testing environment.

- Amazon Elastic Compute Cloud (Amazon EC2) c5a.24xlarge instance
- 96 vCPUs, 192 GiB RAM
- Ubuntu 22.04.2 LTS

5.2　Formal Specification

We have formalized the mdTLS, specifying the detailed operations conducted by each entity during the handshake and record phases in the form of rules. For cryptographic primitives like hash, signature, and PRF (Pseudo-Random Function) [15], we used the built-in functions provided by Tamarin. Details of all rules can be found in the spthy file uploaded to our github [4]. The script below illustrates an example of the detailed operations concerning ServerHello messages. In the handshake phase, when the server receives a ClientHello message from the client, it responds by sending a ServerHello message to initiate mutual authentication. In this process, mdTLS sends a ServerKeyExchange message, a signed delegation, a Diffie-Hellman public key, and a ServerCertificate message. The delegation in this context consists of the server's public key, the middlebox's public key and identification information, and a warrant providing an explanation of the delegation.

```
rule Server_Hello:
  let
        server_hello_msg
          = < 'server_hello', ~ns, server_chosen_details >
                ...
        server_key_exchange = s_dhe_pub
        server_key_exchange_signed
          = < server_key_exchange, sign(h(server_key_exchange)
                , ltk) >
        server_cert = < $S, pk(ltk) >
        warrant = ~warrant_fresh
        proxy_delegation = < pk(ltk), $M, mb_pubkey, warrant >
        proxy_delegation_signed = sign(h(proxy_delegation), ltk)

        Y_d = calcY_d(~y, 'G_skp')
        y_d_x = pointx(Y_d)
        c = h(proxy_delegation)
        s_d = multp( plus(multp(ltk, y_d_x), c), inv(~y) )
        proxy_delegation_signed_pair
          = < proxy_delegation, proxy_delegation_signed, <y_d_x, s_d> >
  in
    [ In( <mb_client_hello_msg, c_mb_extension> )
      , !PrivateKey('server', $S, ltk)    ]
  --[
      ServerSendDelegation(ltk_pub, mb_pubkey, warrant, proxy_delegation)
    ]->
    [ Out( <server_hello_msg, server_key_exchange_signed
          , proxy_delegation_signed_pair, s_extension
            , server_cert> ) ...    ]
```

5.3   Formal Verification

A Tamarin-based formal model is a set of multiple rules, and these single rules are made up of three basic components. Facts represent detailed information about the current execution in the model. States are multisets of facts. During formal verification, user-defined functions called rules can add or remove facts from the state. This is often denoted as l → [a] → r, indicating that fact "l" is removed from the state and replaced by fact "r", with this process traced through the action denoted as "a." Tamarin, following these principles, can verify whether a lemma, which is desired to be satisfied throughout the protocol, holds even as the state changes in the operation. Tamarin's verification process is based on tracing the protocol's state through actions. To evaluate the security of our protocol, we defined nine security lemmas and one source lemma. Among them, security lemmas consist of six security lemmas of maTLS and three security lemmas related to the proxy signature scheme. As previously noted, we described three security lemmas associated with proxy signatures. Prior to describing them, we described an additional description of a source lemma designed to assist Tamarin in accurately verifying the formal specifications.

Source Lemma. A source lemma is a concept used for formally verifying the security lemmas that a security protocol must adhere to during its execution. When conducting formal verification of an overall protocol, Tamarin adopts a strategy of deconstructing the protocol into smaller, more manageable components for analysis. The verification outcomes for these individual subsets are then used as supporting evidence to confirm that the entire protocol operates correctly and meets its prescribed security lemmas. However, during the verification process of these subsets, if Tamarin encounters difficulties in distinguishing between variables as nonce values or ciphertexts, it may face challenges in completing the verification. This is commonly referred to as a "partial deconstruction". To address such issues, it becomes necessary to establish a source lemma that precisely specifies the origin of these variables. From this source lemma, a refined source is generated, comprising a new set of sources. All security lemmas are subsequently verified using these refined sources, underscoring the importance of validating the source lemma to ensure the accurate computation of these refined sources [8,40]. When we initially omitted the definition of source lemmas, the formally specified mdTLS model yielded 120 partial deconstructions. Consequently, we defined source lemmas to enable Tamarin to discern the origins of these problematic variables. Upon closer analysis, it was determined that the issue of partial deconstruction occurred in 4 distinct segments, one of which pertained to the scenario where a middlebox received an encrypted request message sent by the client. To resolve this particular issue, we formulated a source lemma indicating that the encrypted message enc received by the middlebox had been transmitted from the client through the OutClientRequest() action, as shown below. By employing this approach, we could generate refined sources in a state of "deconstructions completed". This strategic use of source lemmas proved instrumental in addressing the partial deconstruction challenge and facilitating the successful verification process within the mdTLS model.

```
All enc msg #i.
    InMbClientRequest( enc, msg ) @ i
    ==> (Ex #j. KU(msg) @ j & j < i)
        | (Ex #j. OutClientRequest( enc ) @ j & j<i)
```

Security Lemma. After resolving the partial deconstruction issue, we verified that our protocol meets the nine security lemmas outlined in Sect. 3.2. In this section, we define three of the nine security goals related to proxy signature scheme. We also defined detailed information about the formulas that convert informal definitions into mathematical formulas called lemmas.

- *Verifiability:* The client must verify whether the middlebox's certificate, the proxy signature, was created with the consent of the server. To verify this lemma, we have to check whether the middlebox generated its certificate based on delegation and warrant sent by the server through the ServerHello message, as specified in *rule Server_Hello.*

```
All warrant mbLtk mbCert #tc.
    ClientReceivedProxySign(warrant, pk(mbLtk), mbCert) @tc
    ==> Ex delegation gy #tmb.
        MbGenerateProxySign(delegation, mbLtk, gy, warrant, mbCert)
        @tmb & KU(gy) @tmb & not(Ex #tmb. KU(mbLtk) @tmb)
        ==> Ex sPub #ts.
            ServerSendDelegation(sPub, pk(mbLtk), warrant, delegation)
            @ts & (#ts < #tmb) & KU(sPub) @ts
```

- *Strong-Unforgeability:* The proxy signer's private key, which is used to generate the proxy signature, must not be revealed. Otherwise, the proxy signature can be forged by an adversary.

```
All warrant mbLtk mbCert #tc.
    ClientReceivedProxySign(warrant, pk(mbLtk), mbCert) @tc
    ==> All delegation gy sPub #tmb.
        (MbGenerateProxySign(delegation, mbLtk, gy, warrant, mbCert) @tmb
        & KU(gy)@tmb & not(Ex #tmb.KU(mbLtk) @tmb))
        & (MbReceiveProxyDelegation(sPub, pk(mbLtk), delegation) @tmb)
        ==> All #ts.
            ServerSendDelegation(sPub, pk(mbLtk), warrant, delegation)@ts & KU(sPub)@ts
            ==> Ex #tmbclient. MbSendPublicKey(pk(mbLtk)) @tmbclient
                & KU(pk(mbLtk)) @tmbclient
```

- *Strong-Identifiability:* The identification of a proxy signer can be proved by its public key. The public key of the middlebox included in the proxy signature sent to the client must be the same as the public key of the middlebox sent to the server for proxy delegation.

```
All warrant mbPub mbCert #tc.
    ClientReceivedProxySign(warrant, mbPub, mbCert)@tc
    ==> All delegation mbLtk gy sPub #tmb.
        (MbGenerateProxySign(delegation, mbLtk, gy, warrant, mbCert)
          @tmb & KU(gy)@tmb & not(Ex #tmb. KU(mbLtk) @tmb))
        & (MbReceiveProxyDelegation(sPub, pk(mbLtk), delegation) @tmb)
        ==> All #ts.
            ServerSendDelegation(sPub, pk(mbLtk), warrant, delegation)
            @ts & KU(sPub)@ts
            ==> Ex #tmbclient. MbSendPublicKey(pk(mbLtk)) @tmbclient
                & KU(pk(mbLtk)) @tmbclient & (mbPub = pk(mbLtk))
```

Results of Verification. The overall result of formal verification is shown in Fig. 4. Figure 4 illustrates that our mdTLS protocol not only satisfies the three security lemmas introduced above but also aligns with the lemmas validated for maTLS. Furthermore, Fig. 5 shows mathematical proofs (verification process) demonstrating the consistent validity of the *verifiability* lemma within our mdTLS protocol among the security lemmas outlined in Fig. 4.

```
/* All well-formedness checks were successful. */

end

================================================================================
summary of summaries:

analyzed: mdTLS_ecdsa.spthy

  source_lemma (all-traces): verified (5660 steps)
  server_authentication (all-traces): verified (10 steps)
  middlebox_authentication (all-traces): verified (12 steps)
  middlebox_path_integrity (all-traces): verified (8 steps)
  path_secrecy (all-traces): verified (2 steps)
  modification_accountability (all-traces): verified (6 steps)
  data_authentication (all-traces): verified (2 steps)
  proxy_verifiability (all-traces): verified (10 steps)
  proxy_strong_unforgeability (all-traces): verified (12 steps)
  proxy_strong_identifiability (all-traces): verified (12 steps)

================================================================================
```

Fig. 4. Overview of formal verification results

As mentioned earlier, Tamarin formally verifies whether the rules always satisfy the lemma, called validity. A typical approach to verifying validity is negating the formulas and checking for inconsistencies. Figure 5 shows the negated lemma for verifiability, followed by verifying whether this formulation leads to contradictions. Following this process, we have validated all six security lemmas mentioned earlier.

```
lemma proxy_verifiability:
  all-traces
  "(∀ warrant mbLtk mbCert #tc.
      (ClientReceivedProxySign( warrant, pk(mbLtk), mbCert ) @ #tc) ⇒
      (∀ delegation ydx sd #tmb.
        ((((MbGenerateProxySign( delegation, mbLtk, ydx, sd, warrant,
                                                          mbCert
          ) @ #tmb) ∧
          (!KU( ydx ) @ #tmb)) ∧
          (!KU( sd ) @ #tmb)) ∧
          (¬(∃ #tmb.1. !KU( mbLtk ) @ #tmb.1))) ⇒
        (∃ sPub #ts.
          ((ServerSendDelegation( sPub, pk(mbLtk), warrant, delegation
            ) @ #ts) ∧
            (#ts < #tmb)) ∧
            (!KU( sPub ) @ #ts)))) ∧
  (∀ warrant mbLtk mbSign #tc.
      (ClientReceivedProxySignForSpb( warrant, pk(mbLtk), mbSign
        ) @ #tc) ⇒
      (∀ delegation ydx sd #tmb.
        ((((MbGenerateProxySignForSpb( delegation, mbLtk, ydx, sd, warrant,
                                                          mbSign
          ) @ #tmb) ∧
          (!KU( ydx ) @ #tmb)) ∧
          (!KU( sd ) @ #tmb)) ∧
          (¬(∃ #tmb.1. !KU( mbLtk ) @ #tmb.1))) ⇒
        (∃ sPub #ts.
          ((ServerSendDelegation( sPub, pk(mbLtk), warrant, delegation
            ) @ #ts) ∧
            (#ts < #tmb)) ∧
            (!KU( sPub ) @ #ts))))"
```

Fig. 5. Proof of verifiability lemmas in Tamarin

6 Discussion

We proposed an ECDSA-based cryptographic protocol. However, during the research, we found new insights for improvement. The insight is to use the Schnorr algorithm instead of ECDSA for the algorithm that generates the digital signature. Boldyreva et al.'s research [6] used Schnorr signature, and they shows better outcomes in terms of both performance and security than ECDSA.

- Performance: Schnorr does not have modular inverse calculations that significantly affect performance.
- Security: Since Schnorr is strongly unforgeable under chosen message attack (SUF-CMA), Schnorr is provably secure in the random oracle model [35].

So we compared the performance of the maTLS and mdTLS protocols assumed that both protocols use the Schnorr signature. To measure the performance of Schnorr, the number of modular multiplication operations was calculated using the square-and-multiply algorithm. This algorithm requires 1.5 modular multiplications per bit on average. Besides, as mentioned in Schnorr's paper [38], we calculated the modular multiplications of the Schnorr verification equation by multiplying by 1.75 per bit. When the security level is set to 128-bit, the related parameters' sizes can be shown below [12].

- Public key size: 3,072 bits
- Private key size: 256 bits
- Hash size: 256 bits

Table 6 shows the number of modular multiplications at each stage. Here, N represents the number of middleboxes. The mdTLS reduces the number of modular multiplications by 51.8% compared to maTLS, demonstrating better performance when using Schnorr than when using ECDSA. Nevertheless, the TLS standard mandates the utilization of the ECDSA algorithm for digital signature creation, rendering the adoption of the Schnorr signature algorithm impractical now (Fig. 6).

Table 6. Modular multiplications in maTLS and mdTLS

Stages	maTLS	mdTLS
Certificate generation	4,293N + 4,293	1,603N + 4,293
Certificate verification	1,792N + 1,792	897N + 1,792
Security parameter blocks	833N + 833	833N + 833
Overall	6,918N + 6,918	3,333N + 6,918

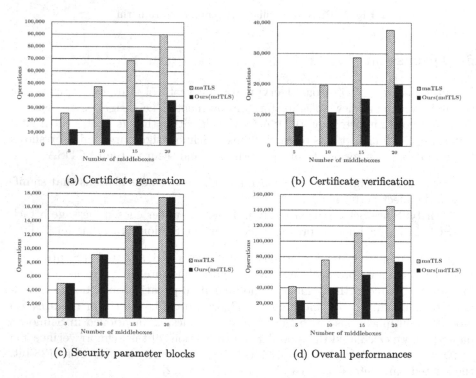

(a) Certificate generation

(b) Certificate verification

(c) Security parameter blocks

(d) Overall performances

Fig. 6. Performance of protocols when using Schnorr

7 Conclusion

In this paper, we proposed a middlebox-delegated TLS protocol in which only middleboxes that have been permitted can participate in the network. To demonstrate the excellence of our proposed protocol, we verified our protocol from two aspects of view: performance and security. In the performance view, we calculated the number of computations in the protocol. We found that the mdTLS reduces about 39% of the computations compared to maTLS. Also, we formally verified that our proposal achieved nine security lemmas: *server/middlebox/data authentication, path integrity, path secrecy, modification accountability, verifiability, strong-unforgeability,* and *strong-identifiability.* Especially among them, the latter three security lemmas are newly defined for our protocol by extending existing concepts. The primary contribution of this work is to show that using the proxy signature scheme can enhance performance efficiency and maintain its security level.

Acknowledgements. This work was partly supported by Institute of Information communications Technology Planning Evaluation (IITP) grant funded by the Korea government (MSIT) (No. 2018-0-00532, Development of High-Assurance (EAL6) Secure Microkernel, 100) and supported by Korea University.

References

1. Apple's Certificate Transparency policy Homepage. https://support.apple.com/en-ng/HT205280. Accessed 21 May 2023
2. Certificate Transparency Homepage. https://certificate.transparency.dev. Accessed 21 May 2023
3. Chrome Certificate Transparency Policy Homepage. https://googlechrome.github.io/CertificateTransparency/ct_policy.html. Accessed 21 May 2023
4. Hackproof Github Homepage. https://github.com/HackProof/mdTLS. Accessed 26 May 2023
5. Anderson, B.: Detecting encrypted malware traffic (without decryption). https://blogs.cisco.com/security/detecting-encrypted-malware-traffic-without-decryption. Accessed 26 Sept 2023
6. Boldyreva, A., Palacio, A., Warinschi, B.: Secure proxy signature schemes for delegation of signing rights. J. Cryptol. **25**, 57–115 (2012)
7. Cooper, D., Santesson, S., Farrell, S., Boeyen, S., Housley, R., Polk, W.: Internet X. 509 public key infrastructure certificate and certificate revocation list (CRL) profile (2008). https://www.rfc-editor.org/rfc/rfc5280.txt. Accessed 23 Sept 2023
8. Cortier, V., Delaune, S., Dreier, J.: Automatic generation of sources lemmas in TAMARIN: towards automatic proofs of security protocols. In: Chen, L., Li, N., Liang, K., Schneider, S. (eds.) ESORICS 2020. LNCS, vol. 12309, pp. 3–22. Springer, Cham (2020). https://doi.org/10.1007/978-3-030-59013-0_1
9. Dang, Q.H.: Secure hash standard (2015). https://nvlpubs.nist.gov/nistpubs/FIPS/NIST.FIPS.180-4.pdf. Accessed 23 Sept 2023
10. Dierks, T., Rescorla, E.: The transport layer security (TLS) protocol version 1.2 (2008). https://www.rfc-editor.org/rfc/rfc5246.txt. Accessed 23 Sept 2023

11. Dolev, D., Yao, A.: On the security of public key protocols. IEEE Trans. Inf. Theory **29**(2), 198–208 (1983)

12. Elaine, B.: Recommendation for key management: part 1 - general (2020). https://nvlpubs.nist.gov/nistpubs/SpecialPublications/NIST.SP.800-57pt1r5.pdf. Accessed 23 Sept 2023

13. Fielding, R., et al.: Hypertext transfer protocol-HTTP/1.1 (1999). https://www.rfc-editor.org/rfc/rfc2616.txt. Accessed 23 Sept 2023

14. Gallagher, S.: Nearly half of malware now use TLS to conceal communications. https://news.sophos.com/en-us/2021/04/21/nearly-half-of-malware-now-use-tls-to-conceal-communications. Accessed 23 Sept 2023

15. Goldreich, O., Goldwasser, S., Micali, S.: How to construct random functions. J. ACM (JACM) **33**(4), 792–807 (1986)

16. Goltzsche, D., et al.: EndBox: scalable middlebox functions using client-side trusted execution. In: 2018 48th Annual IEEE/IFIP International Conference on Dependable Systems and Networks (DSN), pp. 386–397. IEEE (2018)

17. Google: Google Transparency Homepage. https://transparencyreport.google.com/overview?hl=en. Accessed 9 May 2023

18. Han, J., Kim, S., Ha, J., Han, D.: SGX-box: enabling visibility on encrypted traffic using a secure middlebox module. In: Proceedings of the First Asia-Pacific Workshop on Networking, pp. 99–105 (2017)

19. Heron, S.: Advanced encryption standard (AES). Netw. Secur. **2009**(12), 8–12 (2009)

20. Jarmoc, J., Unit, D.: SSL/TLS interception proxies and transitive trust. Black Hat Europe (2012)

21. Johnson, D., Menezes, A., Vanstone, S.: The elliptic curve digital signature algorithm (ECDSA). Int. J. Inf. Secur. **1**, 36–63 (2001)

22. Kim, S., Park, S., Won, D.: Proxy signatures, revisited. In: Han, Y., Okamoto, T., Qing, S. (eds.) ICICS 1997. LNCS, vol. 1334, pp. 223–232. Springer, Heidelberg (1997). https://doi.org/10.1007/bfb0028478

23. Laurie, B., Langley, A., Kasper, E.: RFC 6962: certificate transparency (2013). https://www.rfc-editor.org/rfc/rfc6962.txt. Accessed 23 Sept 2023

24. Lee, H., et al.: maTLS: how to make TLS middlebox-aware? In: NDSS (2019)

25. Mambo, M., Usuda, K., Okamoto, E.: Proxy signatures: delegation of the power to sign messages. IEICE Trans. Fundam. Electron. Commun. Comput. Sci. **79**(9), 1338–1354 (1996)

26. Meier, S., Schmidt, B., Cremers, C., Basin, D.: The TAMARIN prover for the symbolic analysis of security protocols. In: Sharygina, N., Veith, H. (eds.) CAV 2013. LNCS, vol. 8044, pp. 696–701. Springer, Heidelberg (2013). https://doi.org/10.1007/978-3-642-39799-8_48

27. Microsoft: Microsoft Azure firewall Homepage. https://learn.microsoft.com/ko-kr/azure/firewall/premium-features. Accessed 9 May 2023

28. Miller, J.: Telegeography homepage. https://blog.telegeography.com/2021-global-internet-map-tracks-global-capacity-traffic-and-cloud-infrastructure. Accessed 9 May 2023

29. National Institute of Standards and Technology: Digital Signature Standard (DSS) (2023). https://nvlpubs.nist.gov/nistpubs/FIPS/NIST.FIPS.186-5.pdf. Accessed 23 Sept 2023

30. National Security Agency: Cybersecurity and Infrastructure Security Agency Homepage. https://www.us-cert.gov/ncas/current-activity/2019/11/19/nsa-releases-cyber-advisory-managing-risk-transport-layer-security. Accessed 9 May 2023

31. Naylor, D., Li, R., Gkantsidis, C., Karagiannis, T., Steenkiste, P.: And then there were more: secure communication for more than two parties. In: Proceedings of the 13th International Conference on emerging Networking EXperiments and Technologies, pp. 88–100 (2017)
32. Naylor, D., et al.: Multi-context TLS (mcTLS): enabling secure in-network functionality in TLS. ACM SIGCOMM Comput. Commun. Rev. **45**(4), 199–212 (2015)
33. O'Neill, M., Ruoti, S., Seamons, K., Zappala, D.: TLS inspection: how often and who cares? IEEE Internet Comput. **21**(3), 22–29 (2017)
34. Panetta, K.: Gartner homepage. https://www.gartner.com/smarterwithgartner/gartner-top-10-strategic-technology-trends-for-2019. Accessed 9 May 2023
35. Pointcheval, D., Stern, J.: Security arguments for digital signatures and blind signatures. J. Cryptol. **13**, 361–396 (2000)
36. Rescorla, E.: HTTP over TLS (2000). https://www.rfc-editor.org/rfc/rfc2818.txt. Accessed 23 Sept 2023
37. Schmidt, B., Meier, S., Cremers, C., Basin, D.: Automated analysis of Diffie-Hellman protocols and advanced security properties. In: 2012 IEEE 25th Computer Security Foundations Symposium, pp. 78–94. IEEE (2012)
38. Schnorr, C.P.: Efficient identification and signatures for smart cards. In: Brassard, G. (ed.) CRYPTO 1989. LNCS, vol. 435, pp. 239–252. Springer, New York (1990). https://doi.org/10.1007/0-387-34805-0_22
39. Sherry, J., Hasan, S., Scott, C., Krishnamurthy, A., Ratnasamy, S., Sekar, V.: Making middleboxes someone else's problem: network processing as a cloud service. ACM SIGCOMM Comput. Commun. Rev. **42**(4), 13–24 (2012)
40. The-Tamarin-Team: Tamarin-Prover Manual. https://tamarin-prover.github.io/manual/master/tex/tamarin-manual.pdf. Accessed 17 May 2023
41. Trach, B., Krohmer, A., Gregor, F., Arnautov, S., Bhatotia, P., Fetzer, C.: Shield-Box: secure middleboxes using shielded execution. In: Proceedings of the Symposium on SDN Research, pp. 1–14 (2018)
42. Wei, C., Li, J., Li, W., Yu, P., Guan, H.: STYX: a trusted and accelerated hierarchical SSL key management and distribution system for cloud based CDN application. In: Proceedings of the 2017 Symposium on Cloud Computing, pp. 201–213 (2017)

PHI: Pseudo-HAL Identification for Scalable Firmware Fuzzing

Seyeon Jeong[1,2], Eunbi Hwang[1], Yeongpil Cho[3], and Taekyoung Kwon[1(✉)]

[1] Graduate School of Information, Yonsei University, Seoul 03722, South Korea
{ebhwang95,taekyoung}@yonsei.ac.kr
[2] Suresofttech Inc., Seongnam-si, Gyeonggi 13453, South Korea
best6653@gmail.com
[3] Department of Computer Science, Hanyang University, Seoul 08826, South Korea
ypcho@hanyang.ac.kr

Abstract. Firmware fuzzing aims to detect vulnerabilities in firmware by emulating peripherals at different levels: hardware, register, and function. HAL-FUZZ, which emulates peripherals through HAL function handling, is a remarkable firmware fuzzer. However, its effectiveness is confined to firmware solely relying on HAL functions, and it necessitates intricate firmware information for best outcomes, thereby limiting its target firmware range. Notably, in commercial firmware, both HAL and non-HAL (which we call "pseudo-HAL") functions are prevalent. Identifying and addressing both is crucial for comprehensive peripheral control in fuzzing. In this paper, we present PHI, a tool designed to identify HAL and pseudo-HAL functions at the register-level. Using PHI, we develop PHI-Fuzz, an enhanced firmware fuzzer operating at the function-level. This fuzzer efficiently manages HAL and pseudo-HAL functions, demanding minimal prior knowledge yet delivering substantial results. Our evaluation demonstrates that PHI identifies HAL functions accessing the MMIO range as effectively as LIBMATCH of HAL-FUZZ, while overcoming its constraints in detecting pseudo-HAL functions. Significantly, when benchmarked against HAL-FUZZ, PHI-Fuzz showcases superior bug-finding capabilities, uncovering crashes that HAL-FUZZ missed.

Keywords: Security · Firmware · Fuzzing · Hardware Abstraction Layer

1 Introduction

Embedded devices play a crucial role in various applications, including the Internet of Things (IoT), aviation, and weapons systems. According to *State of IoT-Spring 2023* [1] report, there was an 18% growth in the number of global IoT connections during 2022, resulting in a total of 14.3 billion active IoT endpoints.

S. Jeong and E. Hwang—Equal contribution.

© The Author(s), under exclusive license to Springer Nature Singapore Pte Ltd. 2024
H. Seo and S. Kim (Eds.): ICISC 2023, LNCS 14562, pp. 60–80, 2024.
https://doi.org/10.1007/978-981-97-1238-0_4

However, when compared to the total vulnerabilities discovered, firmware vulnerabilities have consistently accounted for about 2% each year since 2017, and as of 2023, 2.41% of firmware vulnerabilities have been identified [2]. Firmware vulnerabilities, which can result from system crashes, reboots, and hangs, are exploitable by attackers aiming to compromise embedded devices. This poses a significant risk to society, thus necessitating dynamic analysis and proactive detection through firmware fuzzing [14,19,20].

Fuzzing, a dynamic bug-finding technique, provides random input values to a program and monitors its executions. AFL (American Fuzz Lop) [24] is a coverage-guided fuzzer that has demonstrated high performance in general software fuzzing and can also be utilized for firmware fuzzing on microcontroller units (MCU) [16,20,25]. However, exploring firmware vulnerabilities through fuzzing techniques can be challenging, particularly for embedded devices with inherent limitations. To address these challenges, recent firmware fuzzing research has proposed emulation-based fuzzing [10–13,18,26]. Firmware emulation enables fuzzing on devices with sufficient power and capacity. Nonetheless, using a general emulator like QEMU [9] can lead to execution failures due to undefined peripheral access during firmware fuzzing. Consequently, how emulators handle peripherals is crucial for successful firmware emulation and fuzzing. Emulation through Hardware-In-The-Loop (HITL) method can result in performance degradation due to communication between hardware and the emulator [19]. Recent studies have focused on peripheral modeling as a way to overcome this limitation. Peripheral modeling techniques can be classified into three types: hardware-level, function-level, and register-level modeling. Function-level and register-level modeling do not require hardware during the modeling phase, resulting in better performance for firmware emulation and fuzzing.

Function-level peripheral modeling involves emulating firmware by hooking a function during emulation and connecting pre-made handlers. Register-level peripheral modeling handles each register during emulation. Compared to register-level modeling, function-level modeling boasts faster processing, as peripheral functions accessing Memory-mapped I/O (MMIO) are processed with a handler. HALucinator, a firmware emulator, implements function-level peripheral modeling using Python handlers achieved through Hardware Abstraction Layer (HAL) function hooking [11]. Building upon this concept, HAL-FUZZ, a firmware fuzzer, integrates HALucinator with UnicornAFL [3]. HALucinator and HAL-FUZZ identify functions to be hooked using LIBMATCH [4], a HAL function identification tool. Although LIBMATCH can identify HAL functions, it requires a software development kit (SDK) containing HAL function object files compiled in the same environment as the target firmware. As a result, LIBMATCH needs extensive information about the firmware despite its limited capabilities in identifying functions.

Many modern firmware implementations utilize not only HAL but also pseudo-HAL functions. Consequently, LIBMATCH may not fully identify all functions in the firmware, limiting the effectiveness of HALucinator and HAL-FUZZ. Additionally, obtaining detailed information about firmware compilation options can be challenging, and the scripts used in LIBMATCH are often not openly available. This makes it difficult to use LIBMATCH in an ideal operating environment. To overcome these limitations, we propose the Pseudo-HAL Identification (PHI) program, which leverages symbolic execution to identify HAL and pseudo-HAL functions at the register-level without relying on specific firmware compilation environments or firmware stripping. Furthermore, we introduce PHI-Fuzz, a function-level firmware fuzzer based on HAL-FUZZ that utilizes PHI's results. With the scalability provided by PHI, PHI-Fuzz can perform more efficient and effective fuzzing compared to existing function-level firmware fuzzers.

Contribution. This paper makes the following contributions.

- **Pseudo-HAL Identification.** We propose PHI, a register-level function identification method for more scalable function-level peripheral modeling.
- **PHI-Fuzz.** We propose PHI-Fuzz, an enhanced and scalable firmware fuzzer operating at the function-level by leveraging PHI.
- For further research, we will release our tool at publication time.

Organization. This paper is organized as follows. Section 2 provides the necessary background and discusses the existing problems. Section 3 presents the design of the proposed system. Section 4 describes the implementation of the system. Section 5 presents the evaluation of the system. Section 6 provides a discussion of the results and limitations. Section 7 reviews the related work. Finally, Sect. 8 concludes the paper.

2 Motivation

In this section, we briefly discuss the background of firmware fuzzing, identify the challenges of existing techniques, and demonstrate their limitations through a series of experiments.

2.1 Background

Firmware in Embedded Devices. Firmware is a type of software that offers low-level control over hardware components, including on-chip and off-chip peripherals, as well as MCUs integrated into embedded systems. Muench et al. [19] classified embedded devices into three categories based on firmware: general OS-based firmware, embedded OS-based firmware, or monolithic firmware. Monolithic firmware (also known as bare-metal firmware) is present in approximately 81% of embedded devices as of 2019 [5]. This firmware type operates by executing simple functions in a continuous loop and is commonly used in small-scale embedded systems. Our study focuses on developing a firmware fuzzing technique that specifically targets monolithic firmware.

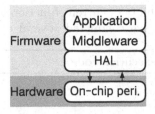

Fig. 1. STM32 firmware architecture

Firmware Fuzzing. Traditional fuzzing techniques for general software often require instrumentation to observe and analyze the behavior of the tested program. However, firmware fuzzing presents additional challenges due to the high dependency on heterogeneous peripherals and the lack of reliable emulation techniques. Fully emulating firmware, including both the processor and peripherals, can be a complex and time-consuming process owing to the wide variety of peripherals available. For firmware testing, partial emulation using the hardware-in-the-loop (HITL) method may be slower than the peripheral modeling method, as it may cause a bottleneck in the communication process between the emulator and the actual hardware being emulated [19,22]. Recently, emulation techniques utilizing peripheral modeling have gained popularity for effective firmware fuzzing [10–13,18,21,26].

HAL (Hardware Abstraction Layer). HAL is a library provided by manufacturers to enhance the convenience of firmware development. By abstracting common functionality for specific devices, HAL makes developers program without relying on a specific hardware target [6]. Since many manufacturers produce various types of hardware, developing firmware based on specific hardware requires a significant loss of productivity to develop firmware that directly accesses the hardware. Using HAL has the advantage of facilitating the development of essential functions when creating firmware. It is presented as higher-layer functions rather than register units, enabling convenient usage through function calls without the need for direct register access. For instance, in implementing the functionality to send data over UART, developers can simply call the *HAL_UART_Transmit()* function without directly manipulating the Data Register. HALucinator [11] leveraged the characteristics of this HAL in firmware emulation. Identified HAL function calls and handled them with pre-made handlers, HALucinator improved emulation efficiency. Unlike HALucinator, which identified HAL functions at the function-level, the PHI proposed in this paper detects not only HAL functions but also various library functions for peripherals HAL functions at the register-level.

2.2 Problem Definition

A central question this study aimed to address is whether function-level fuzzing, as a peripheral modeling method, is more efficient than register-level fuzzing.

We also examined the scalability of current function-level emulation techniques. To answer these questions, we conducted several experiments as part of our research.

Example 1 Firmware execution code

```
1: int main(){
2:     char a[5];
3:     char b = HAL_uart_getc();
4:     a[b] = 1;
5: }
```

Example 2 Firmware execution code

```
1: int main(){
2:     char a[5];
3:     data = HAL_UART_Receive_IT(huart, pData, Size);
4:     strcpy(a, data);
5: }
```

Efficiency of Function-Level Emulation for Fuzzing. This paper investigates the use of different levels of peripheral modeling for firmware fuzzing, including hardware, function, and register-levels. While hardware-level modeling necessitates physical devices, function-level and register-level modeling can be achieved through emulation. To compare the performance of firmware fuzzing at the function and register-levels, we conducted an experiment using recent fuzzers, including HAL-Fuzz, P^{2}IM, Fuzzware, and HEFF. HAL-Fuzz employs function-level modeling, while P^{2}IM and Fuzzware utilize register modeling. HEFF uses dual-level modeling at both functional and register-levels [15]. We tested these fuzzers on the Drone firmware [12], and the results are presented in Table 9. The experiment indicates that the fuzzing speed of register-level fuzzers (including dual-level fuzzers) is approximately half as fast as the fuzzing speed of HAL-FUZZ, a function-level fuzzer. These results suggest that function-level fuzzing is a more efficient approach.

The difference in fuzzing speed between function-level and register-level fuzzing (including dual-level) is due to the additional processing overhead incurred by register-level fuzzing as it handles all accessed registers (also partially handles accessed registers). Firmware vulnerabilities can arise from processing inputs received through peripherals. We provide two examples of vulnerabilities resulting from buffer overflow in this paper. In Example 1, a vulnerability occurs in line 4, where an external input is received through the HAL function and stored as a variable. In Example 2, an external input is saved as a variable, leading to a vulnerability. While both examples use HAL functions, the vulnerabilities arise outside of the HAL function, not within it. In the above-mentioned case, register-level emulation handles all accesses made inside the HAL function, whereas function-level emulation handles functions with pre-made handlers, thus avoiding any processing overhead.

Table 1. Peripheral related functions in CNC firmware

Firmware	Pseudo-HAL	HAL
CNC	dirn_wr	HAL_DeInit
	enable_tim_clock	HAL_DisableCompensationCell
	enable_tim_interrupt	HAL_EnableCompensationCell
	enable_usart_clock	HAL_GPIO_DeInit
	g540_timer_init	HAL_GPIO_EXTI_IRQHandler
	g540_timer_start	HAL_GPIO_Init
	g540_timer_stop	HAL_GPIO_ReadPin
	gpio_clr	HAL_GPIO_TogglePin
	gpio_init	HAL_GPIO_WritePin
	gpio_rd	HAL_Init
	gpio_set	HAL_RCC_ClockConfig
	gpio_toggle	HAL_RCC_DeInit
	mc_dwell	HAL_RCC_GetHCLKFreq
	set_step_period	HAL_RCC_GetOscConfig
	set_step_pulse_delay	HAL_RCC_GetPCLK1Freq
	set_step_pulse_time	HAL_RCC_GetPCLK2Freq
	step_isr_disable	HAL_RCC_GetSysClockFreq
	step_isr_enable	HAL_RCC_MCOConfig
	step_timer_init	HAL_RCC_NMI_IRQHandler
	step_wr	HAL_RCC_OscConfig
	SystemClock_Config	
	SystemCoreClockUpdate	
	SystemInit	
	TIM2_IRQHandler	
	usart_getc	
	usart_init	
	usart_putc	
	usart_tstc	
Total(#)	28	20

The Necessity of Identifying Pseudo-HAL Functions. Figure 1 illustrates the structure of STM32 firmware, where the HAL acts as an intermediate layer between hardware and software, directly writing values to MCU registers or controlling peripheral devices. The HAL is a universal library commonly employed by developers to manage peripheral devices in firmware implementation. Tools like HALucinator and HAL-FUZZ are used to identify and hook these HAL functions for handling. The HAL function identification program proposed in [11], called LIBMATCH, is currently employed for this purpose. This enables firmware to operate without requiring physical peripheral devices or separate peripheral emulations. However, LIBMATCH has two significant limitations due to its reliance on a context-matching technique between the target firmware and the HAL function object file to extract HAL function information.

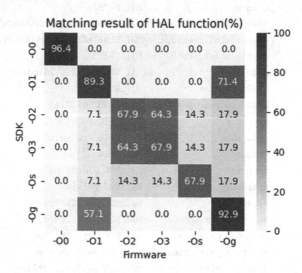

Fig. 2. Result of libmatch HAL function identification according to SDK and firmware combination by compile optimization level

A Lot of Information is Required. The first limitation of LIBMATCH is that it necessitates the SDK (object file of the HAL functions) to be compiled in an environment with the same compiler version and optimization level as the target firmware. Figure 2 displays the LIBMATCH function identification results for six types of compile optimization levels of the target firmware and their corresponding SDKs. The x-axis represents the optimization options for firmware, while the y-axis represents the optimization options for the SDK. For example, in Fig. 2, the matrix (0,0) represents 96.4% of the matching HAL function ratio when the firmware is built with the -O0 option and the SDK is built with the -O0 option, using the libmatch extraction method. When the optimization levels match (6 out of 36), a high matching rate ranging from 67.9% to 96.4% is achieved. However, in most cases where the optimization levels do not match (30 out of 36), searching for a function is either impossible or, even if a match is identified, the matching rate is below 20%. This indicates that Libmatch has a high dependency on the SDK files. If it fails to find an SDK that matches the optimization options of the target firmware, the matching ratio of HAL functions decreases.

Unidentified Functions Exist. The second limitation of LIBMATCH is that it can only identify HAL functions, as the required SDK file contains only HAL function information. Consequently, functions other than HAL functions cannot be identified by LIBMATCH. However, as demonstrated in the CNC [7] firmware example in Table 1, not all firmware exclusively depends on HAL functions to control their peripherals. In such cases, developers define and utilize functions

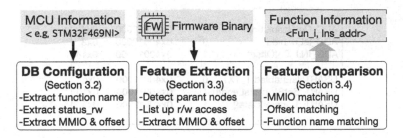

Fig. 3. PHI system flow

that behave like HAL but can be controlled in smaller units for convenience. These functions, referred to as pseudo-HAL functions in this study, perform functions using registers assigned to peripheral devices while accessing within the range of the HAL functions and MMIO. Therefore, for scalable function-level firmware fuzzing, it is crucial to identify both HAL and pseudo-HAL functions.

2.3 Our Approach

We propose the use of pseudo-HAL function identification for effective and scalable firmware fuzzing at the function-level. Pseudo-HAL functions are identified based on register access patterns at the register-level. This can be accomplished through symbolic execution of MMIO and identifying characteristic offset information for each function. This approach reduces the reliance on the SDK compilation environment and enables fuzzing of a wider range of firmware than HAL-FUZZ. In the next section, we will provide a detailed description of our PHI system.

3 System Design

3.1 System Overview

In this section, we present an overview of the PHI (Pseudo-HAL Identification) system, which involves a two-input, three-step process, as illustrated in Fig. 3. The user provides the target firmware and the corresponding MCU (Microcontroller Unit) name as inputs. The MCU name is used for selecting the appropriate DB (Database) file, while the firmware is utilized for feature extraction to identify functions related to peripheral devices. The PHI process comprises three steps: DB configuration, feature extraction, and feature comparison. DB configuration (Sect. 3.2) is the first step, which involves creating a DB for each MCU prior to the PHI operation and selecting the appropriate DB based on the input MCU name. The second step, feature extraction (Sect. 3.3), extracts the function features from the firmware using symbolic execution. This step is the most computationally intensive and involves the extraction of three features for each peripheral access. In the final step, feature comparison (Sect. 3.4), the functions used in the firmware are identified by matching the extracted features with the DB. The extracted files in this step are utilized for fuzzing.

```
    ...
ADC_GetResolution          0    0x40012000    0x4
ADC_IsEnabled              0    0x40012000    0x8
ADC_INJ_SetOffset          1    0x40012000    0x14
    ...
USART_IsEnabledIT_TXT      0    0x40011000    0xc
USART_SetStopBitsLength    1    0x40011000    0x10
USART_TransmitData9        1    0x40011000    0x4
    ...
```

Fig. 4. Example of DB

3.2 DB Configuration

The process of configuring the DB includes two primary steps: DB creation and DB selection. DB creation involves extracting the features of peripheral functions used in each MCU from MMIO (Memory-Mapped Input/Output) and offset that can be called from the embedded board, and converting them into a database. This process is essential for obtaining the necessary information to accurately map the functions used in the firmware to the MCU. It involves analyzing the registers used and their corresponding states, as well as dividing the base address and offset of each peripheral device to enable further classification. As a result, the database structure can be represented as $<func\_i, state\_rw, peri\_addr, offset>$. Figure 4 illustrates an example of a database (DB). DB includes the name of low-level functions ($func\_i$), whether the function involves reading or writing to the MMIO registers ($state\_rw$), the MMIO address associated with the function ($peri\_addr$), and the register access offset ($offset$). For the indication of reading or writing to MMIO registers, 0 represents the state of reading from the MMIO register, and 1 represents the state of writing to the MMIO register. In the first row of the Fig. 4, $ADC\_GetResolution$ represents the function name, 0 indicates reading from the MMIO register, 0x40012000 indicates the base address of peripheral and 0x4 indicates the offset for accessing the MMIO register.

DB selection, on the other hand, is the process of selecting the appropriate DB based on the MCU name input for PHI. This step is crucial for effective and accurate PHI operation. These DBs are stored in a single folder, and DB selection is the process of selecting a DB corresponding to the entered MCU name. The reason for configuring various DBs is that the register addresses used for each MCU are different, and selecting the correct DB ensures the proper mapping of peripheral functions to the specific MCU.

3.3 Feature Extraction

The feature extraction step extracts the features of functions called when the target firmware is executed using symbolic execution, a static analysis technique. Typically, to identify functions at the function-level, an object file containing function information is necessary, as in the case of LIBMATCH results. However,

Table 2. Information of USART

Register		Offset
Status Register	SR	0x00
Data Register	DR	0x04
Baud Rate Register	BRR	0x08
	CR1	0x0C
Control Register	CR2	0x10
	CR3	0x14
Guard Time and Prescalar Register	GTPR	0x18

this paper proposes a register-level function detection approach that extracts function features from all register-level accesses without requiring detailed function information, such as function names. As a result, we leverage symbolic execution to identify functions at the register-level without relying on detailed information, instead of using a matching method that requires such information. This approach is possible because peripheral registers in firmware are assigned to specific memory ranges, such as the MMIO range of 0x40000000–0x5fffffff for ARM Cortex-M4 MCUs, for example.

Consider the case of USART, which manages asynchronous serial communication between computers. In an ARM Cortex-M4 MCU, the peripheral base address for USART is 0x40011000, and offsets such as SR, DR, BRR, CR, and GTPR are allocated to it, as shown in Table 2. By utilizing these offsets and their corresponding USART functions, which control USART using the related registers, it is possible to identify functions at the register-level without the need for detailed information, such as function names. MMIO ranges, peripheral base addresses, and offset information can be obtained from the datasheet for each MCU, facilitating the construction of this information.

Therefore, to extract the features of functions related to firmware peripherals, the following steps are performed:

1. List the functions that access the MMIO range.
2. Check the base address and offset used by each function.
3. Record whether the function reads or writes to that memory.

To accomplish this, the top-level parent node is first extracted from the target firmware. Then, the function call flow within the firmware is checked, starting from all parent nodes. All accesses that read or write memory information within the MMIO address range are recorded. These accesses are listed by creating the tuple <*instruction address (ins_addr), block address (block_addr), state_rw, peri_addr, and offset*>. Typically, functions can access the MMIO range multiple times, and memory reads/writes can occur sequentially. If a function has a continuous sequence of the same type of operation, such as read/read/read/... or write/write/write/..., the sequence of accesses is summarized into a single input. However, if both read and write operations occur in the same function with the same offset, they are summarized as a write operation because the same offset is read and written when writing to a specific register for a function.

3.4 Feature Comparison

In the feature comparison step, a list of functions for fuzzing is extracted by matching the feature extraction results, which consist of instruction address, block address, status (read or write), peripheral base address, and offset, with the previously constructed database. These function names are used as keys when connecting to a function handler after function hooking. The corresponding searching for a function result field is the same as that of $<func\_i, ins\_addr>$. In this step, the corresponding results are extracted to a file and used for function hooking during fuzzing.

4   Implementation

In this study, we implemented PHI, PHI-Fuzz, and a handler. PHI takes the firmware binary and the name of the MCU on which the firmware is loaded as input, then selects the DB corresponding to the MCU name. The PHI is implemented as a Python script consisting of 479 lines, which configures the function information DB, totaling 972 lines of code.

To configure the DB and identify the pseudo-HAL, PHI utilizes angr [8], a symbolic execution tool. The angr functions used include Control-Flow Graph (CFG) analysis and Data Dependency Graph (DDG) results. The CFG functions were divided into CFGFast and CFGEmulated. CFGFast was employed to extract the parent node, while CFGEmulated (with a call depth of 7) was used to extract the DDG.

PHI-Fuzz is implemented based on HAL-Fuzz and receives the PHI result as an addr.yaml file, saves it, and fuzzes the target firmware through a modified handler. The essential handler functions for fuzzing were implemented by adding them to the existing HAL function handler file. Specifically, the existing HAL function handler was connected with the pseudo-HAL function, which played a similar role, to enable fuzzing. Functions discovered through PHI that could not be replaced with existing functions were implemented and added to the existing handler file.

5   Evaluation

The evaluation of PHI-Fuzz was experimentally conducted to answer the following research questions:

- **RQ1:** How scalable is a PHI that uses only firmware images for identification?
- **RQ2:** How effective is the PHI in terms of function identification?
- **RQ3:** How good is the PHI-Fuzz in Bug finding?

Table 3. Firmware tested in Sect. 5.2, 5.3, 5.4

Firmware	MCU	OS	Library	Peripherals			
				GPIO	UART	I2C	SPI
UART_transmit	STM32F469NI	Baremetal	HAL	✓	✓		
UART_receive		Baremetal		✓	✓		
I2C_receive		Baremetal		✓	✓	✓	
SPI_receive		Baremetal		✓	✓		✓
UART_HyperTerminal_IT [11]		Baremetal		✓	✓		
Drone [12]	STM32F103RB	Baremetal	HAL	✓	✓	✓	
CNC [12]		Baremetal	HAL, Pseudo-HAL	✓	✓	✓	
Baremetal_I2C	STM32F469NI	Baremetal	Pseudo-HAL	✓	✓	✓	
FreeRTOS_I2C		FreeRTOS		✓	✓	✓	
Baremetal_UART		Baremetal		✓	✓		
FreeRTOS_UART		FreeRTOS		✓	✓		
RIOT_I2C_receive		RIOT OS		✓		✓	
RIOT_I2C_transmit		RIOT OS		✓	✓	✓	
RIOT_SPI_receive		RIOT OS		✓			✓
RIOT_UART	STM32F103RB	RIOT OS	Pseudo-HAL	✓	✓		
RIOT_SPI		RIOT OS		✓	✓		✓
RIOT_I2C		RIOT OS		✓	✓	✓	

5.1 Experimental Setup

Experimental Environment. Experiments for PHI and PHI-Fuzz evaluation were conducted in an Intel® Core™ i7-8700 CPU @ 3.20 GHz, 8 GB RAM, and Ubuntu 18.04.4 LTS (VM) environment.

Experiment Data. Table 3 presents the information on the firmware used to evaluate PHI and PHI-Fuzz. The firmware was based on STM32F469NI and STM32F103RB, with the source code collected from an open-source project on GitHub and then ported for use. The per firmware included GPIO, UART, I2C, and SPI for evaluation. In total, four HAL-based firmware and ten pseudo-HAL-based firmware were created and used for the experiments. Additionally, one HALucinator benchmark firmware and two P^2IM benchmark firmware were used in the experiment. The firmware was compiled without optimization using the 2018_q4 (gcc8) version. The HAL object file required for Libmatch, a program that compares with PHI, was also compiled with the 2018_q4 (gcc8) version and without optimization.

Table 4. PHI result of UART_Hyperterminal_IT by Optimization level

Optimization level		Total(#)	Result(%)
-O0	No optimization	16	69
-O1	Reduced code size, execution time	15	75
-O3	Optimization of inline functions and registers	15	75
-Os	Omit optimizations that increase code size	15	75
-Og	Remove optimizations that confuse debugging	15	75

5.2 Scalability of PHI (RQ1)

To demonstrate PHI's scalability, this study shows that identifying pseudo-HAL functions is feasible with only the MCU name, without relying on detailed firmware information. To validate this claim, function identification experiments were conducted on compiled firmware at various optimization levels, and the function identification rates were compared with LIBMATCH's HAL function identify results when the compiler versions of the SDK file and the target firmware differed. The reason for demonstrating scalability through results obtained with different compilation options is that LIBMATCH, which uses the specific SDK, exhibits varying results depending on compilation options, as shown in Fig. 2. Therefore, by achieving consistent results without using the SDK, PHI establishes its scalability. Table 4 presents the PHI results for the UART_Hyperterminal_IT [11] firmware compiled at different optimization levels using the same source code. Optimization led to a reduction of one in the total number of peripheral-related functions (HAL functions), but at all optimization levels, 15 identical pseudo-HAL function identifications were possible. In comparison, LIBMATCH's identification rate varies depending on the compilation level of the SDK and firmware, unlike PHI, which not only requires the SDK but also shows consistent identification results in target firmware compiled at each optimization level.

As an additional experiment, a comparison experiment was conducted by detecting with a different compiler. While the original experimental firmware and SDK files were compiled with 2018_q4 (gcc8), for this experiment, only the experimental firmware was compiled with 2016_q4 (gcc6) to compare the results in the unideal environment. Figure 5 and 6 show the results of PHI and LIBMATCH with four types of firmware that utilize HAL functions and compiled with 2018_q4 (gcc8) and 2016_q4 (gcc6) each. Figure 5 represents the identification results in an ideal environment for using LIBMATCH. As a result, PHI exhibited an average exploration rate of around 69%, while LIBMATCH showed an average exploration rate of approximately 75%. Figure 6 illustrates the results of experiments conducted using firmware compiled with 2016_q4 (gcc6), which did not occur in an ideal environment. PHI, since it doesn't rely on the SDK, produced the same results as the exploration with the firmware compiled with 2018_q4 (gcc8). However, LIBMATCH did not achieve the same results. LIBMATCH detected only

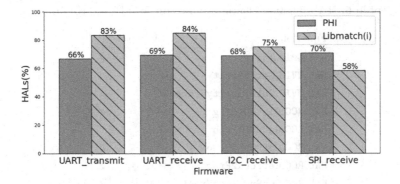

Fig. 5. Comparison of HAL function identification rates between PHI and LIBMATCH. The figure shows the execution outcome of the LIBMATCH with the ideal compiler version.

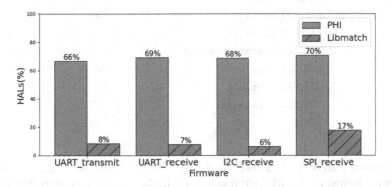

Fig. 6. Comparison of HAL function identification rates between PHI and LIBMATCH. The figure shows the execution outcome of the LIBMATCH without the ideal compiler version.

NVIC-related functions, resulting in detection performance of up to 17% or less. As a result of these experiments, it was confirmed that PHI can explore functions consistently across various compilation optimization options and compiler versions, demonstrating its scalability as a program. With this scalable feature of PHI, it is possible to detect peripheral-related functions in commercially available firmware without prior information. These detection results can subsequently be used for vulnerability exploration through PHI-Fuzz. The experimental results related to this will be presented in Sect. 5.4.

5.3 Effectiveness of PHI (RQ2)

In Sect. 5.2, it was observed that LIBMATCH's identification rate is favorable when the SDK is in an ideal environment. Therefore, in this section, we compare LIBMATCH and our approach in the ideal environment. Generally, the HAL function identification rate of PHI closely resembled LIBMATCH's

Table 5. HAL function identification result for SPI_receive firmware

Function	Libmatch	PHI
HAL_GPIO_Init		✓
HAL_NVIC_SetPriority	✓	
HAL_NVIC_SetPriorityGroup	✓	
HAL_RCC_ClockConfig	✓	✓
HAL_RCC_GetHCLKFreq	✓	
HAL_RCC_GetPCLK1Freq	✓	✓
HAL_RCC_GetPCLK2Freq	✓	✓
HAL_RCC_GetSysClockFreq	✓	✓
HAL_RCC_OscConfig	✓	✓
HAL_SPI_Init		✓
HAL_SPI_MspInit		
HAL_SPI_Receive		✓
HAL_SPI_Transmit		✓
HAL_SPI_TransmitReceive		✓
HAL_UART_Init		✓
HAL_UART_MspInit	✓	
HAL_UART_Transmit	✓	✓
Total	10	12

rate (as shown in Fig. 5). However, for UART_transmit, UART_receive, and I2C_receive firmware, LIBMATCH displayed a higher search rate than PHI. What could be the reason? The functions identified by LIBMATCH but not by PHI were NVIC-related functions, specifically *HAL_NVIC_SetPriority* and *HAL_NVI C_SetPriorityGrouping*. PHI failed to identify these functions because the NVIC-related DB configuration was not established in PHI since the access address was outside the MMIO range. Conversely, for SPI_receive firmware, PHI exhibited a higher search rate than LIBMATCH. In Table 5, while PHI did not identify two NVIC-related functions, LIBMATCH could not identify four other SPI-related functions. This confirms that LIBMATCH cannot identify all HAL functions, whereas PHI can identify functions that LIBMATCH cannot.

Additionally, Table 6 shows the results of another function identification experiment using 10 firmware that call pseudo-HAL functions instead of HAL functions. While LIBMATCH had a detection rate of 0%, PHI could identify functions at a significantly high rate of 92.3%. As a result, PHI can identify HAL functions with performance similar to or even superior to LIBMATCH, which has access to all SDK information, even without utilizing the SDK. Additionally, PHI can also identify pseudo-HAL functions that were previously inaccessible for exploration with LIBMATCH. Furthermore, similar to the results in Sect. 5.2, PHI's effectiveness in detecting a wider range of peripheral-related functions allows for more efficient fuzzing, making it beneficial.

Table 6. Pseudo-HAL function identification (%)

Firmware	Libmatch	PHI
Baremetal_I2C	0	68.1
FreeRTOS_I2C	0	63.6
Baremetal_UART	0	64.2
FreeRTOS_UART	0	64.2
RIOT_I2C_receive	0	60
RIOT_I2C_transmit	0	62.5
RIOT_SPI_receive	0	60
RIOT_UART	0	64.7
RIOT_SPI	0	92.3
RIOT_I2C	0	84.2

Table 7. Fuzzing experiment

Firmware	HAL-Fuzz	PHI-Fuzz
UART_receive	O	O
I2C_receive	O	O
UART_HyperTerminal_IT	O	O
Drone	O	O
CNC	X	O
Baremetal_I2C	X	O
FreeRTOS_I2C	X	O
Baremetal_UART	X	O
FreeRTOS_UART	X	O

5.4 Effectiveness of PHI-Fuzz in Bug Finding (RQ3)

To demonstrate the effectiveness of PHI-Fuzz, the fuzzing results of PHI-Fuzz and HAL-Fuzz were compared. Table 7 represents the results of testing the feasibility of fuzzing on nine firmware, using HAL-Fuzz and PHI-Fuzz. Among the experimental firmware, UART_receive, I2C_receive, UART_HyperTerminal_IT, and Drone contain HAL functions, and both HAL-Fuzz and PHI-Fuzz can be used to fuzz these samples. However, CNC, Baremetal_ I2C, FreeRTOS_I2C, Baremetal_UART, and FreeRTOS_UART contain pseudo-HAL functions, and can only be fuzzed using PHI-Fuzz.

Table 8 shows the execution results of HAL-FUZZ and PHI-Fuzz on Drone and CNC. The experimental results reveal that both fuzzers could run on Drone, but only PHI-Fuzz was capable of running on CNC. PHI-Fuzz outperformed in terms of fuzzing execution speed and execution path on Drone, as more functions were identified and handled. Furthermore, PHI-Fuzz discovered six unique

Table 8. Fuzzing experiment with Drone and CNC firmware

Firmware	HAL-Fuzz			PHI-Fuzz		
	Exec	#Path	#Crash	Exec	#Path	#Crash
Drone	2,981,648	473	✗	3,511,621	491	✗
CNC	✗	✗	✗	4,020,289	958	6

Table 9. Drone firmware fuzzing Performance Comparison in terms of execution speed & a number of basic blocks.

	HAL-Fuzz [3]	P^{2}IM [12]	HEFF [15]	Fuzzware [20]	PHI-Fuzz
Modeling level	Function	Register	Dual	Register	Function
Function scalable	HAL	HAL	HAL	HAL	HAL
		Pseudo-HAL	Pseudo-HAL	Pseudo-HAL	Pseudo-HAL
Speed(exec/s)	49	20	21	23	53
Executed BB (#)	254	519	707	377	210

crashes not detected by HAL-FUZZ, indicating that PHI-Fuzz demonstrated superior performance in finding bugs.

6   Discussion and Limitation

The results presented in Sect. 5.2 demonstrate that PHI can effectively identify both pseudo-HAL and HAL functions independently of firmware information, as shown in Sect. 5.3. Moreover, due to its scalability, PHI can efficiently find bugs, as discussed in Sect. 5.4. Furthermore, the HAL function identification results in Table 5 reveal that PHI outperforms LIBMATCH, since it identified four out of the five SPI-related functions that LIBMATCH failed to identify. However, LIBMATCH has not yet identified *HAL_RCC_GetHCLKFreq* and *HAL_UART_MspInit*. Therefore, to achieve high function coverage during fuzzing, a dual identification technique can be employed. This approach involves first identifying function information through LIBMATCH and then executing PHI to identify functions related to all peripheral devices within the MMIO range.

Table 9 compares the fuzzing performance of firmware fuzzers at various levels. As seen in the table, PHI-Fuzz exhibits more than twice the speed compared to register-level fuzzers and is 8% faster than the function-level firmware fuzzer HAL-FUZZ, achieving the best results in terms of fuzzing speed. However, it also obtained the lowest number of executed basic blocks. This is because register-level firmware fuzzers process all registers, resulting in a larger number of executed basic blocks. On the other hand, function-level firmware fuzzers execute a relatively smaller number of basic blocks since they have predefined handlers for each function call. In this context, PHI explored and handled more functions than HAL-FUZZ, leading to the execution of the fewest basic blocks.

7 Related Work

Firmware fuzzing for an MCU target requires firmware emulation. Unlike general software, firmware depends on various peripheral devices, making peripheral device emulation the core of firmware emulation. To address this dependency problem of peripheral devices, various firmware emulation studies have been conducted. In this section, we introduce the firmware emulation technique and the latest fuzzers that utilize it.

7.1 Firmware Emulation

In WYCINWYC [19], firmware emulation is divided into two categories: full emulation, which emulates both the core and peripheral devices of the firmware, and partial emulation, which emulates only the core device and handles peripheral device emulation through physical hardware or peripheral modeling. Full emulation requires significant engineering effort, as all peripherals must be directly configured into the emulator. In particular, in the case of MCUs, which can have various manufacturers and peripheral devices, directly emulating all of them incurs high costs. On the other hand, partial emulation is proposed to mitigate the inefficient development effort of peripheral devices required during full emulation. This method was studied using hardware-in-the-loop (HITL) and peripheral modeling techniques.

The hardware-in-the-loop emulation handles peripheral access by using real peripheral hardware [17,23]. This approach performs firmware emulation by communicating with peripherals not supported by the emulator using actual peripheral hardware. However, its availability is limited due to the requirement of actual peripheral hardware. On the other hand, peripheral modeling emulates I/O processing for peripheral devices through a model of the peripheral device [10–13,26]. This method does not use actual peripheral devices, making it easier to use and reducing engineering efforts. Muench et al. [19] demonstrated that emulation through peripheral modeling is more effective than the HITL method and improves emulation performance.

7.2 Hardware-Level Emulation

Peripheral modeling can be categorized into hardware-level, function-level, and register-level modeling based on the modeling level of the peripheral device. Pretender [13] models a peripheral device based on hardware values obtained by inputting values for the actual device. The modeling process uses machine learning, and firmware fuzzing is performed using the implemented model. This is different from the HITL method in that the hardware is used only during the peripheral modeling phase. Thus, fuzzing can proceed without an actual device, relying solely on the modeled result. However, a drawback of this approach is that various hardware is eventually required for the peripheral modeling phase. In contrast, PHI makes it possible to identify functions related to peripheral devices using only firmware binary images and MCU names, without the need for actual hardware at any stage. This enables more scalable fuzzing than Pretender and other peripheral modeling-based approaches.

7.3   Function-Level Emulation

HALucinator [11] is an emulator that allows developers to model peripheral devices of MCU devices directly using the Hardware Abstraction Layer (HAL). Compared to full emulation, which requires detailed modeling of the register unit, HALucinator reduces overhead by allowing developers to directly model the HAL, which is commonly used in many MCU target operating systems. When HAL functions are called, HALucinator handles them by using modeled function handlers. Moreover, HALucinator provides emulation for each peripheral device in the HAL layer, making it possible to fuzz without emulating complex hardware. PHI-Fuzz uses a self-modified HAL-Fuzz function handler for fuzzing. Furthermore, PHI's ability to identify pseudo-HAL functions addresses the limitation of HALucinator, which could only identify HAL functions.

7.4   Register-Level Emulation

Compared to HALucinator, which focuses on handling functions, P^2IM [12] is designed for dynamic testing and fuzzing of individual I/O devices at the register-level. When the firmware is executed in the emulator, P^2IM classifies the access pattern of the peripheral's MMIO registers into categories such as CR, SR, DR, and C&SR using a proposed heuristic and performs peripheral device modeling with each register handling method. As a result, P^2IM does not require prior knowledge of which specific peripheral devices are connected to the MCU since peripheral device handling is performed automatically. PHI leverages P^2IM's register access pattern classification to identify peripheral functions. By analyzing the MMIO information output through DDG, PHI classifies peripherals and calculates the used offset, categorizing them into memories such as SR, DR, and CR. Through this classification process, PHI identifies the accesses performed by the HAL and pseudo-HAL functions. In contrast to P^2IM, which automatically creates and operates a handler during fuzzing, PHI-Fuzz requires only a pre-written function handler for the identified function, enabling faster fuzzing.

Laelaps [10] performed firmware emulation through dynamic symbolic execution when an undefined peripheral device access occurred in the emulator while being emulated through QEMU. µEmu [26] analyzed register access patterns for peripheral access via symbolic execution, prior to firmware fuzzing. During symbolic execution, rules for responding to unknown peripheral accesses are inferred, stored in the Knowledge Base (KB), and referenced in the firmware analysis. To address the limitations of Laelaps and µEmu, Fuzzware [20] proposes a solution for limiting fuzzing coverage expansion through path removal during symbolic execution and partial input overhead. PHI also leverages symbolic execution to extract the called functions. Function identification information is provided through Angr, a symbolic execution tool. The offset used when the address of the called function is in the MMIO range is extracted, and function matching is performed through this information.

8 Conclusion

This study aims to improve firmware fuzzing efficiency by identifying both HAL and pseudo-HAL functions at the register-level and implementing PHI and PHI-Fuzz as firmware fuzzers based on HAL-FUZZ. The proposed method was able to identify HAL functions accessing the MMIO range at a comparable level to LIBMATCH, while also addressing the limitation of LIBMATCH in identifying pseudo-HAL functions. PHI-Fuzz proved to be more effective in bug finding than HAL-FUZZ, as it discovered additional crashes not found by HAL-FUZZ. However, there are still some functions that LIBMATCH can identify but PHI cannot. To address this, future work will involve conducting a study that combines LIBMATCH and PHI to increase the function identification rate.

Acknowledgement. This work was supported by Institute of Information & communications Technology Planning & Evaluation (IITP) grant funded by the Korea government (MSIT) (RS-2023-00229400, Development of user authentication and privacy preserving technology for a secure metaverse environment) and by Institute of Information & communications Technology Planning & Evaluation (IITP) grant funded by the Korea government (MSIT) (No. RS-2023-00230337, Advanced and Proactive AI Platform Research and Development Against Malicious Deepfakes).

References

1. State of IoT_spring-2023. https://iot-analytics.com/product/state-of-iot-spring-2023/
2. National vulnerability database. https://nvd.nist.gov/vuln/. Accessed 1 June 2021
3. HAL_Fuzz. https://github.com/ucsb-seclab/hal-fuzz. Accessed 1 June 2021
4. Libmatch. https://github.com/subwire/libmatch. Accessed 1 June 2021
5. 2019 Embedded markets study (2019). https://www.embedded.com/wp-content/uploads/2019/11/EETimes_Embedded_2019_Embedded_Markets_Study.pdf. Accessed 1 June 2021
6. Description of STM32F4 HAL and low-layer drivers. https://www.st.com/resource/en/user_manual/dm00105879-description-of-stm32f4-hal-and-ll-drivers-stmicroelectronics.pdf
7. P^2 IM real-world firmware samples. https://github.com/RiS3-Lab/p2im-real_firmware/tree/d4c7456574ce2c2ed038e6f14fea8e3142b3c1f7. Accessed 1 June 2021
8. Angr. https://github.com/angr/angr
9. Bellard, F.: QEMU, a fast and portable dynamic translator. In: Proceedings of the USENIX Annual Technical Conference, FREENIX Track. Berkeley, CA, USA, April 2005
10. Cao, C., Guan, L., Ming, J., Liu, P.: Device-agnostic firmware execution is possible: a concolic execution approach for peripheral emulation. In: Annual Computer Security Applications Conference, pp. 746–759 (2020)

11. Clements, A.A., et al.: Halucinator: firmware re-hosting through abstraction layer emulation. In: Proceedings of the 29th USENIX Security Symposium, pp. 1201–1218 (2020)
12. Feng, B., Mera, A., Lu, L.: P2im: scalable and hardware-independent firmware testing via automatic peripheral interface modeling. In: Proceedings of the 29th USENIX Security Symposium, pp. 1237–1254 (2020)
13. Gustafson, E., et al.: Toward the analysis of embedded firmware through automated re-hosting. In: Proceedings of the International Symposium on Research in Attacks, Intrusions and Defenses (RAID), pp. 135–150. Beijing, China, September 2019
14. He, Y., et al.: Rapidpatch: firmware hotpatching for real-time embedded devices. In: 31th USENIX Security Symposium (USENIX Security 22) (2022)
15. Hwang, E., Lee, H., Jeong, S., Cho, M., Kwon, T.: Toward fast and scalable firmware fuzzing with dual-level peripheral modeling. IEEE Access **9**, 141790–141799 (2021)
16. Klees, G., Ruef, A., Cooper, B., Wei, S., Hicks, M.: Evaluating fuzz testing. In: Proceedings of the 2018 ACM SIGSAC Conference on Computer and Communications Security (CCS), pp. 2123–2138. Toronto, Canada, October 2018
17. Koscher, K., Kohno, T., Molnar, D.: SURROGATES: enabling near-real-time dynamic analyses of embedded systems. In: Proceedings of the 9th USENIX Workshop Offensive Technologies, Washington, DC, USA, August 2015
18. Mera, A., Feng, B., Lu, L., Kirda, E., Robertson, W.: DICE: automatic emulation of DMA input channels for dynamic firmware analysis. In: Proceedings of the 2021 IEEE Symposium on Security and Privacy (SP), pp. 302–318. Los Alamitos, CA, USA, May 2021
19. Muench, M., Stijohann, J., Kargl, F., Francillon, A., Balzarotti, D.: What you corrupt is not what you crash: challenges in fuzzing embedded devices. In: Proceedings of the Network and Distributed System Security Symposium (NDSS). San Diego, CA, USA, January 2018
20. Scharnowski, T., et al.: Fuzzware: using precise MMIO modeling for effective firmware fuzzing. In: 31st USENIX Security Symposium (USENIX Security 22), pp. 1239–1256 (2022)
21. Spensky, C., et al.: Conware: automated modeling of hardware peripherals. In: Proceedings of the 2021 ACM Asia Conference on Computer and Communications Security (Asia CCS), pp. 95–109 (2021)
22. Wright, C., Moeglein, W.A., Bagchi, S., Kulkarni, M., Clements, A.A.: Challenges in firmware re-hosting, emulation, and analysis. J. ACM Comput. Surv. (CSUR) **54**(1), 1–36 (2021)
23. Zaddach, J., Bruno, L., Francillon, A., Balzarotti, D., et al.: AVATAR: a framework to support dynamic security analysis of embedded systems' firmwares. In: Proceedings of the Network and Distributed System Security Symposium (NDSS), vol. 23, pp. 1–16. San Diego, CA, USA, February 2014
24. Zalewski, M.: American funzz lop. https://lcamtuf.coredump.cx/afl/. Accessed 1 June 2021
25. Zheng, Y., Davanian, A., Yin, H., Song, C., Zhu, H., Sun, L.: FIRM-AFL: high-throughput greybox fuzzing of IoT firmware via augmented process emulation. In: Proceedings of the 28th USENIX Security Symposium (USENIX Security 19), pp. 1099–1114. Santa Clara, CA, USA, August 2019
26. Zhou, W., Guan, L., Liu, P., Zhang, Y.: Automatic firmware emulation through invalidity-guided knowledge inference. In: Proceedings of the 30th USENIX Security Symposium (USENIX Security 21) (2021)

Lightweight Anomaly Detection Mechanism Based on Machine Learning Using Low-Cost Surveillance Cameras

Yeon-Ji Lee⬛, Na-Eun Park⬛, and Il-Gu Lee⁽⊠⁾⬛

Sungshin Women's University, Seongbuk-Gu, Seoul 02844, Korea
`iglee19@gmail.com`

Abstract. As the need for on-site monitoring using surveillance cameras increases, there has been a growing interest in automation research incorporating machine learning. However, traditional research has not resolved the performance and resource efficiency trade-offs. Traditional research often utilizes high-resolution images to enhance detection performance. However, surveillance cameras, being Internet of Things devices, are constrained by limited resources, making high-resolution images less suitable for their operation. Therefore, we proposed a lightweight learning model that is more efficient and with minimal performance degradation. The proposed model reduces the resolution of the image until the performance is maintained, finding where the trade-off is resolved for each dataset. It is also utilized for real-time detection by determining the probability values of detection at an appropriate resolution. Using this, we suggested a real-time lightweight fire detection algorithm. The proposed mechanism is approximately 30 times more memory efficient while maintaining the detection performance of traditional methods.

Keywords: surveillance camera · anomaly detection · CNN

1 Introduction

The need for onsite monitoring using surveillance cameras for public management, security, and safety has recently increased. However, interpreting surveillance camera footage is a human task, and as individuals monitor multiple cameras simultaneously, there are clear limitations regarding efficiency and accuracy [1]. When humans manage surveillance cameras, issues arise related to human resources, maintenance costs for installing and managing cameras, and other associated costs [2].

Research on anomaly detection using machine learning is being actively pursued to address these issues [3–6]. Deep learning, a subset of machine learning, allows training without human intervention and delivers high-level results in object detection, data classification, and natural language processing [3]. In particular, the CNN (convolutional neural networks) model, which directly learns

H. Seo and S. Kim (Eds.): ICISC 2023, LNCS 14562, pp. 81–92, 2024.
https://doi.org/10.1007/978-981-97-1238-0_5

features from datasets, is being utilized for anomaly detection in various fields ranging from medicine to agriculture [4]. However, traditional research has been increasing the resolution of images to the maximum, using ultra-high-resolution images as datasets or relying on high-quality images to enhance the accuracy of CNN models [5]. IoT devices, including surveillance cameras, are constrained in energy, memory, and cost [7,8]. High-quality datasets can maintain high model performance but are unsuitable for real-time surveillance camera detection [6,9]. Various research has been conducted for lightweight CNN learning [10–13]. However, traditional studies have not effectively addressed the trade-off between model performance and cost, underscoring the need for further research in this area.

The proposed model identifies the optimal resolution where the CNN model can maintain its performance on the fire dataset and suggests a more efficient fire detection mechanism. The suggested mechanism maintained a lowered camera resolution and switched to a clearer quality when the likelihood of fire detection exceeded a threshold. The contributions of this study are as follows.

- By classifying the fire dataset based on the fire size and adjusting the resolution to identify the point at which accuracy is maintained, we have addressed the trade-off issue between performance and cost, a limitation of previous research.
- We proposed a universal mechanism not limited to surveillance cameras, making it easier for lightweight CNN learning to be applied across various research and environments.
- We proposed a lightweight fire detection mechanism that maintains the performance of fire detection while reducing memory consumption by 31.8 times.

The structure of this study is as follows: In Sect. 2, we investigate and analyze research aimed at improving overheads in deep learning training and memory consumption. Section 3 introduces the proposed model and suggests a lightweight fire detection mechanism. Section 4 analyzes the experimental environment, content, and results, and Sect. 5 concludes with an introduction to future research.

2   Related Works

Various studies are being conducted to address issues like training time and memory consumption in data learning using images. This section compares and analyzes previous research, describing the limitations of past studies and the contributions of our proposed research.

In the study proposed by [10], a lightweight, intelligent CNN model was designed to reduce the computational cost of the model. The research addressed power consumption limitations when converting analog signals to digital signals and the computational cost aspects of the image sensor module. Two lightweight CNN models were implemented by reducing the bit precision of the analog-digital converter (ADC) to save power and reduce the number of parameters. The paper experimented with the designed pipeline in MobileNetv2 and GhostNet architectures to assess their generalization capability and performance. While the study demonstrated the generalization ability and reduced power consumption of the model, it could not resolve the slight decrease in model accuracy when reducing ADC bit precision. Additionally, there were limitations related to the dataset, this paper uses high-quality, high-capacity, advanced datasets to improve model performance, making it unsuitable for use in lightweight models.

In the study [11] aimed at addressing power consumption in image and video processing and computational cost issues of computer vision applications, an intelligent compression system was proposed to solve the power consumption problem during wireless capsule endoscopy video processing. A deep learning-based classification feed-back loop was proposed to determine the importance of images. Important images were enhanced to include additional content, while the less important ones were compressed into lower quality for storage. In this study, we conducted compression and classification experiments on wireless capsule endoscopy (WCE) videos to evaluate the performance of the proposed model, verify the gain of the intelligent compression system, and predict the number of additional transmittable images. The experiments demonstrated the study's contributions by verifying that achieving high compression rates and classification accuracy is possible while maintaining video quality. However, we did not consider the processing time complexity, and the learning and experiments were limited to specific gastrointestinal organs and lesion presence in the data, making it unclear whether we could achieve the same performance in other learning scenarios.

Study [12] aimed at enhancing the speed of predicting anomalies to detect fire situations. It is emphasized that while recognizing patterns with high accuracy is vital, optimization for real-time execution is also critical. The research adopts the capabilities of Deeplabv3+ and the OpenVINO toolkit to propose an approach close to real-time detection, with experiments and evaluations focusing on process acceleration. The results showed an achieved inference process acceleration of 70.46% to 93.46%. When using a GPU with FP16 precision, the inference process speed was approximately double compared to FP32. This study contributes by considering the accuracy of the detection model and process acceleration and speed in time complexity. However, its limitation lies in analyzing only the impact from a temporal perspective without considering memory availability and accuracy.

In a study [13] using a CNN model trained on actual fire incident images, a custom framework for fire detection was presented using transfer learning. The gradient-weighted class activation mapping (Grad-CAM) method was employed to visualize the fire and pinpoint its location. Experiments were conducted using a composite large-scale dataset formed by merging the fire detection dataset, DeepQuestAI, Saied, Carlo, and Bansal datasets, and the detection performance was evaluated. Experimental results revealed that while the detection accuracies of GoogLeNet, VGG16, and ResNet50 were 88.01%, 64.48%, and 92.54%, respectively, the proposed EfficientNetB0 model exhibited an improved accuracy of 92.68%. However, while traditional research analyses considered model lightweightness and computational costs, this study did not further analyze other metrics besides accuracy. Moreover, while the study introduced EfficientNetB0 as a better method, supposedly lighter than the similarly performing ResNet50, it does not provide concrete evidence to confirm the lightweight nature of the model.

Table 1 summarizes the preceding research that was analyzed.

Table 1. Related research summary table.

Ref	Features	Limitation
[10]	– Research on lightweight, intelligent CNN models for reduced computational cost	– Uses high-quality, high-capacity datasets – It unsuitable for use in lightweight models
	– Proposed method to reduce power consumption by decreasing the bit precision of ADC	– Failed to address the decrease in model accuracy when ADC bit precision is reduced
[11]	– Research on intelligent compression systems to address power consumption issues during wireless capsule endoscopy video processing	– Time complexity was not considered
	– Proposed deep learning-based classification feedback loop based on importance	– The data used for training and experiments was limited to specific conditions such as lesions and specific digestive organs
[12]	– Acceleration of the process speed for fire situation detection models	– Various complexities are mentioned, but only time complexity is considered, without accounting for spatial complexities like memory availability
	– Research on optimization for real-time execution	– Did not conduct performance analysis
[13]	– Proposed fire detection framework using transfer learning	– While lightweight and computational cost aspects are mentioned, these metrics are not considered in the experiments
	– Fire visualization and location identification using Grad-CAM	– No evidence is provided to support the claim of proposing a lightweight model

This research showed that not many actively considered optimization among traditional image and video processing studies. Most previous studies either analyzed performance aspects alone or focused on optimization excluding performance, thereby conducting performance analyses limited to specific areas. Some studies that considered accuracy and complexity simultaneously couldn't resolve the trade-off relationship where an increase in accuracy led to increased complexity and improving the complexity aspect resulted in a decrease in accuracy. Therefore, we proposed a mechanism that detects fire by finding the optimal resolution point while maintaining the CNN model performance to address the trade-off issue and enhance fire detection efficiency.

3   Proposed Mechanism

This section details the proposed preprocessing steps and mechanism, elaborating on each stage in depth. First, we explained the criteria used to divide the fire dataset used in the experiment into large fires, medium fires, and small fires. We then discuss how adjusting the resolution helps determine two threshold values. Subsequently, based on the details mentioned above, we discussed the proposed lightweight fire detection mechanism.

3.1   Adjusting Resolution

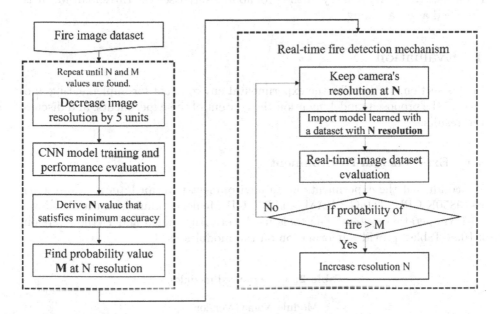

Fig. 1. Flowchart of the mechanism for real-time fire detection.

This study aimed to reduce memory while maintaining performance by reducing image resolution to a point where accuracy is sustained. However, for data where the target object size being detected affects performance, performance differs based on that size. For example, in a medical imaging dataset for tumor detection, one can differentiate between early, middle, and terminal stages based on the tumor size. The early stage would require higher resolution compared to the advanced stage. For reliable experiments, it is necessary to measure the performance separately based on the size of the dataset.

The flow of image resolution adjustment is depicted on the left side of Fig. 1. The original image dataset has a dimension of 224 pixels. After adjusting it from 100 to 1, we aimed to identify the resolution point N where performance remained close to the original. When fire is detected using the model with the lowest performance, we calculate the predicted probability estimates for fire classification to derive the average detection likelihood, denoted as M.

3.2 Lightweight Fire Detection Model

After deriving N and M, we proposed a lightweight fire detection mechanism, the diagram shown on the right side of Fig. 1. N represents the threshold value for the minimum resolution, while M serves as the real-time fire detection threshold. In the proposed mechanism, surveillance cameras operate at resolution N, but if they detect a probability exceeding M, they update to a higher resolution. In this context, 'probability' refers to the model's estimation of the likelihood of a fire. When the resolution is 'N,' if the probability exceeds 'M,' the model increases the resolution and performs the detection again in the zone where all models converge in accuracy. If the probability surpasses the threshold 'M,' it is classified as an anomaly.

4 Evaluation

In this section, we describe the experimental environment for implementing and testing the proposed model, mention the content of the experiments, and discuss the results.

4.1 Experimental Environment

We conducted the experiments in an environment with an Intel(R) Core(TM) i9-10850K CPU, 32.0 GB RAM, and 930 GB Memory, running on the Windows 10 Pro operating system. The tools used were Anaconda3 and Python version 3.10.9. Table 2 provides information on the modules used.

Table 2. Table of used modules.

Module Name	Version
keras	2.10.0
sklearn	1.0.2
numpy	1.23.5
matplotlib	3.5.3
tensorflow	2.10.0
glob	2.69.1
pandas	1.4.2
seaborn	0.11.2

The fire-detection dataset is used [14], an image dataset for detecting fires. This study only used a portion of the dataset, and the fire images were manually verified and categorized into large, medium, and small fires. A large fire is where the fire occupies more than half of the image, a medium fire occupies less than half but more than a quarter of the image, and a small fire takes up less than a quarter of the image. Each large, medium, and small fire is trained separately, and the control group of normal images is used identically in all three models. Table 3 shows the ratio and number of images used in each experiment.

Table 3. Distribution of datasets used by experiment.

Experiment	Image Type	Train	Test	Valid
large-fire Classification	large-fire image	140	40	20
	normal image	140	40	20
medium-fire Classification	medium-fire image	140	40	20
	normal image	140	40	20
small-fire Classification	small-fire image	140	40	20
	normal image	140	40	20

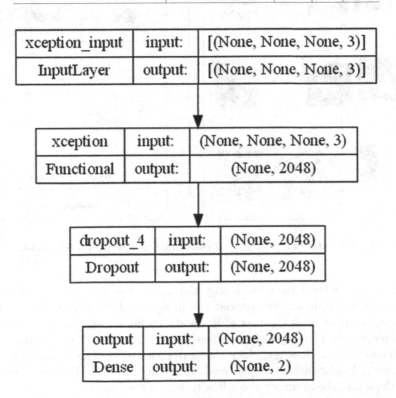

Fig. 2. Layers and input values for the exception model being used.

In the experiment, we used a transfer learning CNN model. Transfer learning models utilize pre-trained models, which can deliver good performance even with data. This made them frequently used models for training with limited images. Figure 3 shows the operational scenario of the real-time fire detection mechanism. As for other parameter values, we used three channels, the Adam optimizer, and binary_crossentropy, for the loss function. We conducted the training for ten epochs.

4.2   Adjustment of Fire Image Resolution

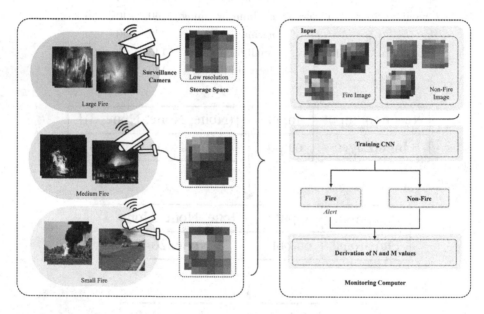

Fig. 3. Operational scenarios of real-time fire detection mechanism.

The first experiment aimed to identify the image resolution range where performance is maintained. We reduced the image resolution from 100 to 1 and conducted a binary classification of fire and non-fire, after which we measured the performance. The experiment adjusted the resolution from 100 to 5 pixels in increments of 5. However, since the performance converged from 20 to 100 pixels, we only visualized and analyzed from 5 to 20 pixels. Figure 4 shows the graph depicting the accuracy according to image resolution.

For the large-fire category, the model maintains an accuracy of 99.3 up to a resolution of 5 pixels. The medium-fire maintains a high accuracy of 96.6 at 5 pixels. However, for the small-fire category, even though it sustains a high accuracy of 95 at a resolution of 20 pixels, it drops to a lower performance of 85 when the resolution is at 5 pixels. Therefore, for each dataset, the maximum points where the performance is maintained while reducing the image resolution are confirmed

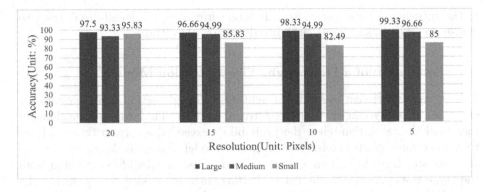

Fig. 4. Evaluation results of detection accuracy by resolution.

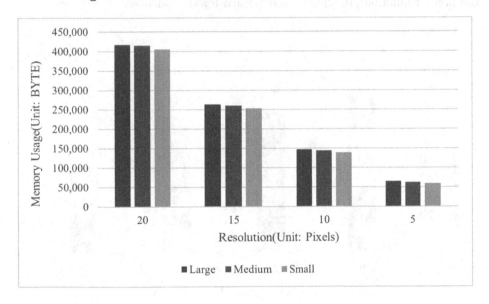

Fig. 5. Evaluation results of memory usage by resolution.

to be 5 for both large and medium-fire and 20 for small-fire. Figure 5 shows the evaluation results of the memory usage at each resolution. The original size of 224 pixcels consumes approximately 4.6 million bytes. At the performance retention point for large-fire and medium-fire, which is 5 pixcels, it uses 59,550 65,307 Bytes, while the small-fire at a resolution of 20 utilizes 405,496416,853 Bytes. This indicates that large and medium-fire can reduce memory size by up to 70 times, whereas small-fire can save memory by a factor of 10.

In the experiment mentioned above, the small-fire detection demonstrated the least effective performance. However, fires typically spread from small to larger ones, and detecting the fire when it is still a small flame is crucial. Therefore, in the subsequent experiment, we will detect fire using the small-fire dataset to devise an efficient and lightweight fire detection algorithm.

4.3   Evaluation of a Lightweight Fire Detection Model

The second experiment evaluated a lightweight fire detection model system for enhanced memory efficiency and effective detection. The proposed mechanism increased the resolution when the probability exceeded a certain threshold, up to a maximum of 20 pixels. The proposed model aimed to detect fires when they are small, so the experiment primarily focused on small-fire detection from the three tests previously conducted. Performance is assessed by measuring the probability, representing the likelihood of matching a particular label. We used the predict function provided by scikit-learn for this purpose.

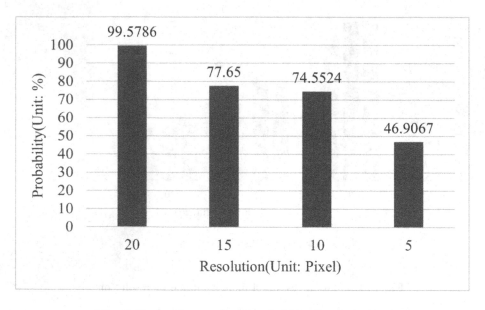

Fig. 6. Evaluation results of probability by resolution.

The probability based on the resolution for small fire is represented in Fig. 6. When the resolution was at 5, it displayed a probability of 46% for fire data. At 10, it showed 74%, and at 20, it converged to 99%.

5   Conclusion

In this study, we proposed a lightweight fire detection model to address the conventional deep learning research limitation of balancing performance with cost. We adjusted the resolution of the images and evaluated the performance for each resolution to determine the threshold value of the proposed model. For the large-fire and medium-fire datasets, a 99.3% accuracy was demonstrated at a resolution of 5, proving 70 times more memory efficient than the original. Furthermore, the small-fire dataset exhibited a 95% accuracy at a resolution of 20, demonstrating it to be ten times more memory efficient. Subsequently, we proposed a two-stage fire detection mechanism, focusing on the small-fire dataset with the lowest performance. This proposed mechanism adjusted the resolution based on the probability of deemed fire and used the measured probability from the small-fire dataset as its threshold. Ultimately, the proposed model proved to be approximately 31 times more memory efficient while maintaining fire detection performance.

However, this study utilized a limited dataset, and various variables may have influenced the experimental results. To derive more reliable results, repetitive testing with vast data is necessary. Therefore, in the future, we plan to conduct experiments targeting a broader and more diverse dataset and aim to derive trustworthy outcomes through repeated experiments.

Acknowledgement. This work is partly supported by the Korea Institute for Advancement of Technology (KIAT) grant funded by the Korea Government (MOTIE) (P0008703, The Competency Development Program for Industry Specialist), and the MSIT under the ICAN (ICT Challenge and Advanced Network of HRD) program (No. IITP-2022-RS-2022-00156310) supervised by the Institute of Information & Communication Technology Planning & Evaluation (IITP).

References

1. Soheil, V., Kin-Choong, Y.: A CNN-RNN combined structure for real-world violence detection in surveillance cameras. Appl. Sci. **12**(3) (2022)
2. Trong, N., Jean, M.: Anomaly detection in video sequence with appearance-motion correspondence. In: 2019 IEEE/CVF International Conference on Computer Vision, ICCV, Seoul Korea (2019)
3. Asif, K., Quadri S.M.K., Saba, B., Junaid, L.: Deep diagnosis: a real-time apple leaf disease detection system based on deep learning. Comput. Electron. Agric. **298** (2022)
4. Amreen, A., Sweta, J., Mahesh, G., Swetha, V.: Tomato plant disease detection using transfer learning with C-GAN synthetic images. Comput. Electron. Agric. **187** (2021)
5. Waqas, A., Umair, N., Muhammad, H.Y., Sergio, A.V.: Lightweight CNN and GRU network for real-time action recognition. In: 2022 12th International Conference on Pattern Recognition Systems, ICPRS, Saint-Etienne, France (2022)
6. Daiki, A., Tomio, G.: Improving image quality using noise removal based on learning method for surveillance camera images. In: 2022 IEEE 4th Global Conference on Life Sciences and Technologies, LifeTech, Osaka, Japan (2022)
7. So-Eun, J., Ye-Sol, O., Ye-Seul, K., Yeon-Ji, L., Il-Gu, L.: Two-step feature selection technique for secure and lightweight internet of things. In: 2023 32nd International Conference on Computer Communications and Networks, ICCCN, Honolulu, HI, USA (2023)

8. Sun-Woo, Y., Na-Eun, P., Il-Gu, L.: Wake-up security: effective security improvement mechanism for low power internet of things. Intell. Autom. Soft Comput. **37**(3), 2897–2917 (2023)
9. Muhammad, A.K., Ridha, H., Aiman, E., Moncef, G.: Distributed inference in resource-constrained IoT for real-time video surveillance. IEEE Syst. J. **17**(1), 1512–1523 (2022)
10. Wilfred, K., Amandeep, K., Deepak, M.: An intelligent system with reduced readout power and lightweight CNN for vision applications. IEEE Trans. Circuits Syst. Video Technol. (2023)
11. Dallel, B., Said, B., Mohammed, K.: An intelligent compression system for wireless capsule endoscopy images. Biomed. Signal Process. Control **70** (2021)
12. Medina, K., Adnan, S., Amila, A., Emir, B.: Early stage flame segmentation with deep learning and intel's OpenVINO toolkit. In: 2023 XXIX International Conference on Information, Communication and Automation Technologies, ICAT (2023)
13. Saima, M., Fayadh, A., Sarfaraz, M., Musheer, A., Emine, S. G., Kemal, P.: Attention based CNN model for fire detection and localization in real-world images. Expert Syst. Appl. **189** (2022)
14. kaggle. https://www.kaggle.com/datasets/tharakan684/urecamain/data. Accessed 06 Oct 2023

Applied Cryptography

Enhancing Prediction Entropy Estimation of RNG for On-the-Fly Test

Yuan Ma[1,2], Weisong Gu[1,2], Tianyu Chen[1(✉)], Na Lv[1], Dongchi Han[1,2], and Shijie Jia[1,2]

[1] SKLOIS, Institute of Information Engineering, CAS, Beijing, China
{mayuan,guweisong,chentianyu,lvna,handongchi,jiashijie}@iie.ac.cn
[2] School of Cyber Security, University of Chinese Academy of Sciences, Beijing, China

Abstract. Random number generators (RNGs) play a vital role in cryptographic applications, and ensuring the quality of the generated random numbers is crucial. At the same time, on-the-fly test plays an important role in cryptography because it is used to assess the quality of the sequences generated by entropy sources and to raise an alert when failures are detected. Moreover, environmental noise, changes in physical equipment, and other factors can introduce variations into the sequence, leading to time-varying sequences. This phenomenon is quite common in real-world scenarios, and it needs on-the-fly test. However, in terms of speed and accuracy, current methods based on mathematical formulas or deep learning algorithms for evaluating min-entropy both fail to meet the requirements of on-the-fly test. Therefore, this paper introduces a new estimator specifically designed for on-the-fly min-entropy estimation. To accurately evaluate time-varying data, we employ an appropriate change detection technology. Additionally, we introduce a new calculation method to replace the original global prediction probability calculation approach for accuracy. We evaluate the performance of our estimator using various kinds of simulated datasets, and compare our estimator with other estimators. The proposed estimator effectively meets the requirements of on-the-fly test.

Keywords: On-the-fly test · Entropy estimation · Prediction estimator · Change detection technology · Confidence interval

1 Introduction

In today's cryptographic engineering applications, random numbers have become increasingly important. For instance, in key distribution and mutual authentication schemes, two communicating parties collaborate to exchange information for key distribution and authentication purposes. These random numbers are generated by random number generators that contains entropy sources, and entropy sources are divided into two categories: stationary sources and time-varying sources. Secure random numbers are often used as security primitives

© The Author(s), under exclusive license to Springer Nature Singapore Pte Ltd. 2024
H. Seo and S. Kim (Eds.): ICISC 2023, LNCS 14562, pp. 95–112, 2024.
https://doi.org/10.1007/978-981-97-1238-0_6

for many cryptographic applications, so it is necessary to evaluate the quality of random numbers.

Current methods for evaluation are mainly divided into two categories: white-box test and black-box test. White-box test, also known as theoretical entropy evaluation, requires an understanding of the internal structure and generation principle of the entropy source. It establishes a mathematical model according to appropriate assumptions to calculate the theoretical entropy of the output sequence [8]. However, given the complex and varied structures of many entropy sources, it becomes challenging to model them accurately, thereby limiting the applicability of theoretical entropy evaluation. Black-box test includes statistical test and statistical entropy evaluation: statistical test uses hypothesis-testing methods to conduct tests on the sequence for some properties, determining whether the tested sequence meets the null hypothesis (indicating randomness) or exhibits statistical defects [13]. Nevertheless, it is worth noting that certain specifically constructed pseudo-random sequences may exhibit favorable statistical properties and successfully pass these tests, posing potential security threats. Statistical entropy does not require the knowledge of the internal structure and generation principle of entropy sources. It evaluates the safety of the random numbers from the perspective of "entropy" [15]. In summary, to meet the requirements of generality and security, statistical entropy evaluation has become an indispensable approach.

Statistical entropy evaluation methods can be categorized into two main categories: those based on mathematical and statistical theories, and those based on deep learning. However, some estimators in the former, represented by the NIST SP800-90B standard, have been found to have overestimation and underestimation problems when faced with some typical datasets during entropy evaluation [21]. The latter has a problem of high time consumption. They both don't perform well in time-varying sequence which is common in reality. Thus, in order to detect RNG failures quickly and reliably, we need an on-the-fly test that is suitable for time-varying datasets.

To design a suitable estimator for on-the-fly test, we need solve two issues. Firstly, as mentioned above, we should update the model in a timely manner, especially for time-varying datasets. To address it, we utilize the change detection technique. Secondly, we introduce a new calculation method for global predictability of entropy estimation [15], specifically designed to handle situations involving small samples or extreme probabilities (i.e., probabilities approaching 0 or 1), which is different from the SP800-90B Standard, because the raw method is no longer suitable for on-the-fly test.

Our goal is to design an entropy estimator which meets the requirement of speed and accuracy for on-the-fly test. We present several significant contributions in this paper:

1) We propose a modified version of the prediction estimators from SP800-90B, enabling an on-the-fly test for evaluating the quality of entropy sources timely. To support the new framework, we proposed two key technologies: change detection technique and new calculation method for global predictability.

2) By leveraging the characteristics of the prediction estimator model and draw-ing inspiration from neural network parameter adjustments during training, we design a novel change detection technique suitable for online entropy esti-mation. Besides, we are the first to address the challenges associated with eval-uating min-entropy in scenarios involving small sample datasets and extreme probabilities. We provide a reasonable solution to this issue, which plays a critical role in on-the-fly test.

3) We compare the performance among our estimator and other existing estima-tors, using different types of simulated datasets with known entropy values. The experimental results show that, our estimator performs well for all dif-ferent types of tested datasets, outperforming the other ones.

The rest of this paper is organized as follows. In Sect. 2, we introduce the definition of min-entropy, along with an overview of the 90B standard. In Sect. 3, we expound and analyze the existing estimators. Section 4 presents our new framework and provides detailed descriptions, including the change detection technique and so on. In Sect. 5, we present a series of experiments comparing our estimator with other estimators. Finally, in Sect. 6, we conclude our paper.

2 Preliminaries

2.1 Min-Entropy

"Entropy" is the unit representing the size of information in communication, which can quantify the randomness of the output sequence [15]. Min-entropy is a conservative way to ensure the quality of random numbers in the worst case. The definition of min-entropy is as follows: we take the next output from an entropy source as a random variable X, which is an independent discrete random variable. If X takes value from the set $A = \{x_1, x_2, ..., x_k\}$ with probability $Pr\{X = x_i\} = p_i$ for $i = 1, ..., k$, the min-entropy of the output is

$$H_{min} = \min_{1 \leq i \leq k}[-\log_2(p_i)] = -\log_2[\max_{1 \leq i \leq k}(p_i)]. \tag{1}$$

If the min-entropy of X is H, then the probability of any value that X can take doesn't exceed 2^{-H}. For a random variable with the possibility of k distinct values, the maximum value that the min-entropy can reach is $log_2 k$, achieved when the variable follows a uniform probability distribution, i.e., $p_1 = p_2 = ... = p_k = 1/k$.

2.2 NIST SP800-90B Standard

The 90B estimation suite is a widely-used standard for calculating statistical entropy [15]. It calculates global predictability and local predictability with an upper bound of 99% confidence, and chooses the maximum value between them to estimate min-entropy. The suite comprises ten distinct entropy estimators that will be discussed in Sect. 3.

Global Predictability: Global predictability is the proportion of all predicted data to be correctly predicted. For a given prediction method, let $p'_{global} = c/n$, where c represents the number of correct predictions and n denotes the number of predictions made. Then, to give a conservative calculation method, 90B calculates p_{global} according to the following equation [7]:

$$p_{global} = \begin{cases} 1 - 0.01^{1/n}, & p'_{global} = 0 \\ \min(1, p'_{global} + 2.576\sqrt{\frac{p'_{global}(1-p'_{global})}{n-1}}), & otherwise \end{cases}, \quad (2)$$

which is the upper bound of the 99% confidence interval on p'_{global}, and it should meet the condition of De Moivre-Laplace Central Limit Theorem, that is: let $X_1, X_2, \ldots, X_n$ be i.i.d Bernoulli random variables with success probability $p \in (0,1)$ such that $np \to \infty$, as $n \to \infty$. Denote $S_n : X_1 + X_2 + \ldots + X_n$ and

$$Y_n^* = \frac{S_n - np}{\sqrt{np(1-p)}}.$$

Then, $\forall\, y \in R$, the theorem states that

$$lim_{n \to \infty}[P(Y_n^* \le y)] = \Phi(y) = \frac{1}{\sqrt{2\pi}} \int_{-\infty}^{y} e^{-t^2/2}\, dt. \quad (3)$$

Local Predictability: Local predictability is based on the longest run of correct predictions, which is valuable mainly when the source falls into a state of very predictable output for a short time [4]. Let l be the number one larger than the longest run of correct predictions. Then local predictability is calculated as

$$0.99 = \frac{1 - p_{local}x}{(l+1-lx)q} \cdot \frac{1}{x^{n+1}}, \quad (4)$$

where $q = 1 - p_{local}$, n represents the number of predictions, and x is the real positive root of the equation $1 - x + qp_{local}^l x^{l+1} = 0$. Then by iterations and the binary search, we can solve the mentioned equation and calculate the local predictability.

3   Related Work

3.1   Statistical Entropy Evaluation

Statistical entropy evaluation is comprised of estimators based on statistic methods and deep learning algorithms. For the former, in 2018, the final NIST SP800-90B test suite published, which is a typical representative of the statistical entropy estimations, which is based on min-entropy and specifies how to design and test entropy sources. It employs ten different estimators to calculate the min-entropy [15]. While it performs well on stationary datasets, it falls short when dealing with time-varying datasets. Before conducting entropy estimation, the

90B standard carries out an initial IID (independent and identically distributed) test. If the dataset meets the IID requirement, the MostCommon Estimator is utilized. Otherwise, the suite employs ten different estimators and selects the minimum value among them. These ten estimators can be divided into two categories: statistic-based and prediction-based. On the one hand, statistic-based estimators treat the test sequence as a whole and employ statistical methods to analyze properties related to entropy sources. On the other hand, prediction-based estimators use a training set comprised of previously observed samples to predict the next sample. By comparing the predicted results with the actual samples, the success rate of prediction is determined, and entropy estimation is performed based on the probability of successful prediction. Prediction-based estimators have a better performance than the other estimators in this standard. A brief introduction of the 10 estimators (Table 1) is as follows.

- **Most Common Value Estimator** performs entropy estimation based on the frequency of the most commonly occurring sample values in the sequence.
- **Collision Estimator** performs entropy estimation based on the collision frequency of samples in the sequence.
- **Markov Estimator** assumes the sequence as a first-order Markov process for entropy estimation.
- **Compression Estimator** is an entropy estimator based on the Maurer's algorithm.
- **T-Tuple Estimator** calculates entropy based on the occurrences of some fixed length repeated tuples.
- **LRS Estimator** calculates entropy based on the occurrences of some longer repeated tuples.
- **MultiMCW Prediction Estimator** utilizes four sliding windows of different sizes to determine the most frequently occurring value for prediction. A scoreboard is employed to determine the appropriate sliding window to use.
- **Lag Prediction Estimator** selects a prediction period ranging from 1 to 128 and also employs a scoreboard to select the optimal period.
- **MultiMMC Prediction Estimator** begins by setting up a dictionary (a two-dimensional array) and a scoreboard (a one-dimensional array). The dictionary is responsible for counting the frequency of prefixes and suffixes, while the scoreboard keeps a record of accurate predictions. After counting, it calculates the min-entropy.
- **LZ78Y Prediction Estimator** creates a dictionary based on patterns observed in the sequences and uses it for prediction.

For the latter, Yang et al. [20] were the first to apply neural networks to entropy source evaluation in 2018. In 2020, Lv et al. [12] conducted a comprehensive study on parameter settings for fully-connected neural networks (FNN) and recurrent neural networks (RNN), achieving accurate estimates of M-sequences with up to 20 stages. In 2019, Zhu et al. [21] combined change detection techniques with neural networks, partially resolving the issue of inaccurate prediction for time-varying sequences, and their model is named CDNN. Furthermore, in 2023, Zhang et al. [10] utilized TPA-LSTM to quantify the unpredictability of

Table 1. 90B Estimators.

Statistic-based	Prediction-based
MostCommon Value Estimator	MultiMCW Prediction Estimator
Collision Estimator	Lag Prediction Estimator
Markov Estimator	MultiMMC Prediction Estimator
Compression Estimator	LZ78Y Prediction Estimator
T-Tuple Estimator	
LRS Estimator	

random numbers, and validated the effectiveness of pruning and quantized deep learning models in the field of random number security analysis. The above methods provide increasingly accurate estimation, but the speed needs to be improved.

In summary, the prediction-based estimators of SP800-90B can provide the same accurate estimation as the deep learning based estimators for stationary datasets and some time-varing datasets, and the former can consume less time.

3.2   On-the-fly Test Technologies

In terms of the on-the-fly test applied in cryptography, Santoro et al. [14] conducted the evaluation of the harmonic series on FPGA in the entropy test in 2009. Then, in 2012, Veljković et al. [16] proposed the online implementation for NIST SP800-22 and Yang et al. [18] improved it in 2015.

At the same time, Yang et al. [19] completed hardware implementations of 4 statistic-based estimators of NIST SP800-90B on FPGA after some simplifications, but it is only aimed at the estimators of the first draft 90B and its accuracy needs to be improved. In 2017, Grujić et al. [6] used the three prediction estimator of NIST SP800-90B to implement the on-the-fly test, but the results is not very accurate because there some mistakes in the second draft standard, and besides, the latest draft is also not suitable because the dictionaries updates laggardly. Then, in 2021, Kim et al. [9] proposed an online estimator that updates the min-entropy estimate as a new sample is received, which is based on the idea of the compression estimate of NIST SP800-90B, and it is implement on software. However, it doesn't perform well in time-varying datasets, even in some stationary datasets. Therefore, new framework should be designed to improve it.

4   New Framework of the 90B's Prediction Estimator for On-the-fly Test

4.1   Design Goal and Principle

Our design goal and principle is to achieve on-the-fly test effectively, so we need to improve speed while ensuring accuracy. We have tested that the minimum of time consumption of estimators based on deep learning is 30 s for processing 1 Mbit of data which can't meet the requirement of on-the-fly test. By contrast, the raw 90B estimators only consume 0.15 s. Therefore, we design the new framework according to the 90B estimators.

Besides, we know that on-the-fly test requires as few estimators as possible to reduce the time consuming, and prediction estimators outperform the other ones [7]. Therefore, while ensuring accuracy, we choose the four prediction estimators included in 90B to modify for on-the-fly test. Last but not least, suitable change detection technology and calculation method of global predictability should be designed to improve the accuracy.

4.2   Framework of Our Estimator

We can observe that the predictors in SP800-90B all feature scoreboards or dictionaries, which serve as key components in the prediction process. However, the estimation accuracy of these predictors in handling time-varying sequences is compromised. This can be attributed to the fact that, even as the datasets change, the scoreboards and dictionaries retain information from the previous datasets. As a result, there is a lag in the response of the dictionaries and scoreboards to data changes during accumulation, leading to prediction errors when applied to new datasets. Therefore, it is imperative to make improvements in this regard.

We have made the following modifications to the aforementioned estimators for conducting on-the-fly test. The entire process is presented in Fig. 1. In it, *point* is the change position, and i is the serial number of the sample. For each estimator, we perform the simultaneous operations of reading in data and outputting results in a serial manner. In step one, considering that the dictionaries and scoreboards have not yet started accumulating data at startup, which may result in erroneous estimation, we exclude the first 4999 samples from undergoing entropy estimation. During this phase, only the dictionaries and scoreboards are accumulated. Then, in the second step, at the point when there are 5000 samples, we calculate the prediction probability as the initial value for the change detection process based on the accumulated dictionaries. Starting from the 5001st sample, we calculate the prediction probability for each subsequently read-in sample. This calculated probability serves as the basis for the change detection technology.

In step three, if the prediction suddenly deviates and exceeds the threshold, we output the calculated min-entropy, clear the dictionaries and scoreboards, and initiate a new round of entropy estimation. Otherwise, as shown in the fourth step, if there is no change appearing, for every I samples input, entropy calculation is performed according to the formula in Sect. 4.4, and the results are outputted without clearing the dictionaries and scoreboards. Throughout this process, the minimum value among the four estimators is selected as the final output result. Here, I refers to the interval between two outputs.

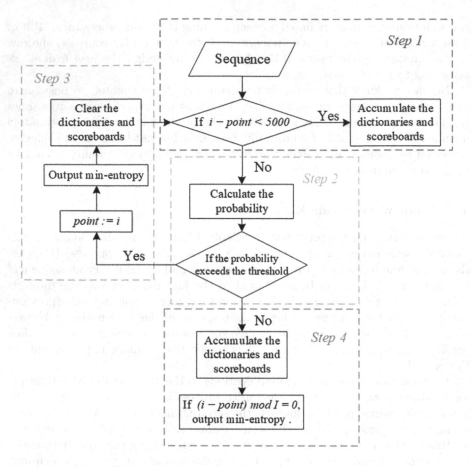

Fig. 1. The flowchart of the new framework.

4.3   Change Detection Module

In Fig. 1, we employ a sequential approach for the four estimators to carry out the accumulation of dictionaries and scoreboards. We then utilize change detection technology to identify changes in the datasets and promptly clear the dictionaries and scoreboards when such changes are detected. This is followed by initiating a new round of dictionaries accumulation and scoreboards counting.

The current change detection technology can be categorized into three types: error rate-based drift detection, data distribution-based drift detection, and multiple hypothesis test drift detection [11]. The latter two methods require more time and resource consumption as they involve additional feature extraction and comparison processing on the data. Consequently, they are not suitable for our on-the-fly test scenario. Error rate-based drift detection, specifically the widely used Drift Detection Method (DDM) [5], offers a viable approach. Its concept is as follows: when the sample dataset exhibits stable distribution, the error rate of the model gradually decreases with the input of data; when there is a change in the probability distribution, the error rate of the model increases. We can reference the DDM approach for our change detection modules, but some adjustments will be necessary in terms of specific details.

For our estimator, when the probability distribution changes, the error rate of our model has a possibility of both an increase and a decrease; when the sample dataset is stable, the error rate is in an almost stable and unchanging state. Besides, Gama et al. [5] set the confidence level for drift to 99%, and the drift level is reached if $p_i + s_i \geq p_{min} + 3 \times s_{min}$, where p_i is the probability corresponding to the first i samples and s_i is the standard deviation of the first i samples. p_{min} is the minimum probability of the previous samples and s_{min} is the corresponding standard deviation. However, the inequality can hold only when the normal approximation of the binomial distribution holds. Therefore, we replace it with another formula for general which mentioned in Sect. 4.4, that is,

$$p_i \geq \frac{p_{min} + \frac{z_{\alpha/2}^2}{2(i_{min}-1)} + z_{\alpha/2}\sqrt{\frac{p_{min}(1-p_{min})}{i_{min}-1} + \frac{z_{\alpha/2}^2}{4(i_{min}-1)^2}}}{1 + \frac{z_{\alpha/2}^2}{i_{min}-1}}, \quad (5)$$

and for the lower bound of confidence interval, we use the formula

$$p_i \leq \frac{p_{max} + \frac{z_{\alpha/2}^2}{2(i_{max}-1)} - z_{\alpha/2}\sqrt{\frac{p_{max}(1-p_{max})}{i_{max}-1} + \frac{z_{\alpha/2}^2}{4(i_{max}-1)^2}}}{1 + \frac{z_{\alpha/2}^2}{i_{max}-1}}, \quad (6)$$

where p_{max} is the maximum probability of the previous samples and $z_{\alpha/2}$ is 2.576 when the confidence level is 99%. This can apply to all situations.

Then, during the estimation, we use the prediction probabilities of four estimators for simultaneous change detection. As long as a probability that exceeds the confidence interval appears, it is determined that a change has occurred and immediately clear the dictionaries and scoreboards. In theory, our method is similar to the hyperparameter update of deep learning algorithms, but more timely than it.

4.4   Optimization of Global Predictability for Small Sample Datasets and Extreme Probability

According to Sect. 2.2, the calculation method of global predictability confidence interval is divided into two situations. When p'_{global} is zero, it uses Clopper-Pearson Exact Method [3]. In other cases, use normal distribution to approximate binomial distribution and calculate the confidence interval.

However, the above method only contains situation when $np > 5$ and $n(1 - p) > 5$, or $p = 0$ or $p = 1$, where n is the sample size and p is the probability. Therefore, we should consider the case that $np \leq 5$ or $n(1 - p) \leq 5$ to make the perfect.

In our proposed online estimator, the dataset was truncated according to the sample distribution and parameter changes due to the use of change detection technology. Besides, in the process of entropy estimation, the probability may approach to 0 or 1. The two factors may make us encounter the case mentioned above, i.e., $np \leq 5$ or $n(1-p) \leq 5$. In this case, the confidence interval calculation of the global prediction probability in 90B standard is no longer valid because it does not meet the condition that the binomial distribution is approximated to normal distribution, that is, the central limit theorem mentioned in Sect. 2.2. Therefore, we need to use a new method to calculate it.

Poisson approximations can do for the above issue to some extent, but it doesn't provide the method of calculating the confidence interval [4]. T-distribution can also handle some small sample issues, but still can't solve the above problem completely [2]. Therefore, we use "Plus Four Confidence Intervals" to handle the small sample issue here. This is proposed by Edwin Bidwell Wilson in 1927, which is an asymmetric interval [17]. It can be used for any probability value between 0 and 1 in the case of the small sample securely. It is obtained by solve the equation of $p : p = \hat{p} \pm z_{\alpha/2}\sqrt{\frac{p(1-p)}{n}}$. $\hat{p}$ is the correct prediction proportion of the sample, and n is the sample size. $z_{\alpha/2}$ is the confidence coefficient, and it equals to 2.576 when the confidence interval is 99%. The result is

$$p = \frac{\hat{p} + \frac{z_{\alpha/2}^2}{2n} \pm z_{\alpha/2}\sqrt{\frac{\hat{p}(1-\hat{p})}{n} + \frac{z_{\alpha/2}^2}{4n^2}}}{1 + \frac{z_{\alpha/2}^2}{n}}. \tag{7}$$

Then, the upper bound of confidence interval of global prediction under the new method is

$$p_{global} = \frac{p'_{global} + \frac{z_{\alpha/2}^2}{2(n-1)} + z_{\alpha/2}\sqrt{\frac{p'_{global}(1-p'_{global})}{n-1} + \frac{z_{\alpha/2}^2}{4(n-1)^2}}}{1 + \frac{z_{\alpha/2}^2}{n-1}}. \tag{8}$$

From the result, according to knowledge of the infinitesimal of higher order of the limit theory, we can see that when $n \to \infty$, the equation is approximate to

$$p_{global} = p'_{global} + z_{\alpha/2}\sqrt{\frac{p'_{global}(1-p'_{global})}{n-1}}. \tag{9}$$

This means that the formula is also applicable to the case of large sample datasets. Besides, when $p'_{global} = 0$, the result is greater than 0, which indicates that it can also handle the situation of endpoint values.

Last but not least, we retain the original local prediction during the process of estimation because it is valid regardless of the sample size and extreme probability. Then, we choose the maximum of the global and local prediction to calculate the min-entropy as the final result.

4.5   Setting of Key Parameters

In this section, we discuss the setting of the parameters. We choose an initial accumulation size of 5000 samples for dictionaries and scoreboards due to the fact that the largest sliding window of the MultiMCW prediction estimator is 4095. If the accumulation size is smaller than 4095, the largest sliding window cannot accumulate dictionaries and scoreboards for the initial samples. This setting is a conservative approach, and it is suitable for other prediction estimators in 90B.

When determining the size of the interval I in Fig. 1, we take into account it both from theoretical and experimental perspectives. On the one hand, as mentioned earlier, the MultiMCW estimator's largest sliding window has a size of 4095. Thus, the interval I should be greater than this value, and we also prove it through the experiment. On the other hand, we conducted an experiment to determine the upper bound. We set the intervals as 2^k, and k takes from 1 to 17, and evaluated sequences that followed IID and non-IID distributions separately. Because the dataset within each segment is stationary after segmentation under change detection technology, we needn't use the time-varying sequence here. For the IID dataset, we select a typical dataset generated by the Oscillator-based

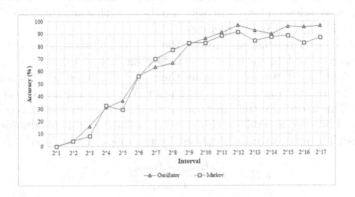

Fig. 2. Accuracy under Different Intervals.

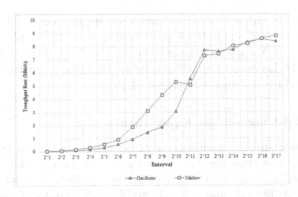

Fig. 3. Throughput Rate under Different Intervals.

model [1]. For the non-IID dataset, we choose one that followed a Markov model. The accuracy and throughput rate under different intervals are depicted in Fig. 2 and Fig. 3.

In the results, we use the line chart to depict the accuracy and throughput rate. We see that the accuracy improves as the interval size increases, and when the interval exceeds 2^{12}, the accuracy starts to fluctuate around 90%. Besides, with larger intervals, the throughput rate grows faster, and when the interval reaches 2^{12}, the throughput rate gradually becomes stable. However, processing too much data at once may consume a significant amount of memory and lead to latency. Therefore, to ensure accuracy and throughput rate, we set the interval range from 2^{12} to 2^{17}. For the sake of convenience in displaying the results throughout the rest of this paper, we set a fixed interval of 50000.

5   Experiment Results and Analysis

5.1   Experiment Setup

Our estimator is implemented in C/C++ language, and we show the results of the other estimators for comparison. In this section, all experiments are conducted on a Windows 11 system with an Intel 11th Gen Intel(R) Core(TM) i7-1195G7 CPU and 16 GB of memory.

During the experiment, we present the results in two ways. Firstly, for the offline estimators such as the estimators in 90B and others based on deep learning algorithms [10,12,21], we only compare their final offline estimation results with the endpoint result of our proposed estimator. We then display the error rate in the figure. This is because their methods are exclusively used in offline scenarios, and it would be unreasonable to choose intermediate output results for the final comparison. The error rate is calculated by the following formula:

$$ErrorRate = \frac{|H_{test} - H_{correct}|}{H_{correct}} \times 100\%, \tag{10}$$

where $H_{correct}$ is the theoretical min-entropy, and H_{test} is the results of the estimators.

Secondly, for the online estimators, including our proposed one and the online estimator based on collision entropy proposed by Kim [9], we plot their estimations in the figures. We do not present the values of the 90B estimators implemented on FPGA because they utilize outdated estimators of the old version of 90B standard, which have some mistakes [6,19].

5.2   Simulated Datasets for Experiments

The datasets used in our experiment can be divided into two categories: stationary datasets and time-varying datasets. The stationary datasets comprise various distribution families, including discrete uniform distribution, discrete near-uniform distribution, and normal distribution rounded to integers. More details are provided below.

- **Discrete Uniform Distribution:** The samples are subject to the discrete uniform distribution and are equally-likely. They come from an IID source.
- **Discrete Near-uniform Distribution:** The samples are subject to the discrete near-uniform distribution with one higher probability than the rest. They come from an IID source.
- **Normal Distribution Rounded To Integers:** The samples are subject to normal distribution and are rounded to integer values. They come from an IID source.

The time-varying datasets consist of two common situations: mutation (i.e., sudden change) and gradient (i.e., gradual change). To represent mutation, we utilize a dataset that undergoes near-uniform distribution with 9 mutations. For the gradient scenario, we employ a Markov model that exhibits a gradient following a linear function curve. The specific details are outlined below.

- **Discrete Near-uniform Distribution with Mutation:** The samples are divided into ten parts and each subject to the discrete near-uniform distribution with different parameter values, i.e., the higher probability. Table 2 shows the changes.
- **Markov Model with Gradient:** The samples are subject to a first-order Markov process of $\{0, 1\}$, and its transfer matrix is $\begin{pmatrix} 1-p & p \\ p & 1-p \end{pmatrix}$, where p changes along a linear function curve:

$$p(i) = \begin{cases} 0.1 + 0.0000004i & , 0 \leq i < 500000 \\ 0.3 & , 500000 \leq i < 1000000 \end{cases}, \tag{11}$$

where i is the serial number of the sample.

Table 2. Discrete Near-uniform Distribution with Mutation.

Serial Number of the Sample	Higher probability
[1, 80000]	0.5
[80001, 230000]	0.8
[230001, 330000]	0.6
[330001, 380000]	0.85
[380001, 400000]	0.7
[400001, 600000]	0.9
[600001, 900000]	0.55
[900001, 1200000]	0.75
[1200001, 1350000]	0.95
[1350001, 1500000]	0.65

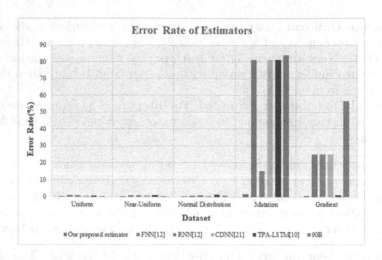

Fig. 4. Comparison of error rate of estimators.

In terms of the dataset size, our proposed online estimator only requires a minimum of 2^{12} samples. However, other offline estimators, as per the 90B standard, necessitate no less than one million samples. To facilitate comparison, we utilize a dataset that follows a discrete near-uniform distribution with 1.5 million samples for the mutation scenario, and other datasets with 1 million samples for the remaining scenarios.

5.3   Experimental Results

In this subsection, we present the results and then analyze them.

1) Offline estimation results
In Fig. 4, we use a column chart to represent the comparison of the error rate of ours and other estimators under different sequences. We find that our online estimator can give better results than raw 90B estimators and other estimators that use deep learning algorithms, especially in time-varying sequences.

2) On-the-fly test results
In the figures, we denote the correct values with red line, and use green "+" dots representing the results of the online estimator based on collision entropy. Ours is shown by blue "x" dots.

Figure 5c shows the estimated results of the simulation dataset from the independent normal distribution entropy source. We observed that the results provided by our estimator and the online estimator based on collision entropy are both close to the correct entropy.

Figure 5a and Fig. 5b show that the online estimator based on collision entropy always provide severely underestimation results on the datasets subject to discrete uniform distribution and discrete near uniform distribution because

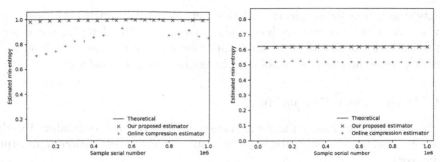

(a) Comparison of min-entropy estimators for uniform source.

(b) Comparison of min-entropy estimators for near-uniform source.

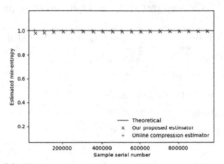

(c) Comparison of min-entropy estimators for normal distribution source.

Fig. 5. Comparison of min-entropy for stationary sequences.

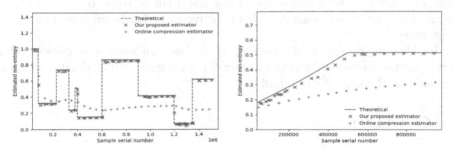

(a) Comparison of min-entropy estimators for near uniform mutation sources.

(b) Comparison of min-entropy estimators for Markov model gradient source.

Fig. 6. Comparison of min-entropy for time-varying sequences.

its algorithm is too simple to mine out the features of the datasets. By contrast,
ours provides almost accurate estimations.

For the time-varying datasets, the online estimator based on collision entropy
completely deviates from the theoretical min-entropy in Fig. 6(a) and Fig. 6(b).
The estimations of ours can approach the theoretical correct values at most

points due to the timely clearing of the dictionaries, although there are some deviations at the inflection points. This is caused by the delay in the change detection technology, and the delay is quite small, which is less than 1000 samples. It proves the effectiveness of our change detection technology.

5.4 Performance Evaluation

In this section, we discuss the performance of our proposed estimator. Firstly, in above results, our estimator can give more accurate estimation than other estimators.

Table 3. Throughput rate under different sequences.

Data type	Throughput rate (Mbit/s)
Uniform	8.92
Near-uniform	8.90
Normal distribution	8.85
Mutation	8.76
Gradient	8.82

Secondly, in terms of time consumption, as is shown in Table 3, the throughput rate of our estimators is stationary under different datasets, which is about 8.85 Mbit/s. Therefore, for on-the-fly test, our estimator is suitable for random number generators with throughput rates less than or equal to 8.7 Mbit/s in terms of conservative estimation, whether software or hardware random number generators.

Besides, in the real world, entropy is an issue on low-power devices. Our estimator consumes 300 Mbit of memory for processing 1Mbit of data, which is the same as the raw 90B standard.

6 Conclusion

In this paper, we design a new estimator based on the 90B prediction estimators for on-the-fly test. This design enhances both speed and accuracy. By employing change detection technology in our proposed new framework, we have achieved excellent performance. Additionally, to address situations involving small sample datasets or extreme probability, we utilize the "Plus Four Confidence Intervals" method to calculate the global predictability. Our estimator achieves a throughput rate exceeding 8.7 Mbit/s, meeting the on-the-fly test requirements of many RNGs. It currently stands as the most accurate technology for evaluating min-entropy. Looking ahead, our future plans involve further improving speed through hardware enhancements and parallel computing, aiming to ensure compatibility with a broader range of entropy sources.

Acknowledgements. This work was supported by the National Natural Science Foundation of China under Grant 62272457.

References

1. Baudet, M., Lubicz, D., Micolod, J., Tassiaux, A.: On the security of oscillator-based random number generators. J. Cryptol. **24**(2), 398–425 (2011)
2. Box, J.F.: Gosset, fisher, and the t distribution. Am. Stat. **35**(2), 61–66 (1981)
3. Clopper, C.J., Pearson, E.S.: The use of confidence or fiducial limits illustrated in the case of the binomial. Biometrika **26**(4), 404–413 (1934)
4. Feller, W.: An Introduction to Probability Theory and Its Applications, Volume 2, vol. 81. John Wiley & Sons, Hoboken (1991)
5. Gama, J., Medas, P., Castillo, G., Rodrigues, P.: Learning with drift detection. In: Bazzan, A.L.C., Labidi, S. (eds.) Advances in Artificial Intelligence – SBIA 2004. SBIA 2004. LNCS, vol. 3171, pp. 286–295. Springer, Berlin, Heidelberg (2004). https://doi.org/10.1007/978-3-540-28645-5_29
6. Grujić, M., Rožić, V., Yang, B., Verbauwhede, I.: Lightweight prediction-based tests for on-line min-entropy estimation. IEEE Embed. Syst. Lett. **9**(2), 45–48 (2017)
7. Kelsey, J., McKay, K.A., Sönmez Turan, M.: Predictive models for min-entropy estimation. In: Guneysu, T., Handschuh, H. (eds.) Cryptographic Hardware and Embedded Systems – CHES 2015. CHES 2015. LNCS, vol. 9293, pp. 373–392. Springer, Berlin, Heidelberg (2015). https://doi.org/10.1007/978-3-662-48324-4_19
8. Killmann, W., Schindler, W.: A design for a physical RNG with robust entropy estimators. In: Oswald, E., Rohatgi, P. (eds.) Cryptographic Hardware and Embedded Systems – CHES 2008. CHES 2008. LNCS, vol. 5154, pp. 146–163. Springer, Berlin, Heidelberg (2008). https://doi.org/10.1007/978-3-540-85053-3_10
9. Kim, Y., Guyot, C., Kim, Y.S.: On the efficient estimation of min-entropy. IEEE Trans. Inf. Forensics Secur. **16**, 3013–3025 (2021)
10. Li, H., Zhang, J., Li, Z., Liu, J., Wang, Y.: Improvement of min-entropy evaluation based on pruning and quantized deep neural network. IEEE Trans. Inf. Forensics Secur. **18**, 1410–1420 (2023)
11. Lu, J., Liu, A., Dong, F., Gu, F., Gama, J., Zhang, G.: Learning under concept drift: a review. IEEE Trans. Knowl. Data Eng. **31**(12), 2346–2363 (2018)
12. Lv, N., et al.: High-efficiency min-entropy estimation based on neural network for random number generators. Secur. Commun. Netw. **2020**, 1–18 (2020)
13. Ruk, A., et al.: A statistical test suite for the validation of random number generators and pseudo-random number generators for cryptographic applications. NIST (2001). http://csrc.nist.gov/rng/rng2.html
14. Santoro, R., Tisserand, A., Sentieys, O., Roy, S.: Arithmetic operators for on-the-fly evaluation of TRNGs. In: Mathematics for Signal and Information Processing, vol. 7444, pp. 253–264. SPIE (2009)
15. Turan, M.S., Barker, E., Kelsey, J., McKay, K.A., Baish, M.L., Boyle, M., et al.: Recommendation for the entropy sources used for random bit generation. NIST Spec. Publ. **800**(90B), 102 (2018)
16. Veljković, F., Rožić, V., Verbauwhede, I.: Low-cost implementations of on-the-fly tests for random number generators. In: 2012 Design, Automation & Test in Europe Conference & Exhibition (DATE), pp. 959–964. IEEE (2012)

17. Wilson, E.B.: Probable inference, the law of succession, and statistical inference. J. Am. Stat. Assoc. **22**(158), 209–212 (1927)
18. Yang, B., Rožić, V., Mentens, N., Dehaene, W., Verbauwhede, I.: Embedded HW/SW platform for on-the-fly testing of true random number generators. In: 2015 Design, Automation & Test in Europe Conference & Exhibition (DATE), pp. 345–350. IEEE (2015)
19. Yang, B., Rožić, V., Mentens, N., Verbauwhede, I.: On-the-fly tests for non-ideal true random number generators. In: 2015 IEEE International Symposium on Circuits and Systems (ISCAS), pp. 2017–2020. IEEE (2015)
20. Yang, J., Zhu, S., Chen, T., Ma, Y., Lv, N., Lin, J.: Neural network based min-entropy estimation for random number generators. In: Beyah, R., Chang, B., Li, Y., Zhu, S. (eds.) Security and Privacy in Communication Networks. SecureComm 2018. LNICS, Social Informatics and Telecommunications Engineering, vol. 255, pp. 231–250. Springer, Cham (2018). https://doi.org/10.1007/978-3-030-01704-0_13
21. Zhu, S., Ma, Y., Li, X., Yang, J., Lin, J., Jing, J.: On the analysis and improvement of min-entropy estimation on time-varying data. IEEE Trans. Inf. Forensics Secur. **15**, 1696–1708 (2019)

Leakage-Resilient Attribute-Based Encryption with Attribute-Hiding

Yijian Zhang[1], Yunhao Ling[1], Jie Chen[1,2(✉)], and Luping Wang[3,4]

[1] Software Engineering Institute, East China Normal University, Shanghai, China
[2] Shanghai Key Laboratory of Trustworthy Computing,
East China Normal University, Shanghai, China
`s080001@e.ntu.edu.sg`
[3] School of Electronic and Information Engineering, Suzhou University
of Science and Technology, Jiangsu, China
[4] Jiangsu Key Laboratory for Elevator Intelligent Safety, Jiangsu, China

Abstract. In this work, we present two generic frameworks for leakage-resilient attribute-based encryption (ABE), which is an improved version of ABE that can be proven secure even when part of the secret key is leaked. Our frameworks rely on the standard assumption (k-Lin) over prime-order groups. The first framework is designed for leakage-resilient ABE with attribute-hiding in the bounded leakage model. Prior to this work, no one had yet derived a generic leakage-resilient ABE framework with attribute-hiding. The second framework provides a generic method to construct leakage-resilient ABE in the continual leakage model. It is compatible with Zhang et al.'s work [DCC 2018] but more generic. Concretely, Zhang et al.'s framework cannot act on some specific ABE schemes while ours manages to do that. Technically, our frameworks are built on the predicate encoding of Chen et al.'s [EUROCRYPT 2015] combined with a method of adding redundancy. At last, several instantiations are derived from our frameworks, which cover the cases of zero inner-product predicate and non-zero inner-product predicate.

Keywords: Leakage-resilient · Attribute-based encryption · Attribute-hiding · Predicate encoding

1 Introduction

Attribute-based encryption (ABE) [18] is a primitive that can provide the confidentiality of data and fine-grained access control simultaneously. In ABE, a ciphertext $\mathsf{ct_x}$ for a message m is associated with an attribute $\mathbf{x} \in \mathcal{X}$, and a secret key $\mathsf{sk_y}$ is associated with a policy $\mathbf{y} \in \mathcal{Y}$. Given a predicate $\mathsf{P} : \mathcal{X} \times \mathcal{Y} \to \{0,1\}$, $\mathsf{ct_x}$ can be decrypted by $\mathsf{sk_y}$ if and only if $\mathsf{P}(\mathbf{x}, \mathbf{y}) = 1$.

The basic security requirement for ABE is *payload-hiding*. Roughly speaking, an adversary holding the secret key such that $\mathsf{P}(\mathbf{x}, \mathbf{y}) = 0$ cannot deduce any information about m from the given ciphertext, and besides, this should be guaranteed even the adversary has more than one such secret key. In some

H. Seo and S. Kim (Eds.): ICISC 2023, LNCS 14562, pp. 113–132, 2024.
https://doi.org/10.1007/978-981-97-1238-0_7

scenarios, the attribute $\mathbf{x}$ may contain user privacy. For example, in the cloud storage [11], the attribute $\mathbf{x}$ contains identity or address, which may be unsuitable to be exposed. *Attribute-hiding* [13] is an additional security requirement, and it concerns the privacy of attribute $\mathbf{x}$. Informally, attribute-hiding says that no information about attribute $\mathbf{x}$ can be disclosed to the adversary.

Recently, due to the emergence of side-channel attacks [1,9,12] which, through various physical methods, can recover part of the secret key, the leakage-resilient cryptography [8] is hence proposed. It is required that a leakage-resilient scheme should be provably secure in the *leakage-resilient model*. In this paper, we are interested in two prominent leakage-resilient models, namely, *bounded leakage model* (BLM) [2] and *continual leakage model* (CLM) [4]. Both of them assume that an adversary obtains leaked information about the secret key sk via a polynomial-time computable leakage function $f : \{0,1\}^{|\mathsf{sk}|} \to \{0,1\}^L$ where $|\mathsf{sk}|$ is the bit length of sk. In the BLM (resp. CLM), the adversary has access to at most $L < |\mathsf{sk}|$ bits leakage on the secret key over the whole lifetime (resp. any time period) of the system. It is necessary to *update* sk periodically in the CLM. Typically, the security of CLM is stronger than BLM [10].

Up to now, various leakage-resilient frameworks have been proposed, while very few of them concentrate on leakage-resilient ABE. There are several generic leakage-resilient frameworks that can convert plain ABE schemes to leakage-resilient ones in the BLM/CLM. The first one is introduced by Yu et al. [20]. Their generic leakage-resilient framework is able to convert the ABE schemes based on pair encoding [3] to leakage-resilient ones. However, their generic leakage-resilient framework cannot provide attribute-hiding feature. Besides, for several concrete constructions, their security must rely on the non-standard computational assumptions, namely, q-type assumptions. Afterward, Zhang et al. [23] proposed a generic leakage-resilient ABE framework from hash proof system, while it also ignores attribute-hiding feature. Another independent work was proposed by Zhang et al. [22]. Their generic leakage-resilient framework is able to convert most ABE schemes based on predicate encoding [19] to leakage-resilient ones. However, their generic leakage-resilient framework cannot guarantee attribute-hiding as well, and besides, cannot act on several specific ABE schemes based on predicate encoding, for example the compact-key ABE for inner-product predicate in [5], to leakage-resilient ones.

In this paper, we will follow the works of Chen et al. [5] and Zhang et al. [22], aimed at presenting two generic leakage-resilient frameworks. The first one can provide the attribute-hiding feature. The second one can convert more ABE schemes to leakage-resilient ones.

1.1   Contributions

In this work, we present two generic frameworks for the design of leakage-resilient ABE. Our contributions can be summarized as follows:

- **Leakage-resilient ABE with attribute-hiding in the BLM.**
  We introduce a new encoding called *attribute-hiding-leakage-resilient*. Based on the attribute-hiding techniques of CGW15 [5] and this new encoding, we present a generic leakage-resilient ABE construction with attribute-hiding, which is provably secure under the k-Lin assumption in the BLM.
- **Leakage-resilient ABE in the CLM.**
  We introduce different redundancy into the secret key and the master key to ensure the security against continual leakage and add a linear map to ensure the generation and update of secret keys. Thus, we present a more generic leakage-resilient ABE in the CLM compared with ZCG+18.

A comparison between our frameworks and previous works is shown in Table 1. Note that, although our second framework in Sect. 4 has the same properties as ZCG+18, it can act on some specific schemes while ZCG+18 cannot do that.

Table 1. Comparison between previous works and ours. "Prime" denotes prime-order groups. "SD" means subgroup assumptions over composite-order groups.

Reference	Leakage model	Attribute-hiding	Prime	Generality	Assumption
YAX+16 [20]	CLM	✗	✗	⊥	SD, q-type
ZZM17 [23]	BLM	✗	✗	⊥	SD
ZCG+18 [22]	CLM	✗	✓	weak	k-Lin
Ours (Sect. 3)	BLM	✓	✓	⊥	k-Lin
Ours (Sect. 4)	CLM	✗	✓	strong	k-Lin

1.2 Technical Overview

Let $(p, G_1, G_2, G_T, g_1, g_2, e)$ denote an asymmetric bilinear group of prime-order p with pairing $e : G_1 \times G_2 \to G_T$. We use mpk, mk to denote the master public key and the master key in ABE, respectively. Let $L \in \mathbb{N}$ be a leakage parameter.

Leakage-Resilient ABE with Attribute-Hiding in the BLM. Based on the ABE with attribute-hiding in CGW15, we propose a generic leakage-resilient ABE construction that possesses attribute-hiding feature even when the secret key can be leaked to the adversary. An overview of our construction is presented as follows[1]:

$$
\begin{aligned}
&\mathsf{mpk} : g_1, g_2, g_1^{\mathbf{w}}, e(g_1, g_2)^{\alpha}, &&\mathsf{mk} : \alpha, \mathbf{w} \\
&\mathsf{sk_y} : \mathbf{z}, \ g_2^r, \ g_2^{r\mathsf{kE}(\mathbf{y},\mathbf{z},\alpha)+r\cdot r\mathsf{E}(\mathbf{y},\mathbf{z},\mathbf{w})}, &&\mathsf{ct_x} : g_1^s, g_1^{s\cdot\mathsf{sE}(\mathbf{x},\mathbf{w})}, m \cdot e(g_1, g_2)^{\alpha s}
\end{aligned}
\tag{1}
$$

---

[1] Strictly speaking, the Eq. (1) is built on composite-order groups. A general approach to transforming schemes over composite-order groups into ones over prime-order groups has been proposed in [5]. Thus, in this section, we decide to abuse constructions over composite-order groups as ones over prime-order groups for simplicity.

where $\mathbf{w} \in \mathcal{W}$ is a set of secret values; $\alpha, r, s \leftarrow \mathbb{Z}_p$; $\mathbf{x} \in \mathcal{X}, \mathbf{y} \in \mathcal{Y}$; $\mathsf{rkE}, \mathsf{rE}, \mathsf{sE}$ are linear encoding algorithms; $\mathbf{z} \in \mathcal{Z}$ and $\mathbf{u}$ are "redundant" information. To achieve attribute-hiding security in the BLM, we require that

- **(attribute-hiding.)** For all $(\mathbf{x}, \mathbf{y}) \in \mathcal{X} \times \mathcal{Y}$ such that $\mathsf{P}(\mathbf{x}, \mathbf{y}) = 0$ and all $\mathbf{z} \in \mathcal{Z}$, the distributions $\{\mathbf{x}, \mathbf{y}, \mathbf{z}, \mathsf{sE}(\mathbf{x}, \mathbf{w}), \mathsf{rE}(\mathbf{y}, \mathbf{z}, \mathbf{w})\}$ and $\{\mathbf{x}, \mathbf{y}, \mathbf{z}, \mathbf{r}\}$ are statistically indistinguishable where the randomness is taken over $\mathbf{w} \leftarrow \mathcal{W}$ and $\mathbf{r} \leftarrow \mathbb{Z}_p^{|\mathsf{sE}(\cdot)| + |\mathsf{rE}(\cdot)|}$.

The above requirement, namely *attribute-hiding* encoding, ensures the attribute-hiding feature. It manages to randomize $\mathbf{x}$ in $\mathsf{sE}(\mathbf{x}, \mathbf{w})$ even after the adversary has got $\mathsf{rE}(\mathbf{y}, \mathbf{z}, \mathbf{w})$ on $\mathsf{sk}_\mathbf{y}$. However, this property only holds when $\mathsf{P}(\mathbf{x}, \mathbf{y}) = 0$ and would be broken by the adversary with leak ability, since he can use the leakage function f to acquire the leakage (i.e., $f(\mathbf{z}, \mathsf{rE}(\mathbf{y}, \mathbf{z}, \mathbf{w}))$) on $\mathsf{sk}_\mathbf{y}$ such that $\mathsf{P}(\mathbf{x}, \mathbf{y}) = 1$. The "redundant" information in $\mathsf{sk}_\mathbf{y}$ is designed to avoid this problem. Inspired by ZCG+18 [22] and LRW11 [14], we additionally require that

- **(attribute-hiding-leakage-resilient.)** For all $(\mathbf{x}, \mathbf{y}) \in \mathcal{X} \times \mathcal{Y}$ such that $\mathsf{P}(\mathbf{x}, \mathbf{y}) = 1$ and $\mathbf{z} \in \mathcal{Z}$, the distributions $\{\mathbf{x}, \mathbf{y}, \mathsf{sE}(\mathbf{x}, \mathbf{w}), f(\mathbf{z}, \mathsf{rE}(\mathbf{y}, \mathbf{z}, \mathbf{w}))\}$ and $\{\mathbf{x}, \mathbf{y}, \mathbf{r}\}$ are identical, where $\mathbf{w} \leftarrow \mathcal{W}$ and $\mathbf{r} \leftarrow \mathbb{Z}_p^{|\mathsf{sE}(\cdot)| + |f(\cdot)|}$.

This encoding guarantees that with the leakage of $\mathsf{sk}_\mathbf{y}$ such that $\mathsf{P}(\mathbf{x}, \mathbf{y}) = 1$, the adversary still cannot reveal the attribute $\mathbf{x}$ under $\mathsf{sE}(\mathbf{x}, \mathbf{w})$ since it seems to be sampled uniformly. Thus, the Eq. (1) achieves attribute-hiding in the BLM.

Leakage-Resilient ABE in the CLM. For the second leakage-resilient ABE framework, we consider the CLM which is stronger than BLM. Although ZCG+18 has proposed a leakage-resilient ABE framework in the CLM, it is not general enough to act on some specific schemes, e.g., compact-key ABE schemes for zero inner-product and non-zero inner-product in CGW15. For these specific schemes, their master keys contain multiple secret values (e.g., α and $\mathbf{w}$), and the adversary can break the security trivially if one of these secret values is leaked. Our solution is to differentiate the redundant information of mk and the redundant information of $\mathsf{sk}_\mathbf{y}$, which provides more possibilities to avoid the leakage on secret values. Thus, we present a new leakage-resilient ABE generic construction:

$$
\begin{aligned}
&\mathsf{mpk} : g_1, g_2, g_1^\mathbf{w}, g_2^\mathbf{w}, e(g_1, g_2)^\alpha, \quad &&\mathsf{mk} : \mathbf{v}, g_2^r, g_2^{\mathsf{mkE}(\mathbf{v}, \alpha) + r \cdot \mathsf{mE}(\mathbf{v}, \mathbf{w})}, \\
&\mathsf{sk}_\mathbf{y} : \mathbf{z}, g_2^r, g_2^{\mathsf{rkE}(\mathbf{y}, \mathbf{z}, \alpha) + r \cdot \mathsf{rE}(\mathbf{y}, \mathbf{z}, \mathbf{w})}, \quad &&\mathsf{ct}_\mathbf{x} : g_1^s, g_1^{s \cdot \mathsf{sE}(\mathbf{x}, \mathbf{w})}, m \cdot e(g_1, g_2)^{\alpha s}
\end{aligned}
\tag{2}
$$

where $\mathsf{mkE}, \mathsf{mE}$ are encoding algorithms; $\mathbf{v} \in \mathcal{V}$ and $\mathbf{z} \in \mathcal{Z}$ serve as redundant information for mk and $\mathsf{sk}_\mathbf{y}$, respectively. Note that this construction is similar to the Eq. (1), while it considers CLM (rather than BLM) and allows the leakage on $\mathsf{sk}_\mathbf{y}$ and mk. Here, we require that

1) **(α-privacy.)** For all $(\mathbf{x}, \mathbf{y}) \in \mathcal{X} \times \mathcal{Y}$ such that $\mathsf{P}(\mathbf{x}, \mathbf{y}) = 0$, the distributions $\{\mathbf{x}, \mathbf{y}, \mathbf{z}, \alpha, \mathsf{sE}(\mathbf{x}, \mathbf{w}), \mathsf{rkE}(\mathbf{y}, \mathbf{z}, \alpha) + \mathsf{rE}(\mathbf{y}, \mathbf{z}, \mathbf{w})\}$ and $\{\mathbf{x}, \mathbf{y}, \mathbf{z}, \alpha, \mathsf{sE}(\mathbf{x}, \mathbf{w}), \mathsf{rE}(\mathbf{y}, \mathbf{z}, \mathbf{w})\}$ are identical where the randomness is taken over $\mathbf{w} \leftarrow \mathcal{W}$.

2) (**α-leakage-resilient.**) For all $(\mathbf{x}, \mathbf{y}) \in \mathcal{X} \times \mathcal{Y}$ such that $P(\mathbf{x}, \mathbf{y}) = 1$ and all $\alpha \in \mathbb{Z}_p, \mathbf{z} \in \mathcal{Z}$, the distributions $\{\mathbf{x}, \mathbf{y}, \alpha, \mathsf{sE}(\mathbf{x}, \mathbf{w}), f(\mathbf{z}, \mathsf{rkE}(\mathbf{y}, \mathbf{z}, \alpha) + \mathsf{rE}(\mathbf{y}, \mathbf{z}, \mathbf{w}))\}$ and $\{\mathbf{x}, \mathbf{y}, \alpha, \mathsf{sE}(\mathbf{x}, \mathbf{w}), f(\mathbf{z}, \mathsf{rE}(\mathbf{y}, \mathbf{z}, \mathbf{w}))\}$ are identical where $\mathbf{w} \leftarrow \mathcal{W}$ and f is a leakage function.

   In addition, the distributions $\{\mathbf{x}, \alpha, \mathsf{sE}(\mathbf{x}, \mathbf{w}), f(\mathbf{z}, \mathsf{mkE}(\mathbf{v}, \alpha) + \mathsf{mE}(\mathbf{v}, \mathbf{w}))\}$ and $\{\mathbf{x}, \alpha, \mathsf{sE}(\mathbf{x}, \mathbf{w}), f(\mathbf{v}, \mathsf{mE}(\mathbf{v}, \mathbf{w}))\}$ are identical.

3) (**re-randomizable.**) There exists a update algorithm for $\mathsf{sk_y}$ and mk.

4) (**delegable.**) There exists an algorithm that takes as input mk and $\mathbf{y}$ and outputs a fresh secret key $\mathsf{sk_y}$.

α-*privacy* and α-*leakage-resilient* are aimed at resisting continual leakage on $\mathsf{sk_y}$ and mk. Since the total leakage bound of the adversary is unlimited in the CLM, *re-randomizable* and *delegable* are proposed to ensure the periodical update for $\mathsf{sk_y}$ and mk. As a specific case, we let $\mathbf{w} := (w_1, \ldots, w_n, \mathbf{u}) \in \mathbb{Z}_p^{n+L}, \mathbf{v} := (\mathbf{v}_0, \mathbf{v}_1, \ldots, \mathbf{v}_n) \in (\mathbb{Z}_p^L)^n$,

$$\mathsf{mkE}(\mathbf{v}, \alpha) \overset{\text{def}}{=} (\alpha, 0, \ldots, 0), \quad \mathsf{mE}(\mathbf{v}, \mathbf{w}) \overset{\text{def}}{=} (\mathbf{v}_0^\top \mathbf{u}, w_1 + \mathbf{v}_1^\top \mathbf{u}, \ldots, w_n + \mathbf{v}_n^\top \mathbf{u}, \mathbf{u})$$

In the above equality, it is best for the adversary to get the leakage on $(\alpha + \mathbf{v}_0^\top \mathbf{u}_0, \mathbf{v}_0, \mathbf{u})$ or $(w_i + \mathbf{v}_i^\top \mathbf{u}_i, \mathbf{v}_i, \mathbf{u})$ if the adversary tries to leak α or w_i. Note that for any $i \neq j$, $\mathbf{v}_i^\top \mathbf{u}$ is statistically independent from $\mathbf{v}_j^\top \mathbf{u}$ due to the randomness of $\mathbf{v}$. Then based on the subspace lemma in LRW11, α or w_i is hidden as long as the adversary gets a limited amount of leakage on mk during a time period. Thus, the randomness of $\mathbf{w}$ is preserved, then α-*privacy* and α-*leakage-resilient* are satisfied. Besides, *re-randomizable* holds since we have published $g_2^{\mathbf{w}}$ in mpk. As for *delegable*, we additionally require a linear map $S : \mathcal{Y} \times \mathcal{V} \to \mathcal{Z}$, which enables the redundant information $\mathbf{z}$ in $\mathsf{sk_y}$ to be computed from $\mathbf{v}$ and $\mathbf{y}$. Thus, $\mathsf{sk_y}$ can be generated from mk and $\mathbf{y}$ correctly. At last, we apply our second framework (in Sect. 4) to compact-key ABE schemes for zero inner-product and non-zero inner-product in CGW15, and hence obtain several leakage-resilient instantiations in Sect. 5.

1.3 Related Work

Other Leakage-Resilient Models. Dziembowski et al. [6] defined the *bounded retrieval model* (BRM), placing rigorous performance requirements on the leakage-resilient scheme. Dodis et al. [7] proposed the *auxiliary input leakage model* (ALM). It only requires that the leakage function f is hard to invert. Besides, Yuen at al. [21] defined the *continual auxiliary leakage model* (CAL) that captures the benefits of both CLM and ALM.

Leakage-Resilient ABE. Lewko et al. [14] proposed the first identity-based encryption (IBE) and ABE which are proved in the CLM. Zhang and Mu [24] constructed a leakage-resilient anonymous inner-product encryption (IPE) scheme over composite-order groups in the BLM. Nishimaki and Yamakawa [17] proposed several constructions of leakage-resilient public-key encryption and leakage-resilient IBE in the BRM, which reach nearly optimal leakage rates under standard assumptions in the standard model. To deal with potential side-channel attacks in the distributed environment, Li et al. [15,16] designed a key-policy ABE in the CAL and a hierarchical ABE in the CLM.

Organization. We recall the related definition and security models in Sect. 2. The first leakage-resilient ABE framework is presented in Sect. 3. The Second leakage-resilient ABE framework is shown in Sect. 4. We present some instantiations in Sect. 5.

2   Preliminaries

Notations. For $n \in \mathbb{N}$, $[n]$ denote the set $\{1, 2, \ldots, n\}$. We use $s \leftarrow \mathcal{S}$ to denote that s is picked randomly from set $\mathcal{S}$. By PPT, we denote a probabilistic polynomial-time algorithm. We use $\overset{c}{\approx}$ and $\overset{s}{\approx}$ to denote two distributions being computationally and statistically indistinguishable, respectively.

2.1   The Definition of ABE

Given attribute universe $\mathcal{X}$, predicate universe $\mathcal{Y}$ and predicate $\mathsf{P} : \mathcal{X} \times \mathcal{Y} \to \{0, 1\}$, an ABE scheme consists of four algorithms (Setup, KeyGen, Enc, Dec):

- Setup(1^λ) $\to$ (mpk, mk). Take as input a security parameter λ. Then return the public parameters mpk and the master key mk.
- KeyGen(mk, $\mathbf{y}$) $\to$ sk$_\mathbf{y}$. Take as input mk, $\mathbf{y} \in \mathcal{Y}$, and return a secret key sk$_\mathbf{y}$.
- Enc(mpk, $\mathbf{x}$, m) $\to$ ct$_\mathbf{x}$. Take as input mpk, an attribute $\mathbf{x} \in \mathcal{X}$, and a message m. Return a ciphertext ct$_\mathbf{x}$.
- Dec(mpk, sk$_\mathbf{y}$, ct$_\mathbf{x}$) $\to$ m or $\bot$. Take as input sk$_\mathbf{y}$ and ct$_\mathbf{x}$. If $\mathsf{P}(\mathbf{x}, \mathbf{y}) = 1$, return message m; otherwise, return $\bot$.

Correctness. For all $(\mathbf{x}, \mathbf{y}) \in \mathcal{X} \times \mathcal{Y}$ such that $\mathsf{P}(\mathbf{x}, \mathbf{y}) = 1$ and all $m \in \mathcal{M}$, it holds that $\Pr\big[\mathsf{Dec}(\mathsf{mpk}, \mathsf{sk}_\mathbf{y}, \mathsf{Enc}(\mathsf{mpk}, \mathbf{x}, m)) = m\big] = 1$ where (mpk, mk) $\leftarrow$ Setup(1^λ, 1^n), sk$_\mathbf{y}$ $\leftarrow$ KeyGen(mk, $\mathbf{y}$).

Additional Algorithm. If we take the presence of continual leakage into account, an extra algorithm should be provided:

- Update(mpk, sk$_\mathbf{y}$) : Take as input a secret key sk$_\mathbf{y}$, and outputs a re-randomized key sk$'_\mathbf{y}$.

It is equivalent to generating a fresh secret key sk$'_\mathbf{y}$ $\leftarrow$ KeyGen(mk, $\mathbf{y}$). We stress that mk can be seen as a secret key sk$_\mathbf{y}$ (where $\mathbf{y}$ is an empty string ϵ) and algorithm Update also acts on mk.

2.2   Security Models

Here, we would define two leakage-resilient models, both of which are parameterized by security parameter λ and leakage bounds $L_{\mathsf{mk}} = L_{\mathsf{mk}}(\lambda)$, $L_{\mathsf{sk}} = L_{\mathsf{sk}}(\lambda)$.

Definition 1. *We say that an ABE scheme is (L_{mk}, L_{sk})-bounded-leakage secure and attribute-hiding if for all* PPT *adversaries $\mathcal{A}$, the advantage function*

$$\mathsf{Adv}_{\mathcal{A}}^{\mathrm{BLR\text{-}AH}}(\lambda) := \left| \Pr\left[b' = b \left| \begin{array}{l} (\mathsf{mpk}, \mathsf{mk}) \leftarrow \mathsf{Setup}(1^{\lambda}) \\ (\mathbf{x}^{(0)}, \mathbf{x}^{(1)}, m^{(0)}, m^{(1)}) \leftarrow \mathcal{A}^{\mathsf{O}_1, \mathsf{O}_2, \mathsf{O}_3}(\mathsf{mpk}) \\ b \leftarrow \{0,1\}; \mathsf{ct}^* \leftarrow \mathsf{Enc}(\mathsf{mpk}, \mathbf{x}^{(b)}, m^{(b)}) \\ b' \leftarrow \mathcal{A}^{\mathsf{O}_1, \mathsf{O}_2, \mathsf{O}_3}(\mathsf{mpk}, \mathsf{ct}^*) \end{array} \right. \right] - \frac{1}{2} \right|.$$

is negligible.

In the above definition, $\mathcal{A}$ has access to oracles $\mathsf{O}_1, \mathsf{O}_2, \mathsf{O}_3$. These oracles maintain sets $\mathcal{H}$ and $\mathcal{R}$ which store some tuples.

- $\mathsf{O}_1(h, \mathbf{y})$: h is a handle to a tuple of $\mathcal{H}$ that must refer to a master key and $\mathbf{y}$ must be a vector in $\mathcal{Y}$. After receiving the input, this oracle finds the tuple t with handle h in $\mathcal{H}$ and answers $\mathcal{A}$ as follows:
  1) If the vector part of t is ϵ, then let $t := (h, \epsilon, \mathsf{mk}, l)$. It runs KeyGen algorithm to obtain a key $\mathsf{sk}_{\mathbf{y}}$ and adds the tuple $(H+1, \mathbf{y}, \mathsf{sk}_{\mathbf{y}}, 0)$ to $\mathcal{H}$. Then it updates $H \leftarrow H + 1$;
  2) Otherwise, it returns $\perp$ to $\mathcal{A}$.
- $\mathsf{O}_2(h, f)$: f is a polynomial-time computable function of constant output size. After receiving the input, it finds the tuple t with handle h in $\mathcal{H}$ and answers $\mathcal{A}$ as follows:
  1) If t is of the form $(h, \epsilon, \mathsf{mk}, l)$, it checks whether $l + |f(\mathsf{mk})| \leq L_{mk}$. If $l + |f(\mathsf{mk})| \leq L_{mk}$ holds, the challenger returns $f(\mathsf{mk})$ to $\mathcal{A}$ and updates $l \leftarrow l + |f(\mathsf{mk})|$. Otherwise, it returns $\perp$ to $\mathcal{A}$;
  2) Else, t is of the form $(h, \mathbf{y}, \mathsf{sk}_{\mathbf{y}}, l)$ and then it checks whether $l + |f(\mathsf{sk}_{\mathbf{y}})| \leq L_{sk}$. If $l + |f(\mathsf{sk}_{\mathbf{y}})| \leq L_{sk}$ holds, the challenger returns $f(\mathsf{sk}_{\mathbf{y}})$ to $\mathcal{A}$ and updates $l \leftarrow l + |f(\mathsf{sk}_{\mathbf{y}})|$. Otherwise, it returns $\perp$.
- $\mathsf{O}_3(h)$: It finds the tuple with handle h in $\mathcal{H}$. If the vector part of the tuple is ϵ, then it returns $\perp$ to $\mathcal{A}$. Otherwise, the tuple is of the form $(h, \mathbf{y}, \mathsf{sk}_{\mathbf{y}}, l)$. It returns $\mathsf{sk}_{\mathbf{y}}$ and then add $\mathbf{y}$ to $\mathcal{R}$.

Note that after $\mathcal{A}$ receives the challenge ciphertext ct^*, only queries on $\mathsf{sk}_{\mathbf{y}}$ such that $\mathsf{P}(\mathbf{x}^{(0)}, \mathbf{y}) = 0$ and $\mathsf{P}(\mathbf{x}^{(1)}, \mathbf{y}) = 0$ are allowed when $\mathcal{A}$ access to $\mathsf{O}_2, \mathsf{O}_3$.

Definition 2. *We say that an* ABE *scheme is (L_{mk}, L_{sk})-continual-leakage secure if for all* PPT *adversaries $\mathcal{A}$, the advantage function*

$$\mathsf{Adv}_{\mathcal{A}}^{\mathrm{CLR\text{-}PH}}(\lambda) := \left| \Pr\left[b' = b \left| \begin{array}{l} (\mathsf{mpk}, \mathsf{mk}) \leftarrow \mathsf{Setup}(1^{\lambda}) \\ (\mathbf{x}, m^{(0)}, m^{(1)}) \leftarrow \mathcal{A}^{\mathsf{O}_1', \mathsf{O}_2', \mathsf{O}_3'}(\mathsf{mpk}) \\ b \leftarrow \{0,1\}; \mathsf{ct}^* \leftarrow \mathsf{Enc}(\mathsf{mpk}, \mathbf{x}, m^{(b)}) \\ b' \leftarrow \mathcal{A}^{\mathsf{O}_1', \mathsf{O}_2', \mathsf{O}_3'}(\mathsf{mpk}, \mathsf{ct}^*) \end{array} \right. \right] - \frac{1}{2} \right|.$$

is negligible.

Here, $\mathcal{A}$ has access to oracles $\mathsf{O}_1', \mathsf{O}_2', \mathsf{O}_3'$. These oracles maintain sets $\mathcal{H}'$ and $\mathcal{R}'$.

- $O'_1(h, \mathbf{y})$: This oracle is similar to O_1 except that the input $\mathbf{y}$ can also be an empty string ϵ. If $\mathcal{A}$ makes a query for $\mathbf{y} = \epsilon$, it will run Update algorithm to get a fresh master key mk' and add the tuple $(H + 1, \epsilon, \mathsf{mk}', 0)$ to the set $\mathcal{H}$.
- $O'_2(h, f)$: This oracle is the same as O_2.
- $O'_3(h)$: This oracle is the same as O_3.

Note that after $\mathcal{A}$ receives the challenge ciphertext ct^*, only queries on $\mathsf{sk}_\mathbf{y}$ such that $\mathsf{P}(\mathbf{x}, \mathbf{y}) = 0$ are allowed when $\mathcal{A}$ access to O'_2, O'_3.

2.3   Assumption

Let $\mathcal{G}$ be a probabilistic polynomial-time algorithm that takes as input a security parameter 1^λ and outputs a group description $\mathbb{G} := (p, G_1, G_2, G_T, g_1, g_2, e)$, where p is a $\Theta(\lambda)$-bit prime and G_1, G_2, G_T are cyclic groups of order p. g_1 and g_2 are generators of G_1 and G_2 respectively and $e : G_1 \times G_2 \to G_T$ is a computationally efficient and non-degenerate bilinear map. We let $g_T = e(g_1, g_2)$ be the generator of G_T.

For $s \in \{1, 2, T\}$ and $a \in \mathbb{Z}_p$, we define $[a]_s = g_s^a$ as the implicit representation of a in G_s. Similarly, for a matrix $\mathbf{A}$ over $\mathbb{Z}_p$, we define $[\mathbf{A}]_s = g_s^\mathbf{A}$, where exponentiations are carried out component-wise. Given $[\mathbf{A}]_1$ and $[\mathbf{B}]_2$, we define $e([\mathbf{A}]_1, [\mathbf{B}]_2) := [\mathbf{A}^\top \mathbf{B}]_T$. Now we review the definition of k-Lin assumption.

Definition 3 (k-Lin Assumption). *Let $s \in \{1, 2, T\}$. We say that the k-Lin assumption holds with respect to $\mathcal{G}$ on G_s if for all PPT adversaries $\mathcal{A}$, the following advantage function is negligible in λ.*

$$\mathsf{Adv}_\mathcal{A}^{k\text{-Lin}}(\lambda) := |\Pr[\mathcal{A}(\mathbb{G}, [\mathbf{A}]_s, [\mathbf{At}]_s) = 1] - \Pr[\mathcal{A}(\mathbb{G}, [\mathbf{A}]_s, [\mathbf{u}]_s) = 1]|$$

where $\mathbb{G} \leftarrow \mathcal{G}(1^\lambda), \mathbf{t} \leftarrow \mathbb{Z}_p^k, \mathbf{u} \leftarrow \mathbb{Z}_p^{k+1}, (a_1, \dots, a_k) \leftarrow \mathbb{Z}_p^k$, then

$$\mathbf{A} := \begin{pmatrix} a_1 & & \\ & \ddots & \\ & & a_k \\ 1 & \cdots & 1 \end{pmatrix} \in \mathbb{Z}_p^{(k+1) \times k} \tag{3}$$

Note that we can trivially set $(\mathbf{a}^\perp)^\top := (a_1^{-1}, \dots, a_k^{-1}, -1)$ such that $\mathbf{A}^\top \mathbf{a}^\perp = \mathbf{0}$.

3   Leakage-Resilient ABE with Attribute-Hiding in the BLM

In this section, we will present the first leakage-resilient ABE framework along with the predicate encoding, generic construction and corresponding security analysis.

3.1   Leakage-Resilient Predicate Encoding

A $\mathbb{Z}_p$-linear leakage-resilient predicate encoding with attribute-hiding for predicate $\mathsf{P} : \mathcal{X} \times \mathcal{Y} \to \{0,1\}$, which contains a set of deterministic algorithms $(\mathsf{rkE}, \mathsf{rE}, \mathsf{sE}, \mathsf{sD}, \mathsf{rD})$, satisfies the following properties:

- **(linearity.)** For all $(\mathbf{x}, \mathbf{y}, \mathbf{z}) \in \mathcal{X} \times \mathcal{Y} \times \mathcal{Z}$, $\mathsf{rkE}(\mathbf{y}, \mathbf{z}, \cdot)$, $\mathsf{rE}(\mathbf{y}, \mathbf{z}, \cdot)$, $\mathsf{sE}(\mathbf{x}, \cdot)$, $\mathsf{sD}(\mathbf{x}, \mathbf{y}, \mathbf{z}, \cdot)$, $\mathsf{rD}(\mathbf{x}, \mathbf{y}, \mathbf{z}, \cdot)$ are $\mathbb{Z}_p$-linear functions. A $\mathbb{Z}_p$-linear function F can be encoded as a matrix $\mathbf{T} = (t_{i,j}) \in \mathbb{Z}_p^{n \times m}$ such that $F : (w_1, \ldots, w_n) \longmapsto (\sum_{i=1}^n t_{i,1} w_i, \ldots, \sum_{i=1}^n t_{i,m} w_i)$.
- **(restricted α-reconstruction.)** For all $(\mathbf{x}, \mathbf{y}) \in \mathcal{X} \times \mathcal{Y}$ such that $\mathsf{P}(\mathbf{x}, \mathbf{y}) = 1$, all $\mathbf{w} \in \mathcal{W}, \mathbf{z} \in \mathcal{Z}$, it holds that $\mathsf{sD}(\mathbf{x}, \mathbf{y}, \mathbf{z}, \mathsf{sE}(\mathbf{x}, \mathbf{w})) = \mathsf{rD}(\mathbf{x}, \mathbf{y}, \mathbf{z}, \mathsf{rE}(\mathbf{y}, \mathbf{z}, \mathbf{w}))$ and $\mathsf{rD}(\mathbf{x}, \mathbf{y}, \mathbf{z}, \mathsf{rkE}(\mathbf{y}, \mathbf{z}, \alpha)) = \alpha$.
- **(x-oblivious α-reconstruction.)** $\mathsf{sD}(\mathbf{x}, \mathbf{y}, \mathbf{z}, \cdot)$, $\mathsf{rD}(\mathbf{x}, \mathbf{y}, \mathbf{z}, \cdot)$ are independent of $\mathbf{x}$. It is a basic requirement for achieving attribute-hiding.
- **(attribute-hiding.)** For all $(\mathbf{x}, \mathbf{y}) \in \mathcal{X} \times \mathcal{Y}$ such that $\mathsf{P}(\mathbf{x}, \mathbf{y}) = 0$ and all $\mathbf{z} \in \mathcal{Z}$, the distributions $\{\mathbf{x}, \mathbf{y}, \mathbf{z}, \mathsf{sE}(\mathbf{x}, \mathbf{w}), \mathsf{rE}(\mathbf{y}, \mathbf{z}, \mathbf{w})\}$ and $\{\mathbf{x}, \mathbf{y}, \mathbf{z}, \mathbf{r}\}$ are identical, where $\mathbf{w} \leftarrow \mathcal{W}$ and $\mathbf{r} \leftarrow \mathbb{Z}_p^{|\mathsf{sE}(\cdot)| + |\mathsf{rE}(\cdot)|}$.
- **(attribute-hiding-leakage-resilient.)** In order to achieve leakage-resilience on $\mathsf{sk}_{\mathbf{y}}$, we require that for all $(\mathbf{x}, \mathbf{y}) \in \mathcal{X} \times \mathcal{Y}$ such that $\mathsf{P}(\mathbf{x}, \mathbf{y}) = 1$ and $\mathbf{z} \in \mathcal{Z}$, the distributions $\{\mathbf{x}, \mathbf{y}, \mathsf{sE}(\mathbf{x}, \mathbf{w}), f(\mathbf{z}, \mathsf{rE}(\mathbf{y}, \mathbf{z}, \mathbf{w}))\}$ and $\{\mathbf{x}, \mathbf{y}, \mathbf{r}\}$ are identical, where $\mathbf{w} \leftarrow \mathcal{W}$ and $\mathbf{r} \leftarrow \mathbb{Z}_p^{|\mathsf{sE}(\cdot)| + |f(\cdot)|}$.

3.2   Generic Construction

An overview of our generic construction has been present in Sect. (1). As mentioned in Sect. 1.2, a general approach [5] to transform schemes over composite-order groups into ones over prime-order groups can be applied to Eq. (1). Concretely, we replace y_1, y_2 with $[\mathbf{A}]_1, [\mathbf{B}]_2$, where $(\mathbf{A}, \mathbf{a}^\perp), (\mathbf{B}, \mathbf{b}^\perp) \leftarrow \mathcal{D}_{k+1,k}$ and other variables are transformed as follows:

$$\alpha \mapsto \mathbf{k} \in \mathbb{Z}_p^{k+1}, \quad u, w_i \mapsto \mathbf{U}, \mathbf{W}_i \in \mathbb{Z}_p^{(k+1) \times (k+1)}, \quad s \mapsto \mathbf{s} \in \mathbb{Z}_p^k, \quad r \mapsto \mathbf{r} \in \mathbb{Z}_p^k,$$

$$g_1^s \mapsto [\mathbf{As}]_1, \quad g_1^{w_i s} \mapsto [\mathbf{W}_i^\top \mathbf{As}]_1, \quad g_2^r \mapsto [\mathbf{Br}]_2, \quad g_2^{w_i r} \mapsto [\mathbf{W}_i \mathbf{Br}]_2$$

The above transformation is also suitable to our second framework in Sect. 4.

Now, we provide the details of our generic construction. Given a $\mathbb{Z}_p$-linear leakage-resilient predicate encoding with attribute-hiding for predicate $\mathsf{P} : \mathcal{X} \times \mathcal{Y} \to \{0,1\}$,

- $\mathsf{Setup}(1^\lambda)$: Let $N \in \mathbb{N}$ be the parameter of the $\mathbb{Z}_p$-linear leakage-resilient predicate encoding with attribute-hiding for predicate P and N is related to 1^λ. Run $\mathbb{G} \leftarrow \mathcal{G}(1^\lambda)$, sample $(\mathbf{A}, \mathbf{a}^\perp), (\mathbf{B}, \mathbf{b}^\perp)$ as in Eq. (3), pick $\mathbf{k} \leftarrow \mathbb{Z}_p^{k+1}, \mathbf{W}_1, \ldots, \mathbf{W}_N \leftarrow \mathbb{Z}_p^{(k+1) \times (k+1)}$. Then pick $\mathbf{r} \leftarrow \mathbb{Z}_p^k, \mathbf{v} \leftarrow \mathcal{V}$, output

$$\mathsf{mpk} := \left(\mathbb{G}; [\mathbf{A}]_1, [\mathbf{W}_1^\top \mathbf{A}]_1, \ldots, [\mathbf{W}_N^\top \mathbf{A}]_1, [\mathbf{A}^\top \mathbf{k}]_T\right), \quad \mathsf{mk} := (\mathbf{B}, \mathbf{k}, \mathbf{W}_1, \ldots, \mathbf{W}_N)$$

- KeyGen(mk, $\mathbf{y}$): Pick $\mathbf{r} \leftarrow \mathbb{Z}_p^k, \mathbf{z} \leftarrow \mathcal{Z}$ and output $\mathsf{sk}_\mathbf{y} := (\mathbf{z}, K_0, \mathbf{K})$, where

$$K_0 := [\mathbf{Br}]_2, \quad \mathbf{K} := \mathsf{rkE}(\mathbf{y}, \mathbf{z}, [\mathbf{k}]_2) \cdot \mathsf{rE}(\mathbf{y}, \mathbf{z}, [\mathbf{W}_1\mathbf{Br}]_2, \ldots, [\mathbf{W}_N\mathbf{Br}]_2)$$

- Enc(mpk, $\mathbf{x}$, m): Pick $\mathbf{s} \leftarrow \mathbb{Z}_p^k$ and output $\mathsf{ct}_\mathbf{x} := (C_0, \mathbf{C}, C_T)$, where

$$C_0 := [\mathbf{As}]_1, \mathbf{C} := \mathsf{sE}(\mathbf{x}, [\mathbf{W}_1^\top \mathbf{As}]_1, \ldots, [\mathbf{W}_N^\top \mathbf{As}]_1), C_T = [\mathbf{k}^\top \mathbf{As}]_T \cdot m$$

- Dec(mpk, $\mathsf{sk}_\mathbf{y}$, $\mathsf{ct}_\mathbf{x}$): output $m' = C_T \cdot e(C_0, \mathsf{rD}(\mathbf{x}, \mathbf{y}, \mathbf{z}, \mathbf{K}))^{-1} \cdot e(\mathsf{sD}(\mathbf{x}, \mathbf{y}, \mathbf{z}, \mathbf{C}), K_0)$.

Correctness. For any $(\mathbf{x}, \mathbf{y}) \in \mathcal{X} \times \mathcal{Y}$ such that $\mathsf{P}(\mathbf{x}, \mathbf{y}) = 1$, we have

$$
\begin{aligned}
&C_T \cdot e(C_0, \mathsf{rD}(\mathbf{x}, \mathbf{y}, \mathbf{z}, \mathbf{K}))^{-1} \\
&= m \cdot [\mathbf{k}^\top \mathbf{As}]_T \cdot e([\mathbf{As}]_1, \mathsf{rD}(\mathbf{x}, \mathbf{y}, \mathbf{z}, \mathsf{rkE}(\mathbf{y}, \mathbf{z}, [\mathbf{k}]_2) \cdot \mathsf{rE}(\mathbf{y}, \mathbf{z}, [\mathbf{W}_1\mathbf{Br}]_2, \ldots, [\mathbf{W}_N\mathbf{Br}]_2)))^{-1} \\
&= m \cdot [\mathbf{k}^\top \mathbf{As}]_T \cdot e([\mathbf{As}]_1, \mathsf{rD}(\mathbf{x}, \mathbf{y}, \mathbf{z}, \mathsf{rkE}(\mathbf{y}, \mathbf{z}, [\mathbf{k}]_2))^{-1} \\
&\qquad \cdot e([\mathbf{As}]_1, \mathsf{rD}(\mathbf{x}, \mathbf{y}, \mathbf{z}, \mathsf{rE}(\mathbf{y}, \mathbf{z}, [\mathbf{W}_1\mathbf{Br}]_2, \ldots, [\mathbf{W}_N\mathbf{Br}]_2)))^{-1} \\
&= m \cdot [\mathbf{k}^\top \mathbf{As}]_T \cdot e([\mathbf{As}]_1, [\mathbf{k}]_2)^{-1} \cdot e([\mathbf{As}]_1, \mathsf{rD}(\mathbf{x}, \mathbf{y}, \mathbf{z}, \mathsf{rE}(\mathbf{y}, \mathbf{z}, [\mathbf{W}_1\mathbf{Br}]_2, \ldots, [\mathbf{W}_N\mathbf{Br}]_2)))^{-1} \\
&= m \cdot e([\mathbf{As}]_1, \mathsf{rD}(\mathbf{x}, \mathbf{y}, \mathbf{z}, \mathsf{rE}(\mathbf{y}, \mathbf{z}, [\mathbf{W}_1\mathbf{Br}]_2, \ldots, [\mathbf{W}_N\mathbf{Br}]_2)))^{-1} \\
&= m \cdot \mathsf{rD}(\mathbf{x}, \mathbf{y}, \mathbf{z}, \mathsf{rE}(\mathbf{y}, \mathbf{z}, e([\mathbf{As}]_1, [\mathbf{W}_1\mathbf{Br}]_2), \ldots, e([\mathbf{As}]_1, [\mathbf{W}_N\mathbf{Br}]_2)))^{-1} \\
&= m \cdot \mathsf{rD}(\mathbf{x}, \mathbf{y}, \mathbf{z}, \mathsf{rE}(\mathbf{y}, \mathbf{z}, e([\mathbf{W}_1^\top \mathbf{As}]_1, [\mathbf{Br}]_2), \ldots, e([\mathbf{W}_N^\top \mathbf{As}]_1, [\mathbf{Br}]_2)))^{-1} \\
&= m \cdot \mathsf{sD}(\mathbf{x}, \mathbf{y}, \mathbf{z}, \mathsf{sE}(\mathbf{x}, e([\mathbf{W}_1^\top \mathbf{As}]_1, [\mathbf{Br}]_2), \ldots, e([\mathbf{W}_N^\top \mathbf{As}]_1, [\mathbf{Br}]_2)))^{-1} \\
&= m \cdot e(\mathsf{sD}(\mathbf{x}, \mathbf{y}, \mathbf{z}, \mathsf{sE}(\mathbf{x}, [\mathbf{W}_1^\top \mathbf{As}]_1, \ldots, [\mathbf{W}_N^\top \mathbf{As}]_1)), [\mathbf{Br}]_2)^{-1} \\
&= m \cdot e(\mathsf{sD}(\mathbf{x}, \mathbf{y}, \mathbf{z}, \mathbf{C}), K_0)^{-1}
\end{aligned}
$$

In the above equality, we exploit *linearity* (for lines 3, 6, 9) and *restricted α-reconstruction* (for lines 4, 8) mentioned in Sect. 3.1. Thus, $C_T \cdot e(C_0, \mathsf{rD}(\mathbf{x}, \mathbf{y}, \mathbf{z}, \mathbf{K}))^{-1} \cdot e(\mathsf{sD}(\mathbf{x}, \mathbf{y}, \mathbf{z}, \mathbf{C}), K_0) = m$ and the correctness follows readily.

3.3   Security

We start by giving some lemmas of [5,14] which will be used throughout the security proof of our framework.

Lemma 1 ([14]). *Let an integer $m \geq 3$ and let p be a prime. Let $\delta \leftarrow \mathbb{Z}_p^m, \tau \leftarrow \mathbb{Z}_p^m$, and let τ' be chosen uniformly from the set of vectors in $\mathbb{Z}_p^m$ which are orthogonal to δ under the dot product modulo p. Let $f : \mathbb{Z}_p^m \rightarrow \mathbf{W}$ be some function. Then there exists any positive constant c, such that $dist((\delta, f(\tau')), (\delta, f(\tau))) \leq p^{-c}$, as long as $|\mathbf{W}| \leq 4 \cdot (1 - \frac{1}{p}) \cdot p^{m-2c-2}$.*

Suppose that $\mathbf{A}$ and $\mathbf{B}$ have the same form as Eq. (3), then we set

$$
\begin{aligned}
\mathsf{PP} &:= \left(\mathbb{G}; \begin{array}{l} [\mathbf{A}]_1, [\mathbf{W}_1^\top \mathbf{A}]_1, \ldots, [\mathbf{W}_N^\top \mathbf{A}]_1, \\ [\mathbf{B}]_2, [\mathbf{W}_1\mathbf{B}]_2, \ldots, [\mathbf{W}_N\mathbf{B}]_2 \end{array} \right), \\
\mathsf{PP}^- &:= (\mathbb{G}; [\mathbf{A}]_1, [\mathbf{W}_1^\top \mathbf{A}]_1, \ldots, [\mathbf{W}_N^\top \mathbf{A}]_1, [\mathbf{B}]_2)
\end{aligned}
\tag{4}
$$

where $\mathbf{W}_1, \ldots, \mathbf{W}_N \leftarrow \mathbb{Z}_p^{(k+1) \times (k+1)}$.

Lemma 2 (Parameter-Hiding[5]). *The following distributions are statistically indistinguishable:*

$$\left\{ \mathsf{PP}, [\mathbf{a}^\perp]_2, \begin{array}{l} [\mathbf{b}^\perp \hat{s}]_1, [\mathbf{W}_1^\top \mathbf{b}^\perp \hat{s}]_1, \dots, [\mathbf{W}_N^\top \mathbf{b}^\perp \hat{s}]_1 \\ [\mathbf{a}^\perp \hat{r}]_2, [\mathbf{W}_1 \mathbf{a}^\perp \hat{r}]_2, \dots, [\mathbf{W}_N \mathbf{a}^\perp \hat{r}]_2 \end{array} \right\} \text{ and}$$

$$\left\{ \mathsf{PP}, [\mathbf{a}^\perp]_2, \begin{array}{l} [\mathbf{b}^\perp \hat{s}]_1, [(\mathbf{W}_1^\top \mathbf{b}^\perp + u_1 \mathbf{b}^\perp) \hat{s}]_1, \dots, [(\mathbf{W}_N^\top \mathbf{b}^\perp + u_N \mathbf{b}^\perp) \hat{s}]_1 \\ [\mathbf{a}^\perp \hat{r}]_2, [(\mathbf{W}_1 \mathbf{a}^\perp + u_1 \mathbf{a}^\perp) \hat{r}]_2, \dots, [(\mathbf{W}_N \mathbf{a}^\perp + u_N \mathbf{a}^\perp) \hat{r}]_2 \end{array} \right\}$$

where $\hat{s}, \hat{r} \leftarrow \mathbb{Z}_p^*, \mathbf{u} := (u_1, \dots, u_N) \leftarrow \mathbb{Z}_p^N$.

Lemma 3 ($\mathbb{H}$-hiding[5]). *The following distributions are statistically indistinguishable:*

$$\{\mathsf{PP}^-, [\mathbf{a}^\perp]_2, [\mathbf{Br}]_2, [\mathbf{W}_1 \mathbf{Br} + \hat{v}_1 \mathbf{a}^\perp]_2, \dots, [\mathbf{W}_N \mathbf{Br} + \hat{v}_N \mathbf{a}^\perp]_2\} \text{ and}$$

$$\{\mathsf{PP}^-, [\mathbf{a}^\perp]_2, [\mathbf{Br}]_2, [\hat{\mathbf{u}}_1]_2, \dots, [\hat{\mathbf{u}}_N]_2\}$$

where $\mathbf{r} \leftarrow \mathbb{Z}_p^k, \hat{\mathbf{v}} := (\hat{v}_1, \dots, \hat{v}_N) \leftarrow \mathbb{Z}_p^N$ *and for* $i = 1, \dots, N, \hat{\mathbf{u}}_i \leftarrow \mathbb{Z}_p^{k+1}$ *subject to the constraint* $\mathbf{A}^\top \hat{\mathbf{u}}_i = (\mathbf{W}_i^\top \mathbf{A})^\top \mathbf{Br}$.

Lemma 4 ($\mathbb{G}$-uniformity[5]). *The following distributions are statistically indistinguishable:*

$$\{\mathsf{PP}^-, [\mathbf{a}^\perp]_1, [\mathbf{As} + \mathbf{b}^\perp \hat{s}]_2, [\mathbf{W}_1^\top (\mathbf{As} + \mathbf{b}^\perp \hat{s})]_1, \dots, [\mathbf{W}_N (\mathbf{As} + \mathbf{b}^\perp \hat{s})]_1\} \text{ and}$$

$$\{\mathsf{PP}^-, [\mathbf{a}^\perp]_2, [\mathbf{As} + \mathbf{b}^\perp \hat{s}]_1, [\hat{\mathbf{w}}_1]_1, \dots, [\hat{\mathbf{w}}_N]_1\}$$

where $\mathbf{s} \leftarrow \mathbb{Z}_p^k, \hat{s} \leftarrow \mathbb{Z}_p^*; \hat{\mathbf{w}}_1, \dots, \hat{\mathbf{w}}_N \leftarrow \mathbb{Z}_p^{k+1}$.

Theorem 1. *If k-Lin assumption holds, the construction described in Sect. 3.2 is $(0, L_{\mathsf{sk}})$-bounded-leakage secure and attribute-hiding. More precisely, for all PPT adversaries $\mathcal{A}$ subject to the restrictions: (1) $\mathcal{A}$ queries O_2 and O_3 at most q times; (2) The leakage on mk is not allowed and the leakage amount of sk are at most L_{sk} bits. There exists an algorithm $\mathcal{B}$ such that $\mathsf{Adv}_{\mathcal{A}}^{\mathrm{BLR\text{-}AH}}(\lambda) \le (2q + 1)\mathsf{Adv}_{\mathcal{B}}^{k\text{-}\mathrm{Lin}}(\lambda) + \mathsf{negl}(\lambda)$.*

Proof. Our proof sketch for the game sequence is shown in Table 2. In Table 2, we use a box to highlight the difference between two adjacent games and the cell marked by "-" means that the corresponding part of $\mathsf{sk_y}$ or ct^* is the same as the last game. For the transition from $\mathsf{Game}_{2,i,1}$ to $\mathsf{Game}_{2,i,2}$, we employ Parameter-Hiding lemma, attribute-hiding encoding and attribute-hiding-leakage-resilient encoding mentioned in Sect. 3.1. In Game_3 and Game_4, m' denotes a random message and $\mathbf{x}'$ denotes a random attribute. Game_0 is the same as $\mathsf{Game}_{\mathrm{BLM\text{-}AH}}$. In Game_4, the advantage of $\mathcal{A}$ is 0.

We denote the advantage of $\mathcal{A}$ in Game_i by $\mathsf{Adv}_i(\lambda)$. Then we will show Theorem 1 by proving the indistinguishability among these games with the following lemmas.

Lemma 5 ($\mathsf{Game}_0 \overset{c}{\approx} \mathsf{Game}_1$). *For all PPT adversary $\mathcal{A}$, there exists an algorithm $\mathcal{B}_1$ such that $|\mathsf{Adv}_0(\lambda) - \mathsf{Adv}_1(\lambda)| \le \mathsf{Adv}_{\mathcal{B}_1}^{k\text{-}\mathrm{Lin}}(\lambda) + 2/p$.*

Table 2. Our proof sketch for the game sequence.

game	i-th queried secret key sk_y			ct^*			justification
	K_0	$\mathsf{rkE}(y,z,\cdot)$	$\mathsf{rE}(y,z,\cdot)$	C_0	$\mathsf{sE}(\cdot,\cdot)$	C_T	
Game_0	$[\mathbf{Br}]_2$	$[\mathbf{k}]_2$	$[\mathbf{W}_k\mathbf{Br}]_2$	$[\mathbf{As}]_1$	$\mathbf{x}^{(b)},\,[\mathbf{W}_j^\top\mathbf{As}]_1$	$e([\mathbf{As}]_1,[\mathbf{k}]_2)\cdot m$	real game
Game_1	-	-	-	$[\mathbf{As}+\mathbf{b}^\perp\hat{s}]_1$	$\mathbf{x}^{(b)},\,[\mathbf{W}_j^\top(\mathbf{As}+\mathbf{b}^\perp\hat{s})]_1$	$e([\mathbf{As}+\mathbf{b}^\perp\hat{s}]_1,[\mathbf{k}]_2)\cdot m$	k-Lin
$\mathsf{Game}_{2,i,1}$	$[\mathbf{Br}+\mathbf{a}^\perp\hat{r}]_2$	-	$[\mathbf{W}_k(\mathbf{Br}+\mathbf{a}^\perp\hat{r})]_2$	-	-	-	k-Lin
$\mathsf{Game}_{2,i,2}$	-	$[\hat{\mathbf{k}}]_2$	$[\mathbf{W}_k(\mathbf{Br}+\mathbf{a}^\perp\hat{r})+\hat{v}_k^\perp\mathbf{a}^\perp]_2$	-	-	-	attribute-hiding, Parameter-Hiding, attribute-hiding-leakage-resilient
$\mathsf{Game}_{2,i,3}$	$[\mathbf{Br}]_2$	-	$[\mathbf{W}_k\mathbf{Br}+\hat{v}_k^\perp\mathbf{a}^\perp]_2$	-	-	-	k-Lin
Game_3	-	-	-	-	-	$e([\mathbf{As}+\mathbf{b}^\perp\hat{s}]_1,[\mathbf{k}]_2)\cdot m'$	statistically identical
Game_4	-	-	-	-	$\mathbf{x}',\,[\mathbf{W}_j^\top(\mathbf{As}+\mathbf{b}^\perp\hat{s})]_1$	-	H-hiding, G-uniformity, attribute-hiding, attribute-hiding-leakage-resilient

Proof. The proof is a simpler case of the proof of Lemma 6, we omit it here. □

Lemma 6 ($\mathsf{Game}_{2,i-1,3} \overset{c}{\approx} \mathsf{Game}_{2,i,1}$). *For all* PPT *adversary* $\mathcal{A}$ *and* $i = 1,\ldots,q$, *there exists an algorithm* $\mathcal{B}_2$ *such that* $|\mathsf{Adv}_{2,i-1,3}(\lambda) - \mathsf{Adv}_{2,i,1}(\lambda)| \leq \mathsf{Adv}_{\mathcal{B}_2}^{k\text{-Lin}}(\lambda) + 2/p$.

Proof. $\mathcal{B}_2$ samples $(\mathbf{A},\mathbf{a}^\perp) \leftarrow \mathcal{D}_{k+1,k}$ along with $\mathbf{W}_1,\ldots,\mathbf{W}_N \leftarrow \mathbb{Z}_p^{(k+1)\times(k+1)}$. We know that $\{\mathbf{Br}+\mathbf{a}^\perp\hat{r} : \mathbf{r} \leftarrow \mathbb{Z}_p^k, \hat{r} \leftarrow \mathbb{Z}_p\}$ is statistically close to the uniform distribution. Then $\mathcal{B}_2$ gets as input $(\mathbb{G},[\mathbf{B}]_2,[\mathbf{t}]_2) = (\mathbb{G},[\mathbf{B}]_2,[\mathbf{Br}+\mathbf{a}^\perp\hat{r}]_2)$ where either $\hat{r} = 0$ or $\hat{r} \leftarrow \mathbb{Z}_p^*$ and proceeds as follows:

Setup. Pick $\mathbf{k} \leftarrow \mathbb{Z}_p^{k+1}, \alpha \leftarrow \mathbb{Z}_p$ and set $\hat{\mathbf{k}} := \mathbf{k}+\alpha\mathbf{a}^\perp$. With $\mathbb{G},\mathbf{A},\mathbf{W}_1,\ldots,\mathbf{W}_n$, $\mathcal{B}_2$ can simulate $\mathsf{mpk} := (\mathbb{G};[\mathbf{A}]_1,[\mathbf{W}_1^\top\mathbf{A}]_1,\ldots,[\mathbf{W}_n^\top\mathbf{A}]_1,[\mathbf{A}^\top\mathbf{k}]_T)$.

Key Queries. When $\mathcal{A}$ makes the j'th **Leak** or **Reveal** key query,

- When $j < i$, since $\mathbf{a}^\perp, \hat{\mathbf{k}}, \mathbf{W}_1,\ldots,\mathbf{W}_n$ and $[\mathbf{B}]_2$ has been known, semi-functional sk_y can be generated properly;
- When $j = i$, $\mathcal{B}_2$ generates

$$\mathsf{sk}_y := \big(\mathbf{z},[\mathbf{t}]_2,\mathsf{rkE}(y,z,[\mathbf{k}]_2)\cdot\mathsf{rE}(y,z,[\mathbf{W}_1\mathbf{t}]_2,\ldots,[\mathbf{W}_N\mathbf{t}]_2)\big)$$

- When $j > i$, it is not hard to know that normal sk_y can also be generated properly;

Challenge. Since $\mathbf{b}^\perp$ is unknown, $\mathbf{As}+\mathbf{b}^\perp\hat{s}$ is statistically close to the uniform distribution. Thus, $\mathcal{B}_2$ would sample $\tilde{\mathbf{s}} \leftarrow \mathbb{Z}_p^{k+1}$ to replace $\mathbf{As}+\mathbf{b}^\perp\hat{s}$. After receiving challenge messages $(m^{(0)},m^{(1)})$ and challenge vectors $(\mathbf{x}^{(0)},\mathbf{x}^{(1)})$, $\mathcal{B}_2$ chooses a random bit $b \in \{0,1\}$ and returns

$$\mathsf{ct}^* := \big([\tilde{\mathbf{s}}]_1,\mathsf{sE}(\mathbf{x}^{(b)},[\mathbf{W}_1^\top\tilde{\mathbf{s}}]_1,\ldots,[\mathbf{W}_N^\top\tilde{\mathbf{s}}]_1),e([\tilde{\mathbf{s}}]_1,[\mathbf{k}]_2)\cdot m^{(b)}\big)$$

Observe that if $\mathbf{t} = \mathbf{Br}$, $\mathcal{B}_2$ has properly simulated $\mathsf{Game}_{2,i-1,3}$ and if $\mathbf{t} = \mathbf{Br}+\mathbf{a}^\perp\hat{r}$, $\mathcal{B}_2$ has properly simulated $\mathsf{Game}_{2,i,1}$. Since $\hat{s},\hat{r} \leftarrow \mathbb{Z}_p^*$ yields a $2/p$ negligible difference in the advantage, Lemma 6 hence holds. □

Lemma 7 ($\mathsf{Game}_{2,i,1} \overset{s}{\approx} \mathsf{Game}_{2,i,2}$). *For $i = 1,\ldots,q$, it holds that* $|\mathsf{Adv}_{2,i,1}(\lambda) - \mathsf{Adv}_{2,i,2}(\lambda)| \approx 0$ *as long as the leakage amount of* sk *are at most* L_{sk} *bits.*

Proof. Given PP as in Eq. (4), we state that $\mathsf{Game}_{2,i,1}$ and $\mathsf{Game}_{2,i,2}$ are statistically indistinguishable if the following distributions $\{\mathsf{PP}, [\mathbf{k}]_2, [\alpha \mathbf{a}^\perp]_2, \mathsf{ct}^*, \mathsf{sk_y}\}$ and $\{\mathsf{PP}, [\mathbf{k}]_2, [\alpha \mathbf{a}^\perp]_2, \mathsf{ct}^*, \mathsf{sk_y'}\}$ are identical where

$$\mathsf{ct}^* = ([\mathbf{As}]_1, \mathsf{sE}(\mathbf{x}^{(b)}, \{[\mathbf{W}_k^\top \mathbf{As}]_1\}_{k\in[N]}), [\mathbf{k}^\top \mathbf{As}]_T \cdot m^{(b)}) \cdot$$

$$\boxed{([\mathbf{b}^\perp \hat{s}]_1, \mathsf{sE}(\mathbf{x}^{(b)}, \{[\mathbf{W}_k^\top \mathbf{b}^\perp \hat{s}]_1\}_{k\in[N]}), [\mathbf{k}^\top \mathbf{b}^\perp \hat{s}]_T)}$$

and $\mathsf{sk_y}, \mathsf{sk_y'}$ are the i'th queried key in $\mathsf{Game}_{2,i,1}$ and $\mathsf{Game}_{2,i,2}$, respectively. Now we consider the following cases:

(1) If $\mathbf{y} \in \mathcal{Y}$ such that $<\mathbf{x}^{(0)}, \mathbf{y}> = 0$ and $<\mathbf{x}^{(1)}, \mathbf{y}> = 0$, we have

$$\mathsf{sk_y} = \big(1, [\mathbf{Br}]_2, \mathsf{rkE}(\mathbf{y}, \mathbf{z}, [\mathbf{k}]_2) \cdot \mathsf{rE}(\mathbf{y}, \mathbf{z}, \{[\mathbf{W}_k \mathbf{Br}]_2\}_{k\in[N]})\big) \cdot$$

$$\big(\mathbf{z}, [\mathbf{a}^\perp \hat{r}]_2, \mathsf{rE}(\mathbf{y}, \mathbf{z}, \{[\mathbf{W}_k \mathbf{a}^\perp \hat{r}]_2\}_{k\in[N]})\big)$$

$$\mathsf{sk_y'} = \big(1, [\mathbf{Br}]_2, \mathsf{rkE}(\mathbf{y}, \mathbf{z}, [\mathbf{k}]_2) \cdot \mathsf{rE}(\mathbf{y}, \mathbf{z}, \{[\mathbf{W}_k \mathbf{Br}]_2\}_{k\in[N]})\big) \cdot$$

$$\boxed{\big(\mathbf{z}, [\mathbf{a}^\perp \hat{r}]_2, \mathsf{rkE}(\mathbf{y}, \mathbf{z}, [\alpha \mathbf{a}^\perp]_2) \cdot \mathsf{rE}(\mathbf{y}, \mathbf{z}, \{[\mathbf{W}_k \mathbf{a}^\perp \hat{r} + \hat{v}_k \mathbf{a}^\perp]_2\}_{k\in[N]})\big)}$$

where $\hat{\mathbf{v}} := (\hat{v}_1, \ldots, \hat{v}_N) \leftarrow \mathbb{Z}_p^N$ and the length of vector $\mathbf{1} := (1, \ldots, 1)$ is equal to the length of $\mathbf{z}$. We observe that it suffices to show that

$$\begin{cases} \mathsf{aux}: \mathsf{PP}, [\mathbf{k}]_2, [\mathbf{B}]_2, [\alpha \mathbf{a}^\perp]_2 \\ \mathsf{ct_x}: [\mathbf{b}^\perp \hat{s}]_1, \mathsf{sE}(\mathbf{x}^{(b)}, \{[\mathbf{W}_k^\top \mathbf{b}^\perp \hat{s}]_1\}_{k\in[N]}), [\mathbf{k}^\top \mathbf{b}^\perp \hat{s}]_T \\ \mathsf{sk_y}: \mathbf{z}, [\mathbf{a}^\perp \hat{r}]_2, \mathsf{rE}(\mathbf{y}, \mathbf{z}, \{[\mathbf{W}_k \mathbf{a}^\perp \hat{r}]_2\}_{k\in[N]}) \end{cases} \text{ and }$$

$$\begin{cases} \mathsf{aux}: \mathsf{PP}, [\mathbf{k}]_2, [\mathbf{B}]_2, [\alpha \mathbf{a}^\perp]_2 \\ \mathsf{ct_x}: [\mathbf{b}^\perp \hat{s}]_1, \mathsf{sE}(\mathbf{x}^{(b)}, \{[\mathbf{W}_k^\top \mathbf{b}^\perp \hat{s}]_1\}_{k\in[N]}), [\mathbf{k}^\top \mathbf{b}^\perp \hat{s}]_T \\ \mathsf{sk_y}: \mathbf{z}, [\mathbf{a}^\perp \hat{r}]_2, \mathsf{rkE}(\mathbf{y}, \mathbf{z}, [\alpha \mathbf{a}^\perp]_2) \cdot \mathsf{rE}(\mathbf{y}, \mathbf{z}, \{[\mathbf{W}_k \mathbf{a}^\perp \hat{r} + \hat{v}_k \mathbf{a}^\perp]_2\}_{k\in[N]}) \end{cases}$$

are indistinguishable. By parameter-hiding in Lemma 2, it suffices to show that:

$$\begin{cases} \mathsf{aux}: \mathsf{PP}, [\mathbf{k}]_2, [\mathbf{B}]_2, [\alpha \mathbf{a}^\perp]_2 \\ \mathsf{ct_x}: [\mathbf{b}^\perp \hat{s}]_1, \mathsf{sE}(\mathbf{x}^{(b)}, \{[(\mathbf{W}_k^\top \mathbf{b}^\perp + u_k \mathbf{b}^\perp)\hat{s}]_1\}_{k\in[N]}), [\mathbf{k}^\top \mathbf{b}^\perp \hat{s}]_T \\ \mathsf{sk_y}: \mathbf{z}, [\mathbf{a}^\perp \hat{r}]_2, \mathsf{rE}(\mathbf{y}, \mathbf{z}, \{[(\mathbf{W}_k \mathbf{a}^\perp + u_k \mathbf{a}^\perp)\hat{r}]_2\}_{k\in[N]}) \end{cases} \text{ and }$$

$$\begin{cases} \mathsf{aux}: \mathsf{PP}, [\mathbf{k}]_2, [\mathbf{B}]_2, [\alpha \mathbf{a}^\perp]_2 \\ \mathsf{ct_x}: [\mathbf{b}^\perp \hat{s}]_1, \mathsf{sE}(\mathbf{x}^{(b)}, \{[(\mathbf{W}_k^\top \mathbf{b}^\perp + u_k \mathbf{b}^\perp)\hat{s}]_1\}_{k\in[N]}), [\mathbf{k}^\top \mathbf{b}^\perp \hat{s}]_T \\ \mathsf{sk_y}: \mathbf{z}, [\mathbf{a}^\perp \hat{r}]_2, \mathsf{rkE}(\mathbf{y}, \mathbf{z}, [\alpha \mathbf{a}^\perp]_2) \cdot \mathsf{rE}(\mathbf{y}, \mathbf{z}, \{[(\mathbf{W}_k \mathbf{a}^\perp + u_k \mathbf{a}^\perp)\hat{r} + \hat{v}_k \mathbf{a}^\perp]_2\}_{k\in[N]}) \end{cases}$$

are indistinguishable. Let $\hat{g}_0 = [\mathbf{b}^\perp \hat{s}]_1, \hat{h}_0 = [\mathbf{a}^\perp \hat{r}]_2$ and set $[\mathbf{a}^\perp] = (\hat{h}_0)^\beta$, we note that

$$\mathsf{sE}(\mathbf{x}^{(b)}, \{[(\mathbf{W}_k^\top \mathbf{b}^\perp + u_k \mathbf{b}^\perp)\hat{s}]_1\}_{k \in [N]}) = \mathsf{sE}(\mathbf{x}^{(b)}, \{[\mathbf{W}_k^\top \mathbf{b}^\perp \hat{s}]_1\}_{k \in [N]}) \cdot \hat{g}_0^{\mathsf{sE}(\mathbf{x}^{(b)}, \mathbf{u})},$$

$$\mathsf{rE}(\mathbf{y}, \mathbf{z}, \{[(\mathbf{W}_k \mathbf{a}^\perp + u_k \mathbf{a}^\perp)\hat{r}]_2\}_{k \in [N]}) = \mathsf{rE}(\mathbf{y}, \mathbf{z}, \{[\mathbf{W}_k \mathbf{a}^\perp \hat{r}]_2\}_{k \in [N]}) \cdot \hat{h}_0^{\mathsf{rE}(\mathbf{y}, \mathbf{z}, \mathbf{u})},$$

$$\mathsf{rkE}(\mathbf{y}, \mathbf{z}, [\alpha \mathbf{a}^\perp]_2) \cdot \mathsf{rE}(\mathbf{y}, \mathbf{z}, \{[(\mathbf{W}_k \mathbf{a}^\perp + u_k \mathbf{a}^\perp)\hat{r} + \hat{v}_k \mathbf{a}^\perp]_2\}_{k \in [N]})$$

$$= \mathsf{rE}(\mathbf{y}, \mathbf{z}, \{[\mathbf{W}_k \mathbf{a}^\perp \hat{r}]_2\}_{k \in [N]}) \cdot \hat{h}_0^{\mathsf{rkE}(\mathbf{y}, \mathbf{z}, \beta\alpha) + \mathsf{rE}(\mathbf{y}, \mathbf{z}, \mathbf{u}) + \mathsf{rE}(\mathbf{y}, \mathbf{z}, \beta\hat{v})}.$$

Since $\mathcal{A}$ can only make **Leak** query on $\mathsf{sk_y}$, according to *attribute-hiding-leakage-resilient* encoding, it holds that $\{\mathbf{x}, \mathbf{y}, \mathsf{sE}(\mathbf{x}, \mathbf{u}), f(\mathbf{z}, \mathsf{rE}(\mathbf{y}, \mathbf{z}, \mathbf{u}))\}$ and $\{\mathbf{x}, \mathbf{y}, \mathbf{r}\}$ are indistinguishable. In other words, the adversary $\mathcal{A}$ cannot get any useful information to distinguish between $\mathsf{sk_y}$ and $\mathsf{sk_y'}$.

(2) If $\mathbf{y} \in \mathcal{Y}$ such that $<\mathbf{x}^{(0)}, \mathbf{y}> \neq 0$ and $<\mathbf{x}^{(1)}, \mathbf{y}> \neq 0$, the proof is also analogous to the proof of last case. Except that we should use *attribute-hiding* encoding, which claims that $\{\mathbf{x}, \mathbf{y}, \mathbf{z}, \mathsf{sE}(\mathbf{x}, \mathbf{u}), \mathsf{rE}(\mathbf{y}, \mathbf{z}, \mathbf{u})\}$ and $\{\mathbf{x}, \mathbf{y}, \mathbf{z}, \mathbf{r}\}$ are indistinguishable.

Finally, Lemma 7 holds. $\square$

Lemma 8 ($\mathsf{Game}_{2,i,2} \overset{c}{\approx} \mathsf{Game}_{2,i,3}$). *For all* PPT *adversary* $\mathcal{A}$ *and* $i = 1, \ldots, q$, *there exists an algorithm* $\mathcal{B}_3$ *such that* $|\mathsf{Adv}_{2,i,2}(\lambda) - \mathsf{Adv}_{2,i,3}(\lambda)| \leq \mathsf{Adv}_{\mathcal{B}_3}^{k\text{-Lin}}(\lambda) + 2/p$

Proof. The proof is completely analogous to Lemma 6. $\square$

Lemma 9 ($\mathsf{Game}_{2,q,3} \overset{s}{\approx} \mathsf{Game}_3$). *For* $i = 1, \ldots, q$, *it holds that* $|\mathsf{Adv}_{2,q,3}(\lambda) - \mathsf{Adv}_3(\lambda)| \approx 0$

Proof. First, pick $\hat{\mathbf{k}} \leftarrow \mathbb{Z}_p^{k+1}, \alpha \leftarrow \mathbb{Z}_p$ and set $\mathbf{k} := \hat{\mathbf{k}} - \alpha \mathbf{a}^\perp$. Given just $(\mathsf{PP}, [\mathbf{a}^\perp]_2, [\hat{\mathbf{k}}]_2)$, we can simulate the setup phase and answer key queries as follows:

Setup. Since $e([\mathbf{A}]_1, [\hat{\mathbf{k}}]_2) := [\mathbf{A}^\top \mathbf{k} - \alpha \mathbf{A}^\top \mathbf{a}^\perp]_T = [\mathbf{A}^\top \mathbf{k}]_T$, then we can simulate $\mathsf{mpk} := (\mathbb{G}; [\mathbf{A}]_1, [\mathbf{W}_1^\top \mathbf{A}]_1, \ldots, [\mathbf{W}_N^\top \mathbf{A}]_1, [\mathbf{A}^\top \mathbf{k}]_T)$.

Key Queries. For the j'th key query for $\mathbf{y}$, we can generate a *semi-functional* secret key properly:

$$\mathsf{sk_y} := \left(\mathbf{z}, [\mathbf{Br}]_2, \mathsf{rkE}(\mathbf{y}, \mathbf{z}, [\hat{\mathbf{k}}]_2) \cdot \mathsf{rE}(\mathbf{y}, \mathbf{z}, \{[\mathbf{W}_k \mathbf{Br} + \hat{v}_k^j \mathbf{a}^\perp]_2\}_{k \in [N]})\right)$$

Challenge. Now, observe that the challenge ciphertext in $\mathsf{Game}_{2,q,3}$ is given by:

$$\mathsf{ct}^* := (C_0 = [\mathbf{As} + \mathbf{b}^\perp \hat{s}]_1, \mathbf{C} := \mathsf{sE}(\mathbf{x}^{(b)}, \{[\mathbf{W}_k^\top (\mathbf{As} + \mathbf{b}^\perp \hat{s})\}_{k \in [N]})]_1),$$

$$C' = e([\mathbf{As} + \mathbf{b}^\perp \hat{s}]_1, [\mathbf{k}]_2) \cdot m^{(b)})$$

where we can rewrite $C' = e([\mathbf{As} + \mathbf{b}^\perp \hat{s}]_1, [\hat{\mathbf{k}}]_2) \cdot \boxed{e([\mathbf{b}^\perp \hat{s}]_1, [\mathbf{a}^\perp]_2)^{-\alpha} \cdot m^{(b)}}$.

Recall that $(\mathsf{mpk}, [\mathbf{B}]_2, \hat{\mathbf{k}})$ and $(C_0, \mathbf{C})$ are statistically independent of $\alpha \leftarrow \mathbb{Z}_p$, then we can say that $e([\mathbf{b}^\perp \hat{s}]_1, [\mathbf{a}^\perp]_2)^{-\alpha}$ is uniformly distributed over $\mathbb{G}_T$. This implies ct^* is identically distributed to semi-functional encryption of a random message in G_T, as in Game_3. Thus, Lemma 9 holds. $\square$

Lemma 10 (Game$_3$ $\overset{s}{\approx}$ Game$_4$). *For $i = 1, \ldots, q$, it holds that $|\mathsf{Adv}_3(\lambda) - \mathsf{Adv}_4(\lambda)| \approx 0$*

Proof. Pick $\hat{\mathbf{k}} \leftarrow \mathbb{Z}_p^{k+1}, \alpha \leftarrow \mathbb{Z}_p$ and set $\mathbf{k} := \hat{\mathbf{k}} - \alpha \mathbf{a}^\perp$. Given just $(\mathsf{PP}^-, [\mathbf{a}^\perp]_2, [\hat{\mathbf{k}}]_2)$, we note that $[\mathbf{W}_i \mathbf{B}]_2$ will not be simulated to ensure $\mathbb{G}$-uniformity holds. But we can still simulate the setup phase and answer key queries as follows:

Setup. We can simulate $\mathsf{mpk} := (\mathbb{G}; [\mathbf{A}]_1, [\mathbf{W}_1^\top \mathbf{A}]_1, \ldots, [\mathbf{W}_N^\top \mathbf{A}]_1, [\mathbf{A}^\top \mathbf{k}]_T)$.

Key Queries. For the j'th key query for $\mathbf{y}$, by $\mathbb{H}$-hiding in Lemma 3, we can simulate a *semi-functional* secret key:

$$\mathsf{sk}_\mathbf{y} := \left(\mathbf{z}, [\mathbf{Br}]_2, \mathsf{rkE}(\mathbf{y}, \mathbf{z}, [\hat{\mathbf{k}}]_2) \cdot \mathsf{rE}(\mathbf{y}, \mathbf{z}, [\hat{\mathbf{u}}_1^j]_2, \ldots, [\hat{\mathbf{u}}_N^j]_2)\right)$$

where for $i = 1, \ldots, N$, $\hat{\mathbf{u}}_i^j \leftarrow \mathbb{Z}_p^{k+1}$ subject to the constraint $\mathbf{A}^\top \hat{\mathbf{u}}_i^j = (\mathbf{W}_i^\top \mathbf{A})^\top \mathbf{Br}$.

Challenge. Now, observe that the challenge ciphertext in Game$_{2,q,3}$ is given by:

$$C_0 = [\mathbf{As} + \mathbf{b}^\perp \hat{s}]_1, \mathbf{C} := \mathsf{sE}(\mathbf{x}^{(b)}, \{[\mathbf{W}_k^\top(\mathbf{As} + \mathbf{b}^\perp \hat{s})]_1\}_{k \in [N]}), C' = e([\mathbf{As} + \mathbf{b}^\perp \hat{s}]_1, [\hat{\mathbf{k}}]_2) \cdot m'$$

where C' is is uniformly distributed over G_T. By $\mathbb{G}$-uniformity in Lemma 4, then

$$\{[\mathbf{As} + \mathbf{b}^\perp \hat{s}]_1, [\mathbf{W}_1^\top(\mathbf{As} + \mathbf{b}^\perp \hat{s})]_1, \ldots, [\mathbf{W}_N^\top(\mathbf{As} + \mathbf{b}^\perp \hat{s})]_1\}$$
$$\overset{s}{\approx} \{[\mathbf{As} + \mathbf{b}^\perp \hat{s}]_1, [\hat{\mathbf{w}}_1]_1, \ldots, [\hat{\mathbf{w}}_N]_1\}$$

where $\hat{\mathbf{w}}_1, \ldots, \hat{\mathbf{w}}_N \leftarrow \mathbb{Z}_p^{k+1}$. Note that $\mathcal{A}$ has no idea any information about $\mathbf{W}_i \mathbf{B}$ from $\mathsf{sk}_\mathbf{y}$ and mpk and hence $\mathbb{G}$-uniformity holds. So we can rewrite $\mathbf{C} := \mathsf{sE}(\mathbf{x}^{(b)}, [\hat{\mathbf{w}}_1]_1, \ldots, [\hat{\mathbf{w}}_N]_1)$. From *attribute-hiding* and *attribute-hiding-leakage-resilient* encoding, we can say that $\mathbf{C}$ is uniformly distributed over $G_1^{\mathsf{sE}(\cdot)}$. Thus, Lemma 10 holds. $\qquad\square$

Finally, we complete the proof of Theorem 1 by showing the above lemmas which imply the indistinguishability between Game$_0$ and Game$_4$.

4 Leakage-Resilient ABE in the CLM

In this section, we present our second leakage-resilient ABE framework, which is compatible with ZCG+18 but more versatile. Note that an overview of this generic construction has been present in Eq. (2).

4.1 Leakage-Resilient Predicate Encoding

We define a $\mathbb{Z}_p$-linear leakage-resilient predicate encoding for predicate $\mathsf{P} : \mathcal{X} \times \mathcal{Y} \to \{0, 1\}$. It consists of a set of deterministic algorithms $(\mathsf{mkE}, \mathsf{mE}, \mathsf{rkE}, \mathsf{rE}, \mathsf{sE}, \mathsf{sD}, \mathsf{rD})$ and satisfies the following properties:

- **(linearity.)** For all $(\mathbf{x}, \mathbf{y}, \mathbf{v}, \mathbf{z}) \in \mathcal{X} \times \mathcal{Y} \times \mathcal{V} \times \mathcal{Z}$, $\mathsf{mkE}(\mathbf{v}, \cdot), \mathsf{mE}(\mathbf{v}, \cdot), \mathsf{rkE}(\mathbf{y}, \mathbf{z}, \cdot)$, $\mathsf{rE}(\mathbf{y}, \mathbf{z}, \cdot), \mathsf{sE}(\mathbf{x}, \cdot), \mathsf{sD}(\mathbf{x}, \mathbf{y}, \mathbf{z}, \cdot), \mathsf{rD}(\mathbf{x}, \mathbf{y}, \mathbf{z}, \cdot)$ are $\mathbb{Z}_p$-linear.

- (**restricted α-reconstruction.**) This property is the same as *restricted α-reconstruction* in Sect. 3.1.
- (**α-privacy.**) For all $(\mathbf{x}, \mathbf{y}) \in \mathcal{X} \times \mathcal{Y}$ such that $\mathsf{P}(\mathbf{x}, \mathbf{y}) = 0$, the distributions $\{\mathbf{x}, \mathbf{y}, \mathbf{z}, \alpha, \mathsf{sE}(\mathbf{x}, \mathbf{w}), \mathsf{rkE}(\mathbf{y}, \mathbf{z}, \alpha) + \mathsf{rE}(\mathbf{y}, \mathbf{z}, \mathbf{w})\}$ and $\{\mathbf{x}, \mathbf{y}, \mathbf{z}, \alpha, \mathsf{sE}(\mathbf{x}, \mathbf{w}), \mathsf{rE}(\mathbf{y}, \mathbf{z}, \mathbf{w})\}$ are identical, where the randomness is taken over $\mathbf{w} \leftarrow \mathcal{W}$.
- (**α-leakage-resilient.**) For all $(\mathbf{x}, \mathbf{y}) \in \mathcal{X} \times \mathcal{Y}$ such that $\mathsf{P}(\mathbf{x}, \mathbf{y}) = 1$ and all $\alpha \in \mathbb{Z}_p, \mathbf{z} \in \mathcal{Z}, \mathbf{v} \in \mathcal{V}$, the distributions $\{\mathbf{x}, \mathbf{y}, \alpha, \mathsf{sE}(\mathbf{x}, \mathbf{w}), f(\mathbf{z}, \mathsf{rkE}(\mathbf{y}, \mathbf{z}, \alpha) + \mathsf{rE}(\mathbf{y}, \mathbf{z}, \mathbf{w}))\}$ and $\{\mathbf{x}, \mathbf{y}, \alpha, \mathsf{sE}(\mathbf{x}, \mathbf{w}), f(\mathbf{z}, \mathsf{rE}(\mathbf{y}, \mathbf{z}, \mathbf{w}))\}$ are identical, where $\mathbf{w} \leftarrow \mathcal{W}$. In addition, the distributions $\{\mathbf{x}, \alpha, \mathsf{sE}(\mathbf{x}, \mathbf{w}), f(\mathbf{v}, \mathsf{mkE}(\mathbf{v}, \alpha) + \mathsf{mE}(\mathbf{v}, \mathbf{w}))\}$ and $\{\mathbf{x}, \alpha, \mathsf{sE}(\mathbf{x}, \mathbf{w}), f(\mathbf{v}, \mathsf{mE}(\mathbf{v}, \mathbf{w}))\}$ are also identical.
- (**delegable.**) There exits a linear algorithm dE such that for all $\alpha \in \mathbb{Z}_p, \mathbf{v} \in \mathcal{V}, \mathbf{z} \in \mathcal{Z}, \mathbf{w} \in \mathcal{W}, \mathbf{y} \in \mathcal{Y}$, it holds that $\mathsf{dE}(\mathbf{y}, \mathsf{mkE}(\mathbf{v}, \alpha) + \mathsf{mE}(\mathbf{v}, \mathbf{w})) = \mathsf{rkE}(\mathbf{y}, \mathbf{z}, \alpha) + \mathsf{rE}(\mathbf{y}, \mathbf{z}, \mathbf{w})$. Note that the algorithm dE implies a linear map $S : \mathcal{Y} \times \mathcal{V} \rightarrow \mathcal{Z}$.
- (**re-randomizable.**) For all $\alpha \in \mathbb{Z}_p, \mathbf{v}, \mathbf{v}' \in \mathcal{V}, \mathbf{w} \in \mathcal{W}$, there exists a linear algorithm mR such that $\mathsf{mR}(\mathbf{v}, \mathbf{v}', \mathsf{mkE}(\mathbf{v}, \alpha) + \mathsf{mE}(\mathbf{v}, \mathbf{w})) = \mathsf{mkE}(\mathbf{v}', \alpha) + \mathsf{mE}(\mathbf{v}', \mathbf{w})$. Similarly, for all $\alpha \in \mathbb{Z}_p, \mathbf{z}, \mathbf{z}' \in \mathcal{Z}, \mathbf{w} \in \mathcal{W}, \mathbf{y} \in \mathcal{Y}$, there exists a linear algorithm kR such that $\mathsf{kR}(\mathbf{z}, \mathbf{z}', \mathsf{rkE}(\mathbf{y}, \mathbf{z}, \alpha) + \mathsf{rE}(\mathbf{y}, \mathbf{z}, \mathbf{w})) = \mathsf{rkE}(\mathbf{y}, \mathbf{z}', \alpha) + \mathsf{rE}(\mathbf{y}, \mathbf{z}', \mathbf{w})$.

4.2 Generic Construction

Given a $\mathbb{Z}_p$-linear leakage-resilient predicate encoding for predicate $\mathsf{P} : \mathcal{X} \times \mathcal{Y} \rightarrow \{0, 1\}$,

- Setup(1^λ): This algorithm is similar to the setup algorithm in Sect. 3.2. Run $\mathbb{G} \leftarrow \mathcal{G}(1^\lambda)$, sample $(\mathbf{A}, \mathbf{a}^\perp), (\mathbf{B}, \mathbf{b}^\perp)$ as in Eq. (3), pick $\mathbf{k} \leftarrow \mathbb{Z}_p^{k+1}, \mathbf{W}_1, \ldots,$ $\mathbf{W}_N \leftarrow \mathbb{Z}_p^{(k+1) \times (k+1)}, \mathbf{r} \leftarrow \mathbb{Z}_p^k, \mathbf{v} \leftarrow \mathcal{V}$, output

$$v := \left(\mathbb{G}; \begin{array}{l} [\mathbf{A}]_1, [\mathbf{W}_1^\top \mathbf{A}]_1, \ldots, [\mathbf{W}_N^\top \mathbf{A}]_1, [\mathbf{A}^\top \mathbf{k}]_T, \\ [\mathbf{B}]_2, [\mathbf{W}_1 \mathbf{B}]_2, \ldots, [\mathbf{W}_N \mathbf{B}]_2 \end{array} \right),$$

$$\mathsf{mk} := \left(\mathbf{v}, [\mathbf{Br}]_2, \mathsf{mkE}(\mathbf{v}, [\mathbf{k}]_2) \cdot \mathsf{mE}(\mathbf{v}, [\mathbf{W}_1 \mathbf{Br}]_2, \ldots, [\mathbf{W}_N \mathbf{Br}]_2) \right)$$

  where we set $K_0 = [\mathbf{Br}]_2, \mathbf{K} = \mathsf{mkE}(\mathbf{v}, [\mathbf{k}]_2) \cdot \mathsf{mE}(\mathbf{v}, [\mathbf{W}_1 \mathbf{Br}]_2, \ldots, [\mathbf{W}_N \mathbf{Br}]_2)$.
- Update$(v, \mathsf{sk}_\mathbf{y})$: If $\mathbf{y} = \epsilon$, then $\mathsf{sk}_\mathbf{y}$ is a master key and we rewrite it as $\mathsf{mk} := (\mathbf{v}, [\mathbf{Br}]_2, \mathbf{K})$. Pick $\tilde{\mathbf{r}} \leftarrow \mathbb{Z}_p^k, \mathbf{v}' \leftarrow \mathcal{V}$, we set $\mathbf{r}' = \mathbf{r} + \tilde{\mathbf{r}}$ and output

$$\mathsf{mk}' := \left(\mathbf{v}', [\mathbf{Br}']_2, \mathsf{mR}(\mathbf{v}, \mathbf{v}', \mathbf{K}) \cdot \mathsf{mE}(\mathbf{v}', [\mathbf{W}_1 \mathbf{B}\tilde{\mathbf{r}}]_2, \ldots, [\mathbf{W}_N \mathbf{B}\tilde{\mathbf{r}}]_2) \right)$$

$$\Downarrow$$

$$\mathsf{mk}' := \left(\mathbf{v}', [\mathbf{Br}']_2, \mathsf{mkE}(\mathbf{v}', [\mathbf{k}]_2) \cdot \mathsf{mE}(\mathbf{v}', [\mathbf{W}_1 \mathbf{Br}']_2, \ldots, [\mathbf{W}_N \mathbf{Br}']_2) \right)$$

Thus, we can generate a new master key mk' with the same distribution as mk. If $\mathbf{y} \in \mathcal{Y}$, $\mathsf{sk}_\mathbf{y}$ is a user secret key. Similarly, we can generate a new secret key $\mathsf{sk}'_\mathbf{y}$ using the algorithm kR.

- KeyGen(mk, $\mathbf{y}$): Parse mk $:= (v, [\mathbf{Br}]_2, \mathbf{K})$. we compute $\mathbf{z} \leftarrow S(\mathbf{y}, \mathbf{v})$ and

$$\mathsf{dE}(\mathbf{y}, \mathbf{K}) = \mathsf{rkE}(\mathbf{y}, \mathbf{z}, [\mathbf{k}]_2) \cdot \mathsf{rE}(\mathbf{y}, \mathbf{z}, [\mathbf{W}_1\mathbf{Br}]_2, \ldots, [\mathbf{W}_N\mathbf{Br}]_2)$$

Then pick $\tilde{\mathbf{r}} \leftarrow \mathbb{Z}_p^k, \mathbf{z}' \leftarrow \mathcal{Z}$ and set $\mathbf{r}' = \mathbf{r} + \tilde{\mathbf{r}}$. Output

$$\mathsf{sk}_{\mathbf{y}} := \big(\mathbf{z}', [\mathbf{Br}']_2, \mathsf{kR}(\mathbf{z}, \mathbf{z}', \mathsf{dE}(\mathbf{y}, \mathbf{K})) \cdot \mathsf{rE}(\mathbf{y}, \mathbf{z}', [\mathbf{W}_1\mathbf{B}\tilde{\mathbf{r}}]_2, \ldots, [\mathbf{W}_N\mathbf{B}\tilde{\mathbf{r}}]_2)\big)$$
$$\Downarrow$$
$$\mathsf{sk}_{\mathbf{y}} := \big(\mathbf{z}', [\mathbf{Br}']_2, \mathsf{rkE}(\mathbf{y}, \mathbf{z}', [\mathbf{k}]_2) \cdot \mathsf{rE}(\mathbf{y}, \mathbf{z}', [\mathbf{W}_1\mathbf{Br}']_2, \ldots, [\mathbf{W}_N\mathbf{Br}']_2)\big)$$

Similar to mk, here we also set $K_0 = [\mathbf{Br}']_2$ and

$$\mathbf{K} = \mathsf{rkE}(\mathbf{y}, \mathbf{z}', [\mathbf{k}]_2) \cdot \mathsf{rE}(\mathbf{y}, \mathbf{z}', [\mathbf{W}_1\mathbf{Br}']_2, \ldots, [\mathbf{W}_N\mathbf{Br}']_2)$$

- Enc($v, \mathbf{x}, m$): Pick $\mathbf{s} \leftarrow \mathbb{Z}_p^k$ and output $\mathsf{ct}_{\mathbf{x}} := (C_0, \mathbf{C}, C_T)$, where

$$C_0 := [\mathbf{As}]_1, \mathbf{C} := \mathsf{sE}(\mathbf{x}, [\mathbf{W}_1^\top\mathbf{As}]_1, \ldots, [\mathbf{W}_N^\top\mathbf{As}]_1), C_T := [\mathbf{k}^\top\mathbf{As}]_T \cdot m$$

- Dec(mpk, $\mathsf{sk}_{\mathbf{y}}, \mathsf{ct}_{\mathbf{x}}$): Parse $\mathsf{sk}_{\mathbf{y}} := (\mathbf{z}, K_0, \mathbf{K}), \mathsf{ct}_{\mathbf{x}} := (C_0, \mathbf{C}, C_T)$ and output $m' = C_T \cdot e(C_0, \mathsf{rD}(\mathbf{x}, \mathbf{y}, \mathbf{z}, \mathbf{K}))^{-1} \cdot e(\mathsf{sD}(\mathbf{x}, \mathbf{y}, \mathbf{z}, \mathbf{C}), K_0)$.

Correctness. Since linearity and restricted α-reconstruction (for $\mathsf{rkE}(\mathbf{y}, \mathbf{z}, \cdot)$, $\mathsf{rE}(\mathbf{y}, \mathbf{z}, \cdot), \mathsf{sE}(\mathbf{x}, \cdot), \mathsf{sD}(\mathbf{x}, \mathbf{y}, \mathbf{z}, \cdot), \mathsf{rD}(\mathbf{x}, \mathbf{y}, \mathbf{z}, \cdot))$ are similar to ones in Sect. 3.1, the correctness also follows Sect. 3.2.

4.3 Security

Theorem 2. *If k-Lin assumption holds, the scheme described in Sect. 4.2 is $(L_{\mathsf{mk}}, L_{\mathsf{sk}})$-continual-leakage secure. More precisely, for all PPT adversaries $\mathcal{A}$ subject to the restrictions: (1) $\mathcal{A}$ makes at most q O_2' and O_3' queries; (2) The leakage amount of mk and sk are at most L_{mk}, L_{sk} bits, respectively. There exists an algorithm $\mathcal{B}$ such that $\mathsf{Adv}_{\mathcal{A}}^{\mathrm{CLR\text{-}PH}}(\lambda) \le (2q+1)\mathsf{Adv}_{\mathcal{B}}^{k\text{-}\mathrm{Lin}}(\lambda) + \mathsf{negl}(\lambda)$.*

Proof. The proof sketch of Theorem 2 is similar to the proof of our first framework. It still designs a sequence of games which are the same as Table 2 except that Game$_4$ is canceled and there is no need to add $\hat{v}_k\mathbf{a}^\perp$ in Game$_{2,i,2}$, Game$_{2,i,3}$ and Game$_3$. Besides, we replace *attribute-hiding* and *attribute-hiding-leakage-resilient* with α-*privacy* and α-*privacy-leakage-resilient*. We omit details due to the page limitation.

5 Instantiations

In this section, we apply our frameworks to the compact-key ABE schemes for zero inner-product and non-zero inner-product in CGW15 and hence obtain several leakage-resilient instantiations.

5.1 Instantiation for the First Framework

Zero Inner-Product Predicate. Let $\mathcal{X} = \mathcal{Y} := \mathbb{Z}_p^n, \mathcal{Z} := \mathbb{Z}_p^L, \mathcal{W} := \mathbb{Z}_p \times \mathbb{Z}_p^n \times \mathbb{Z}_p^L$, where n is the dimension of vector space. Let $L_{\sf sk} = (L - 2c - 1)\log p$ where c is a fixed positive constant. Pick $(u, \mathbf{w}, \mathbf{u}) \leftarrow \mathcal{W}, \mathbf{z} \leftarrow \mathcal{Z}$, then we have

- $\mathsf{rkE}(\mathbf{y}, \mathbf{z}, \alpha) := (\alpha, \mathbf{0}) \in \mathbb{Z}_p^{L+1},$
- $\mathsf{rE}(\mathbf{y}, \mathbf{z}, (u, \mathbf{w}, \mathbf{u})) := (\mathbf{y}^\top \mathbf{w} + \mathbf{z}^\top \mathbf{u}, \mathbf{u}),$
- $\mathsf{sE}(\mathbf{x}, (u, \mathbf{w}, \mathbf{u})) := u\mathbf{x} + \mathbf{w} \in \mathbb{Z}_p^n,$
- $\mathsf{sD}(\mathbf{x}, \mathbf{y}, \mathbf{z}, \mathbf{c}) := \mathbf{c}^\top \mathbf{y},$
- $\mathsf{rD}(\mathbf{x}, \mathbf{y}, \mathbf{z}, (d', \mathbf{d})) := d' - \mathbf{z}^\top \mathbf{d}$

5.2 Instantiations for the Second Framework

Zero Inner-Product Predicate. Let $\mathcal{X} = \mathcal{Y} := \mathbb{Z}_p^n, \mathcal{V} := \mathbb{Z}_p^{(n+1) \times L}, \mathcal{Z} := \mathbb{Z}_p^L, \mathcal{W} := \mathbb{Z}_p \times \mathbb{Z}_p^n \times \mathbb{Z}_p^L$, where n is the dimension of vector space. Let $L_{\sf mk} = L_{\sf sk} = (L - 2c - 1)\log p$ where c is a fixed positive constant. Pick $(u, \mathbf{w}, \mathbf{u}) \leftarrow \mathcal{W}, \mathbf{v} \leftarrow \mathcal{V}, \mathbf{z} \leftarrow \mathcal{Z}$. We denote the i's row vector by $\mathbf{v}_{i-1}^\top \in \mathbb{Z}_p^{1 \times L}$ for $i = 1, 2, \ldots, n+1$ and the last n rows by $\mathbf{v} \in \mathbb{Z}_p^{n \times L}$, respectively. Define

- $\mathsf{mkE}(\mathbf{v}, \alpha) := (\alpha, \mathbf{0}) \in \mathbb{Z}_p^{n+L+1},$
- $\mathsf{mE}(\mathbf{v}, (u, \mathbf{w}, \mathbf{u})) := (\mathbf{v}_0^\top \mathbf{u}, \mathbf{w} + \mathbf{v}\mathbf{u}, \mathbf{u}),$
- $\mathsf{rkE}(\mathbf{y}, \mathbf{z}, \alpha) := (\alpha, \mathbf{0}) \in \mathbb{Z}_p^{L+1},$
- $\mathsf{rE}(\mathbf{y}, \mathbf{z}, (u, \mathbf{w}, \mathbf{u})) := (\mathbf{y}^\top \mathbf{w} + \mathbf{z}^\top \mathbf{u}, \mathbf{u}),$
- $\mathsf{sE}(\mathbf{x}, (u, \mathbf{w}, \mathbf{u})) := u\mathbf{x} + \mathbf{w} \in \mathbb{Z}_p^n,$
- $\mathsf{sD}(\mathbf{x}, \mathbf{y}, \mathbf{z}, \mathbf{c}) := \mathbf{c}^\top \mathbf{y},$
- $\mathsf{rD}(\mathbf{x}, \mathbf{y}, \mathbf{z}, (d', \mathbf{d})) := d' - \mathbf{z}^\top \mathbf{d}$

Non-zore Inner-Product Predicate. Let $\mathcal{X} = \mathcal{Y} := \mathbb{Z}_p^n, \mathcal{V} := \mathbb{Z}_p^{n \times L}, \mathcal{Z} := \mathbb{Z}_p^L, \mathcal{W} := \mathbb{Z}_p \times \mathbb{Z}_p^n \times \mathbb{Z}_p^L$. Pick $(u, \mathbf{w}, \mathbf{u}) \leftarrow \mathcal{W}, \mathbf{v} \leftarrow \mathcal{V}, \mathbf{z} \leftarrow \mathcal{Z}$. Define

- $\mathsf{mkE}(\mathbf{v}, \alpha) := (\alpha, \mathbf{0}) \in \mathbb{Z}_p^{n+L+1},$
- $\mathsf{mE}(\mathbf{v}, (u, \mathbf{w}, \mathbf{u})) := (u, \mathbf{w} + \mathbf{v}\mathbf{u}, \mathbf{u}),$
- $\mathsf{rkE}(\mathbf{y}, \mathbf{z}, \alpha) := (\alpha, \mathbf{0}) \in \mathbb{Z}_p^{L+2},$
- $\mathsf{rE}(\mathbf{y}, \mathbf{z}, (u, \mathbf{w}, \mathbf{u})) := (u, \mathbf{y}^\top \mathbf{w} + \mathbf{z}^\top \mathbf{u}, \mathbf{u}),$
- $\mathsf{sD}(\mathbf{x}, \mathbf{y}, \mathbf{z}, \mathbf{c}) := \mathbf{c}^\top \mathbf{y} \cdot (\mathbf{x}^\top \mathbf{y})^{-1},$
- $\mathsf{rD}(\mathbf{x}, \mathbf{y}, \mathbf{z}, (d', d, \mathbf{d})) := d' + d \cdot (\mathbf{x}^\top \mathbf{y})^{-1} - \mathbf{z}^\top \mathbf{d},$
- $\mathsf{sE}(\mathbf{x}, (u, \mathbf{w}, \mathbf{u})) := u\mathbf{x} + \mathbf{w} \in \mathbb{Z}_p^n$

Acknowledgments. This work was supported by National Natural Science Foundation of China (61972156, 62372180), NSFC-ISF Joint Scientific Research Program (61961146004), Innovation Program of ShanghaiMunicipal Education Commission (2021-01-07-00-08-E00101) and the "Digital Silk Road" Shanghai International Joint Lab of Trustworthy Intelligent Software (22510750100), University natural science research project in Jiangsu Province (22KJB520035), Open project of "Jiangsu Key Laboratory for Elevator Intelligent Safety" (JSKLESS202104) and Special teaching project of Jiangsu Computer Society (JSCS2022049).

References

1. Agrawal, D., Archambeault, B., Rao, J.R., Rohatgi, P.: The EM side-channel(s). In: Kaliski, B.S., Kocs, C.K., Paar, C. (eds.) Cryptographic Hardware and Embedded Systems - CHES 2002. Lecture Notes in Computer Science, vol. 2523, pp. 29–45. Springer, Berlin (2002). https://doi.org/10.1007/3-540-36400-5_4

2. Akavia, A., Goldwasser, S., Vaikuntanathan, V.: Simultaneous hardcore bits and cryptography against memory attacks. In: Reingold, O. (ed.) Theory of Cryptography. Lecture Notes in Computer Science, vol. 5444, pp. 474–495. Springer, Berlin (2009). https://doi.org/10.1007/978-3-642-00457-5_28
3. Attrapadung, N.: Dual system encryption via doubly selective security: framework, fully secure functional encryption for regular languages, and more. In: Nguyen, P.Q., Oswald, E. (eds.) Advances in Cryptology - EUROCRYPT 2014. Lecture Notes in Computer Science, vol. 8441, pp. 557–577. Springer, Berlin (2014). https://doi.org/10.1007/978-3-642-55220-5_31
4. Brakerski, Z., Kalai, Y.T., Katz, J., Vaikuntanathan, V.: Overcoming the hole in the bucket: public-key cryptography resilient to continual memory leakage. In: 2010 IEEE 51st Annual Symposium on Foundations of Computer Science, pp. 501–510. IEEE (2010)
5. Chen, J., Gay, R., Wee, H.: Improved dual system ABE in prime-order groups via predicate encodings. In: Oswald, E., Fischlin, M. (eds.) Advances in Cryptology - EUROCRYPT 2015. Lecture Notes in Computer Science(), vol. 9057, pp. 595–624. Springer, Berlin (2015). https://doi.org/10.1007/978-3-662-46803-6_20
6. Crescenzo, G.D., Lipton, R., Walfish, S.: Perfectly secure password protocols in the bounded retrieval model. In: Halevi, S., Rabin, T. (eds.) Theory of Cryptography. Lecture Notes in Computer Science, vol. 3876, pp. 225–244. Springer, Berlin (2006). https://doi.org/10.1007/11681878_12
7. Dodis, Y., Kalai, Y.T., Lovett, S.: On cryptography with auxiliary input. In: Proceedings of the Forty-First Annual ACM Symposium on Theory of Computing, pp. 621–630 (2009)
8. Dziembowski, S., Pietrzak, K.: Leakage-resilient cryptography. In: 2008 49th Annual IEEE Symposium on Foundations of Computer Science, pp. 293–302. IEEE (2008)
9. Halderman, J.A., et al.: Lest we remember: cold-boot attacks on encryption keys. Commun. ACM **52**(5), 91–98 (2009)
10. Kalai, Y.T., Reyzin, L.: A survey of leakage-resilient cryptography. IACR Cryptol. ePrint Arch. **2019**, 302 (2019)
11. Kim, I., Hwang, S.O., Park, J.H., Park, C.: An efficient predicate encryption with constant pairing computations and minimum costs. IEEE Trans. Comput. **65**(10), 2947–2958 (2016)
12. Kocher, P., et al.: Spectre attacks: exploiting speculative execution. In: 2019 IEEE Symposium on Security and Privacy (SP), pp. 1–19. IEEE (2019)
13. Lewko, A., Okamoto, T., Sahai, A., Takashima, K., Waters, B.: Fully secure functional encryption: attribute-based encryption and (hierarchical) inner product encryption. In: Gilbert, H. (ed.) Advances in Cryptology - EUROCRYPT 2010. Lecture Notes in Computer Science, vol. 6110, pp. 62–91. Springer, Berlin (2010). https://doi.org/10.1007/978-3-642-13190-5_4
14. Lewko, A., Rouselakis, Y., Waters, B.: Achieving leakage resilience through dual system encryption. In: Ishai, Y. (ed.) Theory of Cryptography. Lecture Notes in Computer Science, vol. 6597, pp. 70–88. Springer, Berlin (2011). https://doi.org/10.1007/978-3-642-19571-6_6
15. Li, J., Yu, Q., Zhang, Y.: Hierarchical attribute based encryption with continuous leakage-resilience. Inf. Sci. **484**, 113–134 (2019)
16. Li, J., Yu, Q., Zhang, Y., Shen, J.: Key-policy attribute-based encryption against continual auxiliary input leakage. Inf. Sci. **470**, 175–188 (2019)

17. Nishimaki, R., Yamakawa, T.: Leakage-resilient identity-based encryption in bounded retrieval model with nearly optimal leakage-ratio. In: Lin, D., Sako, K. (eds.) Public-Key Cryptography - PKC 2019. Lecture Notes in Computer Science(), vol. 11442, pp. 466–495. Springer, Cham (2019). https://doi.org/10.1007/978-3-030-17253-4_16

18. Sahai, A., Waters, B.: Fuzzy identity-based encryption. In: Cramer, R. (ed.) Advances in Cryptology – EUROCRYPT 2005. Lecture Notes in Computer Science, vol. 3494, pp. 457–473. Springer, Berlin (2005). https://doi.org/10.1007/11426639_27

19. Wee, H.: Dual system encryption via predicate encodings. In: Lindell, Y. (ed.) Theory of Cryptography. Lecture Notes in Computer Science, vol. 8349, pp. 616–637. Springer, Berlin (2014). https://doi.org/10.1007/978-3-642-54242-8_26

20. Yu, Z., Au, M.H., Xu, Q., Yang, R., Han, J.: Leakage-resilient functional encryption via pair encodings. In: Liu, J., Steinfeld, R. (eds.) Information Security and Privacy. Lecture Notes in Computer Science(), vol. 9722, pp. 443–460. Springer, Cham (2016). https://doi.org/10.1007/978-3-319-40253-6_27

21. Yuen, T.H., Chow, S.S., Zhang, Y., Yiu, S.M.: Identity-based encryption resilient to continual auxiliary leakage. In: Pointcheval, D., Johansson, T. (eds.) Advances in Cryptology - EUROCRYPT 2012. Lecture Notes in Computer Science, vol. 7237, pp. 117–134. Springer, Berlin (2012). https://doi.org/10.1007/978-3-642-29011-4_9

22. Zhang, J., Chen, J., Gong, J., Ge, A., Ma, C.: Leakage-resilient attribute based encryption in prime-order groups via predicate encodings. Des. Codes Crypt. 86(6), 1339–1366 (2018)

23. Zhang, L., Zhang, J., Mu, Y.: Novel leakage-resilient attribute-based encryption from hash proof system. Comput. J. 60(4), 541–554 (2017)

24. Zhang, M., Mu, Y.: Token-leakage tolerant and vector obfuscated IPE and application in privacy-preserving two-party point/polynomial evaluations. Comput. J. 59(4), 493–507 (2016)

Constant-Deposit Multiparty Lotteries on Bitcoin for Arbitrary Number of Players and Winners

Shun Uchizono[1(✉)], Takeshi Nakai[2], Yohei Watanabe[1,3], and Mitsugu Iwamoto[1]

[1] The University of Electro-Communications, Tokyo, Japan
{uchizono,watanabe,mitsugu}@uec.ac.jp
[2] Toyohashi University of Technology, Aichi, Japan
nakai@cs.tut.ac.jp
[3] National Institute of Advanced Industrial Science and Technology, Tokyo, Japan

Abstract. Secure lottery is a cryptographic protocol that allows multiple players to determine a winner from them uniformly at random, without any trusted third party. Bitcoin enables us to construct a secure lottery to guarantee further that the winner receives reward money from the other losers. Many existing works for Bitcoin-based lottery use deposits to ensure that honest players never be disadvantaged in the presence of adversaries. Bartoletti and Zunino (FC 2017) proposed a Bitcoin-based lottery protocol with a constant deposit, i.e., the deposit amount is independent of the number of players. However, their scheme is limited to work only when the number of participants is a power of two. We tackle this problem and propose a lottery protocol applicable to an arbitrary number of players based on their work. Furthermore, we generalize the number of winners; namely, we propose a secure (k, n)-lottery protocol. To the best of our knowledge, this is the first work to address Bitcoin-based (k, n)-lottery protocol. Notably, our protocols maintain the constant deposit property.

Keywords: Secure lottery · Bitcoin · Fairness · Elimination tournament

1 Introduction

1.1 Backgrounds

Consider a bet in which each of the n players gambles one dollar. The champion is randomly chosen from them and he/she receives the sum of the bets, n dollars, as a reward. Secure lottery is a cryptographic protocol that allows us to play such games fairly [12–14, 18]. That is, it ensures that no honest player is disadvantaged in the presence of adversarial players who do not follow procedures.

One of the crucial issues in constructing a secure lottery is how to deal with the abort attack, which terminates in the middle of a protocol to avoid losing.

© The Author(s), under exclusive license to Springer Nature Singapore Pte Ltd. 2024
H. Seo and S. Kim (Eds.): ICISC 2023, LNCS 14562, pp. 133–156, 2024.
https://doi.org/10.1007/978-981-97-1238-0_8

To counter the attack, we must enforce an adversary to tell the lottery result to all honest parties. Such a property is typically defined as *fairness*, which ensures that at the end of a protocol, either all parties learn the output or none of them learn it. Unfortunately, it is known that fairness cannot be achieved without any additional assumption such as the honest majority or trusted third parties [11].

Another fundamental challenge is how to force losers to pay winners. Since a typical cryptographic protocol treats no monetary entity, we cannot require a protocol to guarantee such a property. To enforce the payoff, we need to introduce a setup for handling monetary operations, e.g., a trusted bank [19,22], e-cash [6,9,17], or decentralized cryptocurrency.

Secure Lottery Based on Cryptocurrency. Using cryptocurrency, e.g., Bitcoin [23] and Ethereum [24], we can construct a secure lottery protocol that forces losers to pay winners without relying upon any trusted third party even in the dishonest majority. Informally, in cryptocurrency-based protocols, parties cooperate to create some transactions at the beginning of the protocol and deposit or bet money. One of the transactions is corresponding to n dollars, the prize money. If a protocol guarantees that only the winner can learn the witness to redeem it, it implies that only the winner can receive the prize.

There is a line of work on achieving a variant of fairness using monetary penalties. The monetary penalty enforces adversaries to follow procedures to avoid losing money, and it allows us to achieve fairness. In secure multi-party computation, many works adopt such a definition, e.g., [5,7,8,15,16,21].

Similarly, it is known that monetary penalties enable us to construct a secure lottery protocol even in the dishonest majority. Back and Bentov [2] showed a secure lottery based on Bitcoin in the two-party setting. Their protocol can enforce a payment from the loser to the winner. Moreover, it guarantees that an aborting party loses money and then another party obtains money as compensation. Afterward, Andrychowicz, Dziembowski, Malinowski, and Mazurek [1] and Bentov and Kumaresan [2], respectively, proposed Bitcoins-based secure lottery protocols that can be applied to an arbitrary number of parties.

In many works of Bitcoin-based secure lotteries, parties must input deposit to achieve fairness in addition to the bet. Indeed, the existing protocol made of Marcin [1] requires parties to input $O(n^2)$ deposits, where n is the number of parties. The deposit is guaranteed to be returned to every honest party at the end of the protocol. On the other hand, for adversarial parties, the deposit is not returned to them but is instead distributed to honest parties as compensation. Even though the protocol promises to refund deposits to honest parties, it is undesirable to require money other than bets. That is to say, too expensive deposits make it difficult for parties to participate in the protocol. Based on the backgrounds, Bartoletti and Zunino [4] proposed a secure lottery protocol with a constant deposit. Independently, Miller and Bentov [20] proposed a secure lottery without any deposit money. However, as pointed out by Bartoletti and Zunino [4], their scheme has an issue of depending on a Bitcoin specific opcode,

MULTIINPUT. To be a generic scheme, it should not rely on a custom scripting language supported by a particular blockchain.

In this paper, we focus on Bartoletti-Zunino work [4]. Informally they realize a constant-deposit protocol based on a single-eliminate tournament, i.e., they use multiple matches between two players to determine one winner of the lottery. However, their protocol assumes that the tournament has a complete binary tree structure. In other words, it has an issue to be applicable only if the number of participants can be expressed in 2^L, where L is a positive integer that refers to the tree depth.

1.2 Our Contribution

This paper presents two contributions. The first one is to solve the issue of the restriction of the number of participants in the Bartolotti and Zunino scheme. That is, we propose $(1, n)$-lottery protocol for an arbitrary positive integer n. Our construction idea is we bias the winning percentage for each match to ensure that all participants are equal even if the tournament is not a complete binary tree.

The second contribution is to generalize the number of winners, namely, we propose a (k, n)-lottery protocol for arbitrary k and n. To realize the protocol, we first construct $(k, k+1)$-lottery protocol. Our (k, n)-lottery protocol is derived from a composition of $(k, k+1)$-lottery protocols. More precisely, in our protocol parties first run $(n-1, n)$-lottery protocol and determine one loser. Afterward, $n-1$ winners run $(n-2, n-1)$-lottery protocol and further determine one loser. Players repeat such a process until deciding $n-k$ losers. To the best of our knowledge, this is the first work to realize (k, n)-lottery protocol based on Bitcoin with a constant deposit.

1.3 Basic Notations

For any positive integer i, let $[i] := \{0, 1, \ldots, i-1\}$. We denote by η a security parameter. We suppose that all players are probabilistic polynomial-time algorithms (PPTA) in a security parameter η.

We construct lottery protocols based on a tournament structure represented as a binary tree, as in [4].

Hereafter, we call a champion to distinguish it from the winners of matches in the tournament. In a binary tree, its leaf nodes refer to players, and the other nodes represent a match (or the winner) of two child nodes. Each node at level l in the tree is identified as a $(l+1)$-bit string. For a node π, we denote its child nodes as $\pi_{\text{left}} = \pi \parallel 0$ and $\pi_{\text{right}} = \pi \parallel 1$. Namely, π is the prefix of its child nodes. We write $\pi \sqsubset \pi'$ if π is a prefix of π'. We note that, since we handle an arbitrary number of players, the tournaments may not be the complete binary tree. Hence, the binary tree in our protocol is represented by $\Pi \subseteq \{\{0, 1\}^l \mid 1 \le l \le L\}$, where the tree has L levels. We denote by P the set of players. Note that, since the players correspond to leaf nodes, it holds $P \subset \Pi$. For a bit string π, $|\pi|$ means the bit length of π. We denote by π_r the root node of a binary tree.

Organization. As a preparation for the introduction of our protocol, we first describe a bitcoin overview in Sect. 2. Section 3 presents several notations and useful lemmas regarding tournament structures. In Sect. 4, we define secure lottery protocol. We show our constructions for $(1, n)$-lottery and (k, n)-lottery in Sects. 5 and 6, respectively. In these sections, we prove security of the protocols according to the security definitions, shown in Sect. 4.

2   A Brief Introduction to Bitcoin

In a blockchain protocol, parties maintain a global *ledger* that holds ordered sets of records, i.e., blocks. To append a new block to the blockchain, parties must race and win to solve a cryptographic puzzle, as known as the *mining* process. The puzzle hardness is parameterized so that the intervals between the growth of blocks are approximately constant at a particular time (about 10 min in Bitcoin). Since each block contains a cryptographic hash function of the previous block, the state of each block is preserved by subsequent blocks. Furthermore, when the blockchain diverges into multiple states, proper parties accept the longest chain. Hence, if an adversary tries to rewrite data contained in a block, it needs to reconstruct the subsequent blocks in addition to the block. The adversary must further make the rewritten chain the longest to get other parties to accept it. However, it is infeasible unless the adversary possesses more than half the computing power of the entire network. That is, a blockchain realizes a tamper-resistant public bulletin board based on the assumption about the computing power of adversaries [3,10].

Bitcoin is a decentralized cryptocurrency based on a blockchain. The Bitcoin ledger manages *transactions* on its blocks. Roughly speaking, a transaction Tx_1 refers to a sender, the amount transferred coins, and the recipient, i.e., it expresses information about "a sender S sends Q coins to a recipient R." The party R can send Q coins to the other party by making a new transaction Tx_2 that refers to Tx_1. Then, Tx_1 becomes a spent transaction and thereafter R cannot re-use it. We can check the balance of a party by referring to all *unspent* transactions corresponding to the party on the blockchain.

Precisely, a transaction form has inputs and outputs. An input specifies a transaction to be used for this remittance. In the above example, the input of Tx_2 is Tx_1('s output). An output (script) specifies the recipient by describing a condition to use the transaction. Typically, the output script contains a signature verification with a public key of the recipient. When a party uses a transaction, he/she needs to write a witness on the transaction as an input script that satisfies the output script of the input transaction. See Fig. 1 that shows the transaction flow in the simplest case. Transaction Tx_2 redeems the previous transaction Tx_1 to use \$$v$. Then, witness w_1 written in the input script of Tx_2 must satisfy the condition ϕ_1, which is the output script of Tx_1. Similarly, to use \$$v$ with reference to Tx_2, it is necessary to create a transaction that holds w in its input script such that $\phi_2(w) = 1$. Hereafter, in the graphical description, an arrow connects the corresponding input and output.

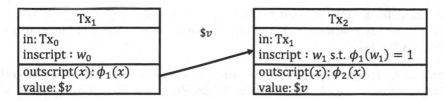

Fig. 1. Graphical description of a transaction flow.

In Bitcoin, by specifying some transactions as inputs, a party can create a transaction to transfer the sum of the coins. Similarly, a single transaction can specify multiple recipients by holding multiple output scripts. Formally, we denote a m-input and l-output transaction in Bitcoin by

$$(\mathsf{in}[m], \mathsf{inscript}[m], \mathsf{value}[l], \mathsf{outscript}[l], \mathsf{lockTime}),$$

where $\mathsf{in}[i]$ is an identifier of the input transaction (i.e., the previous one), $\mathsf{inscript}[i]$ is the corresponding input script (i.e., a witness), $\mathsf{value}[i]$ is the number of coins, $\mathsf{outscript}[i]$ refers to the corresponding output script, and $\mathsf{lockTime}$ specifies the earliest time when the transaction appears on the ledger. Namely, the miners do not approve the transaction until the time specified by $\mathsf{lockTime}$. Note that the sum of the input coins must match the sum of the output coins.

A transaction excluding the input script $(\mathsf{in}[m], \mathsf{value}[l], \mathsf{outscript}[l], \mathsf{lockTime})$ is called the *simplified form*. Typically, as described above, the output script contains a signature verification algorithm to specify the recipient. The input script of the next transaction states a signature in its simplified form in order to prove the creator is the specified recipient.

3   Tournaments with Uniform Winning Probability

3.1   Tournaments with a Single Champion

First, we discuss the case where the champion is only one. In cases of tournaments based on complete binary trees, it is obvious that every party has an equivalent chance to be champion by equating win probabilities of all matches by $1/2$. On the other hand, if it is not a complete binary tree, i.e., the number of matches differs from player to player, then it is necessary to bias the winning probabilities to make the tournament equal for all players. We here present several useful lemmas to make fair tournaments even in such cases. (We show the proofs in Appendix A.)

Let us consider a tournament that may not be a complete binary tree and consider the biased probabilities of each match to make it fair. Suppose a match π of which child nodes are π_{left} and π_{right}. We consider two subtrees such that its root nodes are π_{left} and π_{right}, and let v_{left}^{π} and v_{right}^{π} be the number of leaf nodes in these subtrees, respectively. (Note that, if the entire tournament form is the complete binary tree, then $v_{\mathrm{left}}^{\pi} = v_{\mathrm{right}}^{\pi}$ always holds.) Based on the above notations, for a node π, we define $\mathsf{BiasedPr}(\pi) := v_{\text{left}}^{\pi}/(v_{\text{left}}^{\pi} + v_{\text{right}}^{\pi})$. We can construct a fair tournament based on any binary tree using this function from the following lemma.

Lemma 1. *For any tournament consisting of a binary tree, if the winning probabilities of each match π is set with $(\mathsf{BiasedPr}(\pi), 1 - \mathsf{BiasedPr}(\pi))$, then the tournament is equal for every player.*

3.2 Tournaments with Multiple Champions

Next, we discuss the case of multiple champions. In this case, we must pay attention to the joint winning probabilities of each set of players not only to the winning probability of individual players. For instance, in order to choose two champions, consider the case of dividing the players half into two groups and running a single champion tournament in each group. In this case, although each player has the same probability of being champion, the problem arises that players in the same group can never win simultaneously. To tackle this issue and deal with an arbitrary number of winners, we construct $(k, k + 1)$-lottery protocol. Thus, we first discuss a single eliminate tournament that determines k champions from $k + 1$ players, $(k, k + 1)$-tournament. Afterward, we show that tournaments applicable to an arbitrary number of champions can be constructed by combining multiple $(k, k + 1)$-tournaments.

To construct a $(k, k + 1)$-tournament, we adopt the single-elimination tournament proceeding as follows: First two players p_1 and p_2 play a match π_b. The winning player is determined to be a champion, and the loser $l_1 \in \{p_1, p_2\}$ plays the next match π_2 with p_2. In a similar way, for $i = 1 \ldots k - 1$, player p_{i+1} and the previous match loser l_{i-1} plays a match π_i. The loser of $(k - 1)$-th match π_{k-1} becomes the only loser of the tournament.

Lemma 2. *If the winning probabilities of match π_i between l_{i-1} and p_{i+1} is set with $(i/(i+1), 1 - i/(i+1))$ for $i = 1 \ldots k - 1$, then the tournament is equal for every player. Moreover, for any subset $S \subset P$ such that $|S| = k$, the probability of winning the parties in S simultaneously is also equivalent.*

We can construct a (k, n)-tournaments for arbitrary k and n by running $(n - j, n - j + 1)$-tournament for $j = 1 \ldots n - k$. Concretely, the winners of $(n - j', n - j' + 1)$-tournament continue the next $(n - j' - 1, n - j')$-tournament to further determine one loser, and the players continue such process until the remaining winners are k players.

Lemma 3. *For any positive integers k and n with $k < n$, if a (k, n)-tournament is composed of sequential executions of $(n - j, n - j + 1)$-tournament for $j = 1 \ldots n - k$, then the probability of being the winner of a tournament is equivalent for every player. Moreover, for any subset $S \subset P$ such that $|S| = k$, the probability of winning the parties in S simultaneously is also equivalent.*

4   Definition of Secure Lottery Protocol

Suppose a game in which each of n player bets \$$\alpha$. A secure (k, n)-lottery protocol is a cryptographic protocol to k champions who obtain \$$(n\alpha/k)$ from them *fairly*. This section presents the security model of this protocol.

Hereafter, we say that player p can freely redeem transaction Tx if p holds a witness that satisfies the output script of Tx. Let *wealth* of player p at round t mean the total amount of coins in transactions such that p can freely redeem at round t. Note that we ignore coins not involved in the protocol. Also, *payoff* of player p refers to the difference between wealth at the beginning of the protocol and at the end.

Before presenting formal descriptions, we discuss an intuitive understanding of security requirements. First, we focus on the case of $k = 1$, i.e., the champion is only one. As a premise, if all players behave honestly, it is necessary to determine the champion uniformly at random. Of course, it is ideal to achieve this property even in the presence of an adversary. However, such a requirement is somewhat too strong to achieve. For instance, an adversary may abort early after the start of a protocol. In this case, since the protocol terminates without determining the champion, it does not fulfill the condition of determining the champion uniformly at random. Thus, in the case where corrupted players exist, we relax the requirement. More concretely, a secure protocol ensures that the expected value of honest parties' payoffs is never negative for the arbitrary strategy of the adversary.

In the case of $k \geq 2$, the requirements are almost similar to the above, however, there is one additional condition that comes from having multiple champions. We require that, if all players are honest, for any set of players $W \subset P$ such that $|W| = k$, the probability that W becomes champions is the same. In other words, it ensures that not only the tournament is fair for individual players, but also is equal for each set of players. It is also necessary that, if an adversary violates this property, its expected payoff becomes negative. This requirement means that adversaries cannot prevent a certain set of players from becoming champions simultaneously without loss.

To capture the above requirements formally, we introduce several notations. Let $\sigma_{\mathcal{A}}$ denote a strategy set of a PPTA adversary $\mathcal{A}$, and let st_0 denote the ledger state at the beginning of the protocol. We denote by $\Omega(p, st_0, t, \sigma_{\mathcal{A}})$ a random variable of wealth of player p at round t. In the case where there is no corrupted party, we describe $\sigma_{\mathcal{A}} = \bot$. Let β and ϵ denote the round number at the beginning and at the end of the protocol, respectively. We define a random variable with respect to payoff as follows.

$$\Phi(p, st_0, \sigma_{\mathcal{A}}) = \Omega(p, st_0, \epsilon, \sigma_{\mathcal{A}}) - \Omega(p, st_0, \beta, \sigma_{\mathcal{A}}) \tag{1}$$

We denote by $E(\Phi(p, st_0, \sigma_{\mathcal{A}}))$ the expected value of the payoff.

Definition 1. *We say a $(1, n)$-lottery protocol Π is secure if Π fulfills the followings except a negligible probability in η:*

- If all players are honest, $E(\Phi(p, st_0, \perp)) = 0$ and $\Omega(p, st_0, \epsilon, \perp) \in \{-\alpha, \alpha(n-1)\}$ for all $p \in P$.
- For all PPTA adversaries $\mathcal{A}$, i.e., if there exist corrupted players, $E(\Phi(p, st_0, \sigma_\mathcal{A})) \geq 0$ holds for all $p \in H$.

Definition 2. We say a (k, n)-lottery protocol Π is secure if Π fulfills the followings except a negligible probability in η:

- If all players are honest, $E(\Phi(p, st_0, \perp)) = 0$ and $\Omega(p, st_0, \epsilon, \perp) \in \{-\alpha, (\alpha/k)(n-k)\}$ for all $p \in P$. Furthermore, $\Pr(\sum_{s \in S} \Omega(s, st_0, \beta, \perp)) = k(n-k)) = \binom{n}{k}^{-1}$ for all $S = \{s_1, \ldots, s_k\} \subset P$.
- For any PPTA adversary $\mathcal{A}$, $E(\Phi(p, st_0, \sigma_\mathcal{A})) \geq 0$ holds for all $p \in H$.
- For any PPTA adversary $\mathcal{A}$, if there exists $S \subseteq H$ such that $|S| \leq k$ and $\Pr(\sum_{s \in S} \Phi(s, st_0, \sigma_\mathcal{A}) = |S|(n-k)) \neq \binom{n-|S|}{k-|S|}^{-1}$, the protocol guarantees that $\sum_{p \in C} E(\Phi(p, st_0, \sigma_\mathcal{A})) < 0$.

To achieve a secure protocol, we require players to input *deposit* in addition to the bets. The deposits play a roll of compensation for honest players when an adversary behaves maliciously. We say that a protocol is constant-deposit if the deposit amount of every player is a constant value independent from the number of players.

5 $(1, n)$-Lottery Protocol with Constant Deposits

This section presents a $(1, n)$-lottery protocol for an arbitrary positive integer n. We suppose that a bet amount of each party is $\alpha = 1$. Our protocol is based on single-elimination tournaments with binary tree structure. The tournament consists of $n - 1$ two-player matches: the winners of the matches at level $l \in [L]$ play at the next level $l-1$, where L is the tree depth. The winner of the match at level 0 obtains \n as a reward. Bartoletti and Zunino's protocol set the winning probability to $1/2$ in each match. To construct a protocol for an arbitrary number of players, it is necessary to modify it so that all players are fair to win even if the tournament is not the complete binary tree. The main idea of our protocol is to bias the probability of winning in each match.

5.1   Building Block: Biased Coin-Tossing Protocol

We denote with τ_{Ledger} the sufficient time to write a transaction on the ledger and confirm it. (It is about 60 min in Bitcoin.) We denote by $K_p(\mathsf{Tx}, \pi, \mathcal{P})$ a key pair of player p for transaction Tx, which corresponds to a match π. $\mathcal{P}$ refers to players' identifiers corresponding to the match. We suppose that the private part of key pairs is kept secret by p. (Note that we write signing and verification keys without distinguishing between them.) We define $\mathbf{K}(\mathsf{Tx}, \pi, \mathcal{P}) := \{K_p(\mathsf{Tx}, \pi, \mathcal{P}) \,|\, p \in P\}$.

Let $(\mathsf{ver}, \mathsf{sig})$ be a signature scheme. Following Bartoletti and Zunino's work, we allow the partial signature that enables to exclude of the input field from the signature subjects. It allows to generate a signature on a transaction before determining the input field of the transaction. Namely, we use the malleability of input fields.

Hereafter, a signature written in the input field of transaction $\mathsf{Tx} = (\mathsf{in}[m],$ $\mathsf{inscript}[m], \mathsf{value}[l], \mathsf{outscript}[l], \mathsf{lockTime})$ is for $(\mathsf{value}[l], \mathsf{outscript}[l], \mathsf{lockTime})$. Below, we omit the inputs of signatures and refer to it as $\mathsf{sig}_{K_p(\mathsf{Tx},\pi,\mathcal{P})}$.

Also, $\mathsf{sig}_{\mathbf{K}(\mathsf{Tx},\pi,\mathcal{P})}$ means the multi-signature with $\mathbf{K}(\mathsf{Tx}, \pi, \mathcal{P})$.

As described the previous section, we construct a protocol based on a tournament structure. Thus, before presenting our lottery protocol, we show a protocol to realize a match between two parties. Since we deal with tournaments not the complete binary tree, it is necessary to bias some matches to ensure all players to have the same probability of winning the tournament. Hence, we construct a match protocol, called a biased coin tossing protocol, that can parameterize the winning probability.

To handle biased probabilities, we introduce a *winner function* to determine the winner in a match. Let a and b be players that hold secrets s_a and s_b, respectively. We consider a match such that the winner depends on s_a and s_b, and define the function to determine the winner as follows.

$$\text{Winner}(s_a, s_b, v_a, v_b) = \begin{cases} a & \text{if } s_a + s_b \,(\text{mod } v_a + v_b) < v_a, \\ b & \text{otherwise.} \end{cases} \tag{2}$$

where v_a and v_b are positive integers. Hereafter, we suppose that s_a and s_b are sampled from $[v_a + v_b]$ uniformly at random.[1] The output $x \in \{a, b\}$ means the winner of the match.

See Protocol 1 and Fig. 2 that shows a protocol of realizing a match π_i in a tournament. (Suppose π_a and π_b be the child nodes of π_i.) A match consists of three types of transactions, Win, Turn1, and Turn2. At the beginning of the protocol, suppose $\mathsf{Win}(\pi_a, a)$ and $\mathsf{Win}(\pi_b, b)$ being on the ledger, which implies that player a and b won the previous matches π_a and π_b, respectively. Now, they play a match π_i. Turn1 is used to aggregate the coins of $\mathsf{Win}(\pi_a, a)$ for the preparation of the match. Turn2 is a transaction of which input is Turn1. See the output script of Turn1. To redeem Turn1, a player must write s_a on the input script of Turn2. Thus, putting Turn2 on the ledger implies to reveal a's secret $s_a^{\pi_i}$. $\mathsf{Win}(\pi_i, a)$ and $\mathsf{Win}(\pi_i, b)$ are transactions of which input is Turn2. See the output script of Turn2. To redeem Turn2, a player must write $s_a^{\pi_i}$ and $s_b^{\pi_i}$ on the input script of the next transaction. Thus, to redeem Turn2, player b must reveal his/her secret $s_b^{\pi_i}$. Furthermore, since $s_a^{\pi_i}$ and $s_b^{\pi_i}$ satisfy either $a = \text{Winner}(s_a^{\pi_i}, s_b^{\pi_i}, v_a, v_b)$ or $b = \text{Winner}(s_a^{\pi_i}, s_b^{\pi_i}, v_a, v_b)$, players can put only one of $\mathsf{Win}(\pi_i, a)$ and $\mathsf{Win}(\pi_i, b)$ on the ledger. The transaction put on the ledger refers to the winner of this match and is used as the input of Turn1 in the next match.

---

[1] In our protocol, players commit the secrets at the beginning of the protocol by using a cryptographic hash function. Thus, more precisely, we need to extend the bit lengths of secrets to an appropriate length by adding multiples of $v_a + v_b$.

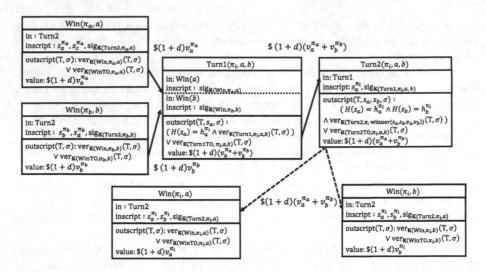

Fig. 2. Graphical description of biased coin-tossing (for match π_i).

5.2 Our Construction of $(1\text{-}n)$-Lottery

The Biased Probability of Each Match in $(1, n)$-Lottery. First, we present the biased probability of each match. Let us consider a match π of which child nodes π_a and π_b. As in Sect. 3.1, we consider two subtrees such that its root nodes are π_a and π_b, and let v_a^π and v_b^π be the number of leaf nodes in these subtrees, respectively. From Lemma 1, we set the winner function in each match π of our $(1, n)$-lottery protocol as $\text{Winner}(s_a^\pi, s_b^\pi, v_a^\pi, v_b^\pi)$.

Our protocol is applicable to an arbitrary binary tree. Let $\Pi \subseteq \{\{0,1\}^n \mid 1 \le n \le L\}$ be a binary tree applied to our protocol, and it has L levels. Based on the binary tree and the biased probability, our protocol proceeds as follows.

Precondition: For all $p \in P$, the ledger contains a transaction Bet_p with value $\$(1 + d)$, and redeemable with key $K_p(\text{Bet}_p)$.

Initialization phase:

1. For all player $p \in P$, p generates the following secret keys locally. Each player p generates all the following key pairs.
   - For all π such that π is leaf and every $p \in P$:
     $K_p(\text{Bet}_p), K_p(\text{CollectW}), K_p(\text{Init}, a)$
   - For all π and every $p \in P$:
     $K_p(\text{Win}, \pi, a), K_p(\text{WinTo}, \pi, a)$
   - For all π such that π is neither leaf nor root and every $a, b \in P$ such that $a, b \sqsubset \pi$:
     $K_p(\text{Turn1To}, \pi, a, b), K_p(\text{Turn1}, \pi, a), K_p(\text{Turn2To}, \pi, a, b), K_p(\text{Turn2}, \pi, a), K_p(\text{Timeout1}, \pi, a, b), K_p(\text{Timeout2}, \pi, a, b)$

Protocol 1. Biased Coin-Tossing $\Pi^W_{a,b}(s_a, s_b, v_a, v_b)$

Setup:

1: The initialization phase was completed, and $\mathsf{Win}(\pi, a)$ and $\mathsf{Win}(\pi, b)$ have been put already on the ledger. Players a and b hold secrets s_a and s_b, respectively. Let τ be the round of the beginning of the protocol.

Procedure:

2: One of the players puts $\mathsf{Turn1}(\pi, a, b)$ on the ledger.

3: a writes s_a on the input script of $\mathsf{Turn2}(\pi, a, b)$, and put the transaction on the ledger.

4: **if** $\mathsf{Turn2}(\pi, a, b)$ does not appear within $\tau + 2\tau_{\text{Ledger}}$ **then**

5:     One of the players puts $\mathsf{Timeout1}(\pi, a, b)$ on the ledger.

6:     One of the players puts $\mathsf{Win}(\pi, b)$ on the ledger.

7: b computes $w = \mathsf{Winner}(s_a, s_b, v_a, v_b)$

8: **if** $w = a$ **then**

9:     b puts $\mathsf{Win}(\pi, a)$ on the ledger.

10: **if** $w = b$ **then**

11:     b puts $\mathsf{Win}(\pi, b)$ on the ledger.

12: **if** $\mathsf{Win}(\pi, x \in \{a, b\})$ does not appear within $\tau + 4\tau_{\text{Ledger}}$ **then**

13:     One of the players puts $\mathsf{Timeout2}(\pi, a, b)$ into the ledger.

14:     One of the players puts $\mathsf{Win}(\pi, a)$ on the ledger.

---

2. For all player $p \in P$, p generates secrets $s_p^{\pi_p}$ for each π_p, such that $(|\pi_p| < L)$, and broadcasts to the other players his/her public keys and hashes $h_p^{\pi_p} = H(s_p^{\pi_p})$.

3. If $h_p^{\pi_p} = h_p^{\pi_p'}$ for some $(p, \pi_p) \neq (p', \pi_p')$, the players abort.

4. Parties agree the time τ_{Init} large enough to fall after the initialization phase.

5. Each player signs all transaction templates in Fig. 3 except for Init, and broadcasts the signatures.

6. Each player verifies the signatures received by the others. Some signature is not valid or missing, the player aborts the protocol.

7. Each player signs Init, and sends the signature to the first player.

8. The first player puts the (signed) transaction Init on the ledger.

9. If Init does not appear within one τ_{Ledger}, then each p redeems Bet_p and aborts.

10. The players put the signed transactions $\mathsf{Win}(p, p)$ on the ledger, for all $p \in P$.

Tournament execution phase: For all levels $l = L \ldots 1$, players proceed as follows: Run $\Pi^W_{a,b}(s_a^{\pi_a}, s_b^{\pi_b}, v_a^{\pi_a}, v_b^{\pi_b})$ for each π, such that $|\pi| = l-1$, in parallel. Then, $v_a^{\pi_a}, v_b^{\pi_b}$ denote the biased probability determined in the manner shown in the above.[2]

Garbage collection phase: If there is some unredeemed $\mathsf{Win}(\pi, p)$ such that π is not the root on the ledger, players put $\mathsf{CollectOrphanWin}(\pi, p)$ on the

---

[2] Only the Win transaction corresponding to the winner of the final match uses the template for the root node. See Fig. 3, and $\mathsf{Win}(\pi_r, a)$ is the corresponding template.

ledger. (If all players behave honestly, this step is not carried out. It is a countermeasure for the transaction insertion attack, shown in Sect. 5.3.)

At step 2, players prepare all transactions that may be used in the protocol. Note that they then signs the transactions using signing keys of all players. Thus, after this step, it is not possible for some players to collude and forge transactions, except for input and input script fields. The number of transactions created in this step is $O(n^2)$, which is derived from the number of possible match combinations. See $\mathsf{Win}(\pi_r, a)$ in Fig. 3 that is a transaction for the champion. At the end of the tournament execution phase, only the champion is freely redeemable a $\mathsf{Win}(\pi_r, a)$ and can obtain $\$(n+d)$, which is the reward and deposit for the champion. Furthermore, $\mathsf{Win}(\pi_r, a)$ holds outputs to return deposits for each player.

5.3   Transaction Insertion Attack

In our scheme, as in the Bartoletti-Zunino scheme, an adversary can turn an honest player who should be the winner into the loser in a match.

The details of the attack are described below.

Settings. Consider a match π with honest player a and malicious player b, where they are winners of the previous matches π_0 and π_1, respectively. Let player c be the loser of π_0, and let π' be the parent node of π. Player b has a freely redeemable transaction T_b with $\$(v_a^\pi + v_b^\pi)(1+d)$ in the external to the protocol.

Procedures. Suppose when honest player a puts $\mathsf{Turn2}(\pi, a, b)$ on the ledger in the biased coin tossing protocol for π, player b realizes that he has lost the match. Then, b redeems T_b through a transaction $\mathsf{Win}(\pi, b)$ by malleating its input and input script fields. (Note that in our scheme, we assume the input malleability.)

Player b can now redeem both his transaction and $\mathsf{Win}(\pi', c)$ by putting $\mathsf{Turn1}(\pi_1, b, c)$ on the ledger. Player a can redeem the pending $\mathsf{Turn2}(\pi, a, b)$ (after its timeout has expired) using $\mathsf{Timeout2}(\pi, a, b)$, and then redeem that with $\mathsf{Win}(\pi, a)$. This transaction is now orphan, i.e. it can no longer be used in the next rounds because its $\mathsf{Win}(\pi', c)$ was already redeemed by b. However, the orphan transaction can be redeemed in the garbage collection phase by $\mathsf{CollectW}(\pi, a)$. Thus, player a can collect $\$(v_a^\pi + v_b^\pi)(1 + d)$ at the garbage collection phase.

As shown above, in order to realize this attack in match π, an adversary needs to invest additional coins $\$(v_a^\pi + v_b^\pi)(1+d)$ into the protocol. The affected honest player can collect $\$d$ by the root $\mathsf{Win}(\pi_r, a)$ and $\$(v_a^\pi + v_b^\pi)(1 + d)$ by the garbage collection. Informally, this adversarial scenario does not affect the security since the honest player who is applied this attack would rather gain due to the deposit. We present security proof of our protocol in the next subsection.

5.4   Security Proof

This section shows security proof of our $(1, n)$-lottery protocol. Our proof is based on the fact that the possible attack strategies for adversaries is only the transaction insertion attack or the rejection of revealing their secrets.

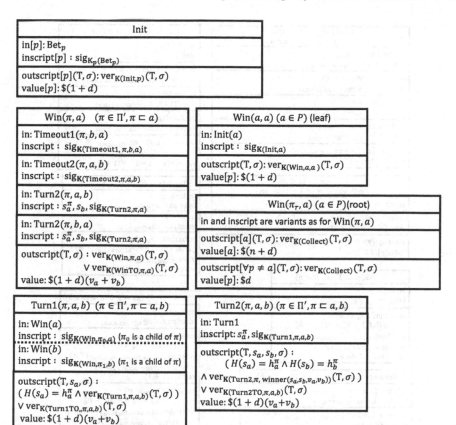

Fig. 3. Transaction templates used in our protocols. Let Π' be the set of nodes excluding leafs and the root. (Part I) Transaction templates for our $(1, n)$-lottery protocol. The dashed line in the inscript field indicates that both inscripts are redeemed at the same time. On the other hand, a solid line indicates that only one of the inscriptions is redeemed.

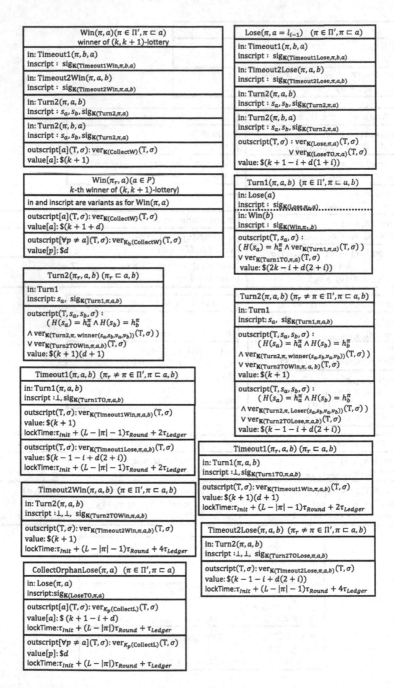

Fig. 4. (Part II) Transaction templates for our $(k, k+1)$-lottery protocol. Let π_i denote i-th match of the protocol. We omit Win and Init descriptions since they are almost the same in Fig. 3. The differences from Fig. 3 are just changes of the values $\$(1+d)$ to $\$(k+d)$.

Theorem 1. *Our $(1,n)$-lottery protocol is secure and constant deposit.*

Proof (Sketch). We prove that our protocol fulfills the Definition 1. In the case of $C = \emptyset$, it is obvious from Lemma 1. If an adversary deviates from the procedure or aborts at some step in the initialization phase, players terminate the protocol. In this case, all honest players do not lose money since no money transfers occur. Thus, we suppose that the initialization phase completes correctly. Below, we discuss two cases in the tournament execution phase, (i) an adversary rejects to reveal its secrets and (ii) an adversary applies the transaction insertion attack, described in Sect. 5.3.

In the case of (i), the biased coin-tossing protocol guarantees that the player who did not reveal the secret is treated as a loser. Thus, no honest player is lost nevertheless an adversary refuses to disclose its secret in any matches.

In the case of (ii), let us consider the case where an adversary applies the transaction insertion attack to a player p at match π. The player p obtains payoff $\$(v_p^\pi + d - 1)$ by CollectOrphanWin at the end of the protocol, as described Sect. 5.3. Note that, in this case, the player p does not reveal his/her secret corresponding to match π. Furthermore, at the beginning of the match, we can express the expected payoff of p as follows

$$\frac{v_p^\pi}{v_p^{\pi_r}} \times \$(n-1) + (1 - \frac{v_p^\pi}{v_p^{\pi_r}}) \times \$(-1) = \$(v_p^\pi - 1) \tag{3}$$

The inequality $v_p^\pi + d - 1 > v_p^\pi - 1$ implies that $E(\Phi(p, st_0, \sigma_\mathcal{A})) > 0$ if $d > 0$. Also, this property holds for an arbitrary positive integer d, our protocol satisfies constant-deposit. From the above, $(1,n)$-lottery protocol is secure.   □

6 (k,n)-Lottery Protocol with Constant Deposits

This section shows our (k,n)-lottery protocol for arbitrary k and n and $(k, k+1)$-lottery protocol for arbitrary k and $k + 1$. We compose a (k,n)-lottery protocol from a composition of $(k, k + 1)$-lottery protocols as follows:

First n parties run $(n-1, n)$-lottery and determine one loser. Thereafter, the remaining $n-1$ winners run $(n-2, n-1)$-lottery and further determine one loser. Parties repeat the similar process until removing $n - k$ players, i.e., resulting in k winners.

6.1 Building Block: Modified Biased Coin-Tossing Protocol

We adopt the single-elimination tournament as described in Lemma 2 to construct a $(k, k+1)$-lottery protocol. That is, it is a tournament where the winner of each match becomes the champion of $(k, k + 1)$-lottery, and the loser moves on to the next match.

Protocol 2. Modified Biased Coin-Tossing $\Pi^{WL}_{a,b}(s_a, s_b, v_a, v_b)$

Setup:
1: The initialization phase was successfully completed, and $\mathsf{Lose}(\pi, a)$ and $\mathsf{Win}(\pi, b)$ have been put already on the ledger. Players a and b hold secrets s^π_a and s^π_b, respectively. Let τ be the round of the beginning of the protocol.

Procedure:
2: One of the players puts $\mathsf{Turn1}(\pi, a, b)$ on the ledger.
3: a writes s^π_a on the input script of $\mathsf{Turn2}(\pi, a, b)$, and put the transaction on the ledger.
4: **if** $\mathsf{Turn2}(\pi, a, b)$ does not appear within $\tau + 2\tau_{\mathsf{Ledger}}$ **then**
5:     One of the players puts $\mathsf{Timeout1}(\pi, a, b)$ on the ledger.
6:     One of the players puts $\mathsf{Win}(\pi, b)$ and $\mathsf{Lose}(\pi, a)$ on the ledger.
7: b computes $w = \mathsf{Winner}(s_a, s_b, v_a, v_b)$
8: **if** $w = a$ **then**
9:     b puts $\mathsf{Win}(\pi, a)$ and $\mathsf{Lose}(\pi, b)$ on the ledger.
10: **if** $w = b$ **then**
11:     b puts $\mathsf{Win}(\pi, b)$ and $\mathsf{Lose}(\pi, a)$ on the ledger.
12: **if** $\mathsf{Win}(\pi, x \in \{a, b\})$ does not appear within $\tau + 4\tau_{\mathsf{Ledger}}$ **then**
13:     One of the players puts $\mathsf{Timeout2Win}(\pi, a, b)$ into the ledger.
14:     One of the players puts $\mathsf{Win}(\pi, a)$ on the ledger.
15: **if** $\mathsf{Lose}(\pi, x \in \{a, b\})$ does not appear within $\tau + 4\tau_{\mathsf{Ledger}}$ **then**
16:     One of the players puts $\mathsf{Timeout2Lose}(\pi, a, b)$ into the ledger.
17:     One of the players puts $\mathsf{Lose}(\pi, a)$ on the ledger.

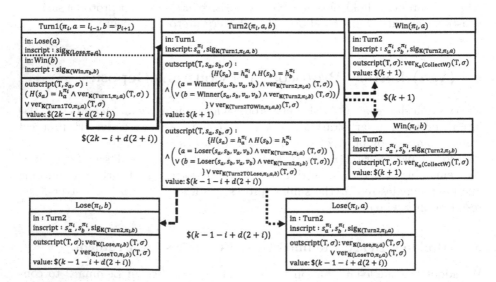

Fig. 5. Graphical description of modified biased coin-tossing (for match π_i). We denote with π_a and π_b child nodes of π_i. Note that Win and Lose redeemed by $\mathsf{Turn1}$ are omitted.

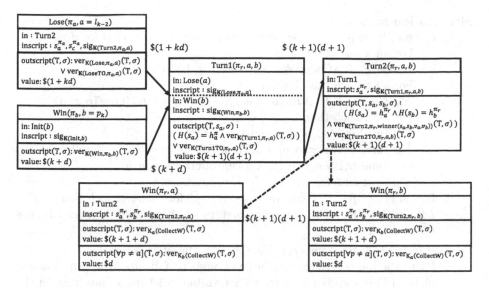

Fig. 6. Graphical description of biased coin-tossing (for match π_r) for the final match of $(k, k+1)$-lottery.

Protocol 1 is insufficient to implement such a tournament since it does not enable the loser to proceed to the next match. Hence, we here modify the protocol to resolve this problem.

See Protocol 2 and Fig. 5 that show the modified protocol. The Loser function described in the Lose transaction returns the inverse of Winner function, i.e., it specifies the loser. That is, unlike Protocol 5.1, the loser also puts Lose transaction of which input is Turn2, and receives coins used in the next match. Moreover, since Turn2 has two output scripts, we set the timeouts for each of Win and Lose by preparing Timeout2Win and Timeout2Lose transactions. If Win or Lose is not published within the time limit, it is dealt with by publishing Timeout2Win or Timeout2Lose respectively. Figure 7 shows flows of procedures when a timeout occurs.

6.2 Our Construction of $(k, k+1)$-Lottery Protocol

Let the bet mount be $\$k$ for each player in this section.

The Biased Probability of Each Match in $(k, k+1)$-Lottery. Suppose a match between p_{i+1} and l_{i-1} in i-th match π_i, where l_{i-1} is the loser of $(i-1)$-th match. From Lemma 2, for $i = 1 \ldots k - 1$, the winning probability of p_{i+1} in π_i is set as $i/(i+1)$.

Based on the biased probability, our protocol proceeds as follows.

Precondition: for all players, the ledger contains a transaction Bet_p with value $\$(1 + d)$, and redeemable with key $K_p(\mathsf{Bet}_p)$.

Initialization phase:

1. For all player $p \in P$, p generates the following secret keys locally.
   - For all π such that $|\pi| = L$:
     $K_p(\mathsf{Bet}_p), K_p(\mathsf{CollectW}), K_p(\mathsf{CollectL}), K_p(\mathsf{Init}, a)$
   - For all π such that $1 \le |\pi| \le L$:
     $K_p(\mathsf{Win}, \pi, a), K_p(\mathsf{WinTo}, \pi, a), K_p(\mathsf{Lose}, \pi, a), K_p(\mathsf{LoseTo}, \pi, a)$
   - For all π such that $1 \le |\pi| < L$:
     $K_p(\mathsf{Turn1To}, \pi, a, b), K_p(\mathsf{Turn1}, \pi, a, b),$
     $K_p(\mathsf{Turn2ToWin}, \pi, a, b), K_p(\mathsf{Turn2ToLose}, \pi, a, b), K_p(\mathsf{Turn2}, \pi, a),$
     $K_p(\mathsf{Timeout1Win}, \pi, a, b), K_p(\mathsf{Timeout1Lose}, \pi, a, b),$
     $K_p(\mathsf{Timeout2Win}, \pi, a, b), K_p(\mathsf{Timeout2Lose}, \pi, a, b)$
2. For all player $p \in P$, p generates secrets $s_p^{\pi_p}$ for each π_p, such that $(|\pi_p| < L)$, and broadcasts to the other players his/her public keys and hashes $h_p^{\pi_p} = H(s_p^{\pi_p})$.
3. If $h_p^{\pi_p} = h_{p'}^{\pi_{p'}}$ for some $(p, \pi_p) \ne (p', \pi_{p'})$, the players abort.
4. Parties agree the time τ_{Init} large enough to fall after the initialization phase. (This step is necessary to determine lockTime values built in the subsequent steps.)
5. Each player signs all the transaction templates in Fig. 3 and 4 except for Init and broadcasts the signatures.
6. Each player verifies the signatures received by the others. some signature is not valid or missing, the player aborts the protocol.
7. Each player signs Init, and sends the signature to the first player.
8. The first player puts the (signed) transaction Init on the ledger.
9. If Init does not appear within one τ_{Ledger}, then each p redeems Bet_p and aborts.
10. The players put the signed transactions $\mathsf{Win}(p, p)$ on the ledger, for all $p \in P$.

Tournament execution phase: For levels $i = k - 1 \ldots 2$, players proceed as follows: Run $\Pi_{a,b}^{\mathsf{WL}}(s_a^{\pi_i}, s_b^{\pi_i}, v_a^{\pi_i}, v_b^{\pi_i})$ for each π, such that $|\pi| = i - 1$.

For level $i = 1$, players proceed as follows: Run $\Pi_{a,b}^{\mathsf{W}}(s_a^{\pi_i}, s_b^{\pi_i}, v_a^{\pi_i}, v_b^{\pi_i})$. Then, v_a^π, v_b^π denote the biased probability determined in the manner shown in the previous subsection.

Garbage collection phase: If there is some unredeemed $\mathsf{Win}(\pi, p)$ such that π is a leaf on the ledger, players put $\mathsf{CollectOrphanWin}(\pi, p)$ on the ledger. Similarly, if there is some unredeemed $\mathsf{Lose}(\pi, p)$ on the ledger, players put $\mathsf{CollectOrphanLose}(\pi, p)$ on the ledger.

At the end of the tournament execution phases, all champions can freely redeem $\mathsf{Win}(\pi, a)$ or $\mathsf{Win}(\pi_r, a)$ as rewards. Also, $\mathsf{Win}(\pi_r, a)$ guarantees that every honest party can collect their deposits. As in Protocol 5.1, the number of transactions prepared at step 5 is $O(n^2)$.

Theorem 2. *Our $(k, k + 1)$-lottery protocol is secure and constant deposit.*

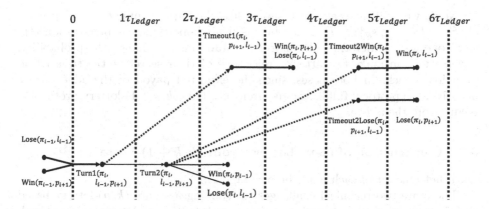

Fig. 7. Graph of the transactions in a tournament round. An arrow from transaction T to T' means that T redeems T'. Thick arrows mean any player can redeem; dashed edges mean any player can redeem, but only after a timeout. Thin arrows mean that only the player who knows the secret on the label can redeem it. $\tau_{Round} := 6\tau_{Ledger}$ refers to the number of rounds in each match.

Proof (Sketch). We prove that our protocol fulfills Definition 2. In the case of $C = \emptyset$, it is obvious from Theorem 2. As in the proof of Theorem 1, we suppose that the initialization phase completes correctly and focuses on the tournament execution phase.

Below, we discuss two cases in the tournament execution phase: (i) an adversary rejects to reveal its secrets, and (ii) an adversary applies the transaction insertion attack, described in Sect. 5.3. The proof of case (i) is omitted since the same argument holds for Theorem 1. For case (ii), we consider further dividing it into the following two cases: (a) an adversary applies the transaction insertion attack to player p_{i+1} at match π_i, where π_i is the first match for p_{i+1}, (b) an adversary applies the attack to player l_{i+1} at match π_i, where l_{i+1} is the loser of the previous match.

Then, the player p_{i+1} obtains payoff $\$(k+d)$ at the end of the protocol. Also, player l_{i-1} at match π_i obtains payoff $\$(1 - i + d)$ by CollectOrphanWin at the end of the protocol. Thus, to confirm that the honest party does not lose by the attack, it requires that the obtained payoff is more than the expected payoff at match π_i. In the case of (a), for any π_i, the expected payoff of player p_i is 0 because p_i because it is fair to the players from Theorem 2.

In the case of (b), The expected payoff of honest l_{i-1} is as follows.

$$\frac{k + 1 - i}{k + 1} \times \$1 + (\frac{i}{k + 1}) \times \$(-k) = \$(1 - i) \tag{4}$$

From this Eq. (4), we can see $E(\Phi(p, st_0, \sigma_{\mathcal{A}})) - E(\Phi(p, st_0, \bot)) > 0$ since $1 - i + d > 1 - i$ for $i \in [k]$ if $d > 0$. It implies that the l_{i-1}'s expected payoff when the adversary applies the transaction insertion attack is larger than their expected payoff when all parties behave honestly.

Next, we confirm that every subset has the same winning probability for all $S = \{s_1, \ldots, s_k\} \subset P$. It is obvious if all honest parties behave honestly since one loser is determined uniformly at random. To change the probability, adversaries can make two attacks: rejections of their secret or the transaction insertion attack. In both cases, since the expected payoff of the adversary is negative, the protocol fulfills the requirement. This $(k, k + 1)$-lottery protocol is secure from the above. □

6.3 Construction of $(k\text{-}n)$-Lottery from $(k, k + 1)$-Lottery

Let a bet amount of each party be $\alpha = n!/k!$.

There are two technical challenges to realizing a secure (k, n)-lottery based on this strategy. The first one is to connect each $(k', k' + 1)$-lottery protocol such that malicious parties cannot escape the protocol in the middle. This issue is derived from the fact that if parties run several lottery protocols sequentially, corrupted players can abort without losing at the initialization process of the next lottery. To circumvent this issue, we aggregate the initialization processes of all protocols in the first $(n - 1, n)$-lottery protocol. That is, players prepare all of the secrets, signing (verification) keys, and transactions used in the entire (k, n)-lottery in the initialization of $(n - 1, n)$-lottery protocol. By this modification, parties can skip all initialization phases after the completion of $(n - 1, n)$-lottery protocol. Note that the number of transactions created in the initialization phase is $O(n^3)$, which can be derived from the number of possible match combinations.

Further, we also slightly change the tournament execution phase, except for the last $(k, k + 1)$ lottery protocol. More concretely, we modify each match protocol, i.e., Fig. 5 and 6, such that Win transactions connect two tournament execution phases. See Appendix B for the modification details.

As the second challenge, it is necessary to ensure that (k, n)-lottery composed of sequential executions of $(n - j, n - j + 1)$-lottery for $j \in [n - k]$ is indeed fair. We present the security proof of our (k, n)-lottery protocol below.

Theorem 3 *Our (k, n)-lottery protocol is secure and constant deposit.*

Proof (Sketch). We prove that our (k, n)-lottery protocol fulfills Definition 2.

As in the proof of our $(k, k + 1)$-lottery protocol, we focus on the payoff obtained by a player who is affected by the transaction insertion attack at π_i^j, where π_i^j is i-th match of j-th $(n - j, n - j + 1)$-lottery protocol.

We denote by w_i^j and l_i^j the winner and loser of match π_i^j, respectively. As in the proof of Theorem 2, we consider further dividing case (ii) into the following two cases: (a) an adversary applies the transaction insertion attack to player l_{i-1}^j at match π_i, (b) the attack to player w_{i+1}^{j-1} at match π_i^j. In the case of (b), the player l_{i-1}^j obtains payoff $\$((n-1)!/\{(k-1)!(n-j+1)(n-j)\} \times (nj-ni-j^2+j)+d)$ at the end of the protocol. Thus, to confirm that the honest party does not lose by the attack, it requires that the obtained payoff is more than the expected payoff at match π_i^j. The expected payoff of honest l_{i-1}^j is as follows.

$$\frac{(n-j+1-i)k}{(n-j+1)(n-j)} \times \$\frac{(n-1)!(n-k)}{k!} + (1 - \frac{(n-j+1-i)k}{(n-j+1)(n-j)}) \times \$(-\frac{(n-1)!}{k!})$$
$$= \$\frac{(n-1)!}{(k-1)!(n-j+1)(n-j)}(nj - ni - j^2 + j).$$

Note that $((n-j+1-i)k)/((n-j+1)(n-j))$ is the winning probability of l_{i-1}^j. From then on, we could prove similar to the proof of our $(k, k+1)$-lottery protocol. A similar calculation in the case of (a) shows no loss. Hence, our (k, n)-lottery is secure. $\qquad\square$

Acknowledgment. This work was supported by JSPS KAKENHI Grant Numbers JP18H05289, JP21H03395, JP21H03441, JP22H03590, JP23H00468, JP23H00479, 23K17455, JP23K16880, JST CREST JPMJCR22M1, JPMJCR23M2, and MEXT Leading Initiative for Excellent Young Researchers.

A   Proofs of Lemmas

Proof of Lemma 1: Let $\pi_{l \in [L]}$ such that $|\pi_l| = l$ be the l-th match for player p. Suppose v_p^l / v_p^{l-1} be the probability that p wins at π_l. Then, the probability that p wins the tournament holds:

$$\frac{1}{v_p^l} \times \frac{v_p^l}{v_p^{l-1}} \times \cdots \times \frac{v_p^1}{v_p^0} = \frac{1}{n_p^0} = \frac{1}{N}.$$

This is also true for any player. $\qquad\square$

Proof of Lemma 2: Let π_i such that $|\pi_i| = i \in [k]$ be the i-th match for player p_{i+1} and l_{i-1}, where l_{i-1} is the loser of $(i-1)$-th match The probability that p wins the tournament holds:

$$1 - \frac{i}{i+1} \times \frac{i+1}{i+2} \times \cdots \times \frac{k}{k+1} = \frac{k}{k+1}.$$

This is also true for any player. Moreover, the probability of winning the parties in S simultaneously equals the probability of losing $p \notin S$. Thus, the probability of winning the parties in S simultaneously is equivalent for any $S \subset P$ such that $|S| = k$. $\qquad\square$

Proof of Lemma 3: For any $j \in [k]$, the winning probability in $(n-j, n-j+1)$-lottery can be expressed by $(n-j-1)/(n-j)$, as shown in Lemma 2. Since the probability of each $(k', k'+1)$-lottery is independent, the probability that a player wins the entire (k, n)-lottery can be written as:

$$\frac{n-1}{n} \times \frac{n-2}{n-1} \times \cdots \times \frac{k}{k+1} = \frac{k}{n}.$$

Moreover, since the losers are chosen uniformly at random in each $(k', k'+1)$-lottery, it is obvious that the winning probability of any set of k players is equivalent.

B   Transaction Templates for Constructing (k, n)-Lottery

To combine multiple $(k, k + 1)$-lottery protocols, we modify Win transactions. See Fig. 8 that shows the point of connection between j-th lottery and $(j + 1)$-th lottery protocols. The output scripts of $\text{Win}(\pi^j, a)$ in j-th lottery are used as input of $\text{Win}(\pi^{j+1}, a)$ in $(j + 1)$-th lottery protocol. Furthermore, $\text{Win}(\pi_r^j, a)$ redistributes $\$d$ to $\text{Win}(\pi, a)$ for deposits of the next lottery. With this modification, $K_p(\text{WinInit}, \pi, a)$ and $K_p(\text{Return}, \pi, a)$ are added to the key pairs prepared in the initialization phase.

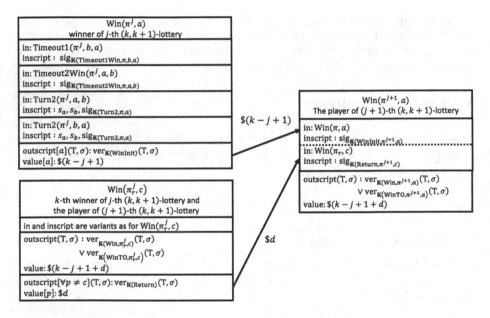

Fig. 8. Graphical description of the connection between j-th lottery and $(j + 1)$-th lottery protocols

References

1. Andrychowicz, M., Dziembowski, S., Malinowski, D., Mazurek, L.: Secure multiparty computations on bitcoin. In: 2014 IEEE Symposium on Security and Privacy, pp. 443–458 (2014). https://doi.org/10.1109/SP.2014.35
2. Back, A., Bentov, I.: Note on fair coin toss via bitcoin. CoRR abs/1402.3698 (2014). http://arxiv.org/abs/1402.3698
3. Badertscher, C., Maurer, U., Tschudi, D., Zikas, V.: Bitcoin as a transaction ledger: a composable treatment. In: Katz, J., Shacham, H. (eds.) Advances in Cryptology - CRYPTO 2017. Lecture Notes in Computer Science(), vol. 10401, pp. 324–356. Springer, Cham (2017). https://doi.org/10.1007/978-3-319-63688-7_11

4. Bartoletti, M., Zunino, R.: Constant-deposit multiparty lotteries on bitcoin. In: Brenner, M., et al. (eds.) Financial Cryptography and Data Security. Lecture Notes in Computer Science(), vol. 10323, pp. 231–247. Springer, Cham (2017). https://doi.org/10.1007/978-3-319-70278-0_15

5. Baum, C., David, B., Dowsley, R.: Insured MPC: efficient secure computation with financial penalties. In: Bonneau, J., Heninger, N. (eds.) Financial Cryptography and Data Security. Lecture Notes in Computer Science(), vol. 12059, pp. 404–420. Springer, Cham (2020). https://doi.org/10.1007/978-3-030-51280-4_22

6. Belenkiy, M., et al.: Making p2p accountable without losing privacy. In: Proceedings of the 2007 ACM Workshop on Privacy in Electronic Society, pp. 31–40. Association for Computing Machinery (2007). https://doi.org/10.1145/1314333.1314339

7. Bentov, I., Kumaresan, R.: How to use bitcoin to design fair protocols. In: Garay, J.A., Gennaro, R. (eds.) Advances in Cryptology - CRYPTO 2014. Lecture Notes in Computer Science, vol. 8617, pp. 421–439. Springer, Berlin (2014). https://doi.org/10.1007/978-3-662-44381-1_24

8. Bentov, I., Kumaresan, R., Miller, A.: Instantaneous decentralized poker. In: Takagi, T., Peyrin, T. (eds.) Advances in Cryptology - ASIACRYPT 2017. Lecture Notes in Computer Science(), vol. 10625, pp. 410–440. Springer, Cham (2017)

9. Chaum, D.: Blind signatures for untraceable payments. In: Chaum, D., Rivest, R.L., Sherman, A.T. (eds.) Advances in Cryptology, pp. 199–203. Springer, Boston (1983). https://doi.org/10.1007/978-1-4757-0602-4_18

10. Choudhuri, A.R., Goyal, V., Jain, A.: Founding secure computation on blockchains. In: Ishai, Y., Rijmen, V. (eds.) Advances in Cryptology - EUROCRYPT 2019. Lecture Notes in Computer Science(), vol. 11477, pp. 351–380. Springer, Cham (2019). https://doi.org/10.1007/978-3-030-17656-3_13

11. Cleve, R.: Limits on the security of coin flips when half the processors are faulty. In: Proceedings of the Eighteenth Annual ACM Symposium on Theory of Computing, STOC '86, pp. 364–369. Association for Computing Machinery, New York, NY, USA (1986). https://doi.org/10.1145/12130.12168

12. Goldschlag, D.M., Stubblebine, S.G.: Publicly verifiable lotteries: applications of delaying functions. In: Hirchfeld, R. (ed.) Financial Cryptography. Lecture Notes in Computer Science, vol. 1465, pp. 214–226. Springer, Berlin (1998). https://doi.org/10.1007/bfb0055485

13. Hall, C., Schneier, B.: Remote electronic gambling. In: Computer Security Applications Conference, Annual, p. 232. IEEE Computer Society (1997). https://doi.org/10.1109/CSAC.1997.646195

14. Konstantinou, E., Liagkou, V., Spirakis, P., Stamatiou, Y.C., Yung, M.: Electronic national lotteries. In: Juels, A. (ed.) Financial Cryptography. Lecture Notes in Computer Science, vol. 3110, pp. 147–163. Springer, Berlin (2004). https://doi.org/10.1007/978-3-540-27809-2_18

15. Kumaresan, R., Bentov, I.: How to use bitcoin to incentivize correct computations. In: Proceedings of the 2014 ACM SIGSAC Conference on Computer and Communications Security, pp. 30–41. Association for Computing Machinery (2014). https://doi.org/10.1145/2660267.2660380

16. Kumaresan, R., Moran, T., Bentov, I.: How to use bitcoin to play decentralized poker. In: Proceedings of the 22nd ACM SIGSAC Conference on Computer and Communications Security, pp. 195–206. Association for Computing Machinery, New York, NY, USA (2015). https://doi.org/10.1145/2810103.2813712

17. Küpçü, A., Lysyanskaya, A.: Usable optimistic fair exchange. In: Pieprzyk, J. (ed.) Topics in Cryptology - CT-RSA 2010. Lecture Notes in Computer Science, vol. 5985, pp. 252–267. Springer, Berlin (2010). https://doi.org/10.1007/978-3-642-11925-5_18

18. Kushilevitz, E., Rabin, T.: Fair e-lotteries and e-Casinos. In: Naccache, D. (ed.) Topics in Cryptology - CT-RSA 2001. Lecture Notes in Computer Science, vol. 2020, pp. 100–109. Springer, Berlin (2001). https://doi.org/10.1007/3-540-45353-9_9

19. Lindell, A.Y.: Legally-enforceable fairness in secure two-party computation. In: Malkin, T. (ed.) Topics in Cryptology - CT-RSA 2008, pp. 121–137. Springer, Berlin Heidelberg, Berlin, Heidelberg (2008). https://doi.org/10.1007/978-3-540-79263-5_8

20. Miller, A., Bentov, I.: Zero-collateral lotteries in bitcoin and ethereum. In: 2017 IEEE European Symposium on Security and Privacy Workshops (EuroS&PW), pp. 4–13 (2017). https://doi.org/10.1109/EuroSPW.2017.44

21. Nakai, T., Shinagawa, K.: Constant-round linear-broadcast secure computation with penalties. Theoret. Comput. Sci. **959**, 113874 (2023). https://doi.org/10.1016/j.tcs.2023.113874

22. Nakai, T., Shinagawa, K.: Secure multi-party computation with legally-enforceable fairness. In: Wang, D., Yung, M., Liu, Z., Chen, X. (eds.) Information and Communications Security. Lecture Notes in Computer Science, vol. 14252, pp. 161–178. Springer, Singapore (2023). https://doi.org/10.1007/978-981-99-7356-9_10

23. Nakamoto, S.: Bitcoin: A peer-to-peer electronic cash system. Decentralized Bus. Rev. (2008)

24. Wood, G.: Ethereum: a secure decentralised generalised transaction ledger. Ethereum Proj. Yellow Pap. **151**, 1–32 (2014)

Single-Shuffle Card-Based Protocols with Six Cards per Gate

Tomoki Ono[1]([⊠]), Kazumasa Shinagawa[2,3], Takeshi Nakai[4], Yohei Watanabe[1,3], and Mitsugu Iwamoto[1]

[1] The University of Electro-Communications, Tokyo, Japan
{onotom,watanabe,mitsugu}@uec.ac.jp
[2] Ibaraki University, Ibaraki, Japan
kazumasa.shinagawa.np92@vc.ibaraki.ac.jp
[3] National Institute of Advanced Industrial Science and Technology, Tokyo, Japan
[4] Toyohashi University of Technology, Aichi, Japan
nakai@cs.tut.ac.jp

Abstract. Card-based cryptography refers to a secure computation with physical cards, and the number of cards and shuffles measures the efficiency of card-based protocols. This paper proposes new card-based protocols for any Boolean circuits with only a single shuffle. Although our protocols rely on Yao's garbled circuit as in previous single-shuffle card-based protocols, our core construction idea is to encode truth tables of each Boolean gate with fewer cards than previous works while being compatible with Yao's garbled circuit. As a result, we show single-shuffle card-based protocols with six cards per gate, which are more efficient than previous single-shuffle card-based protocols.

Keywords: Card-based cryptography · Secure computation · Garbled circuit

1 Introduction

1.1 Background and Motivation

Secure computation protocols allow parties to collaboratively compute a function while keeping each party's input hidden from the other party. Although secure computation protocols are usually implemented on computers, *card-based cryptography* [3,4], which is an area focusing on secure computation using physical cards (without computers), has also been eagerly investigated. Let us give an example of a secure card-based AND protocol called the *five-card trick* [3]. Suppose that each of Alice and Bob has two cards, ♣ and ♡, and a ♡ is placed face-down on a table. Alice (resp., Bob) puts their cards face-down on the left side (resp., the right side) of ♡, following the encoding rule: the order of the cards is ♣♡ if the input is zero; it is ♡♣ if the input is one. After shuffling the five face-down cards without changing the order of the sequence, they face up the cards. The output of the AND protocol is one if the consecutive three heart cards appear; it is zero otherwise.

The major efficiency measures of card-based cryptography are the number of cards and shuffles. The fewer cards and shuffles card-based protocols are realized, the easier it is to execute them. In this work, we focus on the implementability of shuffles; it is unclear how to implement shuffles that yield desired probability distributions, though various attempts have been made thus far [7,11,16,17,21, 22,27,28]. For this reason, we devote effort to constructing card-based protocols with the minimum number of shuffles and as few cards as possible.

A well-known approach to constructing card-based protocols for any function is to realize card-based protocols for a Boolean gate such as AND and XOR since any function can be realized by combining Boolean gates [4,12,15]. Hence, improving card-based protocols for Boolean gates is one of the mainstream research topics [1,2,4–6,8,9,12–14,18–20,24,25]. However, this approach increases the number of shuffles required for the resulting card-based protocols for any function (or Boolean circuit) since the number of shuffles depends on the number of gates consisting of the Boolean circuit. Therefore, we aim to directly propose card-based protocols for any Boolean circuit consisting of various Boolean gates, not any Boolean gate, with a single shuffle. Note that, as stated in [23], it is impossible to realize card-based protocol for any non-trivial function without shuffles; The lower bound of shuffles required for secure card-based protocols is one.

1.2 Prior Works

Shinagawa and Nuida [23] showed a single-shuffle card-based protocol for any n-variable Boolean function $f : \{0,1\}^n \rightarrow \{0,1\}^m$ with $24q + 2n$ cards, where q is number of gates in the Boolean circuit. Tozawa et al. [26] improved the Shinagawa–Nuida protocol and reduced the number of cards to $8q + 2n$ without additional shuffles.

Kuzuma et al. [10] focused on a restricted class of Boolean circuits and showed single-shuffle card-based protocols for an n-variable AND function with $4n - 2$ cards and an n-variable XOR function with $2n$ cards. Note that, allowing multiple shuffles, Nishida et al. [15] showed a card-based protocol with $2n + 6$ cards for any n-variable Boolean circuit $f : \{0,1\}^n \rightarrow \{0,1\}$, which is the most efficient protocol in terms of the number of cards.

1.3 Our Contribution

This paper proposes new single-shuffle card-based protocols based on Yao's garbled circuits [29]. The core construction idea is to encode truth tables of each Boolean gate with fewer cards than previous protocols while being compatible with Yao's garbled circuit. Unlike previous single-shuffle card-based protocols such as Shinagawa–Nuida [23] and Tozawa et al. [26], each output of the truth table is represented by a single card, and we add two more extra cards to make the truth tables encoded with single cards compatible with Yao's technique. As

Table 1. A comparison among protocols with one shuffle for any Boolean circuit. q, n, and m are the number of gates, bit-length of the input, and bits-length of the output, respectively.

	Format	Number of cards	Shuffle type
Shinagawa–Nuida [23]	committed	$24q + 2n$	uniform closed
Tozawa et al. [26]	committed	$8q + 2n$	uniform closed
Our protocol (Sect. 3.6)	non-committed	$6q + 2n$	uniform
Our protocol (Sect. 3.7)	committed	$6q + 2(n + m)$	uniform

a result, we show two single-shuffle card-based protocols for any Boolean circuit $f : \{0,1\}^n \to \{0,1\}^m$ with six cards per gate: One is a non-committed-format protocol with $2n + 6q$ cards, and the other is a committed-format protocol with $2(n + m) + 6q$ cards, where q is the number of gates in f, and a protocol is said to be *committed* if it outputs cards face-down and the output follows the same encoding rule as the input.

Table 1 shows a comparison among the existing protocols and our protocols. Since the number of gates q is greater than or equal to the number of the output gates m, our protocol is more efficient than those of Shinagawa–Nuida [23] and Tozawa et al. [26] in terms of the number of cards. It should be noted that our protocols use a uniform shuffle, which is not closed (see Sect. 2.2 for the definition), although Shinagawa–Nuida [23] and Tozawa et al. [26] used a uniform closed shuffle.

1.4 Organization

In Sect. 2, we introduce basic definitions. In Sect. 3, we construct our single-shuffle protocols both in the non-committed-format setting and the committed-format setting. In Sect. 4, we conclude our paper.

2 Preliminaries

For an integer $k \geq 1$, we denote the k-th symmetric group by S_k. For two permutations $\pi_1, \pi_2 \in S_k$, the composition of them is denoted by $\pi_2 \circ \pi_1$. Here, permutations are applied from right to left, i.e., $\pi_2 \circ \pi_1 \in S_k$ means that permutation π_1 is applied and then π_2 is applied. For two subsets $A, B \subseteq S_k$, we define $AB := \{\pi_A \circ \pi_B \mid \pi_A \in A, \pi_B \in B\}$.

2.1 Syntax of Boolean Circuits

A Boolean circuit C is defined by a 6-tuple (n, m, q, L, R, G) where $n \geq 1$ is the number of input wires, $m \geq 1$ is the number of output wires, $q \geq 1$ is the number of gates, L and R are functions that specify the left and right wires in each gate, respectively, and G is a function that specifies the truth table of each gate. The detailed specification is given in the following.

- The number of wires in C is $n + q$, where n wires are the input wires and q wires are the output wires of gates. Each input wire corresponds to $1, 2, \ldots, n$, and each output wire of gates corresponds to $n + 1, n + 2, \ldots, n + q$. The last m wires $n + q - m + 1, n + q - m + 2, \ldots, n + q$ correspond to the output wires of C. A gate g is identified with the output wire of g, i.e., each gate also corresponds to $n + 1, n + 2, \ldots, n + q$.
- Each gate g has two input wires: the left input wire of g is $L(g)$ and the right input wire of g is $R(g)$. We assume that $L(g) \leq R(g) < g$, i.e., the input wires $L(g), R(g)$ are smaller than g, and the left wire is smaller than or equal to the right wire. This restriction prevents the loop of the circuit.
- A wire w, which is not an output wire of C is called the inner wire, i.e., each inner wire corresponds to $1, 2, \ldots, n + q - m$. An inner wire is an input wire or an input wire of some gate. An inner wire w can be branched, i.e., there might exist two or more gates having w as its input wire, or some gate can be taken w as the left and right input wires.
- For an inner wire w, $L^{-1}(w)$ is defined by the set of all gates whose left input wire is w, i.e., $L^{-1}(w) = \{g \in \{n+1, n+2, \ldots, n+q\} \mid L(g) = w\}$. We define $R^{-1}(w)$ in the same way.
- For a gate g, $G(g)$ represent the truth table of g. When g computes a function $f : \{0,1\}^2 \to \{0,1\}$, $G(g)$ represents a 4-bit binary string defined by

$$G(g) = (f(0,0), f(0,1), f(1,0), f(1,1)).$$

In this paper, for simplicity, we assume that all gates are the NAND gates, i.e., $G(g) = (1,1,1,0)$ for all gates g. This is based on the fact that any Boolean circuit $f : \{0,1\}^n \to \{0,1\}^m$ can be constructed by only NAND gates. We note that our protocol can also be applied to a circuit with other gates.

Example of Boolean Circuit. A Boolean circuit $C = (3, 1, 3, L, R, G)$ is given in Fig. 1, where the number of the input wires is $n = 3$, the number of the output wires is $m = 1$, and the number of the gates is $q = 3$. Each input wire corresponds to $1, 2, 3$ and each gate corresponds to $4, 5, 6$. The functions L and R are defined by $L(4) = 1, R(4) = 2, L(5) = 3, R(5) = 4, L(6) = 4$ and $R(6) = 5$. Then we have $L^{-1}(1) = \{4\}, R^{-1}(1) = \emptyset, L^{-1}(2) = \emptyset, R^{-1}(2) = \{4\}, L^{-1}(3) = \{5\}, R^{-1}(3) = \emptyset, L^{-1}(4) = \{6\}, R^{-1}(4) = \{5\}, L^{-1}(5) = \emptyset$ and $R^{-1}(5) = \{6\}$. Since all gates are the NAND gates, $G(g) = (1,1,1,0)$ for all $4 \leq g \leq 6$.

2.2   Card-Based Protocols

In this paper, we use two-colored cards: the front side of a card is either ♣ or ♡, and the back side is ?. All cards with the same suit are indistinguishable, and the backs of all cards are also indistinguishable.

In card-based protocols, three operations are used: permutation, shuffle, and turn. Let k be the number of cards. A permutation operation (perm, π) for $\pi \in S_k$ is a deterministic operation that rearranges the order of the cards according to π. A shuffle operation (shuffle, $\Pi, \mathcal{F}$) for a subset $\Pi \subseteq S_k$ and a probability

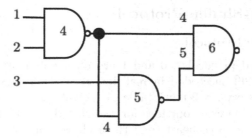

Fig. 1. An example of Boolean circuits

distribution $\mathcal{F}$ over Π is a probabilistic operation that randomly rearranges the order of the cards according to a permutation $\pi \in \Pi$ drawn from $\mathcal{F}$. It is assumed that no player can know which permutation π is actually drawn from $\mathcal{F}$. A turn operation (turn, T) for $T \subseteq \{1, 2, \ldots, k\}$ is a deterministic operation that turns over cards in T from face-down to face-up or from face-up to face-down.

Let S be a shuffle (shuffle, $\Pi, \mathcal{F}$). If $\mathcal{F}$ is a uniform distribution, S is called a uniform shuffle. If Π is a subgroup of S_k, S is called a closed shuffle. If S is uniform and closed, it is called a uniform closed shuffle.

2.3   Card-Based Garbled Circuits

Shinagawa–Nuida [23] developed a card-based garbled circuit, which is a card-based protocol based on garbled circuits. Tozawa et al. [26] improved the card-based garbled circuit in terms of the number of cards. A card-based garbled circuit consists of three phases: initialization phase, garbling phase, and evaluation phase as follows:

Initialization phase: Given a Boolean circuit $f : \{0,1\}^n \rightarrow \{0,1\}^m$ and a sequence of input commitments to $x_1, x_2, \ldots, x_n$, it outputs a sequence of face-down cards I, which we call an initial state. The objective of this phase is to encode the circuit and its input into a sequence of face-down cards.

Garbling phase: Given an initial state I, it outputs two sequences of face-down cards $\widetilde{C}$ and $\widetilde{X}$, which we call a garbled circuit and a garbled input, respectively. The objective of this phase is to randomize the inputs and the intermediate values of the circuit without changing the functionality of the circuit.

Evaluation phase: Given a garbled circuit $\widetilde{C}$ and a garbled input $\widetilde{X}$, it outputs the output value or a commitment of the output value. The purpose of this phase is to obtain the output value by evaluating each gate of the garbled circuit $\widetilde{C}$ with the garbled input $\widetilde{X}$.

3 Our Single-Shuffle Protocols

3.1 Idea of Our Protocol

In many card-based protocols , 0 and 1 are represented by ♡♣ and ♣♡, respectively, and [26] succeeded in realizing garbled circuits with eight cards that by encoding every 2×2 truth table with eight cards.

Here, we briefly describe our idea for realizing the garbled circuits with *six* cards that consist of three hearts and three clubs. For instance, we represent the truth table of the NAND and AND gates as follows, where 0 and 1 are represented by ♣ and ♡, respectively.

NAND	0	1		AND	0	1
0	♡	♡		0	♣	♣
1	♡	♣		1	♣	♡

Facing down cards in the above truth table conceals all values in the truth table, but the negation of them is not possible due to the encoding rule with one card that prevents us from converting the NAND gate to the AND gate[1]. To overcome this obstacle, we append two ♣ to the NAND truth table as the third column and permute it. Then we have the following and by deleting the third column, we obtain the truth table of AND in a committed format.

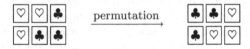

3.2 Preliminaries for Our Protocol

In our protocol, each input wire is represented by two cards ♣♡ and each gate is represented by six cards ♣♣♣♡♡♡. Since we have n input wires and q gates, we use $2n + 6q$ cards in total.

To clarify the position of the cards, we define $2n + 6q$ indices: $P_i[a]$ ($1 \leq i \leq n$ and $a \in \{0,1\}$) and $P_g[b][c]$ ($n + 1 \leq g \leq n + q, b \in \{0,1\}$, and $c \in \{0,1,2\}$). Two indices $P_i[0], P_i[1]$ correspond to the input wire i and six indices $P_g[0][0], P_g[1][0], P_g[0][1], P_g[1][1], P_g[0][2], P_g[1][2]$ correspond to the gate g. We assume that all indices are distinct. We give an example of distinct $2n + 6q$ indices in the following:

- $P_i[a] = 2i - 1 + a$ for $1 \leq i \leq n$ and $a \in \{0,1\}$;
- $P_g[b][c] = 2n + 1 + 6(g - (n + 1)) + 3b + c$ for $n + 1 \leq g \leq n + q, b \in \{0,1\}$, and $c \in \{0,1,2\}$.

The above indices are consecutive from 1 to $2n + 6q$.

---

[1] The reason utilizing eight cards in [26] comes from this point.

3.3   Initialization Phase

Given a Boolean circuit $f : \{0,1\}^n \to \{0,1\}^m$ and a sequence of input commitments to $x_1, x_2, \ldots, x_n$, the initialization phase makes a sequence of face-down cards on the indices of the position $P_i[a]$ and $P_g[b][c]$.

First, the sequence of input commitments is arranged as follows:

$$\underbrace{\overset{P_1[0]\ P_1[1]}{\boxed{?}\ \boxed{?}}}_{x_1}\ \underbrace{\overset{P_2[0]\ P_2[1]}{\boxed{?}\ \boxed{?}}}_{x_2}\ \cdots\ \underbrace{\overset{P_n[0]\ P_n[1]}{\boxed{?}\ \boxed{?}}}_{x_n}.$$

For each gate $g \in \{n+1, n+2, \ldots, n+q\}$, we identify the indices $P_g[a][b]$ ($a \in \{0,1\}$ and $b \in \{0,1,2\}$) with the cells of a 2×3 matrix as follows:

$P_g[0][0]$	$P_g[0][1]$	$P_g[0][2]$
$P_g[1][0]$	$P_g[1][1]$	$P_g[1][2]$

Then, we place six cards $\boxed{\clubsuit}\,\boxed{\clubsuit}\,\boxed{\clubsuit}\,\boxed{\heartsuit}\,\boxed{\heartsuit}\,\boxed{\heartsuit}$ as follows:

$\boxed{\heartsuit}$	$\boxed{\heartsuit}$	$\boxed{\clubsuit}$
$\boxed{\heartsuit}$	$\boxed{\clubsuit}$	$\boxed{\clubsuit}$

We note that the above matrix represents the NAND gate: for two inputs $a, b \in \{0,1\}$, the card on $P_g[a][b]$ is $\boxed{\clubsuit}$ if $a = b = 1$ and $\boxed{\heartsuit}$ otherwise. It can be regarded as the NAND gate by $\clubsuit = 0, \heartsuit = 1$. We also note that two additional $\boxed{\clubsuit}$s on $P_g[0][2], P_g[1][2]$ are needed to garble the gate as explained in Sect. 3.1.

Then, we apply a turn operation so that all cards are face-down. Now we have a sequence of $2n + 6q$ face-down cards on the indices of the position $P_i[a]$ and $P_g[b][c]$. This is the output of this phase.

3.4   Garbling Phase

Next, the protocol proceeds to the garbling phase. This phase just applies a uniform shuffle (shuffle, $\Pi, \mathcal{F}$) to the sequence of $2n + 6q$ cards outputted by the initialization phase. In the following, we will define $\Pi \subseteq S_{2n+6q}$ by three steps: (1) defining four permutations, (2) defining a shuffle for randomizing a wire, and (3) composing all shuffles.

Defining Four Permutations. For an input wire $i \in \{1, 2, \ldots, n\}$, a permutation π_i is defined by

$$\pi_i := (P_i[0], P_i[1]).$$

It represents the bit flip of the i-th input commitment. For a gate $g \in \{n+1, n+2, \ldots, n+q\}$, a permutation π_g is defined by

$$\pi_g := (P_g[0][0], P_g[0][2]) \circ (P_g[1][0], P_g[1][2]) \circ (P_g[0][1], P_g[1][1]).$$

It represents the bit flip of the truth table of g as follows:

$$
\boxed{\heartsuit}\,\boxed{\heartsuit}\,\boxed{\clubsuit} \quad \xrightarrow{\pi_g} \quad \boxed{\clubsuit}\,\boxed{\clubsuit}\,\boxed{\heartsuit}
$$
$$
\boxed{\heartsuit}\,\boxed{\clubsuit}\,\boxed{\clubsuit} \qquad\qquad \boxed{\clubsuit}\,\boxed{\heartsuit}\,\boxed{\heartsuit}.
$$

For a gate g, a permutation τ_g is defined by

$$
\tau_g := (P_g[0][0], P_g[1][0]) \circ (P_g[0][1], P_g[1][1]).
$$

It represents a swap of the rows of the truth table of g as follows:

$$
\boxed{1}\,\boxed{3}\,\boxed{5} \quad \xrightarrow{\tau_g} \quad \boxed{2}\,\boxed{4}\,\boxed{5}
$$
$$
\boxed{2}\,\boxed{4}\,\boxed{6} \qquad\qquad \boxed{1}\,\boxed{3}\,\boxed{6}.
$$

A permutation σ_g is defined by

$$
\sigma_g := (P_g[0][0], P_g[0][1]) \circ (P_g[1][0], P_g[1][1]).
$$

It represents a swap of the columns of the truth table of g as follows:

$$
\boxed{1}\,\boxed{3}\,\boxed{5} \quad \xrightarrow{\sigma_g} \quad \boxed{3}\,\boxed{1}\,\boxed{5}
$$
$$
\boxed{2}\,\boxed{4}\,\boxed{6} \qquad\qquad \boxed{4}\,\boxed{2}\,\boxed{6}.
$$

Defining a Shuffle for Randomizing a Wire. For a wire $w \in \{1, 2, \ldots, n+q\}$, a permutation $\widehat{\pi}_w$ is defined by

$$
\widehat{\pi}_w := \pi_w \circ \prod_{g \in L^{-1}(w)} \tau_g \circ \prod_{g' \in R^{-1}(w)} \sigma_{g'}.
$$

By applying it, the value of the wire w is flipped and for each gate g, the rows of g are swapped if w is the left input wire of g and the columns of g are swapped if w is the right input wire of g. Define $\Pi_w := \{\mathrm{id}, \widehat{\pi}_w\}$. A uniform shuffle (shuffle, $\Pi_w, \mathcal{F}_w$) is a shuffle that randomizes the value of the wire w and all gates having w as input.

Composing All Shuffles. The subset $\Pi \subseteq S_{6q+2n}$ is defined by

$$
\Pi := \Pi_1 \Pi_2 \cdots \Pi_{n+q-m} = \{\pi'_1 \circ \pi'_2 \circ \cdots \pi'_{n+q-m} \mid \pi'_i \in \Pi_i\}.
$$

The uniform shuffle (shuffle, $\Pi, \mathcal{F}$) is now obtained. We note that it is a shuffle by composing $n + q - m$ uniform shuffles (shuffle, $\Pi_w, \mathcal{F}_w$).

3.5   Evaluation Phase

Finally, the protocol proceeds to the evaluation phase. In this phase, the players evaluate the circuit by opening cards as follows. Let v_w ($1 \leq w \leq n+q-m$) be an indeterminate on $\{0, 1\}$. The protocol proceeds by determining these values and finally outputs $v_{n+q-m+1}, v_{n+q-m+2}, \ldots, v_{n+q}$ as the output values.

First, the players open all cards corresponding to the input wires: the value of v_i $(1 \leq i \leq n)$ is set to the value of the i-th commitment according to the encoding rule $\boxed{\clubsuit}\boxed{\heartsuit} = 0$ and $\boxed{\heartsuit}\boxed{\clubsuit} = 1$. Next, each gate $g = n+1, \ldots, n+q$ is evaluated (in this order) by opening the card on the position $P_g[v_{L(g)}][v_{R(g)}]$: the value of v_g is set to the value of the card according to the encoding rule $\boxed{\clubsuit} = 0$ and $\boxed{\heartsuit} = 1$. Note that the values of $v_{L(g)}$ and $v_{R(g)}$ are determined before g is executed since $L(g) \leq R(g) < g$. By repeating this process, we finally obtain the output values $v_{n+q-m+1}, v_{n+q-m+2}, \ldots, v_{n+q}$.

3.6 Description of Our Protocol in the Non-committed Format

We summarize our protocol in the following.

1. First, we enter the initialization phase. Given a Boolean circuit f and the input commitments to $x_1, \ldots, x_n$, this phase outputs a sequence of $6q + 2n$ face-down cards as an initial state.
2. Next, we enter the garbling phase. Given an initial state, this phase applies a shuffle (shuffle, $\Pi, \mathcal{F}$) defined in Sect. 3.4. We regard the resulting sequence of $2n$ cards corresponding to the input commitments as the garbling input and the remaining sequence of $6q$ cards as the garbled circuit.
3. Finally, we enter the evaluation phase. This phase opens the garbled input and some cards of the garbled circuit. We output a m-bit string corresponding to the cards of the output gates.

In the following, we prove the correctness and security of our protocol.

Correctness: Recall that for each wire $1 \leq w \leq n+q-m$, the permutation $\widehat{\pi}_w$ is defined as follows:

$$\widehat{\pi}_w := \pi_w \circ \prod_{g \in L^{-1}(w)} \tau_g \circ \prod_{g' \in R^{-1}(w)} \sigma_{g'}.$$

Let w be a wire and g be a gate such that $L(g) = w$ (resp., $R(g) = w$). From the definition of $\widehat{\pi}_w$, we can observe that the bit flip introduced by $\widehat{\pi}_w$ and the swap of columns (resp., rows) introduced by τ_g (resp., $\sigma_{g'}$) is synchronized, which guarantees that the functionality of the circuit remains the same. Therefore, this protocol is correct.

Security: In order to prove the security, it is sufficient to show that the opened values v_i $(1 \leq i \leq n+q-m)$ except the output values are independently and uniformly random bits. (We note that once this fact is proven, a simulator can be constructed in the same way as Shinagawa–Nuida [23].) In the following, we prove this fact by reverse induction from $n+q-m$ to 1.

Let A_w be the shuffle for randomizing a wire w, i.e., $A_w := (\text{shuffle}, \Pi_w, \mathcal{F}_w)$. First, v_{n+q-m} is a uniformly random bit due to the effect of uniform shuffles A_{n+q-m} and $\{A_w \mid w \in L^{-1}(n+q-m) \cup R^{-1}(n+q-m)\}$. Next, suppose that $v_{i+1}, v_{i+2}, \ldots, v_{n+q-m}$ are independently and uniformly random bits.

The uniform property of v_i is obvious due to the effect of uniform shuffles A_i and $\{A_w \mid w \in L^{-1}(i) \cup R^{-1}(i)\}$. Since A_i does not appear in the wires greater than i, the randomness introduced by the shuffle A_i is independent from $v_{i+1}, v_{i+2}, \ldots, v_{n+q-m}$. Thus $v_i, v_{i+1}, \ldots, v_{n+q-m}$ are also independently and uniformly random bits.

Therefore, v_i $(1 \leq i \leq n + q - m)$ are independently and uniformly random bits. This proves the security.

3.7   Our Protocol in the Committed Format

Although our protocol in Sect. 3.6 is a non-committed-format protocol, we can convert it to a committed-format protocol by appending $2m$ additional cards, where m is the number of the output wires. The committed-format protocol is the same as our non-committed-format protocol except that for each output gate $g \in \{n + q - m + 1, \ldots, n + q\}$, we use the eight-card truth table as in Tozawa et al. [26] instead of our six-card truth table. More concretely, we use a truth table of an output gate g as follows:

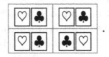

The shuffle in the committed-format protocol can be defined in the same way as in Sect. 3.4. By applying it, we obtain a committed-format protocol. Since each output gate requires two additional cards, the number of cards in this protocol is $6q + 2n + 2m$.

4   Conclusion

This paper proposed new single-shuffle card-based protocols for any Boolean circuit. Our protocols are based on Yao's garbled circuit as in previous single-shuffle protocols [23,26]. Namely, the truth tables of gates in the Boolean circuit are garbled (or randomized) while keeping the output of the circuit consistent. Our core technique to reduce the number of cards is to propose a new encoding of the truth table: each value of the truth table is represented by one card, whereas the previous works used two cards per value. We also used two additional cards to apply Yao's technique to our protocol. Therefore, our protocols require only six cards per gate. Specifically, we proposed a non-committed single-shuffle card-based protocol with $6q + 2n$ cards and then modified it to make it a committed protocol with $2m$ additional cards. Since our protocols require uniform shuffles, it would be interesting to construct a committed card-based protocol with single uniform closed shuffles and a comparable number of cards to ours.

Acknowledgment. This work was supported by JSPS KAKENHI Grant Numbers JP23H00468, JP23H00479, JP23K17455, JP23K16880, JP22H03590, JP21K17702, JP21H03395, JP21H03441, JP18H05289, JST CREST JPMJCR22M1, JPMJCR23M2, and MEXT Leading Initiative for Excellent Young Researchers.

References

1. Abe, Y., Hayashi, Y., Mizuki, T., Sone, H.: Five-card AND protocol in committed format using only practical shuffles. In: 5th ACM on ASIA Public-Key Cryptography Workshop, APKC '18, pp. 3–8. ACM, New York (2018). https://doi.org/10.1145/3197507.3197510
2. Abe, Y., Hayashi, Y., Mizuki, T., Sone, H.: Five-card AND computations in committed format using only uniform cyclic shuffles. New Gener. Comput. **39**(1), 97–114 (2021). https://doi.org/10.1007/s00354-020-00110-2
3. den Boer, B.: More efficient match-making and satisfiability: the five card trick. In: Quisquater, J.J., Vandewalle, J. (eds.) Advances in Cryptology - EUROCRYPT '89. Lecture Notes in Computer Science, vol. 434, pp. 208–217. Springer, Berlin (1989). https://doi.org/10.1007/3-540-46885-4_23
4. Crépeau, C., Kilian, J.: Discreet solitary games. In: Stinson, D.R. (ed.) Advances in Cryptology - CRYPTO' 93. Lecture Notes in Computer Science, vol. 773, pp. 319–330. Springer, Berlin (1994). https://doi.org/10.1007/3-540-48329-2_27
5. Kastner, J., Koch, A., Walzer, S., Miyahara, D., Hayashi, Y., Mizuki, T., Sone, H.: The minimum number of cards in practical card-based protocols. In: Takagi, T., Peyrin, T. (eds.) Advances in Cryptology-ASIACRYPT 2017. LNCS, vol. 10626, pp. 126–155. Springer, Cham (2017). https://doi.org/10.1007/978-3-319-70700-6_5
6. Koch, A.: The landscape of security from physical assumptions. In: IEEE Information Theory Workshop, pp. 1–6. IEEE, NY (2021). https://doi.org/10.1109/ITW48936.2021.9611501
7. Koch, A., Walzer, S.: Foundations for actively secure card-based cryptography. In: Farach-Colton, M. (ed.) 10th International Conference on Fun with Algorithms (FUN 2021). Leibniz International Proceedings in Informatics (LIPIcs), vol. 157, pp. Art.-Nr.: 17. Schloss Dagstuhl - Leibniz-Zentrum für Informatik GmbH (LZI) (2020). https://doi.org/10.4230/LIPIcs.FUN.2021.17
8. Koch, A., Walzer, S., Härtel, K.: Card-based cryptographic protocols using a minimal number of cards. In: Iwata, T., Cheon, J. (eds.) Advances in Cryptology - ASIACRYPT 2015. Lecture Notes in Computer Science(), vol. 9452, pp. 783–807. Springer, Berlin (2015). https://doi.org/10.1007/978-3-662-48797-6_32
9. Koyama, H., Toyoda, K., Miyahara, D., Mizuki, T.: New card-based copy protocols using only random cuts. In: ASIA Public-Key Cryptography Workshop, pp. 13–22. ACM, NY (2021), https://doi.org/10.1145/3457338.3458297
10. Kuzuma, T., Isuzugawa, R., Toyoda, K., Miyahara, D., Mizuki, T.: Card-based single-shuffle protocols for secure multiple-input AND and XOR computations. In: APKC '22: Proceedings of the 9th ACM on ASIA Public-Key Cryptography Workshop, APKC@AsiaCCS 2022, Nagasaki, Japan, 30 May 2022, pp. 51–58. ACM (2022)
11. Miyamoto, K., Shinagawa, K.: Graph automorphism shuffles from pile-scramble shuffles. New Gener. Comput. **40**, 199–223 (2022). https://doi.org/10.1007/s00354-022-00164-4
12. Mizuki, T., Sone, H.: Six-card secure AND and four-card secure XOR. In: Deng, X., Hopcroft, J.E., Xue, J. (eds.) Frontiers in Algorithmics. Lecture Notes in Computer Science, vol. 5598, pp. 358–369. Springer, Berlin (2009). https://doi.org/10.1007/978-3-642-02270-8_36
13. Mizuki, T., Uchiike, F., Sone, H.: Securely computing XOR with 10 cards. Australas. J. Combin. **36**, 279–293 (2006)

14. Niemi, V., Renvall, A.: Secure multiparty computations without computers. Theor. Comput. Sci. **191**(1–2), 173–183 (1998). https://doi.org/10.1016/S0304-3975(97)00107-2

15. Nishida, T., Hayashi, Y., Mizuki, T., Sone, H.: Card-based protocols for any boolean function. In: Jain, R., Jain, S., Stephan, F. (eds.) Theory and Applications of Models of Computation. LNCS, vol. 9076, pp. 110–121. Springer, Cham (2015). https://doi.org/10.1007/978-3-319-17142-5_11

16. Nishimura, A., Hayashi, Y., Mizuki, T., Sone, H.: An implementation of non-uniform shuffle for secure multi-party computation. In: ACM International Workshop on ASIA Public-Key Cryptography, AsiaPKC '16, pp. 49–55. ACM, New York (2016). https://doi.org/10.1145/2898420.2898425

17. Nishimura, A., Hayashi, Y., Mizuki, T., Sone, H.: Pile-shifting scramble for card-based protocols. IEICE Trans. Fundam. **101**(9), 1494–1502 (2018). https://doi.org/10.1587/transfun.E101.A.1494

18. Nishimura, A., Nishida, T., Hayashi, Y.I., Mizuki, T., Sone, H.: Card-based protocols using unequal division shuffles. Soft. Comput. **22**, 361–371 (2018)

19. Nishimura, A., Nishida, T., Hayashi, Y., Mizuki, T., Sone, H.: Five-card secure computations using unequal division shuffle. In: Dediu, A.H., Magdalena, L., Martín-Vide, C. (eds.) Theory and Practice of Natural Computing. LNCS, vol. 9477, pp. 109–120. Springer, Cham (2015). https://doi.org/10.1007/978-3-319-26841-5_9

20. Ruangwises, S., Itoh, T.: AND protocols using only uniform shuffles. In: van Bevern, R., Kucherov, G. (eds.) Computer Science-Theory and Applications. LNCS, vol. 11532, pp. 349–358. Springer, Cham (2019). https://doi.org/10.1007/978-3-030-19955-5_30

21. Saito, T., Miyahara, D., Abe, Y., Mizuki, T., Shizuya, H.: How to implement a non-uniform or non-closed shuffle. In: Martín-Vide, C., Vega-Rodríguez, M.A., Yang, M.S. (eds.) Theory and Practice of Natural Computing. LNCS, vol. 12494, pp. 107–118. Springer, Cham (2020). https://doi.org/10.1007/978-3-030-63000-3_9

22. Shinagawa, K., Miyamoto, K.: Automorphism shuffles for graphs and hypergraphs and its applications. IEICE Trans. Fundam. **E106.A**(3), 306–314 (2023). https://doi.org/10.1587/transfun.2022CIP0020

23. Shinagawa, K., Nuida, K.: A single shuffle is enough for secure card-based computation of any boolean circuit. Discret. Appl. Math. **289**, 248–261 (2021)

24. Stiglic, A.: Computations with a deck of cards. Theor. Comput. Sci. **259**(1–2), 671–678 (2001). https://doi.org/10.1016/S0304-3975(00)00409-6

25. Toyoda, K., Miyahara, D., Mizuki, T., Sone, H.: Six-card finite-runtime XOR protocol with only random cut. In: ACM Workshop on ASIA Public-Key Cryptography, APKC '20, pp. 2–8. ACM, New York (2020). https://doi.org/10.1145/3384940.3388961

26. Tozawa, K., Morita, H., Mizuki, T.: Single-shuffle card-based protocol with eight cards per gate. In: Genova, D., Kari, J. (eds.) Unconventional Computation and Natural Computation. Lecture Notes in Computer Science, vol. 14003, pp. 171–185. Springer, Cham (2023). https://doi.org/10.1007/978-3-031-34034-5_12

27. Ueda, I., Miyahara, D., Nishimura, A., Hayashi, Y., Mizuki, T., Sone, H.: Secure implementations of a random bisection cut. Int. J. Inf. Sec. **19**(4), 445–452 (2020). https://doi.org/10.1007/s10207-019-00463-w

28. Ueda, I., Nishimura, A., Hayashi, Y., Mizuki, T., Sone, H.: How to implement a random bisection cut. In: Martin-Vide, C., Mizuki, T., Vega-Rodriguez, M. (eds.) Theory and Practice of Natural Computing. Lecture Notes in Computer Science(),

vol. 10071, pp. 58–69. Springer, Cham (2016). https://doi.org/10.1007/978-3-319-49001-4_5

29. Yao, A.C.C.: How to generate and exchange secrets (extended abstract). In: FOCS, pp. 162–167. IEEE Computer Society (1986). http://dblp.uni-trier.de/db/conf/focs/focs86.html/Yao86

Efficient Result-Hiding Searchable Encryption with Forward and Backward Privacy

Takumi Amada[1(✉)], Mitsugu Iwamoto[1], and Yohei Watanabe[1,2]

[1] The University of Electro-Communications, Tokyo, Japan
{t.amada,mitsugu,watanabe}@uec.ac.jp
[2] National Institute of Information and Communications Technology, Tokyo, Japan

Abstract. Dynamic searchable symmetric encryption (SSE) realizes efficient update and search operations for encrypted databases, and there has been an increase in this line of research in the recent decade. Dynamic SSE allows the leakage of insignificant information to ensure efficient search operations, and it is important to understand and identify what kinds of information are insignificant. In this paper, we propose an efficient dynamic SSE scheme Laura under the small leakage, which leads to appealing security requirements such as forward privacy, (Type-II) backward privacy, and result hiding. Laura is constructed based on Aura (NDSS 2021) and is almost as efficient as Aura while only allowing less leakage than Aura. We also provide experimental results to show the concrete efficiency of Laura.

Keywords: Dynamic searchable encryption · Backward Privacy · Encrypted database

1 Introduction

Searchable symmetric encryption (SSE) [11,24] provides a way to search a large database efficiently (e.g., cloud storage) for *encrypted* data. In particular, SSE that supports update operations is called *dynamic SSE* [20], which has attracted attention over the past decade [8,16,19,20,22,23].

Forward and Backward Privacy. Dynamic SSE aims to efficiently perform keyword searches on encrypted data while revealing some insignificant information to the server. A common understanding of what kinds of leakage are insignificant has been updated by exploring *leakage-abuse attacks* [3,7,17,28] against SSE. In particular, *file injection attacks* demonstrated by Zhang et al. [28] showed that *forward privacy* [5], which guarantees that the adversary cannot learn if newly-added files contain previously-searched keywords, must be a de facto standard security requirement for dynamic SSE.

Backward privacy [6], which guarantees that search operations reveal no useful information on previously-deleted files even if they contain searched keywords,

© The Author(s), under exclusive license to Springer Nature Singapore Pte Ltd. 2024
H. Seo and S. Kim (Eds.): ICISC 2023, LNCS 14562, pp. 170–193, 2024.
https://doi.org/10.1007/978-981-97-1238-0_10

has been spotlighted since it sounds like another natural security requirement. However, it is more difficult to achieve backward privacy than forward privacy since it is just like we require the server to forget previously-stored information. For example, we have to hide even information about when and which files are added and/or deleted to meet backward privacy. Therefore, one of the current major research interests in dynamic SSE is how efficiently we construct dynamic SSE schemes with backward privacy.

Importance of Result-Hiding SSE. As described above, leakage-abuse attacks tell us which information should not be leaked during update and search operations. Existing attacks are classified into *passive* and *active* ones. Passive attacks (e.g., [17]) aim to identify keywords behind search queries from admitted leakage information and seem more likely to happen in the real world than active attacks (e.g., [28]), which require that the server can force the client to upload arbitrary files. A major drawback of passive attacks is that they also require partial information of the stored data as extra information in addition to the leakage profiles. This is quite an unrealistic assumption. Hence, the subsequent works (e.g., [3,7]) have attempted to weaken the assumption. Recently, Bkackstone et al. [3] showed passive attacks that only require 5% of the client's data, whereas the Islam et al.'s seminal work [17] requires at least 95% of the client's data. In particular, it is worth noting that their attacks only use *access pattern leakage*, which is a standard leakage profile of dynamic SSE. Although there are, fortunately, countermeasures such as volume-hiding techniques [18], they significantly decrease the efficiency of dynamic SSE schemes. Thus, it becomes more important to seek efficient constructions of *result-hiding schemes*, which are dynamic SSE schemes mitigating access pattern leakage.

1.1 Our Contribution

In this paper, we propose Laura, a new result-hiding dynamic SSE scheme with forward and Type-II backward privacy, which is the most investigated security level of backward privacy. Laura is constructed based on Aura [25]; Laura is built from only symmetric-key primitives, specifically, from any pseudorandom function (PRF), any symmetric-key encryption (SKE), and any approximate membership query (AMQ) data structure. Laura achieves better practical efficiency to Aura and requires less leakage than Aura; this is the reason why we call our scheme Laura, which stands for Low-leakage Aura.

We give experimental results to show the concrete efficiency of Laura and v-Laura, which is a variant of Laura; their deletion and search procedures are almost as efficient as Aura, and their addition procedures are substantially more efficient than Aura. For example, Laura and v-Laura take less than a second to add 200,000 entries, while Aura takes about a minute. For concrete efficiency comparison among Laura, v-Laura, and Aura, see Sect. 6.

As a side result, we also figure out that in Aura (as well as Laura and v-Laura), the client is assumed to never re-add any keyword-identifier pair (w, id) once deleted, where id is a file identifier. This assumption seems reasonable in practice since id should be replaced with a new one if the client wants to re-add a

172   T. Amada et al.

Table 1. Efficiency comparison among Type-II backward-private dynamic SSE schemes. Suppose that the client has performed search and update operations t times in total. d and n are the total numbers of distinct keywords and files, respectively. a_w, n_w, and $n_{w,\mathrm{del}}^{(\mathrm{srch})}$ are the total numbers of all updates for w, files currently containing a keyword w, and times a keyword w has been affected by search operations since the last search for w, respectively. It clearly holds $a_w \geq \widehat{n}_w \geq n_w$, where $\widehat{n}_w := n_w + n_{w,\mathrm{del}}^{(\mathrm{srch})}$. N is the total numbers of (document, keyword) pairs, i.e., $N := \Sigma_w n_w$. Let $N' := \Sigma_w \widehat{n}_w$ and $\widehat{N} := \Sigma_w a_w$. Namely, it holds $\widehat{N} \geq N' \geq N$. $|\sigma|$ and $|\mathsf{EDB}|$ denote bit-lengths of client's state information and encrypted database. RT and RH stand for roundtrips and result hiding, respectively. SK indicates whether the scheme is constructed from only symmetric-key primitives. RU stands for re-updatability, which allows the client to re-add a previously-deleted entry (w, id) to EDB.

	$|\sigma|$	$|\mathsf{EDB}|$	Update		Search		RT	RH	SK	RU
			Comp.	Comm.	Comp.	Comm.				
SD_a [12]	$\mathcal{O}(1)$	$\mathcal{O}(\widehat{N})$	$\mathcal{O}(\log \widehat{N})^\dagger$	$\mathcal{O}(\log \widehat{N})^\dagger$	$\mathcal{O}(\widehat{a}_w)^\sharp$	$\mathcal{O}(\widehat{n}_w)$	2	✓	✓	✓
SD_d [12]	$\mathcal{O}(1)$	$\mathcal{O}(\widehat{N})$	$\mathcal{O}(\log^3 \widehat{N})$	$\mathcal{O}(\log \widehat{N})$	$\mathcal{O}(\widehat{a}_w)^\sharp$	$\mathcal{O}(n_w)$	2	✓	✓	✓
Fides [6]	$\mathcal{O}(d)$	$\mathcal{O}(N')$	$\mathcal{O}(1)$	$\mathcal{O}(1)$	$\mathcal{O}(\widehat{n}_w)$	$\mathcal{O}(\widehat{n}_w)$	3	✓	—	✓
Aura [25] (+EKPE [14])	$\mathcal{O}(d)$	$\mathcal{O}(\widehat{N})$	$\mathcal{O}(1)^\ddagger$	$\mathcal{O}(1)$	$\mathcal{O}(\widehat{n}_w)$	$\mathcal{O}(n_w)$	1	—	✓	—
Laura (Sect. 4.2)	$\mathcal{O}(d)$	$\mathcal{O}(N')$	$\mathcal{O}(1)^\ddagger$	$\mathcal{O}(1)$	$\mathcal{O}(\widehat{n}_w)$	$\mathcal{O}(\widehat{n}_w)$	3	✓	✓	—
v-Laura (Sect. 5.1)	$\mathcal{O}(d)$	$\mathcal{O}(N')$	$\mathcal{O}(1)^\ddagger$	$\mathcal{O}(1)$	$\mathcal{O}(\widehat{n}_w)$	$\mathcal{O}(\widehat{n}_w)$	2	✓	✓	—
s-Laura (Sect. 5.2)	$\mathcal{O}(d)$	$\mathcal{O}(N')$	$\mathcal{O}(1)^\ddagger$	$\mathcal{O}(1)$	$\mathcal{O}(\widehat{n}_{w,\mathrm{del}}^{(\mathrm{srch})})^\sharp$	$\mathcal{O}(\widehat{n}_w)$	3	✓	✓	✓

† Amortized analysis.
‡ To be precise, the deletion procedure depends on the time complexity of the underlying AMQ structure, which is $\mathcal{O}(1)$ in almost all existing constructions.
♯ Let $\widehat{a}_w := a_w + \log \widehat{N}$ and $\widehat{n}_{w,\mathrm{del}}^{(\mathrm{srch})} := \widehat{n}_w \cdot n_{w,\mathrm{del}}^{(\mathrm{srch})}$ for compact notations.

previously-deleted file whose identifier is id. We also show a variant of Laura, called s-Laura, that removes the assumption, i.e., it allows the client to re-add previous-deleted entries to the encrypted database, although s-Laura requires extra search costs.

Efficiency Comparison. We compare the asymptotic efficiency of dynamic SSE schemes with forward and Type-II backward privacy in Table 1. Note that we evaluate the server-side complexities of update and search algorithms. Although the efficiency of Laura and v-Laura seems comparable to Fides [6] and Aura [25], Laura and v-Laura has clear advantages over them; Fides employs public-key primitives such as trapdoor permutations for its building block. Moreover, Fides returns a (tentative) search result that contains deleted identifiers. Therefore, the client themself has to remove such deleted ones to obtain the correct search result. Although Laura and v-Laura also require for the client to remove deleted identifiers, the client can easily find them thanks to the underlying approximate membership query (AMQ) data structure. Aura achieves the minimum roundtrip, however, the size of encrypted databases is large. Furthermore, Aura reveals the access pattern and therefore is *not* a result-hiding scheme. Among the dynamic SSE schemes that satisfy all properties (RH, SK, and RU) listed in the table, s-Laura is more efficient than SD_a and SD_d.

2 Preliminaries

Notations. For any integer $a \in \mathbb{Z}$, let $[a] := \{1, 2, \ldots, a\}$. For a finite set $\mathcal{X}$, we use $x \xleftarrow{\$} \mathcal{X}$ to represent processes of choosing an element x from X uniformly at random. For a finite set $\mathcal{X}$, we denote by $\mathcal{X} \leftarrow x$ and $|\mathcal{X}|$ the addition x to $\mathcal{X}$ and cardinality of $\mathcal{X}$, respectively. Concatenation is denoted by $\|$. In the description of the algorithm, all arrays, strings, and sets are initialized to empty ones. We consider probabilistic polynomial time (PPT) algorithms. For any non-interactive algorithm A, out $\leftarrow$ A(in) means that A takes in as input and outputs out. In this paper, we consider two-party interactive algorithms between a client and a server, and it is denoted by $(\mathsf{out_C}; \mathsf{out_S}) \leftarrow \mathsf{A}(\mathsf{in_C}; \mathsf{in_S})$, where $\mathsf{in_C}$ and $\mathsf{in_S}$ are input of client and server, respectively and $\mathsf{out_C}$ and $\mathsf{out_S}$ are output of client and server, respectively. If necessary, we mention the transcript trans and describe the algorithm as $\langle(\mathsf{out_C}; \mathsf{out_S}), \mathsf{trans}\rangle \leftarrow \mathsf{A}(\mathsf{in_C}; \mathsf{in_S})$. The security parameter and negligible function are denoted by κ and $\mathsf{negl}(\cdot)$, respectively.

Pseudorandom Functions (PRFs). A family of functions $\pi := \{\pi_{\mathsf{k_{PRF}}} : \{0, 1\}^* \to \{0, 1\}^m\}_{\mathsf{k_{PRF}} \in \{0,1\}^\kappa}$, where $m = \mathsf{poly}(\kappa)$, is said to be a (variable-input-length) PRF family if for sufficiently large $\kappa \in \mathbb{N}$ and all PPT algorithm D, it holds $|\Pr[\mathsf{D}^{\pi(\mathsf{k_{PRF}},\cdot)}(1^\kappa) = 1 \mid \mathsf{k_{PRF}} \xleftarrow{\$} \{0, 1\}^\kappa] - \Pr[\mathsf{D}^{\mathsf{R}(\cdot)}(1^\kappa) = 1 \mid \mathsf{R} \xleftarrow{\$} \mathcal{R}]| < \mathsf{negl}(\kappa)$, where $\mathcal{R}$ is a set of all mappings $\mathsf{R} : \{0, 1\}^* \to \{0, 1\}^m$.

Symmetric-Key Encryption (SKE). An SKE Π_{SKE} consists of three PPT algorithms $\Pi_{\mathrm{SKE}} = (\mathsf{G}, \mathsf{E}, \mathsf{D})$. G takes a security parameter κ as input and outputs a secret key $\mathsf{k_{SKE}}$, and E takes a plaintext m and $\mathsf{k_{SKE}}$ as input and outputs the ciphertext c. D takes c with $\mathsf{k_{SKE}}$ and outputs m or $\bot$ as a symbol of failure. In this paper, we assume Π_{SKE} is CPA security. For formal definitions, we refer the readers to [21]. Also, if necessary, we explicitly describe a nonce used in an SKE. Specifically, for nonce r, the encryption and decryption algorithms are denoted by $\mathsf{E}(\mathsf{k_{SKE}}, \mathsf{m}; r)$ and $\mathsf{D}(\mathsf{k_{SKE}}, \mathsf{c}; r)$, respectively. The ciphertext is treated as $r\|\mathsf{c}$. Note that (nonce-based) CTR and CBC modes in block ciphers satisfy CPA security and the above properties.

Approximate Membership Query (AMQ) Structure. Probabilistic data structures, known as Approximate Membership Query (AMQ) data structures, provide membership queries with compact data sizes by allowing "false positives." The most appealing feature of AMQ structures is to make the false-positive probability small enough by setting specific parameters appropriately. We consider AMQ structures that support both insertion and deletion operations. While the Bloom filter [4], one of the well-known AMQ structures, does not support deletion, recent ones, such as the cuckoo filter [15] and quotient filter [2], do.

  Formally, an arbitrary set $\mathcal{U} \in \{0, 1\}^*$, an AMQ data structure $\Pi_{\mathrm{AMQ}} = (\mathsf{AMQ.Gen}, \mathsf{AMQ.Insert}, \mathsf{AMQ.Delete}, \mathsf{AMQ.Lookup})$ consists of the following PPT algorithms:

- $(\mathcal{T}, \mathsf{aux}) \leftarrow \mathsf{AMQ.Gen}(\mathcal{U}, \mathsf{par})$: it takes $\mathcal{U}$ and a parameter par as input, and outputs an initial structure $\mathcal{T}$ and auxiliary information aux. The parameter par depends on the construction of the specific AMQ structure.
- $\mathcal{T}' \leftarrow \mathsf{AMQ.Insert}(\mathcal{T}, x, \mathsf{aux})$: it takes as input a data structure $\mathcal{T}$, an element $x \in \mathcal{U}$ to be added, and aux, and outputs an updated structure $\mathcal{T}'$.
- $\mathcal{T}' \leftarrow \mathsf{AMQ.Delete}(\mathcal{T}, x, \mathsf{aux})$: it takes as input a data structure $\mathcal{T}$, an element $x \in \mathcal{U}$ to be deleted, and aux, and outputs an updated structure $\mathcal{T}'$.
- $\mathtt{true}/\mathtt{false} \leftarrow \mathsf{AMQ.Lookup}(\mathcal{T}, x, \mathsf{aux})$: it takes as input a data structure $\mathcal{T}$, an element $x \in \mathcal{U}$ to be queried, and aux, and outputs $\mathtt{true}$ or $\mathtt{false}$.

AMQ structures meet the following two properties. Due to the page limitation, we omit the formal description and will give it in the full version.

- *Completeness*: Let $\mathcal{S}$ be a set of elements that have been inserted (and not deleted). For all $x \in \mathcal{S}$, it holds $\mathsf{AMQ.Lookup}(\mathcal{T}, x, \mathsf{aux}) = \mathtt{true}$, where $\mathcal{T}$ is the corresponding structure.
- *Bounded False-Positive Probability*: Let $n := |\mathcal{S}|$. Then, there exists $\mu_n \in (0, 1]$ such that it holds $\Pr[\mathsf{AMQ.Lookup}(\mathcal{T}, x, \mathsf{aux}) = \mathtt{true}] \leq \mu_n$ for any $x \in \mathcal{U} \setminus \mathcal{S}$.

3   Dynamic SSE

3.1   Notation for Dynamic SSE

$\Lambda := \{0, 1\}^\lambda$ is a set of possible keywords (sometimes called a *dictionary*), where $\lambda = \mathsf{poly}(\kappa)$. A document f_{id} has its unique identifier $\mathsf{id} \in \{0, 1\}^\ell$, which is irrelevant to the contents of f_{id}, where $\ell = \mathsf{poly}(\kappa)$. A counter t represents the global counter through the protocol; it is initialized to 0 at setup and incremented for each search or update operation. A database $\mathsf{DB}^{(t)}$ at t is represented as a set of keyword-identifier pairs (w, id), i.e., $\mathsf{DB}^{(t)} := \{(w_i, \mathsf{id}_i)\}_{i=1}^{N(t)}$, where $N(t)$ is the number of pairs stored in the server at t. We denote $\mathsf{ID}^{(t)}$ by a set of identifiers in $\mathsf{DB}^{(t)}$. That is, $\mathsf{ID}^{(t)} := \{\mathsf{id} \mid \forall w \in \Lambda, (w, \mathsf{id}) \in \mathsf{DB}^{(t)}\}$. Similarly, $\mathcal{W}^{(t)}$ is denoted by a set of keywords in $\mathsf{DB}^{(t)}$, i.e., $\mathcal{W}^{(t)} := \{w \mid \forall \mathsf{id} \in \mathsf{ID}^{(t)}, (w, \mathsf{id}) \in \mathsf{DB}^{(t)}\}$.

3.2   Model

Dynamic SSE consists of three PPT algorithms (Setup, Update, Search). Firstly, the client runs Setup to generate a secret key, initial state information, and an initial encrypted database, which is sent to the server. The client interacts with the server and runs Update and Search repeatedly to add or delete a pair (w, id) and search for keywords.

Definition 1 (Dynamic SSE). *A Dynamic SSE* $\Sigma :=$ (Setup, Update, Search) *over* Λ *consists of the following PPT algorithms:*

- $(k, \sigma^{(0)}, \mathsf{EDB}^{(0)}) \leftarrow \mathsf{Setup}(1^\kappa)$: *it is an non-interactive algorithm that takes a security parameter* κ *as input and outputs a secret key* k, *initial state information* $\sigma^{(0)}$, *and initial encrypted database* $\mathsf{EDB}^{(0)}$.

- $(\sigma^{(t+1)}; \mathsf{EDB}^{(t+1)}) \leftarrow \mathsf{Update}(k, \mathsf{op}, \mathsf{in}, \sigma^{(t)}; \mathsf{EDB}^{(t)})$: *it is an interactive algorithm that takes k, an operation label $\mathsf{op} \in \{\mathsf{add}, \mathsf{del}\}$, the corresponding input* $\mathsf{in} := (w, \mathsf{id})$, *and $\sigma^{(t)}$ as input of the client and encrypted database $\mathsf{EDB}^{(t)}$ as input of the server, and outputs updated state information $\sigma^{(t+1)}$ for the client and updated encrypted database $\mathsf{EDB}^{(t+1)}$ for the server.*

- $(\mathcal{X}_q^{(t)}, \sigma^{(t+1)}; \mathsf{EDB}^{(t+1)}) \leftarrow \mathsf{Search}(k, q, \sigma^{(t)}; \mathsf{EDB}^{(t)})$: *it is an interactive algorithm that takes k, a searched keyword q, and $\sigma^{(t)}$ as input of the client and encrypted database $\mathsf{EDB}^{(t)}$ as input of the server, and outputs updated state information $\sigma^{(t+1)}$ and a search result $\mathcal{X}_q^{(t)}$ for the client and updated encrypted database $\mathsf{EDB}^{(t+1)}$ for the server.*

Briefly, the correctness of the above model ensures that it holds $\mathcal{X}_q^{(t)} = \{\mathsf{id} \in \mathsf{ID}^{(t)} \mid (q, \mathsf{id}) \in \mathsf{DB}^{(t)}\}$ with overwhelming probability for any keyword $q \in \Lambda$. For a formal definition, we refer the readers to [8].

3.3   Security

Dynamic SSE guarantees that the (honest-but-curious) server does not learn any information beyond some explicit information leakage during a sequence of operations. Therefore, such information leakage is characterized as a leakage function $\mathcal{L} := (\mathcal{L}_{\mathsf{Setup}}, \mathcal{L}_{\mathsf{Upd}}, \mathcal{L}_{\mathsf{Srch}})$, where $\mathcal{L}_{\mathsf{Setup}}$, $\mathcal{L}_{\mathsf{Upd}}$, and $\mathcal{L}_{\mathsf{Srch}}$ are functions that refer to information leaked during Setup, Update, and Search, respectively.

$\mathcal{L}$-**Adaptive Security.** We define $\mathcal{L}$-adaptive security of SSE in a simulation-based manner. We consider two experiments: a real experiment Real in which the Dynamic SSE scheme is performed in the real world and an ideal experiment Ideal that at most leaks a leakage function $\mathcal{L}$. Specifically, a real experiment Real_D is performed by the client and a PPT algorithm $\mathsf{D} = (\mathsf{D}_1, \mathsf{D}_2, \ldots, \mathsf{D}_{Q+1})$, while ideal experiment $\mathsf{Ideal}_{\mathsf{D}, \mathsf{S}, \mathcal{L}}$ is performed by D and a simulator $\mathsf{S} = (\mathsf{S}_0, \mathsf{S}_1, \ldots, \mathsf{S}_Q)$ with leakage function $\mathcal{L}$. In each experiment, D adaptively queries and attempts to distinguish between the two experiments. If D cannot distinguish between them, D has not learned more information than the leakage function $\mathcal{L}$; we call this $\mathcal{L}$-adaptive security. Each experiment is formally given in Fig. 1, and the security definition is as follows [27].

Definition 2 ($\mathcal{L}$-Adaptive Security). *Let Σ be a Dynamic SSE scheme. Σ is $\mathcal{L}$-adaptively secure, with regard to a leakage function $\mathcal{L}$, if for any PPT algorithm D, any sufficiently large $\kappa \in \mathbb{N}$, and any $Q := \mathsf{poly}(\kappa)$, there exists a PPT algorithm S s.t. $|\mathrm{Pr}\left[\mathsf{Real}_\mathsf{D}(\kappa, Q) = 1\right] - \mathrm{Pr}\left[\mathsf{Ideal}_{\mathsf{D}, \mathsf{S}, \mathcal{L}}(\kappa, Q) = 1\right]| < \mathsf{negl}(\kappa)$.*

Real Experiment: $\mathsf{Real}_D(\kappa, Q)$	Ideal Experiment: $\mathsf{Ideal}_{D,S,\mathcal{L}}(\kappa, Q)$
1: $(k, \sigma^{(0)}, \mathsf{EDB}^{(0)}) \leftarrow \mathsf{Setup}(1^\kappa)$	1: $(\mathsf{EDB}^{(0)}, \mathsf{st_S}) \leftarrow \mathsf{S}_0(\mathcal{L}_{\mathsf{Setup}}(\kappa))$
2: $\mathsf{st_D} := \{\mathsf{EDB}^{(0)}\}$	2: $\mathsf{st_D} := \{\mathsf{EDB}^{(0)}\}$
3: **for** $t = 1$ **to** Q **do**	3: **for** $t = 1$ **to** Q **do**
4: $\mathsf{query} \leftarrow \mathsf{D}_t(\mathsf{st_D})$	4: $\mathsf{query} \leftarrow \mathsf{D}_t(\mathsf{st_D})$
5: **if** $\mathsf{query} = (\mathsf{upd}, \mathsf{op}, \mathsf{in})$ **then**	5: **if** $\mathsf{query} = (\mathsf{upd}, \mathsf{op}, \mathsf{in})$ **then**
6: $\langle(\sigma^{(t)}; \mathsf{EDB}^{(t)}), \mathsf{trans}^{(t)}\rangle$	6: $\langle(\mathsf{st'_S}; \mathsf{EDB}^{(t)}), \mathsf{trans}^{(t)}\rangle$
$\leftarrow \mathsf{Update}(k, \mathsf{op}, \mathsf{in}, \sigma^{(t-1)}; \mathsf{EDB}^{(t-1)})$	$\leftarrow \mathsf{S}_t(\mathsf{st_S}, \mathcal{L}_{\mathsf{Upd}}(t, \mathsf{op}, \mathsf{in}); \mathsf{EDB}^{(t-1)})$
7: **if** $\mathsf{query} = (\mathsf{srch}, q)$ **then**	7: **if** $\mathsf{query} = (\mathsf{srch}, q)$ **then**
8: $\langle(\sigma^{(t)}, \mathcal{X}_q^{(t-1)}; \mathsf{EDB}^{(t)}), \mathsf{trans}^{(t)}\rangle$	8: $\langle(\mathsf{st'_S}; \mathsf{EDB}^{(t)}), \mathsf{trans}^{(t)}\rangle$
$\leftarrow \mathsf{Search}(k, q, \sigma^{(t-1)}; \mathsf{EDB}^{(t-1)})$	$\leftarrow \mathsf{S}_t(\mathsf{st_S}, \mathcal{L}_{\mathsf{Srch}}(t, q); \mathsf{EDB}^{(t-1)})$
9: $\mathsf{st_D} \leftarrow (\mathsf{EDB}^{(t)}, \mathsf{trans}^{(t)})$	9: $\mathsf{st_D} \leftarrow (\mathsf{EDB}^{(t)}, \mathsf{trans}^{(t)})$
10: $b \leftarrow \mathsf{D}_{Q+1}(\mathsf{st_D})$	10: $\mathsf{st_S} := \mathsf{st'_S}$
11: **return** b	11: $b \leftarrow \mathsf{D}_{Q+1}(\mathsf{st_D})$
	12: **return** b

Fig. 1. Real and ideal experiments.

We also define one-time $\mathcal{L}$-adaptive security, which is $\mathcal{L}$-adaptive security under the restriction that a keyword-identifier pair is never re-added once deleted.

Forward and Backward Privacy. The well-known security notions for update operations are *forward privacy* [5] and *backward privacy* [6].

Forward privacy, roughly speaking, ensures that while running an update of a keyword-identifier pair (q, id), no information about the keyword q is exposed to the server. This means that the keyword q cannot be associated with all previous searches and update operations. Forward privacy is an important security requirement since Zhang et al. [28] showed effective attacks against non-forward-private dynamic SSE schemes. The formal definition is as follows:

Definition 3 (Forward Privacy [5]). *Let Σ be a $\mathcal{L}$-adaptively secure dynamic SSE scheme. Σ is forward private if $\mathcal{L}_{\mathsf{Upd}}$(for $\mathsf{op} = \mathsf{add}$) can be written as $\mathcal{L}_{\mathsf{Upd}}(t, \mathsf{add}, (q, \mathsf{id})) = \mathcal{L}'(t, \mathsf{add}, \mathsf{id})$, where $\mathcal{L}'$ is stateless function.*

On the other hand, loosely speaking, backward privacy guarantees that while running a search for a keyword q, the least possible (ideally, no) information about the deleted pair (q, id) is leaked to the server. However, if leakage regarding deletion operations is to be completely eliminated, significant costs are required due to efficiency trade-offs. Therefore, Bost et al. [6] introduced three levels of backward privacy: from Type-I with the least leakage to Type-III with the most leakage. In this paper, we focus on Type-II backward privacy, which achieves a good balance between security levels and achievable efficiency. To describe their definition, we define several functions of leaked information as follows. Let $\mathcal{Q}^{(t)}$ be the set of all operations of each counter $u \in [t]$, and its elements are described as $(u, q) \in \mathcal{Q}^{(t)}$ for a search for a keyword q and $(u, \mathsf{op}, (q, \mathsf{id})) \in \mathcal{Q}^{(t)}$ for an update of a keyword-identifier pair (q, id), where $\mathsf{op} \in \{\mathsf{add}, \mathsf{del}\}$.

- **Search pattern** $\mathsf{SP}_q^{(t)}$: A set of counters at which the keyword q has been searched. That is, $\mathsf{SP}_q^{(t)} := \{u \mid (u, q) \in \mathcal{Q}^{(t)}\}$.
- **Access pattern** $\mathsf{TimeDB}_q^{(t)}$: A set of pairs of an identifier $\mathsf{id} \in \mathsf{ID}^{(t)}$ that includes a keyword q at t and a counter u when the corresponding keyword-identifier pair (q, id) was added. That is,

$$\mathsf{TimeDB}_q^{(t)} := \left\{ (u^{\mathsf{add}}, \mathsf{id}) \;\middle|\; \begin{array}{l} (u^{\mathsf{add}}, \mathsf{add}, (q, \mathsf{id})) \in \mathcal{Q}^{(t)} \\ \wedge \; \forall u^{\mathsf{del}}, (u^{\mathsf{del}}, \mathsf{del}, (q, \mathsf{id})) \notin \mathcal{Q}^{(t)} \end{array} \right\},$$

where we assume $u^{\mathsf{add}} < u^{\mathsf{del}}$ without the loss of generality.
- **Update pattern** $\mathsf{Update}_q^{(t)}$: It is a set of counters for all update operations on q, i.e., $\mathsf{Update}_q^{(t)} := \{u \mid (u, \mathsf{add}, (q, \mathsf{id})) \in \mathcal{Q}^{(t)} \vee (u, \mathsf{del}, (q, \mathsf{id})) \in \mathcal{Q}^{(t)}\}$.

Using the above functions, Type-II backward privacy is defined as follows.

Definition 4 (Type-II Backward Privacy [6]**).** *Let Σ be a $\mathcal{L}$-adaptively secure dynamic SSE scheme. Σ is Type-II backward private if $\mathcal{L}_{\mathsf{Upd}}$ and $\mathcal{L}_{\mathsf{Srch}}$ can be written as:*

$$\mathcal{L}_{\mathsf{Upd}}(t, \mathsf{op}, (q, \mathsf{id})) = \mathcal{L}'(t, \mathsf{op}, q) \text{ and } \mathcal{L}_{\mathsf{Srch}}(t, q) = \mathcal{L}''(\mathsf{SP}_q^{(t)}, \mathsf{TimeDB}_q^{(t)}, \mathsf{Update}_q^{(t)}),$$

where $\mathcal{L}'$ and $\mathcal{L}''$ are stateless functions.

Result Hiding. As mentioned in the introduction, taking into account the recent progress in leakage abuse attacks, it is important to realize an efficient dynamic SSE scheme that never leaks identifiers of search results. Such a scheme is called a *result-hiding* one. Although several result-hiding schemes [6,12] are already known, to the best of our knowledge, there is no formal definition of the result-hiding property. Therefore, we first define it formally. We consider the following leakage functions.

- **Concealed access pattern** $\mathsf{Time}_q^{(t)}$: It is a set of counters contained in $\mathsf{TimeDB}_q^{(t)}$. That is, $\mathsf{Time}_q^{(t)} := \{u \mid \exists \mathsf{id} \text{ s.t. } (u, \mathsf{id}) \in \mathsf{TimeDB}_q^{(t)}\}$.
- **Deletion history** $\mathsf{DelHist}_q^{(t)}$: It is a set of pairs of two counters at which each of addition and deletion operations is performed on the same (q, id) pair. That is,

$$\mathsf{DelHist}_q^{(t)} := \left\{ (u^{\mathsf{add}}, u^{\mathsf{del}}) \;\middle|\; \begin{array}{l} \exists \mathsf{id} \text{ s.t. } (u^{\mathsf{add}}, \mathsf{add}, (q, \mathsf{id})) \in \mathcal{Q}^{(t)} \\ \wedge \; (u^{\mathsf{del}}, \mathsf{del}, (q, \mathsf{id})) \in \mathcal{Q}^{(t)} \end{array} \right\}.$$

Although $\mathsf{DelHist}_q^{(t)}$ is a well-known leakage function to define Type-III backward privacy, we also use it to define the result-hiding property.

Definition 5 (Result-Hiding Dynamic SSE). *Let Σ be a $\mathcal{L}$-adaptively secure dynamic SSE scheme. Σ is called a result-hiding scheme if $\mathcal{L}_{\mathsf{Upd}}$ and $\mathcal{L}_{\mathsf{Srch}}$ can be written as:*

$$\mathcal{L}_{\mathsf{Upd}}(t, \mathsf{op}, (q, \mathsf{id})) = \mathcal{L}'(t, \mathsf{op}, q) \ and \ \mathcal{L}_{\mathsf{Srch}}(t, q) = \mathcal{L}''(\mathsf{SP}_q^{(t)}, \mathsf{Time}_q^{(t)}, \mathsf{DelHist}_q^{(t)}),$$

where $\mathcal{L}'$ and $\mathcal{L}''$ are stateless functions.

Namely, result-hiding schemes do not leak any identifiers during updates and searches. Note that the search operation may leak all information related to the counters of update operations on q since the result-hiding property should be a property in which result-hiding schemes reveal no information on identifiers *themselves* contained in search results.

Remark 1. One may think that the result-hiding property conflicts with a common use case of dynamic SSE, where the server returns both a search result and the corresponding actual documents. The property prevents the server from returning the actual documents unless the client reveals the search result to the server; the reveal means the leakage of the access pattern and makes the result-hiding property meaningless! Nevertheless, in such a common use case, the result-hiding property should be valuable since the client can choose whether the client reveals the access pattern. Of course, the property would be more appealing in other use cases, e.g., where actual documents are stored on another server.

4   Laura: Low-Leakage Aura

We propose a new efficient dynamic SSE scheme that meets forward privacy, Type-II backward privacy, and the result-hiding property. Although the construction approach of our scheme is based on Aura, our scheme allows less leakage than Aura. Thus, we call our scheme Laura, which stands for low-leakage Aura.

4.1   Construction Idea

Construction Overview of Aura. Sun et al. [25] introduced a core building block of Aura, called symmetric revocable encryption (SRE). Briefly speaking, SRE supports *puncturable decryption*. In SRE, plaintexts are encrypted along with a tag. A decryption key associated with a certain revoked set, containing revoked tags, cannot decrypt ciphertexts related to the revoked tags. In Aura, SRE's puncturable decryption functionality allows the server to decrypt ciphertexts without leaking deleted entires as follows. When adding (w, id), the client encrypts id with a tag τ and the ciphertext is stored on the server. When deleting (w, id), the client adds the corresponding tag τ to a revoked tag set $\mathcal{R}_w$ on w, stored in the local storage. When searching for w, the client retrieves the revoked tag set $\mathcal{R}_w$ and generates a decryption key associated with $\mathcal{R}_w$. The server decrypts ciphertexts with the key and obtains id if the corresponding tag τ' is not revoked (i.e., $\tau' \notin \mathcal{R}_w$); it obtains $\perp$ otherwise due to the punc-turable decryption functionality. Therefore, the client can delegate the process of removing deleted entries to the server; it does not leak when and which identities have been deleted. The client just receives and outputs the search result from the server. Consequently, Aura is the first (efficient) dynamic SSE that supports both non-interactive search operations and Type-II backward privacy. However, there is still room for improvement as follows:

1) Although a Bloom filter [4] is used to compress the revoked tag set $\mathcal{R}_w$, the client has to store them on the local storage. It is desirable to reduce the amount of local storage on the client side (i.e., state information) as much as possible.
2) Aura employs *logical deletion*; for a deletion operation of (w, id), an entry $(\mathsf{del}, (w, \mathsf{id}))$ is added to an encrypted database EDB. As a result, the size of EDB in Aura is $\widehat{N} = \sum_w a_w$, where a_w is the total number of updates for w.
3) As seen above, the server decrypts the ciphertexts and gets the access patterns. Namely, Aura is not a result-hiding scheme.

Our Approach. A common approach to realizing result-hiding schemes is to have the client decrypt the search results [6,9,12]. With this approach in mind, our scheme is based on Aura combined with Etemad et al.'s forward-private scheme [14], which are *not* result-hiding schemes; we no longer employ SRE but the concept of revoked tags. The construction idea for Laura is to perform a *variant of* logical deletion using tags; sending the server a revoked tag τ of a deleted pair (w, id), instead of the (encrypted) pair itself, when deleting (w, id). Therefore, the client does not have to remember the tags. Laura maintains the revoked tags with an (arbitrary) AMQ data structure that supports deletion operations, whereas Sun et al. [25] only considered the Bloom filter for Aura. Hence, the client easily finds the deleted entries with the AMQ.Lookup algorithm, which leads to the result-hiding property while keeping efficiency.[1]

Moreover, we also achieve a smaller EDB through re-addition techniques [14, 26]: for a search query on w, the server retrieves all values related to the query from EDB and deletes them. After getting the search result, the client re-adds all entries except for deleted ones for the next search. We summarize what our approach resolves.

1) Laura achieves a smaller (concrete) storage size on the client side than Aura.
2) Laura achieves a smaller $|\mathsf{EDB}| = N' = \sum_w (n_w + n_{w,\mathsf{del}}^{(\mathsf{srch})})$ than Aura, where $n_{w,\mathsf{del}}^{(\mathsf{srch})}$ is the total number of times a keyword w has been affected by search operations since the last search for w. It clearly holds $\widehat{N} \geq N'$.

---

[1] Though the server needs to send the AMQ structure to the client during the search operation, the size of the structure is reasonably small. For example, if we select the cuckoo filter [15] as the AMQ structure, its size is 0.79 MB for 100,000 deleted entries with the false-positive probability $p = 10^{-4}$. As a reference, according to the Aura paper [25], SD_d [12] requires 8,58 MB of total communication costs for search.

Algorithm: Laura

Setup(1^κ)

Client:

1: $k_{\mathrm{PRF}}, k_{\mathrm{RH}}, k_{\mathrm{SKE}} \xleftarrow{\$} \{0,1\}^\kappa$
2: $(\mathcal{T}, \mathsf{aux}) \leftarrow \mathsf{AMQ.Gen}(\{0,1\}^\lambda, \mathsf{par})$
3: $\mathsf{fc}_w, \mathsf{sc}_w, \mathsf{Index}[] := \varepsilon$ // ε is an empty value
4: **return** $\left(k := (k_{\mathrm{PRF}}, k_{\mathrm{RH}}, k_{\mathrm{SKE}}), \sigma^{(0)} := (\mathsf{sc}_w, \mathsf{fc}_w), \mathsf{EDB}^{(0)} := (\mathsf{Index}, \mathcal{T}, \mathsf{aux})\right)$

Update($k, \mathsf{add}, (w, \mathsf{id}), \sigma^{(t)}; \mathsf{EDB}^{(t)}$)

Client:

1: $\tau \leftarrow \pi(k_{\mathrm{RH}}, w\|\mathsf{id})$
2: **if** sc_w is undefined **then**
3:    $(\mathsf{sc}_w, \mathsf{fc}_w) := (0, 0)$
4: $\mathsf{fc}_w := \mathsf{fc}_w + 1$ // increment fc_w
5: $\mathsf{K}_w^{(\mathsf{sc}_w)} \leftarrow g(k_{\mathrm{PRF}}, w\|\mathsf{sc}_w)$ // generate the PRF key for address
6: $\mathsf{addr} \leftarrow h(\mathsf{K}_w^{(\mathsf{sc}_w)}, \mathsf{fc}_w),\quad \mathsf{val} \leftarrow E(k_{\mathrm{SKE}}, \tau\|\mathsf{id})$
7: Send $\mathsf{trans}^{(t)} := (\mathsf{addr}, \mathsf{val})$ to the server
8: **return** $\sigma^{(t+1)} := (\mathsf{sc}_w, \mathsf{fc}_w)_{w \in \mathcal{W}^{(t+1)}}$

Server:

10: $\mathsf{Index}[\mathsf{addr}] := \mathsf{val}$
11: **return** $\mathsf{EDB}^{(t+1)} := (\mathsf{Index}, \mathcal{T}, \mathsf{aux})$

Update($k, \mathsf{del}, (w, \mathsf{id}), \sigma^{(t)}; \mathsf{EDB}^{(t)}$)

Client:

1: **if** fc_w is defined **then**
2:    $\tau \leftarrow \pi(k_{\mathrm{RH}}, w\|\mathsf{id})$
3:    Send $\mathsf{trans}_1^{(t)} := \tau$ to the server
4: **return** $\sigma^{(t+1)} := \sigma^{(t)}$

Server:

6: $\mathcal{T}' \leftarrow \mathsf{AMQ.Insert}(\mathcal{T}, \tau, \mathsf{aux})$
7: **return** $\mathsf{EDB}^{(t+1)} := (\mathsf{Index}, \mathcal{T}', \mathsf{aux})$

Fig. 2. Setup and Update of our dynamic SSE scheme Laura.

3) Laura is a result-hiding scheme. Furthermore, compared to existing these schemes, Laura achieves compression of EDB and efficient removal of deleted entries due to the AMQ data structure.

In addition to the above benefits, Laura is more practically efficient than Aura. We will see that in Sect. 6.

4.2 Our Construction

Let $\pi : \{0,1\}^* \rightarrow \{0,1\}^\lambda$ and $g : \{0,1\}^* \rightarrow \{0,1\}^\kappa$ be (variable-input-length) PRF families and $h : \{0,1\}^* \rightarrow \{0,1\}^\eta$ be a hash function, where λ and η are polynomials in κ. Let $\Pi_{\mathrm{AMQ}} = (\mathsf{AMQ.Gen}, \mathsf{AMQ.Insert}, \mathsf{AMQ.Delete},$

Algorithm: Laura

$\mathsf{Search}(k, q, \sigma^{(t)}; \mathsf{EDB}^{(t)})$

Client:

1: $\mathsf{K}_q^{(\mathsf{sc}_w)} \leftarrow g(\mathsf{k}_{\mathrm{PRF}}, q\|\mathsf{sc}_q)$

2: Send $\mathsf{trans}_1^{(t)} := (\mathsf{K}_q^{(\mathsf{sc}_w)}, \mathsf{fc}_q)$ to the server

Server:

3: **for** $i = 1$ **to** fc_q **do**

4:    $\mathtt{addr} \leftarrow h(\mathsf{K}_q^{(\mathsf{sc}_w)}, i)$, $\mathtt{val} := \mathsf{Index}[\mathtt{addr}]$, $\mathcal{C}_q^{(t)} \leftarrow \mathtt{val}$

5:    $\mathsf{Index}[\mathtt{addr}] := \mathsf{NULL}$ // delete old addresses

6: Send $\mathsf{trans}_2^{(t)} := (\mathcal{C}_q^{(t)}, \mathcal{T}, \mathsf{aux})$ to the client // Send copy of $\mathcal{T}$

Client:

7: **for** $\forall \mathsf{c} \in \mathcal{C}_q^{(t)}$ **do**

8:    $\tau\|\mathsf{id} \leftarrow \mathsf{D}(\mathsf{k}_{\mathrm{SKE}}, \mathsf{c})$ // the first λ MSBs of $\mathtt{val}$ is tag

9:    **if** $\mathsf{AMQ.Lookup}(\mathcal{T}, \tau, \mathsf{aux}) = \mathbf{true}$ **then** // logical deletion of (q, id)

10:       $\mathcal{D}_q^{(t)} \leftarrow \tau$

11:    **else** // search result

12:       $\mathcal{X}_q^{(t)} \leftarrow \mathsf{id}$, $\mathcal{Y}_q^{(t)} \leftarrow (\tau, \mathsf{id})$

13: $\mathsf{sc}_q := \mathsf{sc}_q + 1$, $\mathsf{fc}_q := |\mathcal{X}_q^{(t)}|$ // update state

14: $\widehat{\mathsf{K}}_q^{(\mathsf{sc}_q)} \leftarrow g(\mathsf{k}_{\mathrm{PRF}}, q\|\mathsf{sc}_q)$ // generate new keys

15: $\mathsf{ctr} := 1$

16: **for** $\forall (\tau, \mathsf{id}) \in \mathcal{Y}_q^{(t)}$ **do**

17:    $\widehat{\mathtt{addr}} \leftarrow h(\widehat{\mathsf{K}}_q^{(\mathsf{sc}_q)}, \mathsf{ctr})$, $\widehat{\mathtt{val}} \leftarrow \mathsf{E}(\mathsf{k}_{\mathrm{SKE}}, \tau\|\mathsf{id})$

18:    $\mathcal{R}_q^{(t)} \leftarrow (\widehat{\mathtt{addr}}, \widehat{\mathtt{val}})$, $\mathsf{ctr} := \mathsf{ctr} + 1$

19: Send $\mathsf{trans}_3^{(t)} := (\mathcal{D}_q^{(t)}, \mathcal{R}_q^{(t)})$ to the server

20: **return** $(\mathcal{X}_q^{(t)}, \sigma^{(t+1)} := (\mathsf{sc}_q, \mathsf{fc}_q)_{q \in \mathcal{W}^{(t+1)}})$

Server:

21: **for** $\forall (\widehat{\mathtt{addr}}, \widehat{\mathtt{val}}) \in \mathcal{R}_q^{(t)}$ **do**

22:    $\mathsf{Index}[\widehat{\mathtt{addr}}] := \widehat{\mathtt{val}}$ // set new addresses and value

23: **for** $\forall \tau \in \mathcal{D}_q^{(t)}$ **do**

24:    $\mathcal{T}' \leftarrow \mathsf{AMQ.Delete}(\mathcal{T}, \tau, \mathsf{aux})$, $\mathcal{T} := \mathcal{T}'$

25: **return** $\mathsf{EDB}^{(t+1)} := (\mathsf{Index}, \mathcal{T}, \mathsf{aux})$

Fig. 3. Search of our dynamic SSE scheme Laura.

AMQ.Lookup) be an AMQ data structure. We propose a dynamic SSE scheme Laura = (Setup, Update, Search) from Π_{AMQ}, π, g, and h. The pseudo-codes for Laura are given in Figs. 2 and 3, and we provide overviews of each algorithm below.

Setup: Setup(1^κ). The client generates a secret key $k := (\mathsf{k}_{\mathrm{SKE}}, \mathsf{k}_{\mathrm{PRF}}, \mathsf{k}_{\mathrm{RH}})$, where $\mathsf{k}_{\mathrm{SKE}}$ is an SKE secret key and $\mathsf{k}_{\mathrm{PRF}}$ and k_{RH} are PRF keys used to compute addresses and tags, respectively. The client initializes two counters fc_w and sc_w, an array Index, and an AMQ data structure $\mathcal{T}$ (along with its auxiliary information aux). The client sets the state information $\sigma^{(0)} := (\mathsf{fc}_w, \mathsf{sc}_w)$, and sends $\mathsf{EDB}^{(0)} := (\mathsf{Index}\mathcal{T}, \mathsf{aux})$ to the server.

Addition: Update(k, add, (w, id), $\sigma^{(t)}$; $\mathsf{EDB}^{(t)}$). First, the client retrieves the file counter fc_w and the search counter sc_w in $\sigma^{(t)}$ and increments fc_w. The client next derives a PRF key $\mathsf{K}_w^{(\mathsf{sc}_w)}$ from the PRF key $\mathsf{k}_{\mathrm{PRF}}$ using the keyword w to calculate an address addr. Also, the client computes a tag τ, which will be sent to the server during the deletion operation, of the pair (w, id) from the PRF key k_{RH}, and encrypts $\tau \| \mathsf{id}$ with the SKE secret key $\mathsf{k}_{\mathrm{SKE}}$. The server adds the ciphertext to $\mathsf{Index}[\mathsf{addr}]$ in $\mathsf{EDB}^{(t)}$.

Deletion: Update(k, del, (w, id), $\sigma^{(t)}$; $\mathsf{EDB}^{(t)}$). The client only computes the tag τ of the pair (w, id) using the PRF key k_{RH} and sends it to the server. The server executes AMQ.Insert to insert τ into the data structure $\mathcal{T}$ in $\mathsf{EDB}^{(t)}$.

Search: Search(k, q, $\sigma^{(t)}$; $\mathsf{EDB}^{(t)}$). First, the client creates the PRF key $\mathsf{K}_q^{(\mathsf{sc}_w)}$ for the search keyword q and sends it together with fc_q to the server. For every $i = 1, \ldots, \mathsf{fc}_q$, the server computes an address $g(\mathsf{K}_q^{(\mathsf{sc}_w)}, i)$ and adds its stored value val to the set $\mathcal{C}_q^{(t)}$. The server sends $\mathcal{C}_q^{(t)}$ and a copy of the data structure $\mathcal{T}$ to the client and frees the memory of all the addresses accessed. For every value $\mathsf{val} \in \mathcal{C}_q^{(t)}$, the client checks whether it has been deleted as follows. The client decrypts val and obtains $\tau \| \mathsf{id}$, and executes AMQ.Lookup with τ to check whether the pair (w, id) has been logically deleted. If AMQ.Lookup outputs false, id is added to the search result $\mathcal{X}_q^{(t)}$. Next, the client re-adds the pairs (w, id) except for the deleted ones. The client increments sc_q, and adds the pairs in the same way to the above addition procedure. The server updates $\mathsf{EDB}^{(t)}$ as in the addition procedure and also receives a tag set $\mathcal{D}_q^{(t)}$ of the deleted entry. For every tag $\tau \in \mathcal{D}_q^{(t)}$, the server executes AMQ.Delete to remove the tags from the data structure $\mathcal{T}$. This re-addition procedure is important to provide forward privacy and reduce the size of EDB and $\mathcal{T}$.

4.3   Security Analysis

Correctness. Before analyzing the security of Laura, we show that it satisfies the correctness. Laura might output wrong search results due to false positives in the underlying AMQ data structure Π_{AMQ}. The correctness error probability depends on the false-positive probability; due to the bounded false-positive probability property, there exists, and we can evaluate an upper bound μ_n of the false-positive probability. Therefore, by setting the parameters of Π_{AMQ} appropriately, one can make the correctness error probability negligible.

Security. To show the security of Laura, we consider a leakage function called *deletion pattern* $\mathsf{DelTime}_q^{(t)}$, which is a set of counters for all deletion operations on w. Namely, $\mathsf{DelTime}_q^{(t)} := \{u^{\mathsf{del}} \mid \exists u^{\mathsf{add}} \text{ s.t. } (u^{\mathsf{add}}, u^{\mathsf{del}}) \in \mathsf{DelHist}_q^{(t)}\}$.

Theorem 1. *If Π_{SKE} is CPA-secure, Π_{AMQ} is an AMQ data structure, π and g are (variable-input-length) PRF families, and h is a random oracle, the dynamic SSE scheme Laura = (Setup, Update, Search) in Figs. 2 and 3 is an one-time*

$\mathcal{L}$-adaptively secure result-hiding scheme that supports forward privacy and Type-II backward privacy, with the following leakage function $\mathcal{L} = (\mathcal{L}_{\mathsf{Setup}}, \mathcal{L}_{\mathsf{Upd}}, \mathcal{L}_{\mathsf{Srch}})$:

$$\mathcal{L}_{\mathsf{Setup}}(1^{\kappa}) = \Lambda, \quad \mathcal{L}_{\mathsf{Upd}}(t, \mathsf{op}, \mathsf{in}) = (t, \mathsf{op}),$$
$$\mathcal{L}_{\mathsf{Srch}}(t, q) = (\mathsf{SP}_q^{(t)}, \mathsf{Update}_q^{(t)}, \mathsf{DelTime}_q^{(t)}),$$

for any t and any $q \in \Lambda$.

Note that $\mathsf{DelTime}_q^{(t)}$ can be derived from $\mathsf{Update}_q^{(t)}$ and op included in $\mathcal{L}_{\mathsf{Upd}}$: $\mathsf{DelTime}_q^{(t)} := \{u \in \mathsf{Update}_q^{(t)} \mid \mathcal{L}_{\mathsf{Upd}}(u, \mathsf{op}, (q, \mathsf{id})) = (u, \mathsf{del})\}$. Since $\mathsf{Time}_q^{(t)}$ and $\mathsf{DelHist}_q^{(t)}$ imply $\mathsf{Update}_q^{(t)}$, our construction clearly meets both Type-II backward privacy and the result-hiding property.

Proof (Sketch). Due to the page limitation, we give a proof sketch. We will provide the detailed proof in the full version. We prove that the simulator S can simulate the update and search operations only with the leakage functions $\mathcal{L}$.

Addition. With leakage $\mathcal{L}_{\mathsf{Upd}}(t, \mathsf{add}, \mathsf{in}) = (t, \mathsf{add})$ for a query $(\mathsf{upd}, \mathsf{add}, \mathsf{in})$, S simulates a transcript $\mathsf{trans}_1^{(t)} := (\mathsf{addr}, \mathsf{c})$. In the real experiment Real, addr and c are η-bit pseudo-random numbers and ciphertexts of $\tau \| \mathsf{id}$, respectively. If h is a random oracle and Π_{SKE} is CPA-secure, addr and c are indistinguishable from an η-bit random string r and a ciphertext c' of $0^{\lambda+l}$, except with negligible probability, respectively. Hence, S can set $\mathsf{trans}_1^{(t)} := (r, \mathsf{c}')$.

Deletion. With leakage $\mathcal{L}_{\mathsf{Upd}}(t, \mathsf{del}, \mathsf{in}) = (t, \mathsf{del})$ for a query $(\mathsf{upd}, \mathsf{del}, \mathsf{in})$, S simulates a transcript $\mathsf{trans}_1^{(t)} := \tau$. If π is a PRF family, τ is indistinguishable from a λ-bit random string r' except with negligible probability. Therefore, S can set $\mathsf{trans}_1^{(t)} := r'$.

Search. With leakage $\mathcal{L}_{\mathsf{Srch}}(t, q) = (\mathsf{SP}_q^{(t)}, \mathsf{Update}_q^{(t)}, \mathsf{DelTime}_q^{(t)})$ for a query (srch, q), S simulates transcripts $\mathsf{trans}_1^{(t)} := (\mathsf{K}_q^{(\mathsf{sc}_w)}, \mathsf{fc}_q)$, $\mathsf{trans}_2^{(t)} := (\mathcal{C}_q^{(t)}, \mathcal{T},$ aux$)$, and $\mathsf{trans}_3^{(t)} := (\mathcal{D}_q^{(t)}, \mathcal{R}_q^{(t)})$. Roughly speaking, due to the security of the underlying PRF g, S can set a κ-bit random string as $\mathsf{K}_q^{(\mathsf{sc}_w)}$. Since fc_q can be derived from $\mathsf{Update}_q^{(t)}$ and $\mathsf{DelTime}_q^{(t)}$, S can simulate $\mathsf{trans}_1^{(t)}$. Since $\mathcal{C}_q^{(t)}$ is a set of all ciphertexts generated during the addition operation for q, S retrieves a ciphertext simulated at every $u \in \mathsf{Update}_q^{(t)} \setminus \mathsf{DelTime}_q^{(t)}$ and sets them as $\mathcal{C}_q^{(t)}$.[2] S easily simulates $\mathcal{T}$ and aux since tags for w, which are entered into AMQ.Insert and AMQ.Delete, are correctly simulated during the deletion operation. Hence, S can simulate $\mathsf{trans}_2^{(t)}$. The set $\mathcal{D}_q^{(t)}$ of deleted tags can also be simulated as above. $\mathcal{R}_q^{(t)}$ can be simulated as in the case of the addition since each $(\widehat{\mathsf{addr}}, \widehat{\mathsf{val}}) \in \mathcal{R}_q^{(t)}$ is generated in the same manner as the addition operation. Therefore, S can simulate $\mathsf{trans}_3^{(t)}$. □

---

[2] To be precise, S has to change the way to retrieve ciphertexts depending on $\mathsf{SP}_q^{(t)}$; S first retrieves ciphertexts re-added at the last search for q, i.e., at $t' = \max \mathsf{SP}_q^{(t)}$, and then retrieves ciphertexts simulated from t' to t.

Algorithm: v-Laura

Setup(1^{κ})

Client:

1: $k_{PRF}, k_{RH}, k_{SKE} \xleftarrow{\$} \{0,1\}^{\kappa}$
2: $fc_w, sc_w, \mathbf{F}[], Index[], Cache[] := \varepsilon$ // ε is an empty value
3: **return** $\left(k := (k_{PRF}, k_{RH}, k_{SKE}), \sigma^{(0)} := (sc_w, fc_w, \mathbf{F}), EDB^{(0)} := (Index, Cache)\right)$

Update(k, add, $(w, id), \sigma^{(t)}; EDB^{(t)}$)

Client:

1: $\tau \leftarrow \pi(k_{RH}, w\|id)$
2: **if** sc_w is undefined **then**
3:     $(sc_w, fc_w) := (0,0)$
4:     $(\mathcal{T}_w, aux) \leftarrow AMQ.Gen(\{0,1\}^{\lambda}, par)$
5:     $\mathbf{F}[w] := (\mathcal{T}_w, aux)$
6: $fc_w := fc_w + 1$ // increment fc_w
7: $K_w^{(sc_w)} \leftarrow g(k_{PRF}, w\|sc_w)$ // generate the PRF key for address
8: $c \leftarrow E(k_{SKE}, id; \tau)$ // Encryption with nonce
9: $addr \leftarrow h(K_w^{(sc_w)}, fc_w), \quad val := \tau\|c$
10: Send $trans_1^{(t)} := (addr, val)$ to the server
11: **return** $\sigma^{(t+1)} := ((sc_w, fc_w)_{w \in \mathcal{W}^{(t+1)}}, \mathbf{F})$

Server:

12: $Index[addr] := val$
13: **return** $EDB^{(t+1)} := (Index, Cache)$

Update(k, del, $(w, id), \sigma^{(t)}; EDB^{(t)}$)

Client:

1: **if** fc_w is defined **then**
2:     $\tau \leftarrow \pi(k_{RH}, w\|id)$
3:     $(\mathcal{T}_w, aux) \leftarrow \mathbf{F}[w]$
4:     $\mathcal{T}_w' \leftarrow AMQ.Insert(\mathcal{T}_w, \tau, aux)$
5:     $\mathbf{F}[w] := (\mathcal{T}_w', aux)$
6: **return** $\sigma^{(t+1)} := ((sc_w, fc_w)_{w \in \mathcal{W}^{(t+1)}}, \mathbf{F})$

Fig. 4. Setup and Update of our dynamic SSE scheme v-Laura.

5 Extensions

5.1 A Variant of Laura: v-Laura

Although Laura is very efficient with small client storage, there is a trade-off between it and the communication cost, as noted in the footnote in Sect. 4.1. Specifically, the server has to send the AMQ structure together with a search result during the search algorithm (line 6 in Fig. 3). The idea to reduce communication cost is to store the AMQ structure on the client side for each keyword, as in Aura. For clients with ample storage or narrow bandwidth, a more suitable and efficient variant scheme than Laura, called v-Laura, can be constructed. At first glance, it seems to be the same as Aura, but the following are differences;

Algorithm: v-Laura

Search($k, q, \sigma^{(t)}; \mathsf{EDB}^{(t)}$)

Client:
1: $\mathsf{K}_q^{(\mathsf{sc}_w)} \leftarrow g(\mathsf{k}_{\mathrm{PRF}}, q \| \mathsf{sc}_q)$
2: $\mathsf{tkn}_q \leftarrow g(\mathsf{k}_{\mathrm{PRF}}, q)$
3: $(\mathcal{T}_q, \mathsf{aux}) := \mathbf{F}[q]$
4: Send $\mathsf{trans}_1^{(t)} := \left(\mathsf{K}_q^{(\mathsf{sc}_w)}, \mathsf{tkn}_q, \mathsf{fc}_q, (\mathcal{T}_q, \mathsf{aux})\right)$ to the server

Server:
5: $\mathcal{C}_q^{(t)} := \mathsf{Cache}[\mathsf{tkn}_q]$
6: **for** $i = 1$ **to** fc_q **do**
7:    $\mathsf{addr} \leftarrow h(\mathsf{K}_q^{(\mathsf{sc}_w)}, i)$, $\mathsf{val} := \mathsf{Index}[\mathsf{addr}]$, $\mathcal{C}_q^{(t)} \leftarrow \mathsf{val}$
8:    $\mathsf{Index}[\mathsf{addr}] := \mathsf{NULL}$ // delete old addresses
9: **for** $\forall \mathsf{val} \in \mathcal{C}_q^{(t)}$ **do**
10:   parse $\mathsf{val} = \tau \| \mathsf{c}$ // the first λ MSBs of val is tag(nonce)
11:   **if** $\mathsf{AMQ.Lookup}(\mathcal{T}_q, \tau, \mathsf{aux}) = \mathbf{true}$ **then** // logical deletion of (w, id)
12:     $\mathcal{C}_q^{(t)} := \mathcal{C}_q^{(t)} \setminus \{\mathsf{val}\}$
13: $\mathsf{Cache}[\mathsf{tkn}_q] := \mathcal{C}_q^{(t)}$
14: Send $\mathsf{trans}_2^{(t)} := \mathcal{C}_q^{(t)}$ to the client
15: **return** $\mathsf{EDB}^{(t+1)} := (\mathsf{Index}, \mathsf{Cache})$

Client:
7: **for** $\forall (\tau, \mathsf{c}) \in \mathcal{C}_q^{(t)}$ **do**
8:    $\mathcal{X}_q^{(t)} \leftarrow \mathsf{D}(\mathsf{k}_{\mathrm{SKE}}, \mathsf{c}; \tau)$ // decrypt c to get search result
9: $(\mathcal{T}_q', \mathsf{aux}) \leftarrow \mathsf{AMQ.Gen}(\{0,1\}^\lambda, \mathsf{par})$
10: $\mathsf{fc}_q := 0$, $\mathsf{sc}_q := \mathsf{sc}_q + 1$, $\mathbf{F}[q] := (\mathcal{T}_q', \mathsf{aux})$ // update state
11: **return** $\left(\mathcal{X}_q^{(t)}, \sigma^{(t+1)} := ((\mathsf{sc}_q, \mathsf{fc}_q)_{q \in \mathcal{W}^{(t+1)}}, \mathbf{F})\right)$

Fig. 5. Search of our dynamic SSE scheme v-Laura.

1) AMQ is used only as a compression of the deleted tag set without SRE functionality. Therefore, efficient AMQs can be selected, not limited to the bloom filter used for SRE in Aura. The v-Laura also achieves efficient search by eliminating SRE processing, which is dominant in Aura searches (see Sect. 5).
2) The server removes the deleted entries using AMQ structure while the client decrypts the search results to achieve result-hiding, similar to Laura.
3) The v-Laura can compress the size of val in EDB with the idea of using τ as a nonce in encryption. In some block cipher modes of CPA-secure Π_{SKE}, the nonce is used for security and is stored with the ciphertext. Since τ plays the role of nonce, it can compress the size of the original nonce.

The pseudo-codes for v-Laura are given in Figs. 4 and 5, and we provide overviews of each algorithm below. However, we omit the same part of Laura.

Setup: Setup(1^κ). The client generates a secret key $k := (\mathsf{k}_{\mathrm{SKE}}, \mathsf{k}_{\mathrm{PRF}}, \mathsf{k}_{\mathrm{RH}})$. The client initializes two counters fc_w and sc_w, and three array Index and Cache and **F**. The client sets the state information $\sigma^{(0)} := (\mathsf{fc}_w, \mathsf{sc}_w, \mathbf{F})$, and sends $\mathsf{EDB}^{(0)} := (\mathsf{IndexCache})$ to the server.

Addition: $\mathsf{Update}(k, \mathsf{add}, (w, \mathsf{id}), \sigma^{(t)}; \mathsf{EDB}^{(t)})$. First, the client calculates an address addr and tag τ, like Laura. Also, the client encrypts id using τ as nonce (i.e., $\mathsf{c} \leftarrow \mathsf{E}(k_{\mathsf{SKE}}, \mathsf{id}; \tau)$) and sends addr and $\mathsf{val} := \tau\|\mathsf{c}$ to the server. The server adds val to $\mathsf{Index[addr]}$ in $\mathsf{EDB}^{(t)}$.

Deletion: $\mathsf{Update}(k, \mathsf{del}, (w, \mathsf{id}), \sigma^{(t)}; \mathsf{EDB}^{(t)})$. The client only computes the tag τ and executes $\mathsf{AMQ.Insert}$ to insert τ into the data structure $\mathcal{T}_w$ for w in $\sigma^{(t)}$.

Search: $\mathsf{Search}(k, q, \sigma^{(t)}; \mathsf{EDB}^{(t)})$. First, the client creates $\mathsf{K}_q^{(\mathsf{sc}_w)}$ and tkn_q with the PRF key k_{PRF} and sends them together with fc_q and $\mathcal{T}_q$ to the server. The server gets $\mathsf{Cache[tkn}_q]$ as a set $\mathcal{C}_q^{(t)}$. For every $i = 1, \ldots, \mathsf{fc}_q$, the server computes an address $g(\mathsf{K}_q^{(\mathsf{sc}_w)}, i)$ and adds its stored value val to the set $\mathcal{C}_q^{(t)}$. For every $\mathsf{val} \in \mathcal{C}_q^{(t)}$, the server parse $\mathsf{val} := \tau\|\mathsf{c}$ and executes $\mathsf{AMQ.Lookup}$ with τ and $\mathcal{T}_q$ to check whether the pair (q, id) has been logically deleted. If $\mathsf{AMQ.Lookup}$ outputs true, val is removed from $\mathcal{C}_q^{(t)}$. Next, the server sets $\mathcal{C}_q^{(t)}$ to $\mathsf{Cache[tkn}_q]$ and updates $\mathsf{EDB}^{(t)}$, and sends $\mathcal{C}_q^{(t)}$ to the client. For every value $\mathsf{val} \in \mathcal{C}_q^{(t)}$, the client decrypts val to obtain id and adds it to the search result $\mathcal{X}_q^{(t)}$. Finally, the client initializes $\mathcal{T}_q$ and fc_q and increments sc_q.

The security of v-Laura and the proof is shown in the full version.

5.2   A Strongly Secure Variant of Laura: s-Laura

As explained in the introduction, Aura implicitly requires every pair of (w, id) to be added at most only once; it does not allow the client to re-add previously deleted pairs. Indeed, Laura and v-Laura work well under the same assumption. In other words, if the client wants to add and delete a pair (w, id) multiple times, those schemes are no longer Type-II backward private. This limitation stems from the fact that the corresponding tag of the pair (w, id) is generated deterministically in those schemes. The extended scheme s-Laura, which stands for strongly-secure Laura, allows to run Update of pair (w, id) any number of times. The basic idea of s-Laura is that the deletion tag of the pair (w, id) changes with each deletion. The client holds extra information dc_w which increments for each deletion regarding w. When pair (w, id) is deleted, a delete tag τ_{dc_w} is generated from τ and dc_w. The client then computes tags $\tau_1, \ldots, \tau_{\mathsf{dc}_w}$ from τ and dc_w, and executes $\mathsf{AMQ.Lookup}$ with τ_i for every $i \in [\mathsf{dc}_w]$ to check whether the pair (w, id) has been logically deleted. If $\mathsf{AMQ.Lookup}$ outputs false for all tags, id is added to the search result $\mathcal{X}_q^{(t)}$. However, the search time of s-Laura increases linearly with the number of deletions, as shown in Table 1. Hence, s-Laura has not been evaluated for implementation in Sect. 6. Efficient construction is a future work.

We give the pseudo-codes for s-Laura in Appendix A, and provide overviews of each algorithm below.

Setup: Setup(1^κ). The client generates a secret key $k := (\mathsf{k}_{\mathrm{SKE}}, \mathsf{k}_{\mathrm{PRF}}, \mathsf{k}_{\mathrm{RH}})$, where $\mathsf{k}_{\mathrm{SKE}}$ is an SKE secret key and $\mathsf{k}_{\mathrm{PRF}}$ and k_{RH} are PRF keys used to compute addresses and tags, respectively. The client initializes three counters fc_w, sc_w, and dc_w, an array Index, and an AMQ data structure $\mathcal{T}$ (along with its auxiliary information aux). The client sets the state information $\sigma^{(0)} := (\mathsf{fc}_w, \mathsf{sc}_w, \mathsf{dc}_w)$, and sends $\mathsf{EDB}^{(0)} := (\mathsf{Index}\mathcal{T}, \mathsf{aux})$ to the server.

Addition: Update($k, \mathsf{add}, (w, \mathsf{id}), \sigma^{(t)}; \mathsf{EDB}^{(t)}$). First, the client retrieves the file counter fc_w and the search counter sc_w in $\sigma^{(t)}$ and increments fc_w. The client next derives a PRF key $\mathsf{K}_{w,0}^{(\mathsf{sc}_w)}$ from the PRF key $\mathsf{k}_{\mathrm{PRF}}$ using the keyword w to calculate an address $\mathtt{addr}$. Also, the client computes a *persistent tag* τ, which will be used to derive an *ephemeral tag* τ_i during the deletion operation, of the pair (w, id) from the PRF key k_{RH}, and encrypts $\tau \| \mathsf{id}$ with the SKE secret key $\mathsf{k}_{\mathrm{SKE}}$. The server adds the ciphertext to $\mathsf{Index}[\mathtt{addr}]$ in $\mathsf{EDB}^{(t)}$.

Deletion: Update($k, \mathsf{del}, (w, \mathsf{id}), \sigma^{(t)}; \mathsf{EDB}^{(t)}$). First, the client retrieves the deletion counter dc_w and increments it. The client computes the persistent tag τ as in the addition operation. Then, the client derives a key $\mathsf{K}_{w,1}^{(\mathsf{sc}_w)}$ from the PRF key $\mathsf{k}_{\mathrm{PRF}}$ using the keyword w and generates an ephemeral tag τ_{dc_w} from the derived key $\mathsf{K}_{w,1}^{(\mathsf{sc}_w)}$, the persistent tag τ, and the counter dc_w. The server executes AMQ.Insert to insert τ into the data structure $\mathcal{T}$ in $\mathsf{EDB}^{(t)}$.

Search: Search($k, q, \sigma^{(t)}; \mathsf{EDB}^{(t)}$). First, the client creates the PRF key $\mathsf{K}_{q,0}^{(\mathsf{sc}_w)}$ for the search keyword q and sends it together with fc_q to the server. For every $i = 1, \ldots, \mathsf{fc}_q$, the server computes an address $g(\mathsf{K}_{w,0}^{(\mathsf{sc}_w)}, i)$ and adds its stored value $\mathtt{val}$ to the set $\mathcal{C}_q^{(t)}$. The server sends $\mathcal{C}_q^{(t)}$ and a copy of the data structure $\mathcal{T}$ to the client and frees the memory of all the addresses accessed. For every value $\mathtt{val} \in \mathcal{C}_q^{(t)}$, the client checks whether it has been deleted as follows. The client decrypts $\mathtt{val}$ and obtains $\tau \| \mathsf{id}$. The client then computes ephemeral tags $\tau_1, \ldots, \tau_{\mathsf{dc}_q}$ from τ and dc_q, and executes AMQ.Lookup with τ_i for every $i \in [\mathsf{dc}_q]$ to check whether the pair (w, id) has been logically deleted. If AMQ.Lookup outputs $\mathtt{false}$ for all ephemeral tags, id is added to the search result $\mathcal{X}_q^{(t)}$. Next, the client re-adds the pairs (w, id) except for the deleted ones. The client increments sc_q, and adds the pairs in the same way to the above addition procedure. The server updates $\mathsf{EDB}^{(t)}$ as in the addition procedure and also receives a set $\mathcal{D}_q^{(t)}$ of the ephemeral tags of the deleted entry. For every ephemeral tag $\tau_i \in \mathcal{D}_q^{(t)}$, the server executes AMQ.Delete to remove the tags from the data structure $\mathcal{T}$. This re-addition procedure is important to provide forward privacy and reduce the size of $\mathcal{T}$.

s-Laura satisfies Theorem 1 which is not one-time. The detailed theorem and the proof are shown in the full version.

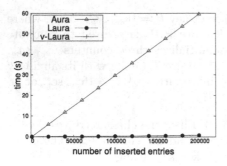

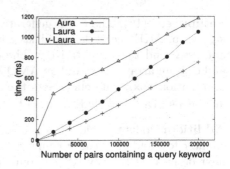

Fig. 6. Addition cost.   **Fig. 7.** Search cost without deletion.

6   Experiments

Implementation. We implemented the proposed protocols Laura and v-Laura in C++ and evaluated their performance comparatively.[3] We compare them with Aura [25] implemented in C++ [1] for each protocol. For instances and technical details of Aura, please refer to [1,25]. These experiments were done in an Ubuntu 22.04.3 LTS server with 756 GB RAM, using Docker (version 24.0.4) [13]. We used AES-GCM for the instantiation of SKE Π_{SKE}. The PRFs π, g, and the random oracle h are realized with AES-GCM and GMAC, respectively. They are implemented using the EVP functions API on the open SSL library (version 3.0.2 15 Mar 2022), and AES-GCM is accelerated by the Intel AES-NI instruction set. For the instance of the AMQ data structure of Laura and v-Laura, we choose the cuckoo filter [15] implemented in [10].

The sizes of keys and outputs of AES and PRF are 128 bits, respectively. The identifier id and each counter (i.e. fc_w, sc_w) are 32-bit integers. For experiments on search, we measure the time it takes the server to get all the decrypted identifiers in the search results. Note that both the client and server run locally and communication costs are not taken into account.

Parameter Setting. Throughout the experiments, we set the false-positive probability $p = 10^{-4}$, which was also considered practically acceptable in the Aura paper [25]. To ensure that false-positive probability, we need to set the maximum number d_w of elements inserted into the AMQ data structure in Laura and v-Laura (resp., the Bloom filter in Aura) at the beginning of the protocol. To be precise, Aura and v-Laura prepares a filter per keyword, while Laura employ only one AMQ structure for the whole system. Therefore, unless otherwise stated, we set $d_w = 1,000$ for Aura and v-Laura and $d_\Lambda = 10,000,000$ for Laura, where d_w and $d_\Lambda = \sum_{w \in \Lambda} d_w$.

Addition Cost. We give the addition costs of Aura, Laura, and v-Laura in Fig. 6. This results surprisingly show a marked performance difference between ours

---

[3] We did not implement *sOurs* since we want to compare dynamic SSE schemes with the same security level. Note that s-Laura is secure even if deleted entries are re-added.

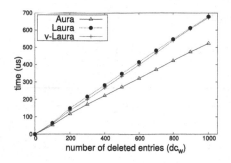
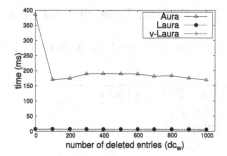

Fig. 8. Deletion cost.   **Fig. 9.** Search cost with deletion.

and Aura. Specifically, Laura and v-Laura takes less than 1.0 s to add 200,000 keyword-identifier pairs, whereas Aura takes 59.5 s. This is due to the concrete construction of the underlying SRE scheme, which requires many resources for the addition.

Search Cost without Deletion. Figure 7 compares the search costs of Aura, Laura, and v-Laura when no entries on w have been deleted. The search costs of the three schemes increase linearly with the number of pairs. When the search results is 200,000 pairs, Laura, v-Laura, and Aura take 1.05 s, 0.75 s and 1.18 s respectively.

Deletion Cost. As can be seen in Fig. 8, the deletion costs for Aura, Laura, and v-Laura are remarkably fast since the deletion procedures of these schemes only require the calculation of the tag corresponding to the pair to be deleted and the insertion to the filter. Specifically, for 1,000 deleted entries, Laura, v-Laura and Aura take 0.68 ms, 0.67 ms and 0.52 ms respectively. The Laura and v-Laura are slightly slower since the cuckoo filter [15] has the property that as more items are inserted to the filter, the frequency of kicked out an item in the insertion also increases.

Search Cost with Deletion. We show the effect of deletion on search costs in Fig. 9. After adding 2,000 pairs of (w, id), we delete pairs and then search for w. Figure 9 shows the search time with the range of the number of the deleted pairs from 0 to 1,000. The Laura and v-Laura are remarkably faster than Aura. Specifically, when deleting 1,000 entries (i.e., 1,000 results of 2,000 entries), Laura, v-Laura and Aura take 0.61 ms, 0.41 ms and 169.0 ms respectively. Compared Aura with v-Laura, it is clear that the computational complexity of SRE is dominant. More interestingly, Aura takes longer when no deletion occurred due to the underlying SRE construction.

Acknowledgment. This work was supported by JSPS KAKENHI Grant Numbers JP21H03395, JP21H03441, JP22H03590, JP23H00468, JP23H00479, JP23K17455, JST CREST JPMJCR23M2, and MEXT Leading Initiative for Excellent Young Researchers.

A   Formal Description of s-Laura

We give the concrete procedures of s-Laura in Figs. 10 and 11.

Algorithm: s-Laura

Setup(1^κ)

Client:

1: $k_{\text{PRF}}, k_{\text{RH}}, k_{\text{SKE}} \xleftarrow{\$} \{0,1\}^\kappa$
2: $(\mathcal{T}, \text{aux}) \leftarrow \text{AMQ.Gen}(\{0,1\}^\lambda, \text{par})$
3: $\text{fc}_w, \text{sc}_w, \text{dc}_w, \text{Index}[] := \varepsilon$ // ε is an empty value
4: **return** $\left(k := (k_{\text{PRF}}, k_{\text{RH}}, k_{\text{SKE}}), \sigma^{(0)} := (\text{sc}_w, \text{fc}_w, \text{dc}_w), \text{EDB}^{(0)} := (\text{Index}, \mathcal{T}, \text{aux}) \right)$

Update($k, \text{add}, (w, \text{id}), \sigma^{(t)}; \text{EDB}^{(t)}$)

Client:

1: $\tau \leftarrow \pi(k_{\text{RH}}, w \| \text{id})$
2: **if** sc_w is undefined **then**
3:     $(\text{sc}_w, \text{fc}_w, \text{dc}_w) := (0,0,0)$
4: $\text{fc}_w := \text{fc}_w + 1$ // increment fc_w
5: $K_{w,0}^{(\text{sc}_w)} := g(k_{\text{PRF}}, w \| \text{sc}_w \| 0)$ // generate the PRF key for address
6: $\text{addr} \leftarrow h(K_{w,0}^{(\text{sc}_w)}, \text{fc}_w)$
7: $\text{val} \leftarrow E(k_{\text{SKE}}, \tau \| \text{id})$
8: Send $\text{trans}_1^{(t)} := (\text{addr}, \text{val})$ to the server
9: **return** $\sigma^{(t+1)} := (\text{sc}_w, \text{fc}_w, \text{dc}_w)_{w \in \mathcal{W}^{(t+1)}}$

Server:

10: $\text{Index}[\text{addr}] := \text{val}$
11: **return** $\text{EDB}^{(t+1)} := (\text{Index}, \mathcal{T}, \text{aux})$

Update($k, \text{del}, (w, \text{id}), \sigma^{(t)}; \text{EDB}^{(t)}$)

Client:

1: **if** dc_w is defined **then**
2:     $\text{dc}_w := \text{dc}_w + 1$
3:     $\tau \leftarrow \pi(k_{\text{RH}}, w \| \text{id})$
4:     $K_{w,1}^{(\text{sc}_w)} := g(k_{\text{PRF}}, w \| \text{sc}_w \| 1)$
5:     $\tau_{\text{dc}_w} \leftarrow \pi(K_{w,1}^{(\text{sc}_w)}, \tau \| \text{dc}_w)$
6:     Send $\text{trans}_1^{(t)} := \tau_{\text{dc}_w}$ to the server
7: **return** $\sigma^{(t+1)} := (\text{sc}_w, \text{fc}_w, \text{dc}_w)_{w \in \mathcal{W}^{(t+1)}}$

Server:

8: $\mathcal{T}' \leftarrow \text{AMQ.Insert}(\mathcal{T}, \tau_{\text{dc}_w}, \text{aux})$
9: **return** $\text{EDB}^{(t+1)} := (\text{Index}, \mathcal{T}', \text{aux})$

Fig. 10. Setup and Update of our dynamic SSE scheme s-Laura.

Algorithm: s-Laura

$\mathsf{Search}(k, q, \sigma^{(t)}; \mathsf{EDB}^{(t)})$

Client:

1: $\mathsf{K}_{q,0}^{(\mathsf{sc}_w)} := g(\mathsf{k_{PRF}}, q\|\mathsf{sc}_w\|0)$

2: Send $\mathsf{trans}_1^{(t)} := (\mathsf{K}_{q,0}^{(\mathsf{sc}_w)}, \mathsf{fc}_q)$ to the server

Server:

3: **for** $i = 1$ **to** fc_q **do**

4:     $\mathsf{addr} \leftarrow h(\mathsf{K}_{q,0}^{(\mathsf{sc}_w)}, i)$, $\mathcal{C}_q^{(t)} \leftarrow \mathsf{Index}[\mathsf{addr}]$

5:     $\mathsf{Index}[\mathsf{addr}] := \mathsf{NULL}$ // delete old addresses

6: Send $\mathsf{trans}_2^{(t)} := (\mathcal{C}_q^{(t)}, \mathcal{T}, \mathsf{aux})$ to the client // Send copy of $\mathcal{T}$

Client:

7: $\mathsf{K}_{q,1}^{(\mathsf{sc}_w)} := g(\mathsf{k_{PRF}}, q\|\mathsf{sc}_q\|1)$

8: **for** $\forall \mathsf{c} \in \mathcal{C}_q^{(t)}$ **do** // define Loop1 for Jump

9:     $\tau\|\mathsf{id} \leftarrow \mathsf{D}(\mathsf{k_{SKE}}, \mathsf{c})$ // the first λ MSBs of val is tag

10:     **for** $i = 1$ **to** dc_q **do**

11:         $\tau_i \leftarrow \pi(\mathsf{K}_{q,1}^{(\mathsf{sc}_w)}, \tau\|i)$

12:         **if** $\mathsf{AMQ.Lookup}(\mathcal{T}, \tau_i, \mathsf{aux}) = \mathbf{true}$ **then**

13:             $\mathcal{D}_q^{(t)} \leftarrow \tau_i$

14:             **Jump Loop1 and next element**

15:     $\mathcal{X}_q^{(t)} \leftarrow \mathsf{id}$, $\mathcal{Y}_q^{(t)} \leftarrow (\mathsf{id}, \tau)$

16: $\mathsf{sc}_q := \mathsf{sc}_q + 1$, $\mathsf{fc}_q := |\mathcal{X}_q^{(t)}|$, $\mathsf{dc}_q := 0$ // update state

17: $\widehat{\mathsf{K}}_{q,0}^{(\mathsf{sc}_q,0)} := g(\mathsf{k_{PRF}}, q\|\mathsf{sc}_q\|0)$ // generate new keys

18: $\mathsf{ctr} := 1$

19: **for** $\forall (\tau, \mathsf{id}) \in \mathcal{Y}_q^{(t)}$ **do**

20:     $\mathcal{R}_q^{(t)} \leftarrow (h(\widehat{\mathsf{K}}_{q,0}^{(\mathsf{sc}_q,0)}, \mathsf{ctr}), \mathsf{E}(\mathsf{k_{SKE}}, \tau\|\mathsf{id}))$ // new $(\widehat{\mathsf{addr}}, \widehat{\mathsf{val}})$ pair

21:     $\mathsf{ctr} := \mathsf{ctr} + 1$

22: Send $\mathsf{trans}_3^{(t)} := (\mathcal{D}_w^{(t)}, \mathcal{R}_q^{(t)})$ to the server

23: **return** $(\mathcal{X}_q^{(t)}, \sigma^{(t+1)} := (\mathsf{sc}_w, \mathsf{fc}_q, \mathsf{dc}_q)_{q \in \mathcal{W}^{(t+1)}})$

Server:

24: **for** $\forall (\widehat{\mathsf{addr}}, \widehat{\mathsf{val}}) \in \mathcal{R}_q^{(t)}$ **do**

25:     $\mathsf{Index}[\widehat{\mathsf{addr}}] := \widehat{\mathsf{val}}$ // set new addresses and value

26: **for** $\forall \tau_i \in \mathcal{D}_q^{(t)}$ **do**

27:     $\mathcal{T}' \leftarrow \mathsf{AMQ.Delete}(\mathcal{T}, \tau_i, \mathsf{aux})$, $\mathcal{T} := \mathcal{T}'$

28: **return** $\mathsf{EDB}^{(t+1)} := (\mathsf{Index}, \mathcal{T}, \mathsf{aux})$

Fig. 11. Search of our dynamic SSE scheme s-Laura.

References

1. Aura. https://github.com/MonashCybersecurityLab/Aura
2. Bender, M.A., et al.: Don't thrash: how to cache your hash on flash. Proc. VLDB Endow. **5**(11), 1627–1637 (2012)
3. Blackstone, L., Kamara, S., Moataz, T.: Revisiting leakage abuse attacks. In: NDSS 2020. The Internet Society (2020)
4. Bloom, B.H.: Space/time trade-offs in hash coding with allowable errors. Commun. ACM **13**(7), 422–426 (1970)

5. Bost, R.: $\sum o\varphi o\varsigma$: forward secure searchable encryption. In: Proceedings of ACM CCS 2016, pp. 1143–1154. ACM (2016)
6. Bost, R., Minaud, B., Ohrimenko, O.: Forward and backward private searchable encryption from constrained cryptographic primitives. In: Proceedings of ACM CCS 2017, pp. 1465–1482. ACM (2017)
7. Cash, D., Grubbs, P., Perry, J., Ristenpart, T.: Leakage-abuse attacks against searchable encryption. In: Proceedings of ACM CCS 2015, pp. 668–679. ACM (2015)
8. Cash, D., et al.: Dynamic searchable encryption in very-large databases: data structures and implementation. In: Proceedings of NDSS 2014. The Internet Society (2014)
9. Chamani, J.G., Papadopoulos, D., Papamanthou, C., Jalili, R.: New constructions for forward and backward private symmetric searchable encryption. In: Proceedings of ACM CCS 2018, pp. 1038–1055. ACM (2018)
10. Cuckoo filter. https://github.com/efficient/cuckoofilter/tree/master
11. Curtmola, R., Garay, J.A., Kamara, S., Ostrovsky, R.: Searchable symmetric encryption: improved definitions and efficient constructions. In: Proceedings of ACM CCS 2006, pp. 79–88. ACM (2006)
12. Demertzis, I., Chamani, J.G., Papadopoulos, D., Papamanthou, C.: Dynamic searchable encryption with small client storage. In: Proceedings of NDSS 2020. The Internet Society (2020)
13. Docker. https://www.docker.com/
14. Etemad, M., Küpçü, A., Papamanthou, C., Evans, D.: Efficient dynamic searchable encryption with forward privacy. PoPETs **2018**(1), 5–20 (2018)
15. Fan, B., Andersen, D.G., Kaminsky, M., Mitzenmacher, M.D.: Cuckoo filter: practically better than bloom. In: Proceedings of CoNEXT 2014, pp. 75–88 (2014)
16. Hahn, F., Kerschbaum, F.: Searchable encryption with secure and efficient updates. In: ACM SIGSAC Conference on Computer and Communications Security, CCS 2014, pp. 310–320. ACM, New York (2014)
17. Islam, M.S., Kuzu, M., Kantarcioglu, M.: Access pattern disclosure on searchable encryption: ramification, attack and mitigation. In: Proceedings of NDSS 2012. The Internet Society (2012)
18. Kamara, S., Moataz, T.: Computationally volume-hiding structured encryption. In: Ishai, Y., Rijmen, V. (eds.) EUROCRYPT 2019. LNCS, vol. 11477, pp. 183–213. Springer, Cham (2019). https://doi.org/10.1007/978-3-030-17656-3_7
19. Kamara, S., Papamanthou, C.: Parallel and dynamic searchable symmetric encryption. In: Sadeghi, A.-R. (ed.) FC 2013. LNCS, vol. 7859, pp. 258–274. Springer, Heidelberg (2013). https://doi.org/10.1007/978-3-642-39884-1_22
20. Kamara, S., Papamanthou, C., Roeder, T.: Dynamic searchable symmetric encryption. In: Proceedings of ACM CCS 2012, pp. 965–976. ACM (2012)
21. Katz, J., Lindell, Y.: Introduction to Modern Cryptography, 2nd edn. CRC Press (2014)
22. Miers, I., Mohassel, P.: IO-DSSE: scaling dynamic searchable encryption to millions of indexes by improving locality. In: Network and Distributed System Security Symposium, NDSS 2017 (2017)
23. Naveed, M., Prabhakaran, M., Gunter, C.: Dynamic searchable encryption via blind storage. In: IEEE Symposium on Security and Privacy, S&P 2014, pp. 639–654 (2014)
24. Song, D.X., Wagner, D.A., Perrig, A.: Practical techniques for searches on encrypted data. In: IEEE S&P 2000, pp. 44–55. IEEE (2000)

25. Sun, S., et al.: Practical non-interactive searchable encryption with forward and backward privacy. In: Proceedings of NDSS 2021. The Internet Society (2021)
26. Wang, J., Chow, S.S.M.: Omnes pro uno: practical multi-writer encrypted database. In: 31st USENIX Security Symposium, USENIX Security 2022, Boston, MA, USA, 10–12 August 2022, pp. 2371–2388. USENIX Association (2022)
27. Watanabe, Y., Ohara, K., Iwamoto, M., Ohta, K.: Efficient dynamic searchable encryption with forward privacy under the decent leakage. In: Proceedings of ACM CODASPY 2022, pp. 312–323. ACM (2022)
28. Zhang, Y., Katz, J., Papamanthou, C.: All your queries are belong to us: the power of file-injection attacks on searchable encryption. In: Proceedings of USENIX Security 2016, pp. 707–720. USENIX Association (2016)

Finsler Encryption

Tetsuya Nagano[1]([✉]) and Hiroaki Anada[2]

[1] University of Nagasaki, Nagasaki 851-2195, Japan
hnagano@sun.ac.jp
[2] Aomori University, Aomori 030-0943, Japan
anada@aomori-u.ac.jp

Abstract. Inspired by previous work with the first example proposed at SecITC 2020, we give a general description of Finsler encryption that is based on a Finsler space, which uses a kind of a differentiable geometry on a smooth manifold, with appropriate quantization as the security parameter. Key generation, encryption and decryption algorithms are introduced in detail, and a further example is presented. Then we analyse security properties of Finsler encryption. First, as the dimension (as another security parameter) increases, the length of the secret key also increases, and hence the computational hardness becomes stronger. Second, we prove indistinguishability against chosen-plaintext attacks.

Keywords: Finsler geometry · Differential geometry · Linear parallel displacement problem · Underdetermined systems of equations · Mapping-decomposition problem

1 Introduction

Finsler encryption is a new cryptographic system that has recently been studied. In previous work [10] proposed at SecITC 2020, an example was given in the case of dimension 2. To capture the intuition, we first state the outline of this system briefly. First of all, we choose a Finsler space with the asymmetric property (See Appendix (2)). Next, the geodesics and the linear parallel displacement must be decided. Both of these are defined by certain differential equations system. And the equation of the energy of a vector is calculated. The key generation is performed using linear parallel displacement of vectors and preserved norms. The obtained key is an $n + 1$-dimensional vector consisting of rational expressions with several parameters as components. The n is the dimension of Finsler space. The encryption algorithm generates the ciphertext by calculating several sums of vectors obtained by substituting several given parameter values. On the other hand, the decryption algorithm is performed based on the value of parameter τ

This work was supported by Institute of Mathematics for Industry, Joint Usage/ Research Center in Kyushu University. (FY2022 Workshop(II) "CRISMATH2022" (2022c006)).

obtained from a system of simultaneous linear equations with unknown plaintext components and homogeneous quadratic equations involving the squared norms of vectors. In the next section, we will present a detailed explanation of the Finsler space used to generate Finsler encryption and its key generation, encryption and decryption. In the following section, we will explain in detail the strength of Finsler encryption, but the intuitive outline is as follows.

If an attacker attempts to decrypt a ciphertext that is encrypted with a public key, he must solve a system of underdetermined equations. This is because, by setting k to be greater than or equal to $n + 1$, the number of unknown variables becomes greater than the number of equations that can be obtained from the ciphertext and the public key. Generally, solutions to underdetermined systems of equations can only be obtained in the form that includes unknown constants, which we call "the property of **SUS**". Therefore, determining one plaintext from countless solutions is impossible. Next, finding a "linear parallel displacement" is an assumably computationally hard problem, which we call the Linear Parallel Displacement problem (**LPD problem**). We emphasize that the problem arises from the structure of asymmetric Finsler spaces, and currently no algorithm to solve it known. The last one is the difficulty of solving the composite mapping problem, which we call **Mapping-decomposition problem**. That is, the energy expression is a product of five regular matrices. It is difficult to decompose the energy function, which is a product of five regular matrices, to obtain the five regular matrices.

In this paper, we formalize Finsler encryption in the case of general dimension n. Then we study the strength of our Finsler encryption. Note that we implicitly use the general theory on Finsler geometry and linear parallel displacement, that can be seen in previous publications.

2   Preliminaries

2.1   Public-Key Encryption

A public-key encryption scheme PKE consists three probabilistic polynomial-time (PPT) algorithms; PKE = (KeyGen, Enc, Dec).

- KeyGen(1^λ) → $(\mathbf{PK}, \mathbf{SK})$. On input the security parameter 1^λ, this PPT algorithm generates a secret key $\mathbf{SK}$ and the corresponding public key $\mathbf{PK}$. It returns $(\mathbf{PK}, \mathbf{SK})$.
- Enc($\mathbf{PK}, m$) → ct. On input the public key $\mathbf{PK}$ and a message m, this PPT algorithm generates a ciphertext ct. It returns ct.
- Dec($\mathbf{SK}, ct$) → $\hat{m}$. On input the secret key $\mathbf{SK}$ and a ciphertext ct, this deterministic polynomial-time algorithm generates a decrypted message $\hat{m}$. It returns $\hat{m}$.

Correctness should hold for PKE. That is; for any 1^λ and any m,

$$\Pr[m = \hat{m} \mid \mathsf{KeyGen}(1^\lambda) \to (\mathbf{SK}, \mathbf{PK}); \mathsf{Enc}(\mathbf{PK}, m) \to ct; \mathsf{Dec}(\mathbf{SK}, ct) \to \hat{m}] = 1.$$

(cf. [19–21]).

2.2 IND-CPA Security of PKE

We prove here the security of indistinguishability against chosen-plaintext attacks is defined by the following experimental algorithm $\mathsf{Exp}_{\mathsf{PKE},\mathbf{A}}^{\text{ind-cpa}}$, where $\mathbf{A}$ is any given PPT algorithm.

$$\mathsf{Exp}_{\mathsf{PKE},\mathbf{A}}^{\text{ind-cpa}}(1^\lambda)$$

$\quad(\mathbf{SK},\mathbf{PK}) \leftarrow \mathsf{KeyGen}(1^\lambda));\ (m_0, m_1) \leftarrow \mathbf{A}(\mathbf{PK})$

$\quad b \in_R \{0,1\};\ ct \leftarrow \mathsf{Enc}(\mathbf{PK}, m_b);\ b' \leftarrow \mathbf{A}(ct)$

$\quad$If $b = b'$ then return 1 else return 0

The advantage of $\mathbf{A}$ over PKE is defined as

$$\mathbf{Adv}_{\mathsf{PKE},\mathbf{A}}^{\text{ind-cpa}}(\lambda) \overset{\text{def}}{=} |\Pr[\mathsf{Exp}_{\mathsf{PKE},\mathbf{A}}^{\text{ind-cpa}}(1^\lambda) = 1] - (1/2)|.$$

PKE is said to be IND-CPA secure if, for any PPT algorithm $\mathbf{A}$, $\mathbf{Adv}_{\mathsf{PKE},\mathbf{A}}^{\text{ind-cpa}}(\lambda)$ is negligible in λ (cf. [18,19]).

3   Finsler Encryption

3.1   Finsler Space

Generally, Finsler space (M, F) over the set of real numbers $\mathbb{R}$ is defined as a pair consisting of a smooth n-dimensional manifold M and a scalar function F on its tangent bundle TM [1–6]. Let $x = (x^1, \cdots, x^n)$ be the coordinate of the base manifold M and $y = (y^1, \cdots, y^n)$ the coordinate of a tangent vector y on $T_x M$. $F = F(x, y)$ is called the Finsler metric or the fundamental function and plays role giving the norm $||y||$ of a tangent vector y. The Finsler metric $F(x, y)$ determines everything in the space. The metric tensor $g_{ij}(x, y)$ which is very important quantity is calculated from $F(x, y)$ as follows:

$$g_{ij}(x, y) := \frac{1}{2}\frac{\partial^2 F^2}{\partial y^i \partial y^j},$$

$$||y||_x = F(x, y) = \sqrt{\sum_{i,j} g_{ij}(x, y)y^i y^j},\ (i, j = 1, \cdots, n).$$

We use the asymmetric property of linear parallel displacement of tangent vectors to construct a new public key encryption.

Necessary objects (See Appendix (2), (3), (4))

(1) Metric tensor field $g_{ij}(x, y)$,
(2) Nonlinear connection $N_j^i(x, y)$,
(3) Horizontal connection $F_{rj}^i(x, y)$,
$\quad$(where the indices $i, j, r = 1, 2, \cdots, n = dim M$)
(4) Geodesic $c = c(t)$

(5) Linear parallel displacement (LPD) Π_c on c is constructed by the solution of the following differential equations:

$$(\star) \quad \frac{dv^i}{dt} + \sum_{j,r} F^i_{jr}(c,\dot{c})v^j\dot{c}^r = 0 \quad (\dot{c}^r = \frac{dc^r}{dt}),$$

and we call the linear map $\Pi_c : v(t_0) \in T_pM \longrightarrow v(t_1) \in T_qM$ a **linear parallel displacement** along c [7,14–17].

(6) The energy $E(v)$ of a vector $v = (v^1, \cdots, v^n)$ on c:

$$E(v) := \sum_{i,j} g_{ij}(c,\dot{c})v^i v^j$$

Example

We introduce 2-dimensional Finsler space as follows (i.e. the case $n = 2$) (cf. [8–10]):

$$M := \mathbb{R}^2$$

$(\star\star)$ $F(x,y,\dot{x},\dot{y}) = \sqrt{a^2\dot{x}^2 + b^2\dot{y}^2} - h_1 x\dot{x} - h_2 y\dot{y}$ (a, b, h_1, h_2 : positive constant),

where (x,y) is the coordinate of the base manifold M, and $(\dot{x},\dot{y})$ is the coordinate of $T_{(x,y)}M$, namely, $x = x^1, y = x^2, \dot{x} = y^1, \dot{y} = y^2$.

Geodesics in this Finsler space are any straight lines. So we choose a geodesic as follows

$$c_m(t) = (c^1(t), c^2(t)) = (\frac{1}{a\sqrt{1+m^2}}t, \frac{m}{b\sqrt{1+m^2}}t) \ (y = \frac{am}{b}x).$$

And the linear transformation $C(\tau)$ on T_pM (p : start point) is

$$C(\tau) := \begin{pmatrix} \tau & -1 \\ 1 & \tau \end{pmatrix}.$$

Then we have 7 parameters $(a, b, h_1, h_2, m, t_0, t_1)$, where t_0, t_1 mean the start point and the end point of the linear parallel displacement on the geodesic c, respectively. In this case the linear parallel displacement $\Pi_{c_m}(t)$ is the solution of $(\star)$ as follows

$$\Pi_{c_m}(t) = \begin{pmatrix} B^1_1 & B^1_2 \\ B^2_1 & B^2_2 \end{pmatrix} \quad \text{(See Appendix (5))},$$

and the energy equation $E(v_1)$ is

$$E(v_1) := <v_1, v_1>_{\dot{c}} = \sum_{i,j} g_{ij}(c,\dot{c})v^i_1 v^j_1 = {}^t v_1 G v_1,$$

where $G = \begin{pmatrix} g_{11} & g_{12} \\ g_{21} & g_{22} \end{pmatrix}$,

$$g_{11} = \frac{1}{a^2 b^2 (m^2 + 1)^2} (b^2 m^4 a^4 + b^2 a^4 + 2b^2 m^2 a^4$$
$$- (h_2 m^4 a^4 + 3b^2 h_1 m^2 a^2 + 2b^2 h_1 a^2)t + (b^2 h_1^2 + b^2 h_1^2 m^2)t^2),$$

$$g_{12} = -\frac{(h_2 a^2 m + b^2 h_1 m^3)\, t - (h_1 h_2 m^3 + h_1 h_2 m)\, t^2}{ab\,(m^2 + 1)^2},$$

$$g_{21} = g_{12},$$

$$g_{22} = \frac{1}{a^2 b^2 (m^2 + 1)^2}(a^2 m^4 b^4 + a^2 b^4 + 2a^2 m^2 b^4$$
$$- (h_1 b^4 + 2a^2 h_2 m^4 b^2 + 3a^2 h_2 m^2 b^2)t + (a^2 h_2^2 m^4 + a^2 h_2^2 m^2)t^2).$$

However, the components $B_1^1, B_2^1, B_1^2, B_2^2$ are expressed by rationalization as follows:

Rationalization of Forms: For new parameters l and τ or t_2, they are changing as follows:

$$l^2 := a^2 b^2 (1 + m^2) - (b^2 h_1 + a^2 h_2 m^2)t_0,$$
$$\tau^2 (\text{or } t_2^2) := l^2 - (b^2 h_1 + a^2 h_2 m^2)t,$$

where l must be elected as t_0 is a rational number. The methods of Rationalization, however, are many (See Sect. 4.5, 2).

3.2　KeyGen, Enc and Dec of Finsler Encryption

The description hereafter is under the assumption that a real number is approximately represented with a rational number that is a ratio of the form (a λ-bit integer)/(a λ-bit integer). Our Finsler encryption scheme FE consists of three polynomial-time (in λ) algorithms KeyGen, Enc and Dec (cf. [11–13]).
KeyGen(1^λ)

Step1. $c(t)$: a geodesic, $p(t_0)$: start point, $q(t_1)$: end point
Step2. v: a vector in $\mathbb{Z}_+^n$ (a plaintext), dv: a positive difference vector , $v_0 = (v_0^i) = v + dv$
Step3. $v_1 = C(\tau)v_0$ ($C(\tau)$ is a regular matrix)
Step4. $v_2 = \Pi_c(t_2)v_1$ ($\Pi_c(t_2)$ is the matrix of LPD)
Step5. $E(v_1) = E(v_2) = \sum_{i=0}^n E_i$ where $E_1, \ldots, E_n \in_R \mathbb{Q}[v_0, \tau, t_2], E_0 := E(v_1) - \sum_{i=1}^n E_i$ (because $E(v_1)$ is preserved by LPD)
Step6. $E(v_1) = E(v_2) = \sum_{i=0}^n \frac{E_i}{f_i v_0^i} f_i v_0^i$ where $f_0, \ldots, f_n \in_R \mathbb{Q}_+; v_0^0 = 1$
Step 7. $V_3 = \Pi_c(\tau)\, {}^t(\frac{E_1}{f_1 v_0^1}, \cdots, \frac{E_n}{f_n v_0^n}) = {}^t(V_3^1, \cdots, V_3^n)$
Step 8. $(\frac{E_0}{f_0}, V_3^1, \cdots, V_3^n)$: an encryption key
PK $:= (\frac{E_0}{f_0}, V_3^1, \cdots, V_3^n)$, **SK** $:= \{(f_0, \cdots, f_n), \Pi_c(t_2), E(v_1)\}$
Return (**PK, SK**).

Note that, for the above **PK** and **SK**, the set of plaintexts should be $\mathbb{Z}_+^n$ and the set of ciphertexts should be a certain subset Cy of $\mathbb{Q}^{(n+1)^2}$.

Next, we obtain the ciphertext ct of a plaintext $v = (v^i)$ by using $1 + (n+1)k$ parameters, where $k > n$ as follows:

$\mathsf{Enc}(\mathbf{PK}, v)$ $//\mathbf{PK} = (\frac{E_0}{f_0}, V_3^1, \cdots, V_3^n)$

Step1. k: Choose a natural number k which is above n.

Step2. α, $\beta_1, \cdots, \beta_{(n+1)k}$: Each other different rational numbers

Step3. $\{v, \tau \leftarrow \alpha, t_2 \leftarrow \beta_1\} \;\to\; e_1 = \frac{1}{k}(\frac{E_0}{f_0}, v_3^1, \cdots, v_3^n)$

$$\vdots \qquad\qquad\qquad \vdots$$

$\{v, \tau \leftarrow \alpha, t_2 \leftarrow \beta_{(n+1)k}\} \;\to\; e_{(n+1)k} = \frac{1}{k}(\frac{E_0}{f_0}, v_3^1, \cdots, v_3^n)$

Step4. $ct_1 := \sum_{i=1}^{k} e_i$, $ct_2 := \sum_{i=k+1}^{2k} e_i$, $\cdots$, $ct_{n+1} := \sum_{i=nk+1}^{(n+1)k} e_i$

Step5. $ct = \{ct_1, \cdots, ct_{n+1}\}$: a ciphertext

Return ct.

Finally, we can decrypt ct and recover the plaintext v by using the secret key $\mathbf{SK} = \{(f_0, \cdots, f_n), \Pi_c(t_2), E(v_1)\}$ as follows:

$\mathsf{Dec}(\mathbf{SK}, ct)$ $//\mathbf{SK} := \{(f_0, \cdots, f_n), \Pi_c(t_2), E(v_1)\}$

Step1. $(f_0, f_1, \cdots, f_n) \to sx := (f_0, f_1 X_1, \cdots, f_n X_n)$

Step2. $\bar{ct}_1 := (ct_1[[1]], \Pi_c^{-1}(\tau)\, {}^t(ct_1[[2]], \cdots, ct_1[[n+1]]))$

$$\vdots \qquad\qquad \vdots \qquad\qquad \vdots$$

$\bar{ct}_{n+1} := (ct_{n+1}[[1]], \Pi_c^{-1}(\tau)\, {}^t(ct_{n+1}[[2]], \cdots, ct_{n+1}[[n+1]]))$

Step3. $EX_1 := <sx, \bar{ct}_1>, \cdots, EX_{n+1} := <sx, \bar{ct}_{n+1}>$

Step4.

$$(I) \quad \begin{cases} EX_1 = EX_{n+1} \\ \;\vdots \quad \vdots \;\; \vdots \\ EX_n = EX_{n+1} \end{cases}$$

(System of simultaneous linear equations with $X_1, \cdots, X_n$)

Step5. $\bar{X}_1, \cdots, \bar{X}_n$: formal solution of simultaneous linear equations (I) with unknown τ

Step6. $EX_1|_{X_1 \leftarrow \bar{X}_1, \cdots, X_n \leftarrow \bar{X}_n} - E(v_1)|_{v_0^1 \leftarrow \bar{X}_1, \cdots, v_0^n \leftarrow \bar{X}_n} = 0$

(algebraic equation of τ)

Step7. Solve the **rational number solution** $\tau = \alpha$ and substitute them for $\bar{X}_1, \cdots, \bar{X}_n$

$$v_0 = (v_0^1, \cdots, v_0^n) = (\bar{X}_1|_{\tau \leftarrow \alpha}, \cdots, \bar{X}_n|_{\tau \leftarrow \alpha})$$

Step8. Finally, obtain the plaintext v as follows

$$v = v_0 - dv.$$

Return v.

Example

In the Finsler space (⋆⋆) in p.4, we put $(a, b, h_1, h_2, m, t_0, t_1) = (1, 1, 1, 1, 1, \frac{1}{2}, 1)$, then

SK:

$$(f_0, f_1, f_2) := (mh_1, at_0h_2, bt_1h_2^2) = (1, \frac{1}{2}, 1)$$

$$\Pi_{c_m}(\tau) = \begin{pmatrix} \frac{\tau+1}{2\tau^2} & -\frac{\tau-1}{2\tau^2} \\ -\frac{\tau-1}{2\tau^2} & \frac{\tau+1}{2\tau^2} \end{pmatrix}.$$

$$E(v_1) = G(v_1, v_1) = {}^t v_2 G v_2 = {}^t v_1 \, {}^t \Pi_c G \Pi_c v_1 = {}^t v_0 \, {}^t C \, {}^t \Pi_c G \Pi_c C v_0$$

$$= \frac{1}{8}(3\tau^2 - 2\tau + 3)(v_0^1)^2 + \frac{1}{4}(1 - \tau^2)v_0^1 v_0^2 + \frac{1}{8}(3\tau^2 + 2\tau + 3)(v_0^2)^2$$

PK:

$$\mathbf{PK} = (\frac{E_0}{f_0}, V_3^1, V_3^2) \quad \text{(See Appendix (6))}.$$

From $E(v_1) = (\frac{E_0}{f_0})f_0 + (\frac{E_1}{f_1 v_0^1})f_1 v_0^1 + (\frac{E_2}{f_2 v_0^2})f_2 v_0^2 \rightarrow V = (\frac{E_1}{f_1 v_0^1}, \frac{E_2}{f_2 v_0^2})$, $(V_3^1, V_3^2) = V_3 = \Pi_c(\tau)V$. Then, **PK** is obtained.

4   Security Analysis

4.1   Strength of SK

In this section, the strength of each secret key $(f_0, \cdots, f_n)$, $\Pi_c(t_2)$ and $E(v_1)$ is stated about the security from a viewpoint of a calculation amount.

1. $(f_0, \cdots, f_n)$: **Each component is arbitrary rational number.**
2. $\Pi_c(t_2)$: The regular matrix $\Pi_c(t_2)$ is derived from a certain simultaneous differential equations. The differential equations are made by the Finsler metric function F. Therefore nobody knows the equations without F(**LPD problem**, see Appendix (1)). Further, in general, the linear parallel displacement of a Finsler space satisfying asymmetric property is asymmetric, namely,

$$\Pi_c^{-1} \neq \Pi_{c^{-1}}$$

   is satisfied. This means that any informations of Π_c^{-1} used in the algorithm of decryption are not obtained from $\Pi_{c^{-1}}$, where c^{-1} is the inverse curve of c. Π_c is an one-way function (cf. [8,9]).
3. $E(v_1)$: The energy of the vector v_1. This equation is directly affected by the matrix $C(\tau)$. If you replace $C(\tau)$ for the following matrix

$$\begin{pmatrix} \tau & 1 \\ \tau - 1 & 1 \end{pmatrix},$$

then the expression of $E(v_1)$ is changed as follows

$$E(v_1) = \frac{1}{8}(4\tau^2 - 4\tau + 3)(v_0^1)^2 + \frac{1}{2}(2\tau - 1)v_0^1 v_0^2 + \frac{1}{2}(v_0^2)^2.$$

Therefore nobody knows three coefficients $\frac{1}{8}(4\tau^2 - 4\tau + 3)$, $\frac{1}{2}(2\tau - 1)$ and $\frac{1}{2}$ without recognition of $C(\tau)$. $C(\tau)$ is completely arbitrary regular matrix. On the other hand, the matrix E is composed by three regular matrixes $C(\tau), \Pi_c(\tau)$ and G, namely,

$$E = {}^tC\,{}^t\Pi_c G \Pi_c C, \quad (E(v_1) = {}^t v_0 E v_0),$$

where G is called the Finsler metric tensor field. If E can be decomposed, then the attacker can get $C(\tau), \Pi_c(\tau)$ and G. Then the attacker can decrypt any ciphertext. However, to decompose E to 5-pieces regular matrix ${}^tC, {}^t\Pi_c, G, \Pi_c, C$ is computationally hard under the assumption of Mapping-Decomposition Problem (cf. [12, 13]).

4.2   Strength of PK

In the encryption algorithm, the ciphertext ct is made from $(1+(n+1)k)$ parameters β_i at Step3. Each component $ct_i (i = 1, \cdots, n+1)$ of $ct = \{ct_1, \cdots, ct_{n+1}\}$ is made by k-pieces parameters β_j $(j = (i-1)k + 1, \cdots, ik)$. Thus, algebraic equations made by the public key **PK** and ct have the property that the number of its unknown variables is more than ones of equations. For example, in the former case $\mathbf{PK} = (\frac{E_0}{f_0}, V_3^1, V_3^2)$, if $k = 2$, we have the following equation: If a ciphertext $ct = (ct_1, ct_2, ct_3) = (ct_{11}, ct_{12}, ct_{13}, ct_{21}, ct_{22}, ct_{23}, ct_{31}, ct_{32}, ct_{33})$,
$ct_1 = (ct_{11}, ct_{12}, ct_{13}) \leftarrow \frac{1}{2}(\frac{E_1}{f_0}, V_3^1, V_3^2)|_{t_2 \leftarrow \beta_1} + \frac{1}{2}(\frac{E_1}{f_0}, V_3^1, V_3^2)|_{t_2 \leftarrow \beta_2}$
$ct_2 = (ct_{21}, ct_{22}, ct_{23}) \leftarrow \frac{1}{2}(\frac{E_1}{f_0}, V_3^1, V_3^2)|_{t_2 \leftarrow \beta_3} + \frac{1}{2}(\frac{E_1}{f_0}, V_3^1, V_3^2)|_{t_2 \leftarrow \beta_4}$
$ct_3 = (ct_{31}, ct_{32}, ct_{33}) \leftarrow \frac{1}{2}(\frac{E_1}{f_0}, V_3^1, V_3^2)|_{t_2 \leftarrow \beta_5} + \frac{1}{2}(\frac{E_1}{f_0}, V_3^1, V_3^2)|_{t_2 \leftarrow \beta_6}$
for example, from ct_1, we have following three equations
$ct_{11} = \frac{1}{2}\frac{E_1}{f_0}|_{t_2 \leftarrow \beta_1} + \frac{1}{2}\frac{E_1}{f_0}|_{t_2 \leftarrow \beta_2}, \quad ct_{12} = \frac{1}{2}V_3^1|_{t_2 \leftarrow \beta_1} + \frac{1}{2}V_3^1|_{t_2 \leftarrow \beta_2}, \quad ct_{13} = \frac{1}{2}V_3^2|_{t_2 \leftarrow \beta_1} + \frac{1}{2}V_3^2|_{t_2 \leftarrow \beta_2}.$
From ct_2,
$ct_{21} = \frac{1}{2}\frac{E_1}{f_0}|_{t_2 \leftarrow \beta_3} + \frac{1}{2}\frac{E_1}{f_0}|_{t_2 \leftarrow \beta_4}, \quad ct_{22} = \frac{1}{2}V_3^1|_{t_2 \leftarrow \beta_3} + \frac{1}{2}V_3^1|_{t_2 \leftarrow \beta_4}, \quad ct_{23} = \frac{1}{2}V_3^2|_{t_2 \leftarrow \beta_3} + \frac{1}{2}V_3^2|_{t_2 \leftarrow \beta_4}$
From ct_3,
$ct_{31} = \frac{1}{2}\frac{E_1}{f_0}|_{t_2 \leftarrow \beta_5} + \frac{1}{2}\frac{E_1}{f_0}|_{t_2 \leftarrow \beta_6}, \quad ct_{32} = \frac{1}{2}V_3^1|_{t_2 \leftarrow \beta_5} + \frac{1}{2}V_3^1|_{t_2 \leftarrow \beta_6}, \quad ct_{33} = \frac{1}{2}V_3^2|_{t_2 \leftarrow \beta_5} + \frac{1}{2}V_3^2|_{t_2 \leftarrow \beta_6}$

Thus, in total, we have 9-pieces unknown variables $v_0^1, v_0^2, \tau, \beta_1, \cdots, \beta_6$ and 9-pieces equations. Here k is known, however. In general, for ct_{11}, the attacker must solve the following equation.

$$\frac{1}{k}\frac{E_1}{f_0}|_{t_2 \leftarrow \beta_1} + \cdots + \frac{1}{k}\frac{E_1}{f_0}|_{t_2 \leftarrow \beta_k} = ct_{11}$$

is satisfied. Namely, let $(v_0^1, v_0^2, \tau, k, t_{21}, \cdots, t_{2k})$ be unknown variables, then the attacker must solve the following equation with $(4+k)$-pieces unknowm variables

$$
\frac{1}{64kt_{21}^4} \times
$$

$$
\begin{aligned}
\Big(&t_{21}^6 \left(3\tau^2(v_0^1)^2 - 6\tau(v_0^1)^2 + 3(v_0^1)^2 - 6\tau^2 v_0^1 v_0^2 + 6v_0^1 v_0^2 + 3\tau^2(v_0^2)^2 \right.\\
&\left. +6\tau(v_0^2)^2 + 3(v_0^2)^2\right)\\
+ &t_{21}^5 \left(-8\tau^2(v_0^1)^2 - 8\tau(v_0^1)^2 + 16(v_0^1)^2 - 8\tau^2 v_0^1 v_0^2 + 48\tau v_0^1 v_0^2 \right.\\
&\left. +8v_0^1 v_0^2 + 16\tau^2(v_0^2)^2 + 8\tau(v_0^2)^2 - 8(v_0^2)^2\right)\\
+ &t_{21}^4 \left(-2\tau^2(v_0^1)^2 + 28\tau(v_0^1)^2 + 10(v_0^1)^2 + 28\tau^2 v_0^1 v_0^2 + 24\tau v_0^1 v_0^2 \right.\\
&\left. -28v_0^1 v_0^2 + 10\tau^2(v_0^2)^2 - 28\tau(v_0^2)^2 - 2(v_0^2)^2\right)\\
+ &t_{21}^3 \left(16\tau^2(v_0^1)^2 + 16\tau(v_0^1)^2 - 32(v_0^1)^2 + 16\tau^2 v_0^1 v_0^2 - 96\tau v_0^1 v_0^2 \right.\\
&\left. -16v_0^1 v_0^2 - 32\tau^2(v_0^2)^2 - 16\tau(v_0^2)^2 + 16(v_0^2)^2\right)\\
+ &t_{21}^2 \left(44\tau^2(v_0^1)^2 - 40\tau(v_0^1)^2 + 68(v_0^1)^2 - 40\tau^2 v_0^1 v_0^2 + 48\tau v_0^1 v_0^2 \right.\\
&\left. +40v_0^1 v_0^2 + 68\tau^2(v_0^2)^2 + 40\tau(v_0^2)^2 + 44(v_0^2)^2\right)\\
+ &24\tau^2(v_0^1)^2 - 48\tau(v_0^1)^2 + 24(v_0^1)^2 - 48\tau^2 v_0^1 v_0^2 + 48v_0^1 v_0^2\\
+ &24\tau^2(v_0^2)^2 + 48\tau(v_0^2)^2 + 24(v_0^2)^2\Big)\\
&+ \cdots\cdots \text{(sum of k-terms)} \cdots\cdots +
\end{aligned}
$$

$$
+ \frac{1}{64kt_{2k}^4} \times
$$

$$
\begin{aligned}
\Big(&t_{2k}^6 \left(3\tau^2(v_0^1)^2 - 6\tau(v_0^1)^2 + 3(v_0^1)^2 - 6\tau^2 v_0^1 v_0^2 + 6v_0^1 v_0^2 + 3\tau^2(v_0^2)^2 \right.\\
&\left. +6\tau(v_0^2)^2 + 3(v_0^2)^2\right)\\
+ &t_{2k}^5 \left(-8\tau^2(v_0^1)^2 - 8\tau(v_0^1)^2 + 16(v_0^1)^2 - 8\tau^2 v_0^1 v_0^2 + 48\tau v_0^1 v_0^2 \right.\\
&\left. +8v_0^1 v_0^2 + 16\tau^2(v_0^2)^2 + 8\tau(v_0^2)^2 - 8(v_0^2)^2\right)\\
+ &t_{2k}^4 \left(-2\tau^2(v_0^1)^2 + 28\tau(v_0^1)^2 + 10(v_0^1)^2 + 28\tau^2 v_0^1 v_0^2 + 24\tau v_0^1 v_0^2 \right.\\
&\left. -28v_0^1 v_0^2 + 10\tau^2(v_0^2)^2 - 28\tau(v_0^2)^2 - 2(v_0^2)^2\right)\\
+ &t_{2k}^3 \left(16\tau^2(v_0^1)^2 + 16\tau(v_0^1)^2 - 32(v_0^1)^2 + 16\tau^2 v_0^1 v_0^2 - 96\tau v_0^1 v_0^2 \right.\\
&\left. -16v_0^1 v_0^2 - 32\tau^2(v_0^2)^2 - 16\tau(v_0^2)^2 + 16(v_0^2)^2\right)\\
+ &t_{2k}^2 \left(44\tau^2(v_0^1)^2 - 40\tau(v_0^1)^2 + 68(v_0^1)^2 - 40\tau^2 v_0^1 v_0^2 + 48\tau v_0^1 v_0^2 \right.\\
&\left. +40v_0^1 v_0^2 + 68\tau^2(v_0^2)^2 + 40\tau(v_0^2)^2 + 44(v_0^2)^2\right)\\
+ &24\tau^2(v_0^1)^2 - 48\tau(v_0^1)^2 + 24(v_0^1)^2 - 48\tau^2 v_0^1 v_0^2 + 48v_0^1 v_0^2\\
+ &24\tau^2(v_0^2)^2 + 48\tau(v_0^2)^2 + 24(v_0^2)^2\Big)\\
&= ct_{11}.
\end{aligned}
$$

Further, from ct_{12} and ct_{13},

$$\frac{1}{k}V_3^1|_{t_2 \leftarrow \beta_1} + \cdots + \frac{1}{k}V_3^1|_{t_2 \leftarrow \beta_k} = ct_{12},$$

$$\frac{1}{k}V_3^2|_{t_2 \leftarrow \beta_1} + \cdots + \frac{1}{k}V_3^2|_{t_2 \leftarrow \beta_k} = ct_{13}$$

are satisfied. After all, $(4+k)$-pieces $(v_0^1, v_0^2, \tau, k, t_{21}, \cdots, t_{2k})$ are unknown variables. Next, from $ct_2 = (ct_{21}, ct_{22}, ct_{23})$, according to the same manner, we have $(4+k)$-pieces $(v_0^1, v_0^2, \tau, k, t_{2(k+1)}, \cdots, t_{2(2k)})$ unknown variables and, further from $ct_3 = (ct_{31}, ct_{32}, ct_{33})$, we have $(4+k)$-pieces $(v_0^1, v_0^2, \tau, k, t_{2(2k+1)}, \cdots, t_{2(3k)})$ unknown variables. Totally, we have $(4+3k)$-pieces $(v_0^1, v_0^2, \tau, k, t_1, \cdots, t_{2(3k)})$ unknown variables. $3k \geq 6$ is true if $k \geq 2$, so unknown variables number satisfies $4 + 3k \geq 10$ if $k \geq 2$. The other side, equation's number is 9, obviously. This means that the simultaneous equations made by 9-pieces algebraic equations are not able to be solved because these are underdetermined on rational numbers (**SUS problem**). In general, if an n-dimensional vector v is a plaintext, then the unknown variables are $n + 2 + (n + 1)k$-pieces because the components of v is n-pieces and other parameters are $(2 + 3k)$-pieces $\{k, \tau, \beta_1, \cdots, \beta_{(n+1)k}\}$. Therefore the equation's number is $(n + 1)^2$ and if $k \geq n + 1$ is satisfied then $n + 2 + (n + 1)k > (n + 1)^2$ is true(Underdetermined system) [13].

4.3   Length of SK

Finally, we remark the length of the secret key $\mathbf{SK} = \{(f_0, \cdots, f_n), \Pi_c(\tau), E(v_1)\}$. The length depend on the dimension n.
$(f_0, \cdots, f_n)$: $n + 1$-pieces arbitrary rational numbers.

$$\Pi_c(\tau) = \begin{pmatrix} \dfrac{a_{11}(\tau)}{b_{11}(\tau)} & \cdots & \dfrac{a_{1n}(\tau)}{b_{1n}(\tau)} \\ \vdots & \ddots & \vdots \\ \dfrac{a_{n1}(\tau)}{b_{n1}(\tau)} & \cdots & \dfrac{a_{nn}(\tau)}{b_{nn}(\tau)} \end{pmatrix}$$

$$E(v_1) = \sum_{i=1}^{n} \frac{a_i(\tau)}{b_i(\tau)}(v_0^i)^2 + \sum_{i<j, i=1, \cdots, n-1, j=2, \cdots, n} \frac{c_{ij}(\tau)}{d_{ij}(\tau)} v_0^i v_0^j,$$

where $a_{ij}(\tau)$ and $b_{ij}(\tau)$ are polynomials of τ of degree p and q and $a_i(\tau), b_i(\tau), c_{ij}(\tau)$ and $d_{ij}(\tau)$ are polynomials of τ of degree r, s, t and w. Therefore all of integer as coefficients of all polynomial $a_{ij}, b_{ij}, a_i, b_i, c_{ij}, d_{ij}$ is $2n + (p+1)n^2 + (q+1)n^2 + rn + sn + t \, {}_nC_2 + w \, {}_nC_2 \approx \alpha n^2 + \beta n + \gamma \,(\alpha, \beta, \gamma :$ certain natural numbers). Thus we can recognize that *the length of the secret key increases linearly to square of the dimension n* (i.e. $\mathcal{O}(n^2)$).

4.4 IND-CPA Security

We prove here the IND-CPA security of FE under the LPD assumption.

To construct the public key **PK** and the secret key **SK** of FE needs some parameters. In the case of the example of Appendix, the values $(a, b, h_1, h_2, m, t_0, t_1, \alpha, f_0, f_1, f_2)$ and the matrix $C(\alpha), \Pi_c(\alpha)$ are needed. In addition the energy form $E(v_1)$ is also needed. Especially, for **PK**, certain methods of rationalization and splitting are essentially needed. The values $(a, b, h_1, h_2, m, t_0, t_1, \alpha, f_0, f_1, f_2, C(\alpha))$ and the method of splitting of $E(v_1)$ decides **PK**, and the values $(a, b, h_1, h_2, m, t_0, t_1, \alpha)$ and the method of rationalization of t_2 decides $\Pi_c(\alpha)$.

Here, we state the LPD assumption [8–10].
Computational problem of linear parallel displacement (LPD Problem)
Suppose that each variable is quantized with λ-bit uniformly. (Note that λ is the security parameter.) Let (M, F) be a Finsler space and p, q be points on M. For a geodesic c from p to q, the problem is stated as the computational problem to find values of the parameters of linear parallel displacement along c from T_pM to T_qM, where T_pM, T_qM are tangent spaces at p, q respectively. Formally,

- **Input:** (p, q, c)
- **Output:** A matrix $\Pi_c(\alpha)$ of linear parallel displacement along c from T_pM to T_qM.

LPD Assumption
For a fixed Finsler space with $H_j^i \neq 0$ (See Appendix (2)), there exists no polynomial time algorithm to solve a random instance of LPD problem.

We will prove the following theorem.

Theorem 41. *FE has the IND-CPA security under LPD assumption.*

Propositions for Theorem. First we consider the following problem;
Problem. Let $\Pi_c(\alpha)$ and $\Pi_c(\alpha')$ be the matrices of the linear parallel displacement made by the values $(a, b, h_1, h_2, m, t_0, t_1, \alpha)$ and $(a, b, h_1, h_2, m, t_0, t_1, \alpha')$, respectively. Then we distinguish $\Pi_c(\alpha)$ and $\Pi_c(\alpha')$, where the method of rationalization is unknown and $(a, b, h_1, h_2, m, t_0, t_1)$ are same values.

We can state the two matrices in the Problem are indistinguishable under LPD assumption.

Proposition 41. *The two matrices in the above Problem are indistinguishable under LPD assumption.*

Proof. We assume that the two matrices in Problem are capable of being identified. This assumption means that m-pieces matrices $\Pi_c(\alpha_1), \cdots, \Pi_c(\alpha_m)$ which are correspondent to the different m values $\alpha_1, \cdots, \alpha_m$ are distinguishable.

Now, we have no information of the method of the rationalization of t_2. Then the general form of $\Pi_c(\alpha)$ is put by

$$
\Pi_c(\alpha) = \begin{pmatrix} \dfrac{a_{11}(\alpha)}{b_{11}(\alpha)} & \dfrac{a_{12}(\alpha)}{b_{12}(\alpha)} \\ \dfrac{a_{21}(\alpha)}{b_{21}(\alpha)} & \dfrac{a_{22}(\alpha)}{b_{22}(\alpha)} \end{pmatrix},
$$

where the forms $a_{11}(\alpha), a_{12}(\alpha), a_{21}(\alpha), a_{22}(\alpha), b_{11}(\alpha), b_{12}(\alpha), b_{21}(\alpha), b_{22}(\alpha)$ are polynomials with respect to unknown value α. If the amount of unknown coefficients of α of all forms $a_{ij}(\alpha), b_{ij}(\alpha)(i, j = 1, 2)$ are m, then all coefficients are solvable under informations of distinguished m-pieces matrices $\Pi_c(\alpha_1), \cdots, \Pi_c(\alpha_m)$. Namely, the general form of $\Pi_c(\alpha)$ is obtained. That means that LPD assumption is broken. Therefore this proposition's assertion is true. $\square$

Further, we have the following proposition.

Proposition 42. *In FE, if parameter values $(a, b, h_1, h_2, m, t_0, t_1, f_0, f_1, f_2, \alpha)$ and the values of entries of the matrix of linear parallel displacement $\Pi_c(\alpha)$ are known, then any ciphertext $ct = \{ct_1, ct_2, ct_3\}$ is solvable. Namely, to decrypt any ciphertext is no need of $E(v_1)$.*

Proof. Let $ct_1 = (ct_{11}, ct_{12}, ct_{13}), ct_2 = (ct_{21}, ct_{22}, ct_{23}), ct_3 = (ct_{31}, ct_{32}, ct_{33})$ be the components of the ciphertext ct, where all $ct_{ij}(i, j = 1, 2)$ are rational numbers.

First, respectively, we can obtain $\overline{ct}_{12}, \overline{ct}_{13}, \overline{ct}_{22}, \overline{ct}_{23}, \overline{ct}_{32}, \overline{ct}_{33}$ from ct_1, ct_2, ct_3 and $\Pi_c(\alpha)$ as follows;

$$
\begin{pmatrix} \overline{ct}_{12} \\ \overline{ct}_{13} \end{pmatrix} = \Pi_c^{-1}(\alpha) \begin{pmatrix} ct_{12} \\ ct_{13} \end{pmatrix}, \begin{pmatrix} \overline{ct}_{22} \\ \overline{ct}_{23} \end{pmatrix} = \Pi_c^{-1}(\alpha) \begin{pmatrix} ct_{22} \\ ct_{23} \end{pmatrix}, \begin{pmatrix} \overline{ct}_{32} \\ \overline{ct}_{33} \end{pmatrix} =
$$
$$
\Pi_c^{-1}(\alpha) \begin{pmatrix} ct_{32} \\ ct_{33} \end{pmatrix}.
$$

Next, we can construct the following simultaneous linear equations of X_1, X_2;

$$
\begin{cases} ct_{11}f_0 + \overline{ct}_{12}f_1X_1 + \overline{ct}_{13}f_2X_2 = ct_{31}f_0 + \overline{ct}_{32}f_1X_1 + \overline{ct}_{33}f_2X_2 \\ ct_{21}f_0 + \overline{ct}_{22}f_1X_1 + \overline{ct}_{23}f_2X_2 = ct_{31}f_0 + \overline{ct}_{32}f_1X_1 + \overline{ct}_{33}f_2X_2. \end{cases}
$$

Finally, the solution X_1, X_2 of the above system leads to the plain text $v = (v^1, v^2)$. In this algorithm, there is no using of $E(v_1)$. $\square$

Proof of Theorem. We consider the following game of any given PPT attacker **A** and our FE, (1) to (5), that is in accordance with the experiment $\mathsf{Exp}_{\mathsf{FE,A}}^{\mathsf{ind\text{-}cpa}}(1^\lambda)$.

(1) The challenger sends the public key **PK** of FE to the attacker.
(2) The attacker gives two plaintext $m_0, m_1 \in \mathbb{Z}_+^2$ to the challenger (We denote a message as m_i instead of v_i to avoid confusion).

(3) The challenger selects $b = 0$ or $b = 1$ at random.
(4) The challenger selects $\alpha \in \mathbb{Q}_+$ at random and sends the ciphertext $ct_b(\alpha)$ (that is encryption of m_b with $\Pi_c(\alpha)$) to the attacker.
(5) The attacker returns a guess b' to the challenger.

Now we consider another game that is the same as the above procedure (1) to (5) *except* that a simulated $ct_b(\alpha, \alpha')$ is used, which is generated using $\Pi_c(\alpha')$ where a random α' is sampled independently of α, while E_0/f_0 is dependent of α. (This is an analogy of the security proof of IND-CPA security of the El Gamal encryption [18, 19]). Then $\Pi_c(\alpha)$ and $\Pi_c(\alpha')$ are indistinguishable under the LPD assumption because of Proposition 41. Therefore the following relation holds.

$$\left| \Pr[b' = b \mid \Pi_c(\alpha)] - \Pr[b' = b \mid \Pi_c(\alpha')] \right| < \varepsilon \tag{1}$$

On the other hand, $ct_b(\alpha, \alpha')$ is actually a one-time pad because α' is sampled uniformly at random and independently of α, and the components of a ciphtertext, except the E_0/f_0, is obtained by multiplying $\Pi_c(\alpha')$. Therefore $Pr[b' = b | \Pi_c(\alpha')] = \dfrac{1}{2}$ is true. Thus, the following holds.

$$\mathbf{Adv}_{\mathsf{FE,A}}^{\text{ind-cpa}}(\lambda) = \left| \Pr[b' = b \mid \Pi_c(\alpha)] - \frac{1}{2} \right| < \varepsilon \tag{2}$$

Therefore, the theorem holds. $\qquad\qquad\qquad\qquad\qquad\qquad\qquad\qquad\qquad$ $\square$

Remark 41. *In the case of the example in Appendix, the determined differential equations (Appendix (4)) is completely solved and the general solution $\Pi_c(t)$ is obtained (Appendix (5)).*
Therefore there is the polynomial time algorithm to generate key $(\mathbf{PK}, \mathbf{SK})$.

4.5   Remarks

In this section, we state other strength, for example, splitting method of $E(v_1)$ and transforming method to rational form for parameter t_2. And any other issues requiring special attention are stated.

1. In Step5 of KeyGen, we treat the splitting $E(v_1) = \sum_{i=0}^{n} E_i$. We first use different parameters t_2, t_3 and make the matrix

$$\widetilde{E} = {}^t C(\tau) \, {}^t \Pi_c(t_3) G(t_2) \Pi_c(t_3) C(\tau)$$

because of $E = {}^t C \, {}^t \Pi_c G \Pi_c C$. Next $\widetilde{E}(v_1) = {}^t v_0 \widetilde{E} v_0$ is calculated and is splitted to $\widetilde{E}(v_1) = \sum_{i=0}^{n} \widetilde{E}_i$. And last, parameter t_3 of each component $\widetilde{E}_i$ is change to t_2. In this way, we have the splitting of $E(v_1) = \sum_{i=0}^{n} E_i$. Therefore, by different splitting of $\widetilde{E}(v_1)$ we have other splitting of $E(v_1)$. The splitting method is arbitrary.

2. In Sect. 2.1, we use the following transformation because of obtaining rational forms of formations in G, Π_c

$$t_2^2 := l^2 - (b^2 h_1 + a^2 h_2 m^2)t.$$

However, many other transformations exist, for example,

$$t_2^4 := l^2 - (b^2 h_1 + a^2 h_2 m^2)t,$$
$$(t_2 + 1)^2 := l^2 - (b^2 h_1 + a^2 h_2 m^2)t,$$
$$(\frac{t_2 + 1}{t_2})^2 := l^2 - (b^2 h_1 + a^2 h_2 m^2)t,$$

$$\vdots$$

The transforming method of the parameter t in the solution$(B_1^1, B_2^1, B_2^1, B_2^2)$ of the differential equation $(\star)$ is arbitrary. By using above transformations, all equations in **PK** and **SK** come to algebraic (or rational), fortunately. However, such thing will not always happen to us. Further, the differential equations(which give geodesics in Appendix (4)) which we must solve and its solutions are always complex.

3. Next, we state the regularity of the simultaneous linear equation (I). In Step4 of $\mathsf{Dec}(\mathbf{SK}, ct)$, for the ciphertext $ct = (ct_1, \cdots, ct_{n+1})$, each inner product $EX_1 := <sx, \bar{ct}_1>, \cdots, EX_{n+1} := <sx, \bar{ct}_{n+1}>$ is expressed as follows:

$$EX_1 = ct_{11}f_0 + \bar{ct}_{12}f_1 X_1 + \cdots + \bar{ct}_{1(n+1)}f_n X_n$$

$$\vdots \qquad \vdots$$

$$EX_{n+1} = ct_{(n+1)1}f_0 + \bar{ct}_{(n+1)2}f_1 X_1 + \cdots + \bar{ct}_{(n+1)(n+1)}f_n X_n$$

Then, the determinant Det of (I)

$$Det = \begin{vmatrix} f_1(\bar{ct}_{12} - \bar{ct}_{(n+1)2}) & \cdots & f_n(\bar{ct}_{1(n+1)} - \bar{ct}_{(n+1)(n+1)}) \\ \vdots & \ddots & \vdots \\ f_1(\bar{ct}_{n2} - \bar{ct}_{(n+1)2}) & \cdots & f_n(\bar{ct}_{n(n+1)} - \bar{ct}_{(n+1)(n+1)}) \end{vmatrix}$$

For example, in the case $n = 2$ in p.7,
$Det = \frac{1}{2}(ct_{12}ct_{23} - ct_{12}ct_{33} + ct_{13}ct_{32} - ct_{13}ct_{22} + ct_{22}ct_{33} - ct_{23}ct_{32})\tau^3$
is satisfied. If $Det = 0$, then we can change β_i so that $Det \neq 0$ is satisfied. Therefore the regularity of (I) is recognized from the ciphertext ct only.

4. The encryption map $PK_{\alpha,\beta_1,\cdots,\beta_{(n+1)k}} : \mathbb{Z}_+^2 \to \mathbb{Q}^9$ defined by parameters $(\alpha, \beta_1, \cdots, \beta_{(n+1)k})$ is one to one if $Det \neq 0$ of (I) is satisfied. Namely, different plaintexts $v, \bar{v}(\neq v)$ don't have the same ciphertext $ct = PK_{\alpha,\beta_1,\cdots,\beta_{(n+1)k}}(v) = PK_{\alpha,\beta_1,\cdots,\beta_{(n+1)k}}(\bar{v})$. On the other hand, if $(\alpha, \beta_1, \cdots, \beta_{(n+1)k}) \neq (\bar{\alpha}, \bar{\beta}_1, \cdots, \overline{\beta_{(n+1)k}})$, $PK_{\alpha,\beta_1,\cdots,\beta_{(n+1)k}}(v) \neq PK_{\bar{\alpha},\bar{\beta}_1,\cdots,\overline{\beta_{(n+1)k}}}(v)$ will happen for a plaintext v.

5. We state the solution of the energy equation

$$EX_1|_{X_1 \leftarrow \bar{X}_1, \cdots, X_n \leftarrow \bar{X}_n} - E(v_1)|_{v_0^1 \leftarrow \bar{X}_1, \cdots, v_0^n \leftarrow \bar{X}_n} = 0.$$

This equation is an algebraic equation of a certain degree in τ. Further the real solution's number is two only. In addition, true solution is rational number. Indeed, in Decryption of the case $n = 2$ in p.7, this is an algebraic equation of degree 4 in τ. How to solve this equation? It, however, is no problem because we have known the method of finding rational solutions, for example, Newton-Raphson method for an algebraic equation.

The next problem is particularly important.

6. Does the energy equation

$$EX_1|_{X_1 \leftarrow \bar{X}_1, \cdots, X_n \leftarrow \bar{X}_n} - E(v_1)|_{v_0^1 \leftarrow \bar{X}_1, \cdots, v_0^n \leftarrow \bar{X}_n} = 0$$

have two rational solutions α_1 and α_2? Further, do α_1 and α_2 yield two integer plaintext $v, \bar{v}$? This means that different plaintext $v, \bar{v}$ have the same ciphertext with different parameters $(\alpha, \beta_1, \cdots, \beta_{(n+1)k}) \neq (\bar{\alpha}, \bar{\beta}_1, \cdots, \overline{\beta_{(n+1)k}})$.
This is an open problem.

7. In 2 above, we state the transformations about t. This is called "coordinate transformation" in differential geometry, in general. Then, the transformation $t = \phi(t_2)$ must satisfy

$$\frac{dt}{dt_2} = \phi'(t_2) \neq 0.$$

If there exist a certain $\tilde{t}$ which satisfies $\phi'(\tilde{t}) = 0$, then we omit such $\tilde{t}$.

5　Conclusion

Based on a Finsler space, we formalized Finsler encryption.

1. We must choose a Finsler space with the asymmetry property (See Appendix (2)).
2. We must choose a geodesic on the Finsler space.
3. We must obtain the linear parallel displacement on the geodesic.
4. The strength is based on the three following open problems (i), (ii), (iii):
   (i) LPD problem (See Appendix (1)),
   (ii) Mapping-decomposition problem: To decompose the matrix $E = {}^tC \, {}^t\Pi_c G \Pi_c C$ is computationally hard (See Sect. 4.1, 3),
   (iii) SUS problem: To solve underdetermined system of equations is very hard (See Sect. 4.2),
   and further, it owes of arbitrariness of $C(\tau)$, splitting of E and the method of rationalization of forms.
5. In Example (p.4), Finsler space is defined as a single (a, b, h_1, h_2), namely, the form (**) expresses the family of Finsler spaces, its amount is about $10^{4\lambda}$ (λ is a security parameter). The parameter m expresses a geodesic, and t_0, t_1 express the start point and the end point. Therefore **the amount of (PK, SK) is about at least $10^{7\lambda}$.**

6. In our Finsler encryption scheme FE, all calculations are over **rational number field** $\mathbb{Q}$ with λ-bit quantization.

Key generation, encryption and decryption were given in detail. For intuitive understanding, an example was presented. Then we analyzed the strength of Finsler encryption. Future direction would be a digital signature scheme on a Finsler space.

Appendix

(1) **LPD problem and LPD assumption**
Computational problem for linear parallel displacement (LPD problem)
Suppose that each variable is quantized with λ-bit, uniformly. Let (M, F) be a Finsler space and p, q be points on M. For a geodesic c from p to q, the problem is stated as the computational problem to find values of the parameters of linear parallel displacement along c from T_pM to T_qM, where T_pM, T_qM are tangent spaces at p, q respectively.
LPD assumption
For a fixed Finsler space with $H_j^i \neq 0$, there exists no polynomial time algorithm to solve a random instance of LPD problem.

(2) Let M be an n-dimensional differentiable real manifold. Let (M, F) be a Finsler space with the metric function F which is $2n$-variable real-valued function on the tangent bundle TM. F plays very important role of which geodesic, linear parallel displacement and norm are determined. Further, we assume that

$$H_j^i(x, y) := \sum_r F_{rj}^i(x, y)y^r + \sum_r F_{rj}^i(x, -y)(-y^r) \neq 0$$

where

$$F_{rj}^i := \frac{1}{2} \sum_k g^{ik} \left(\frac{\delta g_{rk}}{\delta x^j} + \frac{\delta g_{kj}}{\delta x^r} - \frac{\delta g_{jr}}{\delta x^k} \right) \quad ((g^{ij}) = (g_{ij})^{-1}),$$

$$\frac{\delta}{\delta x^i} := \frac{\partial}{\partial x^i} - \sum_{r,j} N_i^r(x, y) \frac{\partial}{\partial y^r}.$$

Hereafter the indices $h, i, j, \cdots, p, q, r, \cdots$ of $\sum$ run from 1 to $n(= dimM)$.
(3)

$$N_j^i(x, y) = \sum_r \gamma_{rj}^i(x, y)y^r - \sum_{p,q,r} C_{jr}^i(x, y)\gamma_{pq}^r(x, y)y^p y^q,$$

where

$$\gamma_{pq}^i(x, y) = \sum_h \frac{1}{2} g^{hi} \left(\frac{\partial g_{ph}}{\partial x^q} + \frac{\partial g_{hq}}{\partial x^p} - \frac{\partial g_{pq}}{\partial x^h} \right),$$

$$C_{jr}^i(x, y) = \sum_h \frac{1}{2} g^{hi} \frac{\partial g_{jh}}{\partial y^r}.$$

(4) Geodesic is the curve which is minimizing of the distance between two points locally. Then, a geodesic $c(t) = (c^i(t))$ satisfies the following equation

$$\frac{d^2 c^i}{dt^2} + \sum_{j,r} F^i_{jr}(c, \dot{c}) \dot{c}^j \dot{c}^r = 0 \quad (\dot{c} = (\dot{c}^i), \dot{c}^i = \frac{dc^i}{dt}),$$

where t is an affine parameter.

(5)

$$B^1_1 = -\frac{1}{(a^2 (b^2 (m^2 + 1) - h_2 m^2 (t + t_0)) - b^2 h_1 (t + t_0))^{3/2}} \times$$

$$\left(a^2 \left(h_2 m^2 (t + t_0) \sqrt{a^2 (b^2 (m^2 + 1) - h_2 m^2 t_0) - b^2 h_1 t_0} \right. \right.$$

$$- b^2 \left(\sqrt{a^2 (b^2 (m^2 + 1) - h_2 m^2 (t + t_0)) - b^2 h_1 (t + t_0)} \right.$$

$$\left. \left. + m^2 \sqrt{a^2 (b^2 (m^2 + 1) - h_2 m^2 t_0) - b^2 h_1 t_0} \right) \right)$$

$$\left. + b^2 h_1 t_0 \sqrt{a^2 (b^2 (m^2 + 1) - h_2 m^2 (t + t_0)) - b^2 h_1 (t + t_0)} \right)$$

$$B^1_2 = \frac{1}{(a^2 (b^2 (m^2 + 1) - h_2 m^2 (t + t_0)) - b^2 h_1 (t + t_0))^{3/2}} \times$$

$$\left(abm \left(b^2 \left(\sqrt{a^2 (b^2 (m^2 + 1) - h_2 m^2 (t + t_0)) - b^2 h_1 (t + t_0)} \right. \right. \right.$$

$$\left. - \sqrt{a^2 (b^2 (m^2 + 1) - h_2 m^2 t_0) - b^2 h_1 t_0} \right)$$

$$+ h_2 \left(t \sqrt{a^2 (b^2 (m^2 + 1) - h_2 m^2 t_0) - b^2 h_1 t_0} \right.$$

$$+ t_0 \sqrt{a^2 (b^2 (m^2 + 1) - h_2 m^2 t_0) - b^2 h_1 t_0}$$

$$\left. \left. \left. - t_0 \sqrt{a^2 (b^2 (m^2 + 1) - h_2 m^2 (t + t_0)) - b^2 h_1 (t + t_0)} \right) \right) \right)$$

$$B^2_1 = \frac{1}{(a^2 (b^2 (m^2 + 1) - h_2 m^2 (t + t_0)) - b^2 h_1 (t + t_0))^{3/2}} \times$$

$$\left(abm \left(a^2 \left(\sqrt{a^2 (b^2 (m^2 + 1) - h_2 m^2 (t + t_0)) - b^2 h_1 (t + t_0)} \right. \right. \right.$$

$$\left. - \sqrt{a^2 (b^2 (m^2 + 1) - h_2 m^2 t_0) - b^2 h_1 t_0} \right)$$

$$+ h_1 \left(t \sqrt{a^2 (b^2 (m^2 + 1) - h_2 m^2 t_0) - b^2 h_1 t_0} \right.$$

$$+ t_0 \sqrt{a^2 (b^2 (m^2 + 1) - h_2 m^2 t_0) - b^2 h_1 t_0}$$

$$\left. \left. \left. - t_0 \sqrt{a^2 (b^2 (m^2 + 1) - h_2 m^2 (t + t_0)) - b^2 h_1 (t + t_0)} \right) \right) \right)$$

$$B_2^2 = -\frac{1}{\left(a^2\left(b^2\left(m^2+1\right)-h_2m^2(t+t_0)\right)-b^2h_1(t+t_0)\right)^{3/2}} \times$$

$$\left(-a^2b^2\left(m^2\sqrt{a^2\left(b^2\left(m^2+1\right)-h_2m^2(t+t_0)\right)-b^2h_1(t+t_0)}\right.\right.$$

$$\left.+\sqrt{a^2\left(b^2\left(m^2+1\right)-h_2m^2t_0\right)-b^2h_1t_0}\right)$$

$$+b^2h_1(t+t_0)\sqrt{a^2\left(b^2\left(m^2+1\right)-h_2m^2t_0\right)-b^2h_1t_0}$$

$$\left.+a^2h_2m^2t_0\sqrt{a^2\left(b^2\left(m^2+1\right)-h_2m^2(t+t_0)\right)-b^2h_1(t+t_0)}\right)$$

(6)

$$\frac{E_0}{f_0} = \frac{1}{64t_2^4} \times$$

$$\left(t_2^6\left(3\tau^2(v_0^1)^2 - 6\tau(v_0^1)^2 + 3(v_0^1)^2 - 6\tau^2v_0^1v_0^2 + 6v_0^1v_0^2 + 3\tau^2(v_0^2)^2 + 6\tau(v_0^2)^2 + 3(v_0^2)^2\right)\right.$$

$$+ t_2^5\left(-8\tau^2(v_0^1)^2 - 8\tau(v_0^1)^2 + 16(v_0^1)^2 - 8\tau^2v_0^1v_0^2 + 48\tau v_0^1v_0^2\right.$$

$$\left.+8v_0^1v_0^2 + 16\tau^2(v_0^2)^2 + 8\tau(v_0^2)^2 - 8(v_0^2)^2\right)$$

$$+ t_2^4\left(-2\tau^2(v_0^1)^2 + 28\tau(v_0^1)^2 + 10(v_0^1)^2 + 28\tau^2v_0^1v_0^2 + 24\tau v_0^1v_0^2\right.$$

$$\left.-28v_0^1v_0^2 + 10\tau^2(v_0^2)^2 - 28\tau(v_0^2)^2 - 2(v_0^2)^2\right)$$

$$+ t_2^3\left(16\tau^2(v_0^1)^2 + 16\tau(v_0^1)^2 - 32(v_0^1)^2 + 16\tau^2v_0^1v_0^2 - 96\tau v_0^1v_0^2\right.$$

$$\left.-16v_0^1v_0^2 - 32\tau^2(v_0^2)^2 - 16\tau(v_0^2)^2 + 16(v_0^2)^2\right)$$

$$+ t_2^2\left(44\tau^2(v_0^1)^2 - 40\tau(v_0^1)^2 + 68(v_0^1)^2 - 40\tau^2v_0^1v_0^2 + 48\tau v_0^1v_0^2\right.$$

$$\left.+40v_0^1v_0^2 + 68\tau^2(v_0^2)^2 + 40\tau(v_0^2)^2 + 44(v_0^2)^2\right)$$

$$+ 24\tau^2(v_0^1)^2 - 48\tau(v_0^1)^2 + 24(v_0^1)^2 - 48\tau^2v_0^1v_0^2 + 48v_0^1v_0^2 + 24\tau^2(v_0^2)^2 + 48\tau(v_0^2)^2 + 24(v_0^2)^2\right),$$

$$V_3^1 = \frac{-1}{64\tau^2t_2^4v_0^1v_0^2} \times$$

$$\left(t_2^6\left(2\tau^3(v_0^1)^3 - 6\tau^2(v_0^1)^3 + 6\tau(v_0^1)^3 - 2(v_0^1)^3 + 3\tau^3(v_0^1)^2v_0^2\right.\right.$$

$$-3\tau^2(v_0^1)^2v_0^2 - 3\tau(v_0^1)^2v_0^2 + 3(v_0^1)^2v_0^2 - 12\tau^3v_0^1(v_0^2)^2$$

$$-12\tau^2v_0^1(v_0^2)^2 + 12\tau v_0^1(v_0^2)^2 + 12v_0^1(v_0^2)^2 + 7\tau^3(v_0^2)^3 + 21\tau^2(v_0^2)^3 + 21\tau(v_0^2)^3 + 7(v_0^2)^3\right)$$

$$+ t_2^5\left(-4\tau^2(v_0^1)^3 + 8\tau(v_0^1)^3 - 4(v_0^1)^3 - 12\tau^3(v_0^1)^2v_0^2 - 12\tau^2(v_0^1)^2v_0^2\right.$$

$$+4\tau(v_0^1)^2v_0^2 + 20(v_0^1)^2v_0^2 - 12\tau^3v_0^1(v_0^2)^2 + 48\tau^2v_0^1(v_0^2)^2$$

$$\left.+76\tau v_0^1(v_0^2)^2 + 16v_0^1(v_0^2)^2 + 24\tau^3(v_0^2)^3 + 40\tau^2(v_0^2)^3 + 8\tau(v_0^2)^3 - 8(v_0^2)^3\right)$$

$$+ t_2^4\left(-8\tau^3(v_0^1)^3 + 20\tau^2(v_0^1)^3 - 24\tau(v_0^1)^3 + 12(v_0^1)^3 - 30\tau^3(v_0^1)^2v_0^2\right.$$

$$+6\tau^2(v_0^1)^2v_0^2 + 26(v_0^1)^2v_0^2 - 26(v_0^1)^2v_0^2 + 56\tau^3v_0^1(v_0^2)^2$$

$$+76\tau^2v_0^1(v_0^2)^2 - 56\tau v_0^1(v_0^2)^2 - 60v_0^1(v_0^2)^2 - 38\tau^3(v_0^2)^3$$

$$\left.-106\tau^2(v_0^2)^3 - 110\tau(v_0^2)^3 - 42(v_0^2)^3\right)$$

$$+ t_2^3\left(8\tau^2(v_0^1)^3 - 16\tau(v_0^1)^3 + 8(v_0^1)^3 + 24\tau^3(v_0^1)^2v_0^2 + 24\tau^2(v_0^1)^2v_0^2\right.$$

$$-8\tau(v_0^1)^2v_0^2 - 40(v_0^1)^2v_0^2 + 24\tau^3v_0^1(v_0^2)^2 - 96\tau^2v_0^1(v_0^2)^2$$

$$\left.-152\tau v_0^1(v_0^2)^2 - 32v_0^1(v_0^2)^2 - 48\tau^3(v_0^2)^3 - 80\tau^2(v_0^2)^3 - 16\tau(v_0^2)^3 + 16(v_0^2)^3\right)$$

$$+ t_2^2 \left(8\tau^2(v_0^1)^3 + 8\tau(v_0^1)^3 - 16(v_0^1)^3 + 52\tau^3(v_0^1)^2 v_0^2 + 44\tau^2(v_0^1)^2 v_0^2 \right.$$
$$+ 36\tau(v_0^1)^2 v_0^2 + 108(v_0^1)^2 v_0^2 - 8\tau^3 v_0^1(v_0^2)^2 + 64\tau^2 v_0^1(v_0^2)^2$$
$$+ 144\tau v_0^1(v_0^2)^2 + 24 v_0^1(v_0^2)^2 + 100\tau^3(v_0^2)^3 + 124\tau^2(v_0^2)^3 + 68\tau(v_0^2)^3 + 44(v_0^2)^3 \right)$$
$$+ 16\tau^3(v_0^1)^3 - 48\tau^2(v_0^1)^3 + 48\tau(v_0^1)^3 - 16(v_0^1)^3 + 24\tau^3(v_0^1)^2 v_0^2$$
$$- 24\tau^2(v_0^1)^2 v_0^2 - 24\tau(v_0^1)^2 v_0^2 + 24(v_0^1)^2 v_0^2 - 96\tau^3 v_0^1(v_0^2)^2$$
$$- 96\tau^2 v_0^1(v_0^2)^2 + 96\tau v_0^1(v_0^2)^2 + 96 v_0^1(v_0^2)^2 + 56\tau^3(v_0^2)^3 + 168\tau^2(v_0^2)^3$$
$$+ 168\tau(v_0^2)^3 + 56(v_0^2)^3 \Big),$$

$$V_3^2 = \frac{1}{64\tau^2 t_2^4 v_0^1 v_0^2} \times$$
$$\left(t_2^6 \left(2\tau^3(v_0^1)^3 - 2\tau^2(v_0^1)^3 - 2\tau(v_0^1)^3 + 2(v_0^1)^3 + 3\tau^3(v_0^1)^2 v_0^2 \right.\right.$$
$$- 25\tau^2(v_0^1)^2 v_0^2 + 25\tau(v_0^1)^2 v_0^2 - 3(v_0^1)^2 v_0^2 - 12\tau^3 v_0^1(v_0^2)^2$$
$$+ 20\tau^2 v_0^1(v_0^2)^2 + 20\tau v_0^1(v_0^2)^2 - 12 v_0^1(v_0^2)^2 + 7\tau^3(v_0^2)^3 + 7\tau^2(v_0^2)^3 - 7\tau(v_0^2)^3 - 7(v_0^2)^3 \Big)$$
$$+ t_2^5 \left(-4\tau^2(v_0^1)^3 + 4(v_0^1)^3 - 12\tau^3(v_0^1)^2 v_0^2 - 4\tau^2(v_0^1)^2 v_0^2 \right.$$
$$+ 52\tau(v_0^1)^2 v_0^2 - 20(v_0^1)^2 v_0^2 - 12\tau^3 v_0^1(v_0^2)^2 + 88\tau^2 v_0^1(v_0^2)^2$$
$$- 44\tau v_0^1(v_0^2)^2 - 16 v_0^1(v_0^2)^2 + 24\tau^3(v_0^2)^3 - 8\tau^2(v_0^2)^3 - 24\tau(v_0^2)^3 + 8(v_0^2)^3 \Big)$$
$$+ t_2^4 \left(-8\tau^3(v_0^1)^3 + 4\tau^2(v_0^1)^3 - 12(v_0^1)^3 - 30\tau^3(v_0^1)^2 v_0^2 \right.$$
$$+ 114\tau^2(v_0^1)^2 v_0^2 - 126\tau(v_0^1)^2 v_0^2 + 26(v_0^1)^2 v_0^2 + 56\tau^3 v_0^1(v_0^2)^2$$
$$- 84\tau^2 v_0^1(v_0^2)^2 - 96\tau v_0^1(v_0^2)^2 + 60 v_0^1(v_0^2)^2 - 38\tau^3(v_0^2)^3$$
$$- 30\tau^2(v_0^2)^3 + 26\tau(v_0^2)^3 + 42(v_0^2)^3 \Big)$$
$$+ t_2^3 \left(8\tau^2(v_0^1)^3 - 8(v_0^1)^3 + 24\tau^3(v_0^1)^2 v_0^2 + 8\tau^2(v_0^1)^2 v_0^2 \right.$$
$$- 104\tau(v_0^1)^2 v_0^2 + 40(v_0^1)^2 v_0^2 + 24\tau^3 v_0^1(v_0^2)^2 - 176\tau^2 v_0^1(v_0^2)^2$$
$$+ 88\tau v_0^1(v_0^2)^2 + 32 v_0^1(v_0^2)^2 - 48\tau^3(v_0^2)^3 + 16\tau^2(v_0^2)^3 + 48\tau(v_0^2)^3 - 16(v_0^2)^3 \Big)$$
$$+ t_2^2 \left(8\tau^2(v_0^1)^3 + 24\tau(v_0^1)^3 + 16(v_0^1)^3 + 52\tau^3(v_0^1)^2 v_0^2 - 28\tau^2(v_0^1)^2 v_0^2 \right.$$
$$+ 148\tau(v_0^1)^2 v_0^2 - 108(v_0^1)^2 v_0^2 - 8\tau^3 v_0^1(v_0^2)^2 + 144\tau^2 v_0^1(v_0^2)^2$$
$$- 96\tau v_0^1(v_0^2)^2 - 24 v_0^1(v_0^2)^2 + 100\tau^3(v_0^2)^3 - 76\tau^2(v_0^2)^3 + 20\tau(v_0^2)^3 - 44(v_0^2)^3 \Big)$$
$$+ 16\tau^3(v_0^1)^3 - 16\tau^2(v_0^1)^3 - 16\tau(v_0^1)^3 + 16(v_0^1)^3 + 24\tau^3(v_0^1)^2 v_0^2$$
$$- 200\tau^2(v_0^1)^2 v_0^2 + 200\tau(v_0^1)^2 v_0^2 - 24(v_0^1)^2 v_0^2 - 96\tau^3 v_0^1(v_0^2)^2$$
$$+ 160\tau^2 v_0^1(v_0^2)^2 + 160\tau v_0^1(v_0^2)^2 - 96 v_0^1(v_0^2)^2 + 56\tau^3(v_0^2)^3$$
$$+ 56\tau^2(v_0^2)^3 - 56\tau(v_0^2)^3 - 56(v_0^2)^3 \Big).$$

References

1. Aikou, T., Kozma, L.: Global aspects of Finsler geometry. In: Handbook of Global Analysis, vol. 1211, pp. 1–39. Elsevier Science B. V., Amsterdam (2008)
2. Bao, D., Chern, S.-S., Shen, Z.: An Introduction to Riemann-Finsler Geometry. Graduate Texts in Math, vol. 200. Springer, New York (2000). https://doi.org/10.1007/978-1-4612-1268-3
3. Chern, S.-S., Shen, Z.: Riemann-Finsler Geometry. Nankai Tracts in Mathematics, vol. 6. World Scientific Publishing Co., Pte. Ltd., Hackensack (2005)

4. Crampin, M.: Randers spaces with reversible geodesics. Publ. Math. Debrecen **67**(3–4), 401–409 (2005)
5. Matsumoto, M.: Foundations of Finsler Geometry and Special Finsler Spaces. Kaiseisha Press, Shigaken (1986)
6. Matsumoto, M.: Finsler geometry in the 20th-century. In: Handbook of Finsler Geometry, vol. 1, 2, pp. 557–966. Kluwer Academic Publishers, Dordrecht (2003)
7. Nagano, T., Innami, N., Itokawa, Y., Shiohama, K.: Notes on reversibility and branching of geodesics in Finsler spaces. Iasi Ploytechic Inst. Bull.-Mathematics. Theoretical Mechanics. Physics Section, pp. 9–28 (2019)
8. Nagano, T., Anada, H.: Public-key encryption scheme using non-symmetry of Finsler spaces. In: Proceedings of Computer Security Symposium 2019, Information Processing Society of Japan, pp. 415–421 (2019). (in Japanese)
9. Nagano, T., Anada, H.: One-wayness of public-key encryption scheme using non-symmetry of Finsler spaces. (Original title: Indistinguishability of Public-Key Encryption Scheme Using Non-symmetry of Finsler Spaces). In: Proceedings of 2020 Symposium on Cryptography and Information Security (SCIS 2020), The Institute of Electronics, Information and Communication Engineers, 3A3-1(1–7) (2020). (in Japanese)
10. Nagano, T., Anada, H.: Approach to cryptography from differential geometry with example. In: Maimut, D., Oprina, A.-G., Sauveron, D. (eds.) SecITC 2020. LNCS, vol. 12596, pp. 110–129. Springer, Cham (2021). https://doi.org/10.1007/978-3-030-69255-1_8
11. Nagano, T., Anada, H.: Mathematical Structure of Finsler Encryption, IPSJ SIG Technical Report, Vol. 2021-CSEC-95 No. 6 (Vol. 2021-SPT-45 No. 6, Vol. 2021-EIP-94 No. 6) (2021)
12. Nagano, T., Anada, H.: Mathematical structure of Finsler encryption and signature. In: Proceedings of 2022 Symposium on Cryptography and Information Security Osaka (SCIS 2022), Japan & Online, 18–21 January 2022. The Institute of Electronics, Information and Communication Engineers, 2A3-2(1–7) (2022)
13. Nagano, T., Anada, H.: Finsler Encryption, 2022: Workshop on interaction between Cryptography, Information Security and Mathematics (CRISMATH 2022), Joint Research Center for Advanced and Fundamental Mathematics-for-Industry. Kyushu University, 20–21 December 2022 (2022)
14. Nagano, T.: Notes on the notion of the parallel displacement in Finsler geometry. Tensor (N.S.) **70**(3), 302–310 (2008)
15. Nagano, T.: On the parallel displacement and parallel vector fields in Finsler geometry. Acta Math. Acad. Paedagog. Nyhazi. **26**(2), 349–358 (2010)
16. Nagano, T.: A note on linear parallel displacements in Finsler geometry. J. Fac. Glob. Commun. **12**, 195–205 (2011)
17. Nagano, T.: On the quantities W, L, K derived from linear parallel displacements in Finsler geometry. J. Fac. Glob. Commun. **14**, 123–132 (2013)
18. ElGamal, T.: A public key cryptosystem and a signature scheme based on discrete logarithms. In: Blakley, G.R., Chaum, D. (eds.) CRYPTO 1984. LNCS, vol. 196, pp. 10–18. Springer, Heidelberg (1985). https://doi.org/10.1007/3-540-39568-7_2
19. Katz, J., Lindell, Y.: Introduction to Modern Cryptography, 2nd edn. CRC Press, Florida (2014)
20. Goldreich, O.: The Foundations of Cryptography - Volume 1, Basic Techniques. Cambridge University Press, Cambridge (2001)
21. Goldreich, O.: The Foundations of Cryptography - Volume 2, Basic Applications. Cambridge University Press, Cambridge (2004)

Feasibility Analysis and Performance Optimization of the Conflict Test Algorithms for Searching Eviction Sets

Zhenzhen Li[1,2], Zihan Xue[1,2], and Wei Song[1,2(✉)]

[1] Key Laboratory of Cyberspace Security Defense, Institute of Information Engineering, Chinese Academy of Sciences, Beijing, China
{lizhenzhen1,xuezihan,songwei}@iie.ac.cn
[2] School of Cyber Security, University of Chinese Academy of Sciences, Beijing, China

Abstract. Cache side-channel attacks have been widely utilized as an intermediate step in some comprehensive attacks. Eviction sets, especially the minimal eviction sets, are essential components of the conflict-based cache side-channel attacks. It is important to develop efficient search algorithms that incur the lowest latency with the highest success rate. Several fast search algorithms have been proposed in recent years, among which conflict test (CT) achieves the highest success rate with the lowest latency. In this paper, we have conducted the first systematic feasibility analysis of the CT algorithm. Besides failing on the commonly known cache architectures where the last-level cache (LLC) is exclusive or non-inclusive, CT is also found and verified failing on two inclusive LLC architectures if it is running in single-core mode. We have further explored three optimizations for improving the speed performance of the CT algorithm, two of which are newly proposed in this paper.

Keywords: Computer micro-architecture · Cache architecture · Cache side-channel attack · Eviction set construction

1 Introduction

As an effective way of obtaining sensitive information from the cache system [10,18,24], cache side-channel attacks have been widely utilized as an intermediate step in some comprehensive attacks, such as reconstructing cryptographic keys [1,6,11,29,30,37], disarming the address space randomization [7,8] in control-flow attacks, retrieving the leaked information at the end of a transient execution attack [14,15], and constantly striking a row of the off-chip memory in a rowhammer attack [9].

Eviction sets, especially the minimal eviction sets [32], are essential components of the conflict-based cache side-channel attacks [34]. In such attacks, an attacker and her victim share the same cache space, typically certain cache sets in the last-level cache (LLC). The attacker needs to control the state of these shared cache sets to monitor the memory accesses of her victim, which are then used to infer security-critical information. To be specific, the attacker occupies (primes) a cache set by accessing an eviction set [9]; therefore, her victim's access to this cache set must incur a cache miss, refilling of the missing cache block, evicting an address from the eviction set, and eventually a prolonged access. Both the address eviction and the prolonged access latency might be observable and used to infer the access of her victim.

All addresses in a minimal eviction set are *congruent* with (mapping to) the targeted cache set [32]. At least W addresses are required for a W-way set-associative cache. Obviously, the key for constructing an eviction set is to find enough congruent addresses. Unfortunately, this is not an easy task on modern processors. LLC is indexed by physical addresses but attackers control only virtual addresses. A complex addressing scheme is utilized by modern Intel processors [17] to randomize the mapping from physical addresses to LLC slices. Attackers are usually forced to search eviction sets at runtime from a large amount of random addresses. It is important to develop efficient search algorithms that incur the lowest latency with the highest success rate. Several fast search algorithms have been proposed in recent years, including *group elimination* (GE) [16,27,32], *prime, prune and probe* (PPP) [19,22], *conflict test* (CT) [23] and *write-after-write* (W+W) [28]. Among these algorithms, CT achieves the highest success rate with the lowest latency (see Table 1), and becomes one of the most widely utilized search algorithms [20,21]. However, there lacks a systematic analysis on the feasibility and the potential optimization of CT while similar analyses have been done for GE [27] and PPP [19].

In this paper, we have conducted the first systematic feasibility analysis of the CT algorithm. Besides sharing a commonly known limitation with other algorithms, that CT fails to work on exclusive or non-inclusive LLCs, CT also fails on two inclusive LLC architectures if the algorithm is running in single-core mode. Based on the result of the feasibility analysis, we have further explored three techniques for further optimizing the CT algorithm, two of which are newly proposed in this paper. Overall, this paper makes the following contributions:

- Conduct a systematic feasibility analysis on CT. For the first time, two inclusive cache architectures are identified as infeasible for single-core CT.
- Optimize the performance of CT by improving the efficiency of the cacheback technique and propose two new techniques.
- Practically evaluate the optimization techniques on both real processors and a behavioral-level cache model.

2   Background

Modern processors are multicore processors adopting a two/three-level cache structure. Each processing core contains a pair of private level-one (L1) instruction and data caches. Some processors, especially the Intel ones, equip each core with a uniformed level-two (L2) cache. A large LLC (L2 or L3) is shared among all cores. This LLC might be divided into multiple slices, whose mapping with physical addresses is decided by an undisclosed hash function (complex addressing scheme [17]) in Intel processors. All levels of caches are set-associative write-back allocated caches. According to [31], all cache levels in the early generations

(Haswell and earlier) and the L1 caches in recent Intel processors utilize the pseudo-LRU (PLRU) replacement policy [5], while L2 and LLC in recent Intel processors adopt some policies derived from RRIP [13]. The situation is similar for most other commercial processors, such as AMD ones. In some rare cases, random replacement policy is used in embedded-level processors [26]. In all cache architectures, LLC acts as the coherence hub. LLC and the private L1/L2 caches maintain either an inclusive relation (Intel's consumer processors), where all cache blocks in the private caches are also stored in the LLC, or a non-inclusive relation (Intel's Xeon and AMD's Ryzen), where cache blocks stored in private caches may not be concurrently stored in the LLC.

Cache side-channel attacks normally fall in two categories: *flush-based* and *conflict-based* attacks. Flush-based attacks use explicit flush instructions (`clflush` on x86 [36]) to invalidate a targeted data out of the cache architecture. These attacks are accurate but require the targeted data is accessible by the attacker, which is a rather strict requirement infeasible in most cross-process side-channel attacks. As an alternative, conflict-based attacks can achieve the similar effect. They evict the targeted data out of the LLC by occupying the corresponding LLC cache set with a collection of attacker's controlled cache blocks, typically called an *eviction set*. An eviction set is a collection of addresses (cache blocks) that contain enough addresses congruent with the targeted data. A sufficiently large number of addresses are also an eviction set as they can evict any cache block by priming the whole caches [33]. However, this type of untargeted eviction introduces undesirable noise [9] and brings down the attack speed [7]. What is really desirable is a minimal eviction containing only the congruent addresses. For simplicity, an "eviction set" beyond this point refers to a minimal eviction set. This paper concentrates on the algorithms for searching eviction sets.

Existing search algorithms for eviction sets can be classified into two categories: *pruning algorithms* which begin with an untargeted eviction set containing a large number of random addresses and prune it into a minimal one, and *inserting algorithms* which begin with an empty collection and gradually fill it with newly found congruent addresses until it becomes an eviction set.

GE and PPP are the two widely utilized pruning algorithms. GE prunes the initial large eviction set in a multi-round process. In each round, the remaining N addresses are divided into $W + 1$ groups. Since a minimal eviction set contains only W addresses, at least one group contains none of the W addresses and should be removed. By sequentially testing whether the address collection remains an eviction set without a certain group, the removable group is found and removed. The prune process continues until a minimal set is produced. GE is robust in tolerating environment noise, as indicated by the high success rate shown in Table 1, but the multi-round prune is slow.

PPP reduces the prune latency by manipulating the PLRU replacement policy [22,23]. It first tries to store addresses of the initial large eviction set into the LLC concurrently by gradually removing the addresses causing self-evictions. The resulted (reduced) eviction set is still untargeted but may fully occupy the

Table 1. Speed comparison of different search algorithms for eviction sets.

CPU	GE		PPP		W+W		CT	
	latency	rate	latency	rate	latency	rate	latency	rate
i7-3770	58 ± 32 ms	74%	0.69 ± 1.7 ms	8.8%	33 ± 41 ms	6.1%	6.0 ± 3.4 ms	69%
i7-6700	82 ± 66 ms	79%	1.0 ± 2.9 ms	0.9%	10 ± 5.3 ms	5.3%	23 ± 21 ms	16%
i7-9700	115 ± 92 ms	85%	0.65 ± 0.68 ms	11%	159 ± 8.5 ms	2.0%	20 ± 17 ms	21%
i7-11700	642 ± 586 ms	24%	0.81 ± 0.04 ms	7.0%	3 ± 1.4 ms	0.4%	12 ± 4.4 ms	2.1%

targeted cache set. Then the attacker incurs an eviction in the targeted cache set by accessing the targeted address, following with a timed re-access of the reduced eviction set. Due to the PLRU replacement policy, it is likely that exactly W addresses (just enough for an eviction set) are found missing in the LLC. However, the probability that the reduced eviction set occupying the targeted cache set is actually low in a large LLC with many cache sets. As shown in Table 1, the success rate of PPP is much lower than GE.

CT is the mostly utilized inserting algorithm. It was initially proposed only for LLCs adopting the random replacement policy [23]. In this case, a congruent address has a $1/W$ probability to evict the targeted cache block. As a random address is a congruent address by a probability of $1/S$, where S is the number of cache sets, one congruent address can be found by probing around SW random addresses. Finding eviction set with W congruent addresses therefore requires probing $\mathcal{O}(SW^2)$ random addresses. This algorithm is also effective for permutation-based replacement, such as LRU and RRIP. Instead of finding congruent addresses by detecting the eviction of the targeted cache block, detecting the prolonged write latency due to the LLC enforced serialization of parallel writes to the same cache set was also found effective [28]. The resulted algorithm, namely $W+W$, was claimed faster than the GE algorithm. However, the accuracy of such serialization detection is found extremely noisy and unstable, which results in low success rates as shown in Table 1.

To compare the speed performance of these algorithms, they are ported to four Intel processors and the result is shown in Table 1. CT seems to provide the most balanced performance in latency and success rate. The search latency is significantly lower than GE while the success rate is much higher than PPP (except for i7-11700). The search latency of W+W is shorter than CT only on i7-6700 and i7-11700 but the success rate is much lower on both processors. This paper concentrates on improving the CT algorithm.

3   Feasibility Analysis

This section conducts a systematic analysis on the feasibility of the CT algorithm on different cache architectures. For the first time, the CT algorithm is found infeasible on two inclusive cache architectures.

3.1 Threat Model

For an eviction set search algorithm, we define a successful attack as finding an eviction set. We assume that the search algorithm is run by an attacker in a restricted user mode environment with the following capabilities and limitations:

- The targeted LLC is shared between the attacker and her victim.
- The amount of memory acquirable by the attacker is not limited by the system, so the attacker can access an arbitraily large range of addresses.
- The attacker either runs in the same core with her victim or occupies a separate core.
- The attacker can flush her own data out of the LLC.
- The attacker can accurately trick her victim into accessing a target address without incurring a large amount of noise.
- Some parameters regarding the cache system are made available, such as the replacement policy, the inclusiveness relation, and the number of sets and ways of each cache level, but neither the virtual to physical page mapping nor the Intel complex addressing scheme [17] is reverse-engineered.

3.2 Necessary Working Conditions

Algorithm 1 illustrates the baseline CT algorithm. Different with other papers [20,23], we explicitly specify the cores running the victim and the attacker. When $C_a = C_v$, the attacker and her victim are running on the same core or even in the same process/thread. This is the typical case for cache side-channel attacks that tries to break the user-mode address randomization [8], leak information through transient execution [14,15], and constantly hammer a targeted DRAM row [9]. We call this the single-core case while the traditional cross-core (process) attack as the cross-core case. As we will soon discover in Sect. 3.3, CT may fail to work on some inclusive cache architectures when running in the single-core case while remains feasible for cross-core.

According to Algorithm 1, a random address a is found congruent with the targeted address x only if accessing a (line 6) causes a miss in the targeted cache

---

Algorithm 1: The baseline CT algorithm

Input: x, target address; W, number of ways; (C_a, C_v), cores running the attacker and her victim.
Output: $\mathcal{E}$, an eviction set for x.

```
 1  function ct(x, W, Ca, Cv)
 2      E ← ∅ // eviction set
 3      Cv:access(x)
 4      while |E| < W do
 5          a ← random()
 6          Ca:access(a)
 7          if not Cv:probe(x) then
 8              E ⋃{a}
 9          end
10      end
11      return E
12  end
```

$$C_a{:}L1 \boxed{a_3|a_4|a_5|a_6} \quad (LRU \text{ --- } MRU)$$

$C_a{:}L1$ [LRU — MRU] $\boxed{a_3|a_4|a_5|a_6}$ $C_v{:}L1$ [LRU — MRU] $\boxed{?|?|?|x}$ $C_a{:}L1$ [LRU — MRU] $\boxed{a_4|a_5|a_6|a_7}$ $C_v{:}L1$ [LRU — MRU] $\boxed{?|?|?|\boxed{x}}$

LLC [LRU — MRU] $\boxed{x|a_0|a_1|a_2|a_3|a_4|a_5|a_6}$ LLC (x) [LRU — MRU] $\boxed{a_0|a_1|a_2|a_3|a_4|a_5|a_6|a_7}$

(a) Before accessing a_7. (b) After accessing a_7.

Fig. 1. Purging x (cross-core case) after accessing a_7 by C_a in a 2-level inclusive cache architecture. ($W_{L1} = 4, W_{LLC} = 8$, all caches use LRU)

set and the cache block containing x is evicted for refilling a. In addition, the eviction of x can be observed by probing x (code highlighted in blue): a timed access of x. If the probe latency is longer than a pre-defined threshold, x is assumed missing and a is identified as congruent. Two necessary conditions for the success of CT can be derived from Algorithm 1:

Condition 1: *Inclusion victim effect.* When an LLC is the targeted cache, the targeted cache block stored in a private L1 cache (the potential inclusion victim [12]), such as the x stored in $C_v{:}L1$ depicted in Fig. 1a, must be purged from the cache architecture when its copy in the LLC is evicted due to a conflict, such as the access of a_7 by C_a shown in Fig. 1b. In other words, CT works only when the targeted LLC is inclusive. Note that this condition is required for the single-core case as well, since x is also purged by a conflict in the LLC.

Condition 2: *Cache filter effect.* When the CT algorithm is used to target an LLC adopting LRU/RRIP replacement policies, the probing of x is observed by the LLC only after x is successfully evicted in the LLC, such as probing x after accessing a_7 as shown in Fig. 1b. The cache filter effect is a by-product of the hierarchical cache architecture where memory accesses hitting in private caches are invisible to the LLC. When the LLC adopts PLRU/RRIP replacement policies, the target address x is possible to be evicted by a fresh access of a new random address a only when x is pushed to the LRU position, as shown in Fig. 1a, by a number of accesses (random addresses) to the cache set after the previous access of x is observed by the LLC. According to Algorithm 1, x is accessed once in the probe for each random address. All of these accesses must be filtered from the LLC (served by private L1/L2 caches); otherwise, x is repeatedly accessed in the LLC and cannot be pushed to the LRU position. This is the first time that such condition has been discovered and we will show in the next section (Sect. 3.3) why CT fails on some inclusive cache architectures (satisfying condition 1) due to the lack of this cache filter effect.

3.3   Feasibility on Different Cache Architectures

Utilizing the two necessary conditions discovered in Sect. 3.2, we have conducted a systematic survey on the feasibility of CT on different cache architectures. We consider the following cache parameters:

- **Cache levels:** cache architectures that have two or three levels of caches.
- **Inclusiveness:** inclusive ($L1 \subseteq LLC$), exclusive ($L1 \neq LLC$) or non-inclusive ($L1 \nsubseteq LLC$) relation between cache levels.

Table 2. Feasibility on different cache architectures.

Architecture	Example	Attack	Feasible
Exclusive or Non-inclusive LLC[a]	AMD Zen 2 and later (Ryzen-7 5700G)	cross-core	No
		single-core	No
Inclusive LLC[b] with private caches using LRU/RRIP	Intel Processors (i7-6700 and Xeon 4110[b])	cross-core	Yes
		single-core	Yes
Three levels of inclusive caches using LRU/RRIP	Early quad/hexa-core processors (Intel Dunnington [2, 25])	cross-core	Yes
		single-core	No
Inclusive LLC using LRU/RRIP with private caches using random	A customized Rocket-Chip processor (Sect. 5.1)	cross-core	Yes
		single-core	No

[a]A non-inclusive LLC may adopt an inclusive directory and CT becomes feasible, such as the Intel Xeon processors [35]. These cache architectures are counted as inclusive LLCs without differentiating the directory from the cache.
[b]Include the non-inclusive LLCs adopting inclusive directories.

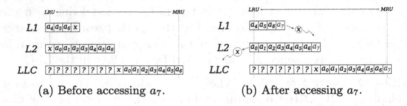

(a) Before accessing a_7.   (b) After accessing a_7.

Fig. 2. A failing example of single-core CT in a 3-level inclusive cache using LRU. ($W_{L1} = 4, W_{L2} = 8, W_{LLC} = 16$)

- **Cache sets and ways**: when the LLC is inclusive, it is assumed that the number of ways in the LLC (W_{LLC}) is no less than it in private caches: $W_{LLC} \geq W_{L2}$ if $L1 \subseteq L2$ or $W_{LLC} \geq W_{L1} + W_{L2}$ otherwise.
- **Replacement policy**: the replacement policy of individual cache can be independently selected among LRU, RRIP or random.
- **Attack scenario**: both cross-core and single-core attacks are considered.

In total, we have surveyed 168 different cache architectures (scenarios) and identified four categories of representative cache architectures as revealed in Table 2:

Exclusive or Non-inclusive LLC: When the LLC is exclusive or non-inclusive, the target x stored in L1 cannot become an inclusion victim and CT fails to work. Nearly all recent AMD Zen 2 and later processors fall in this category and are naturally immune to the CT algorithm. Intel Xeon processors adopt a non-inclusive LLC but utilize an inclusive directory. Due the inclusiveness of the directory, they are still vulnerable to CT. We count them as inclusive LLCs.

Inclusive LLC with private caches using LRU/RRIP: This is the common category for nearly all Intel processors. The inclusive LLC ensures the inclusion victim effect. As for the cache fitler effect, since LRU/RRIP is adopted by the private caches, the repeatedly probing of x ensures that x is pinned in the L1 and all accesses to x are invisible to LLC until x is evicted from the LLC. Note that we deliberately leave an exception here for simplicity. As described by the next category, a three-level inclusive LLC using LRU/RRIP can break the condition for the cache filter effect.

Three levels of inclusive caches using LRU/RRIP: This is an exception of the previous category. CT works in the cross-core case but fails in the single-core case due to the lack of the filter effect. A failing example is presented in Fig. 2. After accessing seven congruent addresses (a_0 to a_6) and probing x, the state of the three-level cache is depicted in Fig. 2a. Note the repeated probing of x is filtered by L1 and invisible to both L2 and LLC. As a result, x is pushed to the LRU position in L2. As demonstrated in Fig. 2b, the following access of a_7 thus evicts x from L2, which consequently purges x also from L1 as it is an inclusion victim. As x is purges from both L1 and L2, the probing of x is observed by LLC, which moves x to the MRU position in LLC and CT fails. The rooting cause is that the probing of x is invisible to the inclusive L2 while $W_{L2} < W_{LLC}$. Early generations of the Intel quad/hexa-core multiprocessors, such as the Intel Dunnington architecture [2, 25] adopts such a three-level inclusive cache architecture. The L2 cache in later generations becomes exclusive, which unfortunately makes them vulnerable to single-core CT.

Inclusive LLC using LRU/RRIP with Private Caches Using Random: This architecture is uncommon as most L1 caches adopt LRU/RRIP replacement policies. However, the single-core CT fails in such an architecture as x is likely evicted from the private caches before it is evicted from the LLC due to the random replacement, which makes the following probing of x observed by the LLC. CT therefore fails due to the lack of the filter effect. In Sect. 5.1, we have configured the cache architecture of a dual-core Rocket-Chip accordingly as a demonstrative example for the failing of single-core CT.

4   Performance Optimization

This section begins with a performance analysis of the baseline CT algorithm. Based on the analysis, three optimization techniques are proposed to improve the efficiency of the CT algorithm.

4.1   Performance Analysis of the Baseline Algorithm

Let us consider a cross-core attack on a two-level inclusive cache using the LRU replacement policy. The latency (L) of searching one eviction set of W congruent addresses can be estimated as:

$$L = (N_{RA} + W) \cdot t_{mem} + (N_v - W) \cdot t_{L1} + N_v \cdot \Delta_{cross} \tag{1}$$

where N_{RA} and N_v are the numbers of accessing random addresses and the victim address x, respectively, while t_{mem}, t_{L1} and Δ_{cross} are the time for one memory access, the time for one access hitting in L1, and the time overhead for one cross-core access, respectively. The total number of LLC misses is $N_{RA} + W$ and $N_v - W$ times of probing x should hit in L1 due to the perfect filter effect.

Due to the LRU replacement policy, the target address x is evicted from the LLC every time when W congruent random addresses are accessed. A total of W^2 congruent random addresses are searched before obtaining an eviction set. We call this number N_{CA}. Since random address is a congruent address with x by a probability of $1/S$, N_{RA} and N_v can be estimated as:

$$N_{RA} = N_v = N_{CA} \cdot S = SW^2 \tag{2}$$

where S is the number of LLC sets. Using Eq. 1, L is rewritten to:

$$L = (SW^2 + W) \cdot t_{mem} + (SW^2 - W) \cdot t_{L1} + SW^2 \cdot t_{cross} \tag{3}$$

$$= SW^2 \cdot [t_{mem} + (t_{L1} + \Delta_{cross})] + W \cdot (t_{mem} - t_{L1}) \tag{4}$$

$$= S \cdot N_{CA} \cdot (t_{mem} + t_v) + W \cdot \Delta_{miss} \tag{5}$$

where t_v and Δ_{miss} are the time for one (cross-core) probing of x and the time overhead of one cache (both L1 and LLC) miss, respectively. According to Eq. 5, the key for reducing L is to decrease N_{CA}, the number of congruent random addresses requiring to be accessed, as all others are constants.

Equation 5 holds true for cross-core attacks on all feasible cache architectures, even when the LLC adopts the random replacement policy. In this case, Eq. 2 remains the same as a random address is a congruent address with x by a probability of $1/S$, accessing a congruent address evicts x by a probability of $1/W$, and x is evicted for W times during the whole search. Consequently, Eq. 4 and 5 remain untouched.

For single-core attacks, Eq. 5 remains valid as long as the L1 adopts LRU/RRIP replacement policies because LRU/RRIP guarantees the perfect filter effect. t_v is reduced to t_{L1} as the cross-core overhead is removed. When both L1 and LLC adopt the random replacement policy, accessing a random address evicts x from the L1 cache by a probability of $1/(S_{L1} \cdot W_{L1})$. Therefore, extra latency is introduced in Eq. 4 and 5:

$$L = SW^2 \cdot (t_{mem} + t_{L1}) + W \cdot (t_{mem} - t_{L1}) + \frac{SW^2}{S_{L1} \cdot W_{L1}} \cdot (t_{LLC} - t_{L1}) \tag{6}$$

$$= S \cdot N_{CA} \cdot (t_{mem} + t_v) + W \cdot \Delta_{miss} + \frac{S \cdot N_{CA}}{S_{L1} \cdot W_{L1}} \cdot \Delta_{L1\text{-miss}} \tag{7}$$

where $t_v = t_{L1}$ and $\Delta_{L1\text{-miss}} = t_{LLC} - t_{L1}$, which is the time overhead of accessing LLC when L1 misses. Similarly, the key for reducing L is to decrease N_{CA} as all others are constants.

4.2   Cacheback: Reducing the Number of Random Accesses

Cacheback is an optimization capable of reducing N_{CA} when the LLC adopts an LRU/RRIP replacement policy. In the baseline CT algorithm, every time the target address x is evicted from the LLC, a total of W congruent addresses are

Algorithm 2: Cacheback after a successful probe

```
1  if not C_v:probe(x) then
2      E ⋃{a}
3      for e in E do
4          C_a:access(e)
5      end
6  end
```

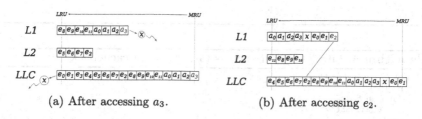

(a) After accessing a_3.   (b) After accessing e_2.

Fig. 3. Problem of cacheback when the order observed by LLC (L2) mismatching with the program order. (According to i7-6700, $W_{L1} = 8, W_{L2} = 4, W_{LLC} = 16$, L2 is exclusive, L2 and LLC adopt RRIP)

accessed but only the last one is identified by the algorithm, because it finally evicts x. When a number of congruent addresses are identified and stored in $\mathcal{E}$ (line 8 in Algorithm 1), these addresses can be used to push x to the LRU position and reduce the total number of congruent addresses (N_{CA}) needed in the search. This cacheback procedure is described in the code extraction of the probe illustrated in Algorithm 2 (replacing the code highlighted blue in Algorithm 1) with the optimization highlighted in red. After the i-th congruent address (e_i) is identified by CT, the number of congruent addresses needed for identifying the next one is reduced to $W - i$. Therefore, N_{CA} is reduced to:

$$N_{CA} = \sum_{i=0}^{W-1} (W - i) = \frac{W^2 + W}{2} \tag{8}$$

Compared with Eq. 2, the total number of congruent addresses needed in the search is roughly reduced by half, so does the search latency.

This optimization is first proposed in the Prime+Scope attack [20]. By further investigation, we find out that the optimization works but not as effective as it should be. There are two reasons for this reduced efficiency: *mismatching access order* and *broken filter effect*. Let us consider an example of single-core attack on a three-level cache depicted in Fig. 3. The access order observed by the LLC might not match with the access order issued by the program. As a result, when the target address x is evicted by accessing address a_3 in Fig. 3a, the access order observed (more importantly the replacement order) by L2 and LLC mismatches with the program order for address e_2[1], assuming 12 congruent addresses (e_0 to e_{11}) have been identified, stored in $\mathcal{E}$, and used for cacheback. a_3 is identified as a

---

[1] Many reasons can cause the mismatch in access order. The filter effect itself is a potential cause as soon shown in Fig. 3b. The imperfect pseudo-LRU used in hardware and the RRIP derivative policies used in L2 and LLC [31] also cause mismatching replacement order and access order. Finally, the L2 in this case (also in modern

---

Algorithm 3: Flush before cacheback

```
1  if not Cᵥ:probe(x) then
2      ℰ⋃{a}
3      for e in ℰ do
4          Cₐ:flush(e)
5      end
6      for e in ℰ do
7          Cₐ:access(e)
8      end
9  end
```

Algorithm 4: Interleavedly re-access target during cacheback

```
1   if not Cᵥ:probe(x) then
2       ℰ⋃{a}
3       for e in ℰ do
4           Cₐ:flush(e)
5       end
6       for e in ℰ do
7           Cₐ:access(e)
8           Cᵥ:access(x) // single-core, Cᵥ = Cₐ
9       end
10  end
```

---

congruent address and stored in $\mathcal{E}$ after probing x (refill x to L1 and LLC as well). According to the cacheback optimization, e_0 to e_{11}, along with a_3 are accessed to push x towards the LRU position in LLC. When the cacheback proceeds to e_2, this address hits in L2 and is swapped to L1 rather than accessing from LLC due to the order mismatch. Consequently, the access of e_2 is invisible to LLC, reducing the effectiveness of the cacheback and the access order in L2 and LLC diverse further away from the program order. To avoid the mismatching access order, we propose to flush all the addresses stored in $\mathcal{E}$ before caching them back, as highlighted in the code extraction of the probe part illustrated in Algorithm 3 (replacing the code highlighted blue in Algorithm 1). In this way, each accessing of e_i forces an insertion at the MRU position in the LLC.

The other problem is the broken filter effect in single-core CT attack when the number of addresses in $\mathcal{E}$ is larger than the associativity of the inner caches: $|\mathcal{E}| \geq W_{L1} + W_{L2}$ for the cache architecture shown in Fig. 3. Let us consider the situation after the cacheback process is finished, the target x is actually evicted from L1 and L2, because the total number of addresses in $\mathcal{E}$ becomes 13 after adding a_3. As a result, LLC observes a re-access of x soon after probing for the next random address. This would put x to the unfavorable MRU position if LLC adopts the LRU replacement. It is even worse for the RRIP replacement policy as a re-access of x promotes it to higher replacement priority [13], which would fail the CT algorithm. To avoid such problem, we propose to interleavedly re-access the target address x during the cacheback process, as shown in Algorithm 4 (replacing the code highlighted blue in Algorithm 1). In this way, CT ensures that x is never evicted from L1.

Intel processor) is exclusive, whose replacement order is also affected by the block swapping between L2 and L1 when a block hits in L2.

Algorithm 5: Extended probing

```
1  r = TRUE
2  r = r and Cᵥ:probe(x)
3  for e in ℰ do
4      r = r and Cₐ:probe(e)
5  end
6  if not r then
7      ℰ ∪ {a}
8  end
```

4.3 *Extended Probing*: Increasing the Probability of Probing

Cacheback is effective only when the LLC adopts an LRU/RRIP replacement policy. If the policy is random, the probability of evicting the target address x is independent for every random address being tested. Cacheback is therefore useless. In this situation, we propose to directly improve the probability of identifying a congruent address in the probing. Instead of probing only the target address x, an attacker can additionally probe all the found congruent addresses stored in $\mathcal{E}$, as they all stored in the same LLC cache set. Algorithm 5 demonstrates the probe (code highlighted blue in Algorithm 1) optimized with the extend probing. If any of the target address x or the addresses stored in $\mathcal{E}$ is probed missing in the LLC, r becomes FALSE, and the random address a is then identified as congruent and added to $\mathcal{E}$.

Assuming the size of $\mathcal{E}$ is $|\mathcal{E}|$, the probability of identifying a congruent address increases from $\frac{1}{W}$ to $\frac{1+|\mathcal{E}|}{W}$, which approaches to 64% when $|\mathcal{E}| = 15$ for a 16-way LLC. Consequently, N_{CA} is reduced from 256 to 54.1, achieving a 79% reduction. However, the search latency does not drop proportionally to the reduction of N_{CA}. In fact, the latency benefit eventually drops to negative with the increasing of $|\mathcal{E}|$, because the total number of accesses issued by probes rises proportionally to $|\mathcal{E}|$. They incur a significant latency overhead when $|\mathcal{E}| \to W$. When $|\mathcal{E}| < W_{\text{L1}}$, addresses in $\mathcal{E}$ likely hit in L1. The extra accesses introduced by the extended probing are served by L1 and the latency overhead is small. When $|\mathcal{E}| \geq W_{\text{L1}}$, the extended probing begins to experience significant amount of L1 misses. The latency overhead would gradually becomes intolerable. There should be an optimal number of addresses applied with the extended probing.

4.4 *Surrogate Targets*: Reducing Victim Accesses

The final optimization is related to reduce the number of probing the target address x. In certain attack scenarios, tricking the victim to probe the target address x (normally cross-core) is a time consuming and noisy procedure ($\Delta_{\text{cross}} \gg t_{\text{L1}}$ in Eq. 4), especially when the victim is non-cooperative or the victim probe is likely bulky (containing unrelated code). As a result, the total time required for constructing an eviction might not be decided by the complexity of the search algorithm but largely by the number of victim accesses [22].

According to Eq. 2, the number of victim access $N_{\text{v}} = N_{\text{CA}} \cdot S$, which is a fairly large number. We would like to significantly reduce N_{v}. Instead of probing the target address x, an attacker can replace x with a found congruent address

Table 3. Cache misses incurred by testing 1000 random addresses.

Scenario	C_0 L1 miss	C_0 L2 miss	C_1 L1 miss	C_1 L2 miss	LLC miss
cross-core	1000 ± 0.0	1000 ± 0.0	1.3 ± 0.5	1.3 ± 0.5	1001 ± 0.5
single-core	1016 ± 1.3	1016 ± 1.3	0 ± 0	0 ± 0	1000 ± 0.03

as the surrogate target, such as e_0 stored in $\mathcal{E}$. The number of total victim access N_v is therefore reduced to the number of victim accesses required for identifying the first congruent address, which is only $S \cdot W$. Note that this effectively convert an originally cross-core attack into a single-core one. Therefore, it is viable only for the cache architectures feasible for the single-core case. It is also worthwhile to point out, this technique is universally effective for all inserting algorithms.

5 Performance Evaluation

The performance of CT with various optimizations is evaluated by running them on actual processors whenever possible. The two assumed failing cache architectures for the single-core case (Sect. 3.3) are first verified. Consequently, the speed benefits of the optimizations proposed in Sect. 4 are measured.

5.1 Feasibility Verification

It is widely understand that CT fails on exclusive/non-inclusive cache architectures. This section concentrates on verifying of the two inclusive cache architectures identified in Table 2 (Sect. 3.3) where the single-core CT fails.

For the **three levels of inclusive caches using LRU/RRIP**, we verify the failing single-core case using a behavioral cache model [27] as we do not have any of the early Intel machines or any open processor implementation adopting a three-level cache architecture. The cache model is configured with two cores. $(C_a, C_v) = (C_0, C1)$ for the cross-core case. Each core contains a 64-set 8-way L1 and an private 512-set 8-way L2, while a 4096-set 12-way LLC is shared between cores. All caches adopt the LRU replacement policy.

The baseline CT is used to test 1000 random addresses for both cross-core and single-core cases. Complying with the analysis provided in Table 2, 1~2 congruent addresses are found in the cross-core case but none in the single-core case. Table 3 reveals the cache misses recorded in all caches. In the cross-core case, testing 1000 random addresses incurs ~1001 misses in the LLC, where the extra 1~2 misses are caused by the eviction of the target addresses x from the LLC, which is confirmed by the matching missing number on core C_1 (C_v). In the single-core case, the number of cache misses incurred by testing 1000 random addresses is ~1016 on L1 but exactly 1000 on LLC. The 16 extra misses on L1 is caused by the eviction of the target address x from the L2, which would lead to re-accessing x on the LLC (broken filter effect). As a result, x is never pushed to the LRU position in the LLC, and CT fails.

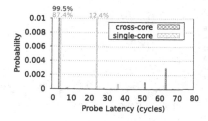

Fig. 4. The latency distribution of probing the target address x.

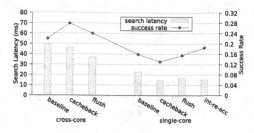

Fig. 5. Search latency and success rate on Intel i7-6700 when various cacheback optimizations are applied.

For the **inclusive LLC using LRU/RRIP with private caches using random**, we manage to configure a dual-core Rocket-Chip [3,4] with a two-level cache architecture where the 1024-set 16-way LLC is inclusive using LRU while the 64-set 8-way L1 uses random. The Rocket-Chip is ported to a FPGA dev board, runs at 50 MHz, and boots with a Linux kernel (ver. 5.11.0).

The baseline CT algorithm runs on this dual-core Rocket-Chip for both cross-core and single-core cases. The cross-core case successfully finds eviction sets with a probability of 13% while the single-core case fails, complying with Table 2. To verify this result, the latency distribution of probing the target address x has been collected and depicted in Fig. 4. For the cross-core case, 99.5% probes hit in L1 ($\sim$4 cycles), while $\sim$0.4% probes miss in LLC (ζ45 cycles). The tested CT algorithm uses random addresses sharing the same page offset with the target address x, providing a theoretical conflicting rate of $1/256$ (0.391%). The 0.4% LLC miss rate matches perfectly with the theory. For the single-core case, only 87.4% probes hit in L1, 12.4% probes hit in LLC ($\sim$25 cycles), and none misses in the LLC. Due to the random replacement policy used in L1, the target address x shall be evicted from the L1 by a probability of $1/8$ (12.5%), in theory. This matches with the 12.4% probes hitting in the LLC. Due to this effect, x is never pushed to the LRU position in LLC, and CT fails.

5.2 Speed Optimization Results

Cacheback (Sect. 4.2) reduces N_{CA} along with the search latency in inclusive LLCs adopting LRU/RRIP replacement policies. We use Intel i7-6700 as our default processor for analyzing the different techniques for improving the effi-

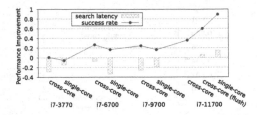

Fig. 6. Search latency and success rate on Intel processors when cacheback is applied.

Table 4. Cross-core CT on Intel processors using cacheback and surrogate targets.

CPU	Baseline		Cacheback		Surrogate Target			
	latency	rate	latency	rate	latency	rate	victim-acc.	reduction
i7-3770	13 ± 4.5 ms	80%	9.5 ± 7.6 ms	81%	6.4 ± 2.6 ms	64%	$3.4K$	89%
i7-6700	49 ± 47 ms	22%	46 ± 54 ms	28%	31 ± 44 ms	16%	$44K$	68%
i7-9700	44 ± 39 ms	20%	33 ± 39 ms	24%	29 ± 36 ms	22%	$43K$	62%
i7-11700	72 ± 54 ms	4.8%	69 ± 58 ms	6.6%	63 ± 50 ms	2.3%	$125K$	37%

ciency of cacheback while the final performance of CT with the optimized cacheback is compared on all the four Intel processors.

Figure 5 demonstrates the search latency and success rate on Intel i7-6700 when different optimization techniques are applied to the cacheback process. In the cross-core case, applying the basic cacheback alone without *flushing before cacheback* (labeled as "flush") or *interleavedly re-access* (labeled as "int-re-acc") already raises the success rate from 22% to 28% and reduces the search latency from 49 ms to 46 ms. Since the target address x is accessed by C_v rather than C_a, caching back $\mathcal{E}$ would not evict x out of the C_v:L1 and the thrashing access pattern observed by the private L1 and L2 caches means the benefit of *flush* is marginal. As shown in Fig. 5, *flush* reduces the search latency but also incurs a drop on the success rate. *int-re-acc* is unnecessary for the cross-core case. We therefore choose the basic cacheback (without *flush* or *int-re-acc*) as the default cacheback optimized CT algorithm. In the single-core case, caching back $\mathcal{E}$ has a much higher probability to evict the target address x out of the private L1 and L2 caches than in the cross-core case. Consequently, applying cacheback itself leads to an substantial drop on the success rate. By applying both *flush* and *int-re-acc*, the success rate is raised from 16% to 19% while the search latency drops from 23 ms to 15 ms. We consequently define the cacheback with both *flush* and *int-re-acc* as the default cacheback optimized CT algorithm for single-core.

Figure 6 demonstrates the performance improvement of cacheback optimized CT compared with the baseline CT on all the four Intel processors. The detail performance figures are also revealed in Table 4 for the cross-care case and Table 5 for the single-core case. The success rate is improved substantially on the more recent processors (later than the 6th generation) and this increase is most visible for the latest i7-11700 where the success rate is raised by 90% for the single-core case. As for the search latency, cacheback is able to reduce the search latency for all processors earlier than the 9th generation. Overall, cacheback is able to

Table 5. Single-core CT on Intel processors using cacheback.

CPU	Baseline		Cacheback	
	latency	rate	latency	rate
i7-3770	6.0 ± 3.4 ms	69%	5.1 ± 5.8 ms	65%
i7-6700	23 ± 21 ms	16%	15 ± 19 ms	19%
i7-9700	20 ± 17 ms	21%	16 ± 18 ms	25%
i7-11700	12 ± 4.4 ms	2.1%	13 ± 9.8 ms	3.9%

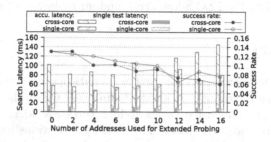

Fig. 7. Success rate and search latency (both single-test and accumulated) of CT running a dual-core Rocket-Chip (L1 LRU and LLC random) with extended probing.

significantly improve the speed performance of CT on all the four tested Intel processors.

The **surrogate targets** (Sect. 4.4) optimization can significantly reduce the number of victim accesses by replacing the probing target from the target address x to the first found congruent address e_0 stored in $\mathcal{E}$. We have tested the CT using surrogate targets on the four Intel processors and the detailed result is revealed in the right-most columns in Table 4. The number of victim accesses is reduced by 37% to, as high as, 89%. This reduction proves the effectiveness of the optimization. The search latency is also significantly reduced to the range achieved by the single-core case. The reason is simply, once the probe target is replaced with e_0, the time consuming cross-core probe becomes the much faster single-core probe. However, the success rate drops to slightly lower than the single-core case. The success rate of single-core case is typically lower than the cross-core case due to its higher noise level. In addition, probing the surrogate targets suffers from a slightly reduced success rate as the found e_0 might not be congruent with x by a small probability due to false-positive errors.

Finally, we demonstrate the performance benefit of the **extended probing** (Sect. 4.3) again using a dual-core Rocket-Chip and configuring the replacement policies of the L1 cache to LRU and the LLC to random. Figure 7 depicts the success rate and the search latency when the probing target is extended with 0 to 16 found congruent addresses stored in $\mathcal{E}$. The search latency is labeled as the "single-test latency" while the accumulated latency for eventually finding an eviction set (latency divided by success rate) is labeled as the "accu. latency". For both cross-core and single-core cases, extending the probe with found congruent addresses reduces the single-test search latency by increasing the success probability of probes. However, the success rate gradually drops with the number of extended probed addresses due to the increased probability of self-evicting the probe targets. The overall impact of applying extended probing is better presented by the accumulated search latency for finding an eviction set. Extending the probe with 2 to 6 addresses reduces the accumulated latency by around 20% for the cross-core case while extending the probe with 4 addresses reduces the accumulated latency by 18% for the single-core case. The result confirms that extending the probe with a small number of found congruent addresses can improve speed when the LLC adopts the random replacement policy.

6   Conclusion

In this paper, we have conducted the first systematic feasibility analysis of the CT algorithm. Besides the commonly known failing case where the LLC is exclusive or non-inclusive, two inclusive cache architectures are identified and verified as failing cases for the single-core CT. Three optimizations have been studied. The performance of the cacheback optimization has been significantly improved (especially for the single-core CT) by introducing flushing before cache back and interleaved re-access during the cacheback. The other two are newly proposed in this paper. Extended probing is effective in reducing the search latency by increasing the success probability of probes on cache architectures where the LLC adopts the random replacement policy. Surrogate targets is effective in reducing the number of victim accesses, which is hugely beneficial when the cross-core probing of the victim address is time consuming.

Acknowledgements. This research was supported by the National Natural Science Foundation of China (No. 62172406) and the CAS Pioneer Hundred Talents Program. Any opinions, findings, conclusions, and recommendations expressed in this paper are those of the authors and do not necessarily reflect the views of the funding parties.

References

1. Acıiçmez, O., Schindler, W., Koç, Ç.K.: Cache based remote timing attack on the AES. In: Abe, M. (ed.) CT-RSA 2007. LNCS, vol. 4377, pp. 271–286. Springer, Heidelberg (2006). https://doi.org/10.1007/11967668_18
2. Alfs, G., Knupffer, N.: Intel fact sheet: Intel corporation's multicore architecture briefing (2008). https://www.intel.com/pressroom/archive/releases/2008/20080317fact.htm
3. Amid, A., et al.: Chipyard: integrated design, simulation, and implementation framework for custom SoCs. IEEE Micro **40**(4), 10–21 (2020)
4. Asanović, K., et al.: The Rocket chip generator. Technical report. UCB/EECS-2016-17, University of California, Berkeley (2016)
5. Berg, C.: PLRU cache domino effects. In: Proceedings of the International Workshop on Worst-Case Execution Time Analysis (WCET) (2006)
6. Bernstein, D.J.: Cache-timing attacks on AES (2005). https://cr.yp.to/antiforgery/cachetiming-20050414.pdf

7. Genkin, D., Pachmanov, L., Tromer, E., Yarom, Y.: Drive-by key-extraction cache attacks from portable code. In: Preneel, B., Vercauteren, F. (eds.) ACNS 2018. LNCS, vol. 10892, pp. 83–102. Springer, Cham (2018). https://doi.org/10.1007/978-3-319-93387-0_5

8. Gras, B., Razavi, K., Bosman, E., Bos, H., Giuffrida, C.: ASLR on the line: practical cache attacks on the MMU. In: Proceedings of the Network and Distributed System Security Symposium (NDSS). Internet Society (2017)

9. Gruss, D., Maurice, C., Mangard, S.: Rowhammer.js: a remote software-induced fault attack in JavaScript. In: Caballero, J., Zurutuza, U., Rodríguez, R.J. (eds.) DIMVA 2016. LNCS, vol. 9721, pp. 300–321. Springer, Cham (2016). https://doi.org/10.1007/978-3-319-40667-1_15

10. İnci, M.S., Gulmezoglu, B., Irazoqui, G., Eisenbarth, T., Sunar, B.: Cache attacks enable bulk key recovery on the cloud. In: Proceedings of the International Conference on Cryptographic Hardware and Embedded Systems (CHES), pp. 368–388. ICAR (2016)

11. Irazoqui, G., Inci, M.S., Eisenbarth, T., Sunar, B.: Wait a minute! a fast, cross-VM attack on AES. In: Stavrou, A., Bos, H., Portokalidis, G. (eds.) RAID 2014. LNCS, vol. 8688, pp. 299–319. Springer, Cham (2014). https://doi.org/10.1007/978-3-319-11379-1_15

12. Jaleel, A., Borch, E., Bhandaru, M., Steely, S.C., Jr., Emer, J.: Achieving non-inclusive cache performance with inclusive caches: temporal locality aware (TLA) cache management policies. In: Proceedings of the Annual IEEE/ACM International Symposium on Microarchitecture (MICRO). IEEE (2020)

13. Jaleel, A., Theobald, K.B., Steely, Jr., S.C., Emer, J.S.: High performance cache replacement using re-reference interval prediction (RRIP). In: Proceedings of the International Symposium on Computer Architecture (ISCA), pp. 60–71. ACM (2010)

14. Kocher, P., et al.: Spectre attacks: exploiting speculative execution. In: Proceedings of the IEEE Symposium on Security and Privacy (S&P), pp. 19–37 (2019)

15. Lipp, M., et al.: Meltdown: reading kernel memory from user space. In: Proceedings of the USENIX Security Symposium (Security), pp. 973–990. USENIX Association (2018)

16. Liu, F., Yarom, Y., Ge, Q., Heiser, G., Lee, R.B.: Last-level cache side-channel attacks are practical. In: Proceedings of the IEEE Symposium on Security and Privacy (S&P). IEEE (2015)

17. Maurice, C., Le Scouarnec, N., Neumann, C., Heen, O., Francillon, A.: Reverse engineering intel last-level cache complex addressing using performance counters. In: Bos, H., Monrose, F., Blanc, G. (eds.) RAID 2015. LNCS, vol. 9404, pp. 48–65. Springer, Cham (2015). https://doi.org/10.1007/978-3-319-26362-5_3

18. Percival, C.: Cache missing for fun and profit (2005)

19. Purnal, A., Giner, L., Gruß, D., Verbauwhede, I.: Systematic analysis of randomization-based protected cache architectures. In: Proceedings of the IEEE Symposium on Security and Privacy (S&P), pp. 987–1002. IEEE (2021)

20. Purnal, A., Turan, F., Verbauwhede, I.: Prime+Scope: overcoming the observer effect for high-precision cache contention attacks. In: Proceedings of the ACM SIGSAC Conference on Computer and Communications Security (CCS), pp. 2906–2920. ACM (2021)

21. Purnal, A., Turan, F., Verbauwhede, I.: Double trouble: combined heterogeneous attacks on non-inclusive cache hierarchies. In: Proceedings of the USENIX Security Symposium (Security), pp. 3647–3664. USENIX Association (2022)

22. Purnal, A., Verbauwhede, I.: Advanced profiling for probabilistic Prime+Probe attacks and covert channels in ScatterCache. arXiv cs.CR (2019)
23. Qureshi, M.K.: New attacks and defense for encrypted-address cache. In: Proceedings of the International Symposium on Computer Architecture (ISCA), pp. 360–371. ACM (2019)
24. Ristenpart, T., Tromer, E., Shacham, H., Savage, S.: Hey, you, get off of my cloud: exploring information leakage in third-party compute clouds. In: Proceedings of the ACM Conference on Computer and Communications Security (CCS), pp. 199–212. ACM (2009)
25. Savage, J.E., Zubair, M.: A unified model for multicore architectures. In: Proceedings of the International Forum on Next-Generation Multicore/Manycore Technologies (IFMT), p. 12. ACM (2008)
26. Shen, S., Li, Z., Song, W.: Methods of extracting parameters of the processor caches. In: Cheng, C.M., Akiyama, M. (eds.) IWSEC 2022. LNCS, vol. 13504, pp. 47–65. Springer, Cham (2022). https://doi.org/10.1007/978-3-031-15255-9_3
27. Song, W., Liu, P.: Dynamically finding minimal eviction sets can be quicker than you think for side-channel attacks against the LLC. In: Proceedings of the International Symposium on Research in Attacks, Intrusions and Defenses (RAID), pp. 427–442. USENIX Association (2019)
28. Thoma, J.P., Güneysu, T.: Write me and I'll tell you secrets – write-after-write effects on Intel CPUs. In: Proceedings of the International Symposium on Research in Attacks, Intrusions and Defenses (RAID). ACM (2022)
29. Tromer, E., Osvik, D.A., Shamir, A.: Efficient cache attacks on AES, and countermeasures. J. Cryptol. **23**(1), 37–71 (2010)
30. Tóth, R., Faigl, Z., Szalay, M., Imre, S.: An advanced timing attack scheme on RSA. In: Networks 2008 - The 13th International Telecommunications Network Strategy and Planning Symposium, vol. Supplement, pp. 1–9 (2008)
31. Vila, P., Ganty, P., Guarnieri, M., Köpf, B.: CacheQuery: learning replacement policies from hardware caches. In: Proceedings of the ACM SIGPLAN Conference on Programming Language Design and Implementation (PLDI). ACM (2020)
32. Vila, P., Köpf, B., Morales, J.F.: Theory and practice of finding eviction sets. In: Proceedings of the IEEE Symposium on Security and Privacy (S&P), pp. 39–54. IEEE (2019)
33. Wong, H.: Intel Ivy Bridge cache replacement policy (2013). https://blog.stuffedcow.net/2013/01/ivb-cache-replacement/
34. Yan, M., Gopireddy, B., Shull, T., Torrellas, J.: Secure hierarchy-aware cache replacement policy (SHARP): defending against cache-based side channel attacks. In: Proceedings of the Annual International Symposium on Computer Architecture (ISCA), pp. 347–360. ACM (2017)
35. Yan, M., Sprabery, R., Gopireddy, B., Fletcher, C.W., Campbell, R.H., Torrellas, J.: Attack directories, not caches: side-channel attacks in a non-inclusive world. In: Proceedings of the IEEE Symposium on Security and Privacy (S&P), pp. 888–904. IEEE (2019)
36. Yarom, Y., Falkner, K.: FLUSH+RELOAD: a high resolution, low noise, L3 cache side-channel attack. In: Proceedings of the USENIX Security Symposium (Security), pp. 719–732. USENIX Association (2014)
37. Zhou, Y., Feng, D.: Side-channel attacks: ten years after its publication and the impacts on cryptographic module security testing (2005). https://eprint.iacr.org/2005/388

Korean Post Quantum Cryptography

Theoretical and Empirical Analysis of **FALCON** and **SOLMAE** Using Their Python Implementation

Kwangjo Kim[✉]

Korea Advanced Institute of Science and Technology (KAIST) and International Research Institute for Cyber Security (IRCS), Yongin, Korea
kkj@kaist.ac.kr

Abstract. Since NIST has recently selected FALCON as one of quantum–resistant digital signatures which uses the hash-and-sign paradigm in the style of Gentry–Peikert–Vaikuntanathan framework and instantiated over NTRU lattices, SOLMAE as a variant of FALCON was submitted to KpqC competition by taking all the pros of FALCON and MITAKA and reducing their cons as much as possible.

In this paper, we suggest the asymptotic computational complexity of FALCON and SOLMAE take $\Theta(n \log n)$ in their `KeyGen`, `Sign` and `Verif` procedures simultaneously, but our computer experiments using their Python implementation exhibit empirically that `KeyGen` of FALCON–512 takes longer time than that of SOLMAE–512 by about a second while the other two procedures are running almost the same time. We show a sample execution of FALCON–512 and SOLMAE–512 with their real value are described in detail for the educational purpose to understand FALCON and SOLMAE easily. We also checked the Gaussian randomness of $\mathcal{N}$-`Sampler` and `UnifCrown` samplers used in SOLMAE only.

Keywords: Lattice-based cryptography · Hash-and-sign paradigm · NTRU trapdoors · Discrete Gaussian sampling · Python implementation

1 Introduction

When Shor [16] has proposed an efficient randomized algorithm on a hypothetical quantum computer in 1999 to integer factorization and discrete logarithm problems in a polynomial time, it was beyond our imagination building for the powerful computing environment at that time. Currently the threat of attacking the current (or classical) secure system by using the quantum computer is expected to be right at our fingertips due to the aggressive road map by IBM quantum computing. We are very concerned about so called *Harvest now, decrypt later* attack [17] which is a surveillance strategy that relies on the acquisition and long-term storage of currently unreadable encrypted data awaiting possible breakthroughs in decryption technology that would render it readable in the future.

H. Seo and S. Kim (Eds.): ICISC 2023, LNCS 14562, pp. 235–260, 2024.
https://doi.org/10.1007/978-981-97-1238-0_13

Due to the substantial amount of research on quantum computers, large-scale quantum computers if built, can break many public-key cryptosystems based on the number–theoretic hard problems in use. In 2016, NIST [14] has initiated Post Quantum Cryptography(PQC) project to solicit, evaluate, and standardize one or more quantum-resistant cryptographic algorithms for Key Encapsulation Mechanism(KEM) and Digital Signature(DS) worldwide. After several rounds, NIST has finally selected CRYSTALS-Kyber for KEM and CRYSTALS-Dilithium, FALCON, and SPHINCS+ for DS in 2022.

Influenced by this NIST PQC project, Korean cryptographic society led by KpqC task force [11] has called for soliciting Korean PQC candidates by the end of Oct. in 2022. By the due of submission, 7 candidates KEM and 8 candidates DS for KpqC competition were submitted and their details are available at https:// kpqc.or.kr/.

SOLMAE which stands for an acronym of quantum–Secure algOrithm for Long–term Message Authentication and Encryption was submitted to KpqC Competition as one of DS candidate algorithms which is a lattice-based signature scheme inspired by several pioneering works based on the hash-then-sign signature paradigm proposed by Gentry, Peikert and Vaikuntanathan [6].

SOLMAE is inspired from FALCON's design. Some of the new theoretical foundations were laid out in the presentation of Mitaka [1] while keeping the security level of FALCON with 5 NIST levels of security I to V. At a high level, SOLMAE removes the inherent technicality of the sampling procedure, and most of its induced complexity from an implementation standpoint, for *free*, that is with no loss of efficiency. This theoretical simplicity translates into faster operations while preserving signatures and verification key sizes, on top of allowing for additional features absent from FALCON, such as enjoying cheaper masking and being parallelizable. We need to evaluate this features with our Python implementation which all the readers can easily understand and compare them.

To the best of our knowledge, there is no the open literature to compare FALCON and SOLMAE directly from the point of their asymptotic complexity and performance. In this paper, after giving a brief description from the specification of FALCON and SOLMAE, we discuss their asymptotic computational complexity of KeyGen, Sign and Verif procedures and evaluate their performance empirically using their Python implementation including Gaussian samplers used in SOLMAE.

The organization of this paper is as follows: In Sect. 2, we define our notations and definition used in this paper. In Sects. 3 and 4, we describe how FALCON and SOLMAE work summarized from their specification, respectively. In Sect. 5, we discuss the asymptotic computational complexity of FALCON and SOLMAE. In Sect. 6, we analyse the $\mathcal{N}$-Sampler and UnifCrown sampler used in SOLMAE only and verify its function by the experiment. In Sect. 7, we suggest the practical execution time of KeyGen, Sign and Verif procedures running 3,000 times for FALCON–512 and SOLMAE–512 by their Python implementation. Finally, we will give concluding remarks and challenging issues.

2 Notations and Definition

To keep the consistency to understand FALCON and SOLMAE correctly, we will use the following notations and definitions used in their specification throughout this paper.

Matrices, Vectors, and Scalars

Matrices will usually be in bold uppercase (e.g. $\mathbf{B}$), vectors in bold lowercase (e.g. $\mathbf{v}$), and scalars - which include polynomials - in italic (e.g. s). We use the row convention for vectors. The transpose of a matrix $\mathbf{B}$ may be noted $\mathbf{B}^t$. It is to be noted that for a polynomial f, we do *not* use f' to denote its derivative in this document.

Quotient Rings

Let $\mathbb{Z}$ and $\mathbb{N}$ denote a set of integers and a set of all numbers starting from 1, respectively. $\mathbb{Q}$ and $\mathbb{R}$ denote a set of rational numbers and a set of real numbers, respectively. For $q \in \mathbb{N}^\times$, we denote by $\mathbb{Z}_q$ the quotient ring $\mathbb{Z}/q\mathbb{Z}$. In FALCON and SOLMAE, an integer modulus $q = 12,289$ is prime, so $\mathbb{Z}_q$ is also a finite field. We denote by $\mathbb{Z}_q^\times$ the group of invertible elements of $\mathbb{Z}_q$, and by φ Euler's totient function: $\varphi(q) = |\mathbb{Z}_q^\times| = q - 1 = 3 \cdot 2^{12}$ since q is prime. The rings $\mathbb{Q}[x]/(\phi)$, $\mathbb{Z}[x]/(\phi)$, and $\mathbb{R}[x]/(\phi)$ where ϕ is a monic minimal polynomial will be interchangeably written as $\mathcal{Q}$, $\mathcal{Z}$, and $K_\mathbb{R}$, respectively for the sake of our convenience.

DFT Representation

For $d = 2^n$, we use $\phi(x) = x^d + 1$. It is a monic polynomial of $\mathbb{Z}[x]$, irreducible in $\mathbb{Q}[x]$ and with distinct roots over $\mathbb{C}$. Then $\zeta_j = exp(i(2j-1)\pi/d)$ for $j = 1, 2, \cdots d$ are roots of $\phi(x)$. For $f = \Sigma f_i x^i \in K_\mathbb{R}$, we define the coefficient representation as $\mathbf{f} = (f_0, f_1, \cdots f_{d-1})$ and Discrete Fourier Transform(DFT) representation $\varphi(f) = (\varphi_1(f), \cdots, \varphi_d(f))$.

Number Fields

Let $a = \sum_{i=0}^{d-1} a_i x^i$ and $b = \sum_{i=0}^{d-1} b_i x^i$ be arbitrary elements of the number field $\mathcal{Q} = \mathbb{Q}[x]/(\phi)$. We note a^* and call (Hermitian) adjoint of a the unique element of $\mathcal{Q}$ such that for any root ζ of ϕ, $a^*(\zeta) = \overline{a(\zeta)}$, where $\bar{\cdot}$ is the usual complex conjugation over $\mathbb{C}$. For $\phi = x^d + 1$, the Hermitian adjoint a^* can be expressed simply:

$$a^* = a_0 - \sum_{i=1}^{d-1} a_i x^{d-i} \tag{1}$$

We extend this definition to vectors and matrices: the adjoint $\mathbf{B}^*$ of a matrix $\mathbf{B} \in \mathcal{Q}^{n \times m}$ (resp. a vector $\mathbf{v}$) is the component-wise adjoint of the transpose of $\mathbf{B}$ (resp. $\mathbf{v}$):

$$\mathbf{B} = \begin{bmatrix} a & b \\ c & d \end{bmatrix} \quad \Leftrightarrow \quad \mathbf{B}^* = \begin{bmatrix} a^* & c^* \\ b^* & d^* \end{bmatrix} \tag{2}$$

Inner Product

The inner product $\langle \cdot, \cdot \rangle$ over $\mathcal{Q}$ and its associated norm $\| \cdot \|$ are defined as:

$$\langle a, b \rangle = \frac{1}{\deg(\phi)} \sum_{0 < i \le d} \varphi_i(a) \cdot \overline{\varphi_i(b)} \tag{3}$$

$$\|a\| = \sqrt{\langle a, a \rangle} \tag{4}$$

These definitions can be extended to vectors: for $u = (u_i)$ and $v = (v_i)$ in $\mathcal{Q}^m$, $\langle u, v \rangle = \sum_i \langle u_i, v_i \rangle$. For our choice of ϕ, the inner product coincides with the usual coefficient-wise inner product:

$$\langle a, b \rangle = \sum_{0 \le i < d} a_i b_i \tag{5}$$

From an algorithmic point of view, computing the inner product or the norm is most easily done using Eq. (3) if polynomials are in FFT representation, and using Eq. (5) if they are in coefficient representation. By substituting $b = a$ in Eqs. (3) and (5), we get

$$\|\varphi(a)\| = \sqrt{d} \cdot \|a\|. \tag{6}$$

where $\| \cdot \|$ is Euclidean norm. Since we know that

$$\|\varphi(a)\| = \sqrt{2} \cdot \|(Re(\varphi_1(a)), Im(\varphi_1(a)), \cdots Re(\varphi_{d/2}(a)), Im(\varphi_{d/2}(a)))\|, \tag{7}$$

we get

$$\|(Re(\varphi_1(a)), Im(\varphi_1(a)), \cdots Re(\varphi_{d/2}(a)), Im(\varphi_{d/2}(a)))\| = \sqrt{\frac{d}{2}} \cdot \|a\|. \tag{8}$$

If $a \in K_{\mathbb{R}}$ follows the d-dimensional standard normal distribution, it is known that

$$(Re(\varphi_1(a)), Im(\varphi_1(a)), \cdots Re(\varphi_{d/2}(a)), Im(\varphi_{d/2}(a))) \text{ follows } \mathcal{N}_{d/2}, \tag{9}$$

where $\mathcal{N}_{d/2}$ denotes continuous Gaussian distribution with zero mean and $\frac{d}{2} \cdot I_d$(*i.e.*, Identity matrix) variance.

Ring Lattices

For the rings $\mathcal{Q} = \mathbb{Q}[x]/(\phi)$ and $\mathcal{Z} = \mathbb{Z}[x]/(\phi)$, positive integers $m \ge n$, and a full-rank matrix $\mathbf{B} \in \mathcal{Q}^{n \times m}$, we denote by $\Lambda(\mathbf{B})$ and call lattice generated by $\mathbf{B}$, the set $\mathcal{Z}^n \cdot \mathbf{B} = \{z\mathbf{B} \mid z \in \mathcal{Z}^n\}$. By extension, a set Λ is a lattice if there exists a matrix $\mathbf{B}$ such that $\Lambda = \Lambda(\mathbf{B})$. We may say that $\Lambda \subseteq \mathcal{Z}^m$ is a q-ary lattice if $q\mathcal{Z}^m \subseteq \Lambda$.

NTRU Lattices

Let q be an integer, and $f \in \mathbb{Z}[x]/(x^d + 1)$ such that f is invertible modulo q (equivalently, $\det[f]$ is coprime to q). Let $h = g/f \bmod q$ and consider the NTRU module associated to h:

$$\mathcal{M}_{\text{NTRU}} = \{(u, v) \in K_{\mathbb{R}}^2 : hu - v = 0 \bmod q\},$$

and its lattice version

$$\mathcal{L}_{\text{NTRU}} = \{(\mathbf{u}, \mathbf{v}) \in \mathbb{Z}^{2d} : [h]\mathbf{u} - \mathbf{v} = 0 \bmod q\}.$$

This lattice has volume q^d. Over $K_{\mathbb{R}}$, it is generated by (f, g) and any (F, G) such that $fG - gF = q$. For such a pair $(f, g), (F, G)$, this means that $\mathcal{L}_{\text{NTRU}}$ has a basis of the form

$$\mathbf{B}_{f,g} = \begin{bmatrix} [f] & [F] \\ [g] & [G] \end{bmatrix}.$$

One checks that $([h], -\text{Id}_d) \cdot \mathbf{B}_{f,g} = 0 \bmod q$, so the verification key is h. The NTRU-search problem is : given $h = g/f \bmod q$, find any $(f' = x^i f, g' = x^i g)$. In its decision variant, one must distinguish $h = g/f \bmod q$ from a uniformly random $h \in R_q := \mathbb{Z}[x]/(q, x^d + 1) = (\mathbb{Z}/q\mathbb{Z})[x]/(x^d + 1)$. These problems are assumed to be intractable for large d.

Discrete Gaussians

For $\sigma, \mu \in \mathbb{R}$ with $\sigma > 0$, we define the Gaussian function $\rho_{\sigma,\mu}$ as $\rho_{\sigma,\mu}(x) = \exp(-|x - \mu|^2/2\sigma^2)$, and the discrete Gaussian distribution $D_{\mathbb{Z},\sigma,\mu}$ over the integers as:

$$D_{\mathbb{Z},\sigma,\mu}(x) = \frac{\rho_{\sigma,\mu}(x)}{\sum_{z \in \mathbb{Z}} \rho_{\sigma,\mu}(z)} \tag{10}$$

The parameter μ may be omitted when it is equal to zero.

Gram-Schmidt Orthogonalization

Any matrix $\mathbf{B} \in \mathcal{Q}^{n \times m}$ can be decomposed as follows:

$$\mathbf{B} = \mathbf{L} \times \tilde{\mathbf{B}} \tag{11}$$

where $\mathbf{L}$ is lower triangular with 1's on the diagonal, and the rows $\tilde{b}_i$'s of $\tilde{\mathbf{B}}$ verify $\langle \tilde{b}_i, \tilde{b}_j \rangle = 0$ for $i \neq j$. When $\mathbf{B}$ is full-rank, this decomposition is unique, and it is called the Gram-Schmidt orthogonalization (or GSO). We also call the Gram-Schmidt norm of $\mathbf{B}$ the following value:

$$\|\mathbf{B}\|_{GS} = \max_{\tilde{b}_i \in \tilde{\mathbf{B}}} \|\tilde{b}_i\| \tag{12}$$

The LDL* Decomposition

The LDL* decomposition writes any full-rank Gram matrix as a product LDL*, where $L \in Q^{n \times n}$ is lower triangular with 1's on the diagonal, and $D \in Q^{n \times n}$ is diagonal. The LDL* decomposition and the GSO are closely related as for a basis $\mathbf{B}$, there exists a unique GSO $\mathbf{B} = \mathbf{L} \cdot \tilde{\mathbf{B}}$, and for a full-rank Gram matrix $\mathbf{G}$, there exists a unique LDL* decomposition $\mathbf{G} = \mathbf{LDL}^*$. If $\mathbf{G} = \mathbf{BB}^*$, then $\mathbf{G} = \mathbf{L} \cdot (\tilde{\mathbf{B}}\tilde{\mathbf{B}}^*) \cdot \mathbf{L}^*$ is a valid LDL* decomposition of $\mathbf{G}$. As both decompositions are unique, the matrices $\mathbf{L}$ in both cases are actually the same. In a nutshell:

$$[\mathbf{L} \cdot \tilde{\mathbf{B}} \text{ is the GSO of } \mathbf{B}] \Leftrightarrow [\mathbf{L} \cdot (\mathbf{B}\tilde{\mathbf{B}}^*) \cdot \mathbf{L}^* \text{ is the LDL}^* \text{ decomposition of } (\mathbf{BB}^*)].$$

(13)

The reason why we present both equivalent decompositions is that the GSO is a more familiar concept in lattice-based cryptography, whereas the use of LDL* decomposition is faster and therefore makes more sense from an algorithmic point of view.

3   How FALCON Works

A group of top-notch cryptographers, Hoffstein, Pipher and Silverman [8] suggested new public–key cryptosystem based on a polynomial ring in 1997 as an alternative to RSA and DH whose difficulties are based on number–theoretic hard problems such as integer factorization and discrete log problem, respectively. They founded the company so–called as NTRU[1] Cryptosystem with Lieman and initiated an open–source lattice-based cryptography consisting of two algorithms: NTRUENCRYPT used for encryption/decryption and NTRUSIGN used for digital signatures. Their security relies on the presumed difficulty of factoring certain polynomials in a truncated polynomial ring into a quotient of two polynomials having very small coefficients.

NTRUSIGN was designed based on the GGH signature scheme [7] which was proposed in 1995 based on solving the closest vector problem (CVP) in a lattice and asymptotically is more efficient than RSA in the computation time for encryption, decryption, signing, and verifying are all quadratic in the natural security parameter. The signer demonstrates knowledge of a good basis for the lattice by using it to solve CVP on a point representing the message; the verifier uses a bad basis for the same lattice to verify that the signature under consideration is actually a lattice point and is sufficiently close to the message point.

On the other hand, Min et al. [12] suggested weak property of malleability of NTRUSIGN using the annihilating polynomial from a given message and signature pair to generate a valid signature. Nguyen and Regev [13] had cryptanalyzed the original GGH signature scheme including NTRUSIGN in 2006 successfully extracting secret information from many known signatures characterized

---

[1] Number Theorists 'R' Us, or Number Theory Research Unit, or N–th degree TRuncated polynomial Ring.

by multivariate optimization problems. Their experiments showed that 90,000 signatures are sufficient to recover the NTRUSign–251 secret key.

In a nutshell, FALCON follows a framework introduced in 2008 by Gentry, Peikert, and Vaikuntanathan [6] which we call the GPV framework for short over the NTRU lattices and uses a typically hash–and–sign paradigm. Their high–level idea is the following:

1. The public key is a long basis of a q–ary lattice.
2. The private key is (essentially) a short basis of the same lattice.
3. In the signing procedure, the signer:
   (a) generates a random value, $salt$;
   (b) computes a target $\mathbf{c} = H(M\|salt)$, where H is a hash function sending input to a random–looking point (on the grid);
   (c) uses his knowledge of a short basis to compute a lattice point $\mathbf{v}$ close to the target $\mathbf{c}$;
   (d) outputs $(salt, \mathbf{s})$, where $\mathbf{s} = \mathbf{c} - \mathbf{v}$.
4. The verifier accepts the signature $(salt, \mathbf{s})$ if and only if:
   (a) the vector $\mathbf{s}$ is short;
   (b) $H(M\|salt) - \mathbf{s}$ is a point on the lattice generated by his public key.

Only the signer should be able to *efficiently* compute v close enough to an arbitrary target. This is a decoding problem that can be solved when a basis of *short* vectors is known. On the other hand, anyone wanting to check the validity of a signature should be able to verify lattice membership. The `KeyGen`, `Sign` and `Verif` procedures for FALCON will be introduced briefly in the later Section by restating the original specification as in [3]. For details, the readers can refer to [3].

3.1 Key Generation of FALCON

For the class of NTRU lattices, a trapdoor pairs is $(h, \mathbf{B}_{f,g})$ where $h = f^{-1}g$, $\mathbf{B}_{f,g}$ is trapdoor basis over $\mathcal{L}_{\mathrm{NTRU}}$ and Pornin & Prest [15] showed that a completion (F, G) can be computed in $O(d \log d)$ time from short polynomials $f, g \in \mathcal{Z}$. In practice, their implementation is as efficient as can be for this technical procedure: it is called `NtruSolve` in FALCON. Their algorithm only depends on the underlying ring and has now a stable version for $\mathbb{Z}[x]/(x^d + 1)$, where $d = 2^n$.

Figure 1 illustrates the flowchart of the key generation procedure for FALCON.

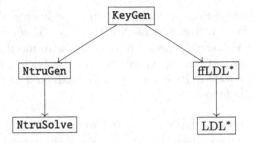

Fig. 1. Flowchart of KeyGen for FALCON

Algorithm 1 describes the pseudo–code for key generation of FALCON.

Algorithm 1: KeyGen of FALCON

Input: A monic polynomial $\phi \in \mathbb{Z}[x]$, a modulus q
Output: A secret key sk, a public key pk

1: $f, g, F, G \leftarrow$ NtruGen ;   /* Solving the NTRU equation */

2: $\mathbf{B} \leftarrow \begin{bmatrix} g & -f \\ G & -F \end{bmatrix}$;

3: $\hat{\mathbf{B}} \leftarrow$ FFT($\mathbf{B}$) ;   /* Compute FFT for each $\{g, -f, G, -F\}$ */
4: $\mathbf{G} \leftarrow \hat{\mathbf{B}} \times \hat{\mathbf{B}}^*$;
5: $\mathbf{T} \leftarrow$ ffLDL*($\mathbf{G}$);   /* Compute the LDL* tree */
6: **for** each leaf of T **do**
7:     $leaf.value \leftarrow \sigma/\sqrt{leaf.value}$;   /* Normalization step */
8: $\mathbf{sk} \leftarrow (\hat{\mathbf{B}}, \mathbf{T})$;
9: $h \leftarrow gf^{-1} \bmod q$;
10: $\mathbf{pk} \leftarrow h$;
11: **return** sk, pk;

3.2   Signing of FALCON

At a high level, the signing procedure in FALCON is at first to compute a hashed value $\mathbf{c} \in \mathbb{Z}_q[x]/(\phi)$ from the message, M and a salt r, then using the secret key, f, g, F, G to generate two short values $(\mathbf{s}_1, \mathbf{s}_2)$ such that $\mathbf{s}_1 + \mathbf{s}_2 h = \mathbf{c} \bmod q$. An interesting feature is that only the *first half* of the signature $(\mathbf{s}_1, \mathbf{s}_2)$ needs to be sent along the message, as long as h is available to the verifier. This comes from the identity $h\mathbf{s}_1 = \mathbf{s}_2 \bmod q$ defining these lattices, as we will see in the Verif algorithm description.

The core of FALCON signing is to use ffSampling (Algorithm 11 in [3]) which applies a randomizing rounding according to Gaussian distribution on the coefficient of $\mathbf{t} = (\mathbf{t}_0, \mathbf{t}_1) \in (\mathbb{Q}[x]/(\phi))^2$ stored in the FALCON Tree, $\mathbf{T}$ at the KeyGen procedure of FALCON.

This fast Fourier sampling algorithm can be seen as a recursive version of Klein's well–known trapdoor sampler, but *cannot be computed in parallel* also known as the GPV sampler. Klein's sampler uses a matrix $\mathbf{L}$ and the norm of Gram–Schmidt vectors as a trapdoor while FALCON are using a tree of non-trivial elements in such matrices. Note that Fouque *et. al.* [4] suggested Gram-Schmidt norm leakage in FALCON by timing side channels in the implementation of the one-dimensional Gaussian samplers.

FALCON cannot output two different signatures for a message. This well-known concern of the GPV framework can be addressed in several ways, for example, making a stateful scheme or by hash randomization. FALCON chose the latter solution for efficiency purposes. In practice, Sign adds a random "salt" $r \in \{0,1\}^k$, where k is large enough that an unfortunate collision of messages is unlikely to happen, that is, it hashes $(r\|M)$ instead of M. A signature is then $\mathtt{sig} = (r, \mathtt{Compress}(\mathbf{s_1}))$.

Figure 2 and Algorithm 2 sketches the signing procedure for FALCON and shows its pseudo-code for FALCON, respectively.

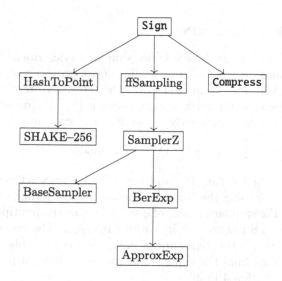

Fig. 2. Flowchart of Sign for FALCON.

Algorithm 2: Sign of FALCON

Input: A message $M \in \{0,1\}^*$, secret key **sk**, a bound γ.
Output: A pair $(r, \mathsf{Compress}(\mathbf{s}_1))$ with $r \in \{0,1\}^{320}$ and $\|(\mathbf{s}_1, \mathbf{s}_2)\| \le \gamma$.
1: $r \leftarrow \mathcal{U}(\{0,1\}^{320})$;
2: $\mathbf{c} \leftarrow \mathsf{HashToPoint}(r\|M, q, n)$;
3: $\mathbf{t} \leftarrow (-\frac{1}{q}\mathsf{FFT}(c) \odot \mathsf{FFT}(F), \frac{1}{q}\mathsf{FFT}(c) \odot \mathsf{FFT}(f))$;   /* $\mathbf{t} = (\mathsf{FFT}(c), \mathsf{FFT}(0)) \cdot \hat{\mathbf{B}}^{-1}$ */
4: **do**
5:          **do**
6:                    $\mathbf{z} \leftarrow \mathsf{ffSampling}_n(\mathbf{t}, T)$;
7:                    $\mathbf{s} = (\mathbf{t} - \mathbf{z})\hat{\mathbf{B}}$;   /* At this point, s follows Gaussian distribution. */
8:          **while** $\|s\|^2 > \gamma$
9:          $(s_1, s_2) \leftarrow \mathsf{FFT}^{-1}(\mathbf{s})$;
10:          $s \leftarrow \mathsf{Compress}(s_2, 8 \cdot \text{sbytelen} - 328)$;   /* Remove 1 byte for the header, and 40 bytes for r */
11: **while**$(s = \bot)$
12: **return** (r, s);

3.3   Verification of FALCON

The last step of the scheme is thankfully simpler to describe. Upon receiving a signature $(r, \mathbf{s})$ and message M, the verifier decompresses $\mathbf{s}$ to a polynomial $\mathbf{s}_1$ and $\mathbf{c} = (0, \mathsf{H}(r\|M))$, then wants to recover the full signature vector $\mathbf{v} = (\mathbf{s}_1, \mathbf{s}_2)$. If $\mathbf{v}$ is a valid signature, the verification identity is $(h, -1) \cdot (\mathbf{c} - \mathbf{v}) = -\mathsf{H}(r\|M) - h\mathbf{s}_1 + \mathbf{s}_2 \bmod q = 0$, or equivalently the verifier can compute

$$\mathbf{s}_2 = \mathsf{H}(r\|M) + h\mathbf{s}_1 \bmod q.$$

This is computed in the ring R_q, and can be done very efficiently for a good choice of modulus q using the Number Theoretic Transform (NTT). FALCON currently follow the standard choice of $q = 12,289$, as the multiplication in NTT format amounts to d integer multiplications in $\mathbb{Z}/q\mathbb{Z}$. The last step is to check that $\|(\mathbf{s}_1, \mathbf{s}_2)\|^2 \le \gamma^2$: the signature is only accepted in this case. The rejection bound γ comes from the expected length of vectors outputted by Sample described as Algorithm 4 in [9].

Since they are morally Gaussian, they concentrate around their standard deviation; a "slack" parameter $\tau = 1.042$ is tuned to ensure that 90% of the vectors generated by Sample will get through the loop:

$$\gamma = \tau \cdot \sigma_{\mathsf{sig}} \cdot \sqrt{2d}.$$

Algorithm 3 shows the pseudo–code of verification procedure of FALCON.

Algorithm 3: Verif of FALCON

Input: A signature $(r, \mathbf{s})$ on M, a public key $\mathbf{pk} = h$, a bound γ.
Output: Accept or Reject.

1: $\mathbf{s}_1 \leftarrow \mathsf{Decompress}(\mathbf{s})$;
2: $\mathbf{c} \leftarrow \mathsf{H}(r\|M)$;
3: $\mathbf{s}_2 \leftarrow \mathbf{c} + h\mathbf{s}_1 \bmod q$;
4: **if** $\|(\mathbf{s}_1, \mathbf{s}_2)\|^2 > \gamma^2$ **then**
5: **return** Reject.
    end
6: **return** Accept.

---

4 How SOLMAE works

SOLMAE is inspired from FALCON's design. Some of the new theoretical foundations were laid out in the presentation of Mitaka [1]. At a high level, it removes the inherent technicality of the sampling procedure, and most of its induced complexity from an implementation standpoint, for *free*, that is with no loss of efficiency. This simplicity translates into faster operations while preserving signatures and verification keys sizes, on top of allowing for additional features absent from FALCON, such as enjoying cheaper masking, and being parallelizable. By using the novel compression techniques and tools of [2], SOLMAE can also obtain smaller signatures and verification keys than those already achieved by FALCON. To sum up, SOLMAE aims to achieve *better performances* for the same security and advantages as FALCON.

While its predecessor FALCON could be summed-up as *an efficient instantiation of the GPV framework*, SOLMAE takes it one step further. The main ingredients in SOLMAE are:

- **Hybrid sampler** is a faster, simpler, parallelizable, and maskable Gaussian sampler to generate signatures;
- **Optimally tuned key generation algorithm**, enhancing the security of the used hybrid sampler to that of FALCON's level[2];
- **Dedicated compression techniques** to reduce bandwidth consumption even further, at no cost on the security according to our analyses.

The KeyGen, Sign and Verif procedures for SOLMAE will be introduced briefly in the later Section by restating the original specification in [9]. For details, the readers can refer to [9].

---

[2] This corresponds to NIST-I and NIST-V requirements.

4.1 Key Generation of SOLMAE

An important concern here is that not all pair $(f, g), (F, G)$ gives good trapdoor pairs for Sample described as Algorithm 4 in [9]. Schemes such as FALCON and MITAKA solve this technicality essentially by sieving among all possible bases to find the ones that reach an acceptable quality for the Sample procedure. This technique is costly, and many tricks were used to achieve an acceptable KeyGen. *This sieving routine was bypassed by redesigning completely how good quality bases can be found.* This improves the running time of KeyGen and also increases the security offered by Sample. In any case, note that NtruSolve's running time largely dominates the overall time for KeyGen: this is not avoidable as the basis completion algorithm requires working with quite large integers and relatively high-precision floating-point arithmetic.

At the end of the procedure, the secret key contains not only the secret basis but also the necessary data for Sign and Sample. This additional information can be represented by elements in $K_{\mathbb{R}}$ and is computed during or at the end of NtruSolve. All-in-all, KeyGen outputs:

$$\mathbf{sk} = (\mathbf{b}_1 = (f, g), \mathbf{b}_2 = (F, G), \widetilde{\mathbf{b}}_2 = (\widetilde{F}, \widetilde{G}), \Sigma_1, \Sigma_2, \beta_1, \beta_2),$$
$$\mathbf{pk} = (h, q, \sigma_{\mathsf{sig}}, \eta),$$

where we recall that $h = g/f \bmod q$. These parameters and a table of their practical values are described more thoroughly in [9].

Informally, they correspond to the following:

- $(f, g), (F, G)$ is a good basis of the lattice $\mathcal{L}_{\mathrm{NTRU}}$ associated to h, with quality $\mathcal{Q}(f, g) = \alpha$, and $\widetilde{\mathbf{b}}_2$ is the Gram-Schmidt orthogonalization of (F, G) with respect to (f, g);
- $\sigma_{\mathsf{sig}}, \eta$ are respectively the standard deviation for signature vectors, and a tight upper bound on the "smoothing parameter of $\mathbb{Z}^{d}$";
- $\Sigma_1, \Sigma_2 \in K_{\mathbb{R}}$ represent covariance matrices for two intermediate Gaussian samplings in Sample;
- the vectors $\beta_1, \beta_2 \in K_{\mathbb{R}}^2$ represent the orthogonal projections from $K_{\mathbb{R}}^2$ onto $K_{\mathbb{R}} \cdot \mathbf{b}_1$ and $K_{\mathbb{R}} \cdot \widetilde{\mathbf{b}}_2$ respectively. In other words, they act as "getCoordinates" for vectors in $K_{\mathbb{R}}^2$. They are used by Sample and are precomputed for efficiency.

Algorithm 4 computes the necessary data for signature sampling, then outputs the key pair. Note that NtruSolve could also compute the sampling data and the public key, but for clarity, the pseudo-code gives these tasks to KeyGen of SOLMAE. Figure 3 sketches the key generation procedure of SOLMAE

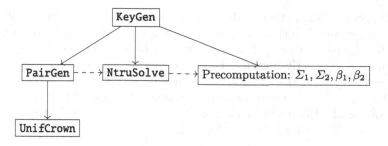

Fig. 3. Flowchart of KeyGen of SOLMAE.

Algorithm 4: KeyGen of SOLMAE

Input: A modulus q, a target quality parameter $1 < \alpha$, parameters $\sigma_{\sf sig}, \eta > 0$

Output: A basis $((f,g),(F,G)) \in R^2$ of an NTRU lattice $\mathcal{L}_{\rm NTRU}$ with $\mathcal{Q}(f,g) = \alpha$;

1: **repeat**
  | $\mathbf{b}_1 := (f,g) \leftarrow \mathtt{PairGen}(q, \alpha, R_-, R_+)\}$
    until f *is invertible modulo* q;
      ;   /* Secret basis computation between R_- and R_+ */
2: $\mathbf{b}_2 := (F,G) \leftarrow \mathtt{NtruSolve}(q,f,g)$:

3: $h \leftarrow g/f \bmod q$;   /* Public key data computation */
4: $\gamma \leftarrow 1.1 \cdot \sigma_{\sf sig} \cdot \sqrt{2d}$;   /* tolerance for signature length */
5: $\beta_1 \leftarrow \frac{1}{\langle \mathbf{b}_1, \mathbf{b}_1 \rangle_K} \cdot \mathbf{b}_1$;   /* Sampling data computation, in Fourier domain */
6: $\Sigma_1 \leftarrow \sqrt{\frac{\sigma_{\sf sig}^2}{\langle \mathbf{b}_1, \mathbf{b}_1 \rangle_K} - \eta^2}$;
7: $\widetilde{\mathbf{b}}_2 := (\widetilde{F}, \widetilde{G}) \leftarrow \mathbf{b}_2 - \langle \beta_1, \mathbf{b}_2 \rangle \cdot \mathbf{b}_1$;
8: $\beta_2 \leftarrow \frac{1}{\langle \widetilde{\mathbf{b}}_2, \widetilde{\mathbf{b}}_2 \rangle_K} \cdot \widetilde{\mathbf{b}}_2$;
9: $\Sigma_2 \leftarrow \sqrt{\frac{\sigma_{\sf sig}^2}{\langle \widetilde{\mathbf{b}}_2, \widetilde{\mathbf{b}}_2 \rangle_K} - \eta^2}$;

10: $\mathsf{sk} \leftarrow (\mathbf{b}_1, \mathbf{b}_2, \widetilde{\mathbf{b}}_2, \Sigma_1, \Sigma_2, \beta_1, \beta_2)$;
11: $\mathsf{pk} \leftarrow (q, h, \sigma_{\sf sig}, \eta, \gamma)$;
12: **return** sk, pk;

The function of two subroutines `PairGen` and `NtruSolve` are described below:

1. The `PairGen` algorithm generates d complex numbers $(x_j e^{i\theta_j})_{j \leq d/2}$, $(y_j e^{i\theta_j})_{j \leq d/2}$ to act as the FFT representations of two *real* polynomial $f^{\mathbb{R}}, g^{\mathbb{R}}$ in $K_{\mathbb{R}}$. The magnitude of these complex numbers is sampled in a planar annulus whose small and big radii are set to match a target $\mathcal{Q}(f,g)$ with

UnifCrown ([9]). It then finds close elements $f, g \in \mathcal{Z}$ by round-off, unless maybe the rounding error was too large. When the procedure ends, it outputs a pair (f, g) such that $\mathcal{Q}(f, g) = \alpha$, where α depends on the security level.

2. NtruSolve is exactly Pornin & Prest's algorithm and implementation [15]. It takes as input $(f, g) \in \mathcal{Z}^2$ and a modulus q, and outputs $(F, G) \in \mathcal{Z}^2$ such that $(f, g), (F, G)$ is a basis of $\mathcal{L}_{\mathrm{NTRU}}$ associated to $h = g/f \bmod q$. It does so by solving the Bézout-like equation $fG - gF = q$ in $\mathcal{Z}$ using recursively the tower of subfields for optimal efficiency.

4.2 Signing of SOLMAE

Recall that NTRU lattices live in $\mathbb{R}^{2d}$. Their structure also helps to simplify the preimage computation. Indeed, the signer only needs to compute $\mathbf{m} = \mathbf{H}(M) \in \mathbb{R}^d$, as then $\mathbf{c} = (0, \mathbf{m})$ is a valid preimage: the corresponding polynomials satisfy $(h, 1) \cdot \mathbf{c} = \mathbf{m}$.

As the same with Sign procedure of FALCON, an interesting feature is that only the *first half* of the signature $(\mathbf{s}_1, \mathbf{s}_2) \in \mathcal{L}_{\mathrm{NTRU}}$ needs to be sent along the message, as long as h is available to the verifier. This comes from the identity $h\mathbf{s}_1 = \mathbf{s}_2 \bmod q$ defining these lattices, as we will see in the Verif algorithm description. [3]

Because of their nature as Gaussian integer vectors, signatures can be encoded to reduce the size of their bit-representation. The standard deviation of Sample is large enough so that the $\lfloor \log \sqrt{q} \rfloor$ least significant bits of one coordinate are essentially random.

In practice, Sign adds a random "salt" $r \in \{0, 1\}^k$, where k is large enough that an unfortunate collision of messages is unlikely to happen, that is, it hashes $(r \| M)$ instead of M — our analysis in this regard is identical to FALCON. A signature is then $\mathtt{sig} = (r, \mathtt{Compress}(s_1))$. SOLMAE cannot output two different signatures for a message like FALCON which was mentioned in Sect. 3.2.

Figure 4 sketches the signing procedure of SOLMAE and Algorithm 5 shows its pseudo–code.

---

[3] The same identity can also be used to check the validity of signatures only with a hash of the public key h, requiring this time send both $\mathbf{s}_1$ and $\mathbf{s}_2$, but we will not consider this setting here.

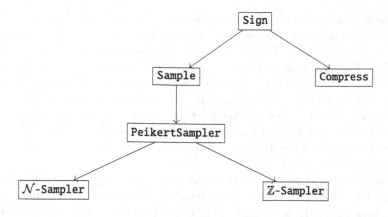

Fig. 4. Flowchart of `Sign` of SOLMAE.

Algorithm 5: `Sign` of SOLMAE

Input: A message $M \in \{0,1\}^*$, a tuple $\mathbf{sk} = ((f,g), (F,G), (\widetilde{F}, \widetilde{G}), \sigma_{\text{sig}}, \Sigma_1, \Sigma_2, \eta)$, a rejection parameter $\gamma > 0$.

Output: A pair $(r, \text{Compress}(\mathbf{s}_1))$ with $r \in \{0,1\}^{320}$ and $\|(\mathbf{s}_1, \mathbf{s}_2)\| \leq \gamma$.

1: $r \leftarrow \mathcal{U}(\{0,1\}^{320})$;
2: $\mathbf{c} \leftarrow (0, \text{H}(r\|M))$;
3: $\hat{\mathbf{c}} \leftarrow \text{FFT}(\mathbf{c})$;
4: **repeat**
   | $(\hat{s}_1, \hat{s}_2) \leftarrow \hat{\mathbf{c}} - \text{Sample}(\hat{\mathbf{c}}, \mathbf{sk})$;   /* $(\mathbf{s}_1, \mathbf{s}_2) \leftarrow D_{\mathcal{L}_{\text{NTRU}}, \mathbf{c}, \sigma_{\text{sig}}}$ */
   until $\|(\text{FFT}^{-1}(\hat{s}_1), \text{FFT}^{-1}(\hat{s}_2))\|^2 \leq \gamma^2$;
5: $s_1 \leftarrow \text{FFT}^{-1}(\hat{s}_1)$;
6: $s \leftarrow \text{Compress}(s_1)$;
   return (r, s);

4.3 Verification of SOLMAE

This is the same as the Verification of FALCON stated in Sect. 3.3.

5 Asymptotic Complexity of FALCON and SOLMAE

To the best of our allowable knowledge as of writing this paper, we will suggest the asymptotic computational complexity of FALCON and SOLMAE algorithms with their pseudo–codes described their specifications based on the following assumptions to make our computation work to be simple:

(i) Multiplication of large integers can be done by integer–type Karatsuba algorithm or Schönhage-Strassen algorithm. However, we assumed multiplication of large integers can be done in $\Theta(1)$.

(ii) The multiplication and division of polynomials in $\mathbb{Z}[x]/(x^d+1)$ or $\mathbb{Q}[x]/(x^d+1)$ are assumed to compute the polynomial–type Karatsuba algorithm or operate pointwise in Fourier domain. It is known that the time complexity of the Karatsuba algorithm and FFT(or FFT^{-1}) are $\Theta(d^{3/2})$ and $\Theta(d\log(d))$, respectively. We assume that all polynomial operations are done in the Fourier domain, so polynomial multiplication and division in $\mathbb{Z}[x]/(x^d+1)$ or $\mathbb{Q}[x]/(x^d+1)$ takes $\Theta(d\log(d))$ time. Since every inverse element of $\mathbb{Z}_q$ is stored in the list and the division of polynomials in $\mathbb{Z}_q[x]/(x^d+1)$ can be done in the NTT domain, the division of polynomials in $\mathbb{Z}_q[x]/(x^d+1)$ also takes $\Theta(d\log d)$.

(iii) Some number of rejection samplings may inevitably happen in FALCON and SOLMAE. If one–loop for rejection sampling takes t times and its probability of the acceptance is p, the expectation value of the total time is $\Sigma_{k=1}^{\infty}p(1-p)^{k-1}\cdot kt = \frac{t}{p} \approx t$ since the value $1/p$ does not influence our asymptotic analysis due to its fixed constant value. So, we may ignore the number of rejections occurred in the rejection sampling. In fact, our experiment reveals that more or less 5 times rejections have occurred.

(iv) Ignore some minor operations and trivial computations which do not affect the total asymptotic complexity so much.

5.1   Asymptotic Complexity of FALCON

Using the previous assumption stated in Sect. 5, Table 1 is the detailed analysis of the asymptotic complexity of KeyGen in FALCON from its algorithm whose total complexity to complete takes $\Theta(d\log d)$.

Table 1. Asymptotic complexity of KeyGen in FALCON

No.	Computation	Complexity	Location	Comment(d is degree)
1	NTRUGen(ϕ, q)	$\Theta(d\log d)$	Step 1 of Algorithm 1	See below[†]
2	FFT(f)	$\Theta(d\log d)$	Step 3 of Algorithm 1	
3	$\mathbf{B} \times \hat{\mathbf{B}}^*$	$\Theta(d\log d)$	Step 4 of Algorithm 1	Polynomial multiplications
4	ffLDL*($\mathbf{G}$)	$\Theta(d\log d)$	Step 5 of Algorithm 1	See below[‡]
5	Normalization	$\Theta(d)$	Step 6–7 of Algorithm 1	d leaf nodes in FALCON tree
6	gf^{-1} mod q	$\Theta(d\log d)$	Step 9 of Algorithm 1	See the beginning of Sect. 5
Total Complexity of KeyGen :	$\Theta(d\log d)$			

† In Algorithm 6: NTRUGen(), Step 2 and Step 5(or 6) take $\Theta(d)$ and $\Theta(d\log d)$, respectively. Since the recurrence relation of NtruSolve is $T(d) = T(d/2) + \Theta(d\log d)$, thus Step 8 in Algorithm 6 takes $\Theta(d\log d)$.

‡ Algorithm 9: ffLDL*($\mathbf{G}$) in [3] recursively calls ffLDL*($\mathbf{G}_0$) and ffLDL*($\mathbf{G}_1$), and other processes such as LDL* and Splitfft both take $\Theta(d)$, so the recursive formula is $T(d) = 2T(d/2) + \Theta(d)$. From this, we can get $T(d) = \Theta(d\log d)$.

Algorithm 6: NTRUGen(ϕ, q)

Input: A monic polynomial $\phi \in \mathbb{Z}[x]$ of degree n, a modulus q
Output: Polynomials f, g, F, G

1: $\sigma \leftarrow 1.17\sqrt{q/2n}$;
2: **for** i *from* 0 *to* $n - 1$ **do**
  $f_i \leftarrow D_{\mathbb{Z}, \sigma_{\{f,g\}}, 0}$;
  $g_i \leftarrow D_{\mathbb{Z}, \sigma_{\{f,g\}}, 0}$;
  end
3: $f \leftarrow \Sigma_i f_i x^i$;
4: $g \leftarrow \Sigma_i g_i x^i$;
5: **if** $NTT(f)$ *contains 0 as a coefficient* **then**
  | restart
  end
6: $\gamma \leftarrow max\{\|(g, -f)\|, \|(\frac{qf*}{ff*+gg*}, \frac{qg*}{ff*+gg*})\|\}$;
7: **if** $\gamma > 1.17\sqrt{q}$ **then**
  | restart
  end
  ;
8: $F, G \leftarrow$ NtruSolve$_{n,q}(f, g)$;
9: **if** $(F, G) = \perp$ **then**
  | restart
  end
  return f, g, F, G;

Tables 2 and 3 are the asymptotic complexity of Sign and Verif in FALCON, respectively whose total complexity to complete takes $\Theta(d \log d)$.

Table 2. Asymptotic complexity of Sign in FALCON

No.	Computation	Complexity	Location	Comment(d is degree)
1	HashToPoint($r\|M, q, n$)	$\Theta(d)$	Step 2 of Algorithm 2	
2	FFT	$\Theta(d \log d)$	Step 3 of Algorithm 2	
3	ffSampling$_n$($\mathbf{t}, T$)	$\Theta(d \log d)$	Step 6 of Algorithm 2	See below †
4	$(\mathbf{t} - \mathbf{z})\hat{\mathbf{B}}$	$\Theta(d \log d)$	Step 7 of Algorithm 2	Polynomial multiplications
5	$\|\mathbf{s}\|^2$	$\Theta(d)$	Step 8 of Algorithm 2	Calculating norm
6	invFFT	$\Theta(d \log d)$	Step 9 of Algorithm 2	
7	Compress	$\Theta(d)$	Step 10 of Algorithm 2	See below ‡
Total Complexity of Sign:		$\Theta(d \log d)$		

† ffSampling$_d$ recursively calls ffSampling$_{d/2}$ two times, and other processes such as splitfft and mergefft take $\Theta(d)$. So, the recursive formula is $T(d) = 2T(d/2) + \Theta(d)$. If we solve this, we get $T(d) = \Theta(d \log d)$.
‡ The compression function converts d degree polynomial into string of length $slen(= 666)$. $slen \approx d$, so it is irrelevant to say that the compression function takes $\Theta(d)$.

Table 3. Asymptotic complexity of `Verif` in FALCON

No.	Computation	Complexity	Location	Comment(d is degree)
1	HashToPoint($r \| m, q, n$)	$\Theta(d)$	Step 1 of Algorithm 3	
2	Decompress(s, $8 \cdot$ sbytelen $- 328$)	$\Theta(d)$	Step 2 of Algorithm 3	More or less on par with `Compress` in Table 2
3	$c - s_2 h \bmod q$	$\Theta(d \log d)$	Step 5 of Algorithm 3	Polynomial multiplication
4	$\|(s_1, s_2)\|^2$	$\Theta(d)$	Step 6 of Algorithm 3	Calculating norm
Total Complexity of `Verif`:		$\Theta(d \log d)$		

5.2   Asymptotic Complexity of SOLMAE

Based on the previous assumption stated in Sect. 5 as the same manner as we analyze the asymptotic complexity of FALCON, Table 4 is the asymptotic complexity of `KeyGen` in SOLMAE whose total complexity to complete takes $\Theta(d \log d)$.

Table 4. Asymptotic complexity of `KeyGen` in SOLMAE

No.	Computation	Complexity	Location	Comment(d is degree)
1	Pairgen	$\Theta(d \log d)$	Step 1 of Algorithm 4	See below †
2	NtruSolve(q, f, g)	$\Theta(d \log d)$	Step 2 of Algorithm 4	Explained in Table 1
3	$g/f \bmod q$	$\Theta(d \log d)$	Step 3 of Algorithm 4	Polynomial operations
4	Key computations	$\Theta(d \log d)$	Step 4–9 of Algorithm 4	Polynomial operations
Total Complexity of `KeyGen`:	$\Theta(d \log d)$			

† In Algorithm 7:PairGen, Steps 1,3,and 5 all take $\Theta(d)$ time. Steps 2 and 4 take $\Theta(d \log d)$ time.

Algorithm 7: `PairGen`

Input: A modulus q, a target quality parameter $1 < \alpha$, two radii parameters $0 < R_- < R_+$

Output: A pair (f, g) with $\mathcal{Q}(f, g) = \alpha$

1: **for** $i = 1$ *to* $d/2$ **do**

$\quad x_i, y_i \leftarrow$ UnifCrown(R_-, R_+) ;   /* see **Algorithm 9** in [9] */

$\quad \theta_x, \theta_y \leftarrow \mathcal{U}(0, 1)$;

$\quad \varphi_{f,i} \leftarrow |x_i| \cdot e^{2i\pi\theta_x}$;

$\quad \varphi_{g,i} \leftarrow |y_i| \cdot e^{2i\pi\theta_y}$;

$\quad$ **end**

2: $(f^{\mathbb{R}}, g^{\mathbb{R}}) \leftarrow \left(\mathsf{FFT}^{-1}((\varphi_{f,i})_{i \leq d/2}), \mathsf{FFT}^{-1}((\varphi_{g,i})_{i \leq d/2}) \right)$;

3: $(\mathbf{f}, \mathbf{g}) \leftarrow (\lfloor f_i^{\mathbb{R}} \rceil)_{i \leq d/2}, (\lfloor g_i^{\mathbb{R}} \rceil)_{i \leq d/2}$;

4: $(\varphi(f), \varphi(g)) \leftarrow (\mathsf{FFT}(\mathbf{f}), \mathsf{FFT}(\mathbf{g}))$;

5: **for** $i = 1$ *to* $d/2$ **do**

$\quad$ **if** $q/\alpha^2 > |\varphi_i(f)|^2 + |\varphi_i(g)|^2$ *or* $\alpha^2 q < |\varphi_i(f)|^2 + |\varphi_i(g)|^2$ **then**

$\quad\quad |$ restart;

$\quad$ **end**

$\quad$ **end**

$\quad$ **return** $(\mathbf{f}, \mathbf{g})$;

Table 5 is the asymptotic complexity of **Sign** in SOLMAE whose total complexity to complete takes $\Theta(d \log d)$.

Table 5. Asymptotic complexity of **Sign** in SOLMAE

No.	Computation	Complexity	Location	Comment(d is degree)
1	$\mathbf{H}(r\|M)$	$\Theta(d)$	Step 2 of Algorithm 5	This is same as HashToPoint()
2	FFT(**c**)	$\Theta(d \log d)$	Step 3 of Algorithm 5	
3	Sample($\hat{c}, sk$)	$\Theta(d \log d)$	Step 4 of Algorithm 5	See below †
4	FFT$^{-1}(\hat{s_1})$	$\Theta(d \log d)$	Step 5 of Algorithm 5	
5	Compress(s_1)	$\Theta(d)$	Step 6 of Algorithm 5	Explained in Table 2
Total Complexity of **Sign**: $\Theta(d \log d)$				

† In Sample (Algorithm 4 in [9],) there are some polynomial multiplications and additions which take $\Theta(d \log d)$ and calls PeikertSampler(Algorithm 5 in [9]) two times. In PeikerSampler, Step 1 takes $\Theta(d)$ (Generating normal vector with N–sampler takes $\Theta(d)$ and multiplying Σ takes $\Theta(d)$ since Σ is a diagonal matrix.). Steps 2, 3, and 5 take $\Theta(d \log d)$ since FFT computation is required. Step 4 takes $\Theta(d)$ simply since the loop iterates d times.

The asymptotic complexity of verification in SOLMAE is omitted since the algorithm is identical to verification in FALCON. Our asymptotic analysis discussed here is the first step to estimate the execution time of FALCON and SOLMAE roughly. We can claim that **KeyGen**, **Sign**, **Verif** procedures take $\Theta(d \log d)$ together with FALCON and SOLMAE here. This analysis does imply that FALCON and SOLMAE show the same execution times regardless of its implemented platform.

6   Gaussian Sampler

Gaussian sampler plays a significant role in preventing quantum–secure signature schemes from secret key leakage attacks described in [13]. FALCON and SOLMAE use discrete Gaussian sampling with fixed and variable center values for efficient and secure sampling. We describe the theoretical significance of $\mathcal{N}$-**Sampler** (Algorithm 10 in [9]) and and the visual analysis **UnifCrown** sampler (Algorithm 9 in [9]) used in SOLMAE specification [9].

6.1 $\mathcal{N}$-**Sampler**

A multivariate normal distribution is a natural distribution that is used in many fields. The process of generating a sample that follows normal distribution is called Gaussian sampling. In SOLMAE, we use an $\mathcal{N}$-**Sampler** (which is the same as the Gaussian sampler) to generate the FFT representation of d–dimensional standard normal distribution. To generate $\mathbb{R}^d$ vector that follows the multivariate normal distribution of mean **0** and variance matrix $\frac{d}{2} \cdot I_d$, we can generate independent $\frac{d}{2}$ many random vectors that follow a bivariate normal distribution with mean **0** and variance matrix $\frac{d}{2} \cdot I_2$, then concatenate them together. Also, sampling bivariate normal distribution with mean **0** and variance matrix $\frac{d}{2} \cdot I_2$ can be done by using Box–Muller transform [5]. We describe how it works: First, generate u_1 and u_2, two independent random numbers, that follow uniform distribution between 0 and 1. Then, compute R and θ as shown below.

$$R = \sqrt{-d \cdot ln(u_1)}, \quad \Theta = 2\pi \cdot u_2 \tag{14}$$

Finally, calculate X and Y, to convert (R, Θ) into Cartesian coordinates.

$$X = R \cdot \cos(\Theta), \quad Y = R \cdot \sin(\Theta) \tag{15}$$

Theorem 1. *(X, Y) in Eq. (15) follows bivariate normal distribution with mean **0** and variance matrix $\frac{d}{2} \cdot I_2$.*

Proof. By using the random variable transform theorem stated in [10], we show that this theorem holds as follows:

$$pdf_{X,Y}(x,y) = pdf_{U_1,U_2}(u_1,u_2) \cdot \begin{vmatrix} \frac{\partial u_1}{\partial x} & \frac{\partial u_1}{\partial y} \\ \frac{\partial u_2}{\partial x} & \frac{\partial u_2}{\partial y} \end{vmatrix}$$

$$= \begin{vmatrix} -\frac{2x}{d} \cdot e^{-\frac{x^2+y^2}{d}} & -\frac{2y}{d} \cdot e^{-\frac{x^2+y^2}{d}} \\ \frac{1}{2\pi} \cdot \frac{-y}{x^2+y^2} & \frac{1}{2\pi} \cdot \frac{x}{x^2+y^2} \end{vmatrix} \left(u_1 = e^{-\frac{x^2+y^2}{d}}, u_2 = \frac{1}{2\pi} \tan^{-1}(\frac{y}{x}) \right)$$

$$= (2\pi)^{-1} \cdot |\Sigma|^{-1/2} exp(-\frac{1}{2}\mathbf{x}^T \Sigma^{-1}\mathbf{x})(\mathbf{x} = (x,y)^T, \Sigma = \frac{d}{2} \cdot I_2)$$

where *pdf* means the *probability density function*. Thus, we see that (X, Y) in Eq. (15) follows the bivariate normal distribution. □

Figure 5 shows 10 bivariate normal samplings using Box–Muller transform generated by Python script.

-1.5600039712701361	-1.1549240059661916
-1.4247377976757196	1.002076190337793
0.9969000368756169	-1.993812973058359
0.7107783282470497	0.0979834381524135
-0.4516874832960174	-0.9235298958094609
0.04449314089974015	1.1053117363335245
-0.9864717691744923	0.020836466309925545
0.887687084897981	-0.010185532828900362
-1.4066801271173832	-0.7906097922917507
0.9722996719071684	-1.6390701046508105

Fig. 5. 10 bivariate normal samplings

To check whether the $\mathcal{N}$-Sampler used in SOLMAE reference implementation generates the multivariate normal distribution of mean zero and variance matrix $\frac{d}{2} \cdot I_d$ properly, we made a checking program in Python script that produces a sample of size 1,000, then plots the random vectors' projections to $\mathbb{R}^2$ and Chi-square QQ-plot using the built-in library provided in Python. Figure 6 illustrates the 2–dimensional plot of this $\mathcal{N}$-Sampler. Figures 6(a) and 6(b) are its scatter plot and QQ–plot, respectively. From this experiment, we can see that this $\mathcal{N}$-Sampler works properly.

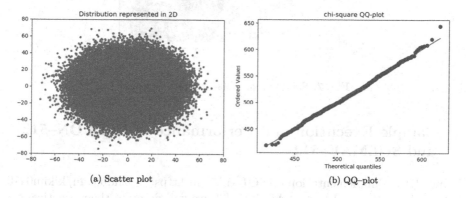

| (a) Scatter plot | (b) QQ–plot |

Fig. 6. Plot of $\mathcal{N}$-Sampler

6.2   UnifCrown Sampler

UnifCrown sampler used in SOLMAE is a method that generates a random vector that follows uniform distribution over $\Omega = \{(x, y) \in \mathbb{R}^2 | R_{min}^2 < x^2 + y^2 < R_{max}^2, x > 0, y > 0\}$ (*i.e.,* the probability density function of random vector (X, Y) is $f_{X,Y}(x, y) = \frac{4}{\pi \cdot (R_{max}^2 - R_{min}^2)} \cdot I_{(R_{min}^2 < x^2 + y^2 < R_{max}^2, x > 0, y > 0)}$). With some calculations, we can easily see that if U_ρ, U_θ follows uniform distribution over $[0, 1]$, $(X, Y) = \sqrt{R_{min}^2 + U_\rho(R_{max}^2 - R_{min}^2)}(\cos(\frac{\pi}{2} \cdot U_\theta), \sin(\frac{\pi}{2} \cdot U_\theta))$ follows uniform distribution over Ω.

To verify this implementation visually, the scatter plot of UnifCrown sampler with 10,000 samples was depicted in Fig. 7. From this, we can see that UnifCrown sampler works properly.

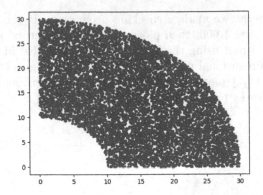

Fig. 7. Scatter plot of UnifCrown Sampler

7 Sample Execution and Performance of FALCON–512 and SOLMAE–512

Using Python implementation of SOLMAE in https://github.com/kjkim0410/SOLMAE_python_512 and FALCON [3], we will describe their practical execution and performance comparison here.

For your clear understanding how FALCON–512 and SOLMAE–512 operate step-by-step, we run the total execution of FALCON–512 and SOLMAE–512 once using the same 512-byte message and same 40-byte salt which was randomly generated by using **urandom()** in Python **os** module as below:

```
Salt: b730f4e48087d8c5d6dcc085a5ad47437fd4da454c4598142b5284a794660a2cf5322d3425c631c2
Length of Salt: 40

Message: bf467a6d349c6409eba490a9ec34443ad9c009b49a0a0e71974893...d147eb98e818e600e8f6
Length of Message: 512
```

Each algorithm generates a set of secret keys (f, g, F, G) and public key (h) at first using its **KeyGen** procedure. Due to the space problem, we printed out the partial output of the intermediate values such as **HashtoPoint, s_0 signature, s_1 signature, norm of signature** with the **allowable bound of signature**. Also, the values of the message, key, and signal are too big, so they are partially expressed in this paper. The full information of executing FALCON–512 and SOLMAE–512 can refer to **FALCON_512_EX2.txt** and **SOLMAE_512_EX2.txt**, respectively at blog https://ircs.re.kr/?p=1769 for details.

7.1 Sample Execution of FALCON–512

The following is a partial printout of key generation, signification, and verification with FALCON–512.

```
f: [-3, 1, 0, -5, 10, -5, 3, 4, 2, 4, 4, ..., 3, -3, 2, -7, 5, 2, 3, 4, -1, -2]
```

```
g: [-3, -3, 4, 5, 5, -6, 10, 1, -4, 3, ..., -9, -3, 1, -2, -7, -3, 7, -2, 0, 2]

F: [23, 10, 2, -16, 14, -26, -20, -1, ..., -7, -14, -24, -21, -23, 18, -1, 44]

G: [-2, 1, 4, 2, -25, 50, 14, 28, -19, ..., -32, -10, -2, 14, 1, -14, -12, 5]

h: [2923, 7873, 9970, 6579, 16, 10828, 337, 8243, ..., 6409, 6857, 2467, 5207]

HashToPoint: [8332, 4711, 5492, 4716, 9558, 8284, ..., 6556, 7525, 11628, 5028]

s0 Signature: [-34, 182,  -7, 82, -86, 113, ..., 204, 212, 349, -65, -89,  -3]

s1 Signature: [-120, -58, 30, 133, 126, 13, ..., -205, -50, 114, -502, 290, 136]

Norm of Signature : 27,222,436
Bound of Signature: 34,034,726

Signature: f8dd47a0abf43635d313e9d5a5dbb7ec2354a805d3...4200000000000000000000000
Length of Signature: 666

Verification result = True
```

7.2   Sample Execution of SOLMAE–512

The following is a partial printout of key generation, signification, and verification with SOLMAE–512.

```
f: [0, 1, -3, -6, -3, 2, -4, 1, -1, 0, ..., 2, -3, -5, 0, -5, -5, -1, 1, -4, 3]

g: [5, 3, 5, 2, 0, 4, -10, -6, -3, 1, -2, ..., 2, 4, -2, 4, -3, 3, 3, 2, 2, -3]

F: [-4, 18, 18, -36, 4, -24, 45, 42, 23, 31, ..., 3, 0, 0, 40, 42, -20, -35, 19]

G: [27, -11, 70, -13, 19, -10, -37, 20, ..., -45, 12, -3, -32, 48, 14, -16, -1]

h: [11703, 2428, 2427, 11917, 9502, 8908, 3567, ..., 6080, 7718, 3106,  11973]

HashToPoint: [8332, 4711, 5492, 4716, 9558, 8284, ..., 6556, 7525, 11628, 5028]

s0 Signature: [74, -6, 253, 187, -285, 210, ..., -225, -195, 364, 325, 138, -44]

s1 Signature: [-50, -47, 198, 13, 218, -201, ..., 114, -234, 5, -119, -41, 170]

Norm of Signature : 30,454,805
Bound of Signature: 33,870,790

Signature: 4ac35f53b674a92dd3ef7f28a9cee2bd2cc48cc8c471d1...9ac8000000000000000000
Length of Signature: 666

Verification result = True
```

7.3   Performance Comparison of FALCON–512 and SOLMAE–512

Note that Python code is not so good tool to evaluate the exact performance of FALCON and SOLMAE. However, we can grab a rough idea of their relative performance which one can work fast. The specification of our test platform is

Intel Core i7–9700 CPU at 3 GHz clock speed with 16 GRAM. We limited our experiment to the relative performance of KeyGen, Sign, and Verif procedures on FALCON–512 and SOLMAE–512 only. We executed 3 cases of each test which is executed 1,000 times iteration.

Tables 6 and 7 indicates the average time in second of KeyGen and Sign and Verif procedures of FALCON–512 and SOLMAE–512, respectively.

Table 6. Average time of KeyGen

	FALCON–512	SOLMAE–512
Test 1	3.6316	2.7346
Test 2	3.6908	2.7633
Test 3	3.7250	2.7306

Table 7. Average time of Sign and Verif

	Time of Sign		Time of Verif	
Algo.	FALCON–512	SOLMAE–512	FALCON–512	SOLMAE–512
Test 1	6.4849×10^{-2}	5.9507×10^{-2}	5.4598×10^{-3}	5.4609×10^{-3}
Test 2	6.4664×10^{-2}	5.9432×10^{-2}	5.4359×10^{-3}	5.3684×10^{-3}
Test 3	6.4900×10^{-2}	5.8873×10^{-2}	5.4271×10^{-3}	5.3648×10^{-3}

Our experiments show almost indistinguishable performances between FALCON–512 and SOLMAE–512 by their Python implementation in Sign and Verif procedures while the KeyGen procedure of FALCON takes longer time than that of SOLMAE. We couldn't check the performance of FALCON–1024 and SOLMAE–1024 due to the deadlock issue of our experiment with the limited precision inherited from Python language. The SOLMAE specification [9] states that the Sign procedure of SOLMAE takes 2 times faster than that of FALCON by the reference implementation of SOLMAE in C language.

8 Concluding Remarks

FALCON is claimed to have the advantage of providing short public keys and signatures as well as high–security levels; plagued by a contrived signing algorithm, not very fast for signing and hard to parallelize; very little flexibility in terms of parameter settings. However, SOLMAE has a simple, fast, parallelizable signing algorithm, with flexible parameters with its novel key generation algorithm.

In this paper, after giving a brief description of the specification of FALCON and SOLMAE, we found that their asymptotic computational complexity of

KeyGen, Sign and Verif procedures take $\Theta(n \log n)$ simultaneously. Also, our computer experiments using their Python implementation exhibit empirically that KeyGen of FALCON–512 only takes longer time than that of SOLMAE–512 by about a second. But we can say that this is not an exact evaluation of their performance by Python implementation.

Further work such as elaborated analysis of computational complexity on FALCON and SOLMAE asymptotically is left to do next.

Acknowledgement. This work was partially supported by Electronics and Telecommunications Research Institute (ETRI) grant funded by the Korean Government (20ZR1300, Core Technology Research on Trust Data Connectome). Jaehyun Kim and Jueun Jung from Seoul National Unviersity, Korea have partially contributed this work while they were intern researchers at IRCS during their summer break in 2023.

References

1. Espitau, T., et al.: Mitaka: a simpler, parallelizable, maskable variant of falcon. In: Dunkelman, O., Dziembowski, S. (eds.) Advances in Cryptology – EUROCRYPT 2022. EUROCRYPT 2022. LNCS, vol. 13277, pp. 222–253. Springer, Cham (2022). https://doi.org/10.1007/978-3-031-07082-2_9
2. Espitau, T., Tibouchi, M., Wallet, A., Yu, Y.: Shorter hash-and-sign lattice-based signatures. In: Dodis, Y., Shrimpton, T. (eds.) Advances in Cryptology – CRYPTO 2022. CRYPTO 2022. LNCS, vol. 13508, pp. 245–275. Springer, Cham (2022). https://doi.org/10.1007/978-3-031-15979-4_9
3. Fouque, P.A., et al: Falcon: fast-fourier lattice-based compact signatures over ntru. https://falcon-sign.info/
4. Fouque, P.A., Kirchner, P., Tibouchi, M., Wallet, A., Yu, Y.: Key recovery from gram-schmidt norm leakage in hash-and-sign signatures over ntru lattices. Cryptology ePrint Archive, Paper 2019/1180 (2019). https://eprint.iacr.org/2019/1180
5. Box, G.E., Muller, M.E.: A note on the generation of random normal deviatess Ann. Math. Stat. 010–611 (1958)
6. Gentry, C., Peikert, C., Vaikuntanathan, V.: Trapdoors for hard lattices and new cryptographic constructions. In: Ladner, R.E., Dwork, C. (eds.) 40th ACM STOC, pp. 197–206. ACM Press, May 2008. https://doi.org/10.1145/1374376.1374407
7. Goldreich, O., Goldwasser, S., Halevi, S.: Public-key cryptosystems from lattice reduction problems. In: Kaliski, B.S. (eds.) Advances in Cryptology – CRYPTO '97. CRYPTO 1997. LNCS, vol. 1294, pp. 112–131. Springer, Berlin, Heidelberg (1997). https://doi.org/10.1007/BFb0052231
8. Hoffstein, J., Pipher, J., Silverman, J.H.: NTRU: a ring-based public key cryptosystem. In: Buhler, J.P. (eds.) Algorithmic Number Theory. ANTS 1998. LNCS, vol. 1423, pp. 267–288. Springer, Berlin, Heidelberg (1998). https://doi.org/10.1007/BFb0054868
9. Kim, K., et al.: Solmae: algorithm specification. Updated SOLMAE, IRCS Blog (2023). https://ircs.re.kr/?p=1714
10. Kim, W.: Mathematical Statistics(in Korean). Minyoungsa, Seoul, Korea (2021)
11. KpqC: Korean post-quantum crytography (2020). https://kpqc.or.kr/
12. Min, S., Yamamoto, G., Kim, K.: Weak property of malleability in NTRUSign. In: Wang, H., Pieprzyk, J., Varadharajan, V. (eds.) Information Security and Privacy. ACISP 2004. LNCS, vol. 3108, pp. 379–390 . Springer, Berlin, Heidelberg (2004). https://doi.org/10.1007/978-3-540-27800-9_33

13. Nguyen, P.Q., Regev, O.: Learning a parallelepiped: cryptanalysis of ggh and ntru signatures. J. Cryptol. **22**(2), 139–160 (2009)
14. NIST: Post-quantum crytography (2016). https://csrc.nist.gov/projects/post-quantum-cryptography
15. Pornin, T., Prest, T.: More efficient algorithms for the NTRU key generation using the field norm. In: Lin, D., Sako, K. (eds.) Public-Key Cryptography – PKC 2019. PKC 2019. LNCS, vol. 11443, pp. 504–533. Springer, Cham (2019). https://doi.org/10.1007/978-3-030-17259-6_17
16. Shor, P.W.: Polynomial-time algorithms for prime factorization and discrete logarithms on a quantum computer. SIAM Rev. **41**(2), 303–332 (1999)
17. Wikipedia: Harvest now, decrypt later (2023). https://en.wikipedia.org/wiki/Harvest_now_decrypt_later

Security Evaluation on KpqC Round 1 Lattice-Based Algorithms Using Lattice Estimator

Suhri Kim, Eunmin Lee, Joohee Lee[✉], Minju Lee, and Hyuna Noh

Sungshin Women's University, Seoul, Republic of Korea
{suhrikim,20211089,jooheelee,20211082,20211056}@sungshin.ac.kr

Abstract. Post-quantum cryptography is expected to become one of the fundamental technologies in the field of security that requires public-key cryptosystems, potentially replacing standards such as RSA and ECC, as it is designed to withstand attacks using quantum computers. In South Korea, there is an ongoing standardization effort called the KpqC (Korean Post-Quantum Cryptography) competition for developing post-quantum cryptography as a national standard. The competition is in its first round, and it has introduced a total of 16 candidate algorithms for evaluation.

In this paper, we analyze the security of five algorithms among the eight lattice-based schemes in the first round of the KpqC competition. We assess their security using M. Albrecht's Lattice Estimator, focusing on problems related to LWE (Learning with Errors) and LWR (Learning with Rounding). Additionally, we compare the security analysis results with the claims in the proposal documents for each algorithm. When an algorithm fails to achieve the level of security in its proposal, we suggest potential types of attacks that need to be considered for further analysis and improvement.

Keywords: Post-Quantum Cryptography · KpqC Competition · LWE · LWR

1 Introduction

In 1994, Peter Shor proposed polynomial-time quantum algorithms for solving discrete logarithm and factoring problems, posing a significant threat to the security of standard public-key cryptosystems such as RSA and ECC [32]. Against this backdrop, there have been active international standardization efforts for Post-Quantum Cryptography (PQC), which aims to provide new standards that are resistant to attacks using quantum computers. Since the end of 2016, the National Institute of Standards and Technology (NIST) in the United States has been conducting a standardization project for PQC in the areas of Key

---

The authors are listed in alphabetical order.

© The Author(s), under exclusive license to Springer Nature Singapore Pte Ltd. 2024
H. Seo and S. Kim (Eds.): ICISC 2023, LNCS 14562, pp. 261–281, 2024.
https://doi.org/10.1007/978-981-97-1238-0_14

Encapsulation Mechanism (KEM) and digital signature. Over three rounds of evaluations, NIST selected one KEM and three signature schemes as standards in 2022 [28]. Currently, there is an ongoing process for additional selections and evaluations in the fourth round and an on-ramp for the digital signature category [29]. Similarly, in South Korea, a national standardization competition for post-quantum cryptography, known as the KpqC competition, began in 2022 [10].

Lattice-based cryptography is a field of post-quantum cryptography that relies on the hard problems related to lattices, including NTRU [19], Learning with Errors (LWE) [9,31], Learning with Rounding (LWR) [30], and Short Integer Solution (SIS) [1]. It has gained significant attention and recognition due to its fast computational speed and balanced performance in terms of communication overhead compared to other post-quantum cryptosystems: in the U.S. NIST standardization competition, the one selected KEM standard and two digital signature schemes out of a total of selected three post-quantum signatures are lattice-based schemes.

In the context of the KpqC competition, the lattice-based submissions in the first round include three and five schemes in the Key Encapsulation Mechanism (KEM) and digital signature categories, respectively. Each of these schemes is built upon specific underlying problems, which are summarized in Table 1.

Table 1. KpqC Competition - Round 1 Lattice-based Submissions

Category	Algorithm	Base Problem
KEM	NTRU+	NTRU, **RLWE**
	SMAUG	**MLWE, MLWR**
	TiGER	**RLWR, RLWE**
Signature	GCKSign	GCK
	HAETAE	**MLWE**, MSIS
	NCC-Sign	**RLWE**, RSIS
	Peregrine	NTRU, RSIS
	SOLMAE	NTRU, RSIS

In this paper, we analyze the security of Learning with Errors (LWE) and Learning with Rounding (LWR) based algorithms, a total of 5 schemes (NTRU+, SMAUG, TiGER, HAETAE, NCC-Sign), among the lattice-based algorithms in the 1st round of the KpqC competition. We analyze the security of the LWE/LWR problem instances used in each algorithm. For security analysis of the LWE/LWR problems, we utilize M. Albrecht's Lattice Estimator [3]. The Lattice Estimator is an open-source tool written in Sage that quantifies specific attack complexities for various types of LWE attacks, including those described in [3]. It takes LWE (LWR) parameters as inputs and computes the attack complexities along with additional parameters required for the respective attack methods.

Using the Lattice Estimator for security analysis, we derive classical security estimation results for the 5 algorithms, as shown in Table 2. For the time complexity calculation of the BKZ algorithm, we employ the Core-SVP model [4], which is consistent with the methods used in the proposal documents for 4 of the 5 algorithms, excluding NCC-Sign. In Table 2, the column 'Claimed' is the claimed security shown in the proposal documents for each algorithm, and 'Estimated' is the security that we estimated by using the Lattice Estimator. For NTRU+, we observed that the description in the specification document is different from the reference implementation which is reflected in our security estimations with respective cases. More precisely, the LWE secret, which is sampled in the encapsulation phase and denoted as r in their scheme description, is sampled from $\{0, 1\}^n$ according to the specification document (See Algorithm 6 and 9 of the NTRU+ document in [10]), while it is sampled from the centered binomial distribution in their implementation. We estimate both cases and denote the security estimation for the NTRU+ version of the specification document in parentheses. Also, for NCC-Sign, we additionally estimated the security without the Core-SVP model shown in the parentheses, since the proposal document of NCC-Sign presented the security result without using the Core-SVP model. The results are summarized as follows.

- We have observed a discrepancy between the claimed attack complexities for NTRU+ and the estimated attack complexities derived using the Lattice Estimator. For the NTRU+576, NTRU+768, and NTRU+864 parameters, we achieve 115.9 bits, 164.7 bits, and 189.2 bits, respectively, for the version of the reference implementation. These values exhibit a difference of 0.1 to 3.7 bits compared to the classical security levels claimed in the specification document. Also, larger gaps were observed between the claimed security and the estimation for the version of the specification document that utilizes the LWE with uniform binary secrets.
- For the SMAUG1280 parameters (Security level V) and TiGER256 (Security level V), classical security levels of 260.3 bits and 263 bits were claimed, but when measured using the Lattice Estimator, the attack complexities were found to be 259.2 bits and 262.0 bits, respectively.
- For HAETAE, the claimed parameters from the proposal document and the security analysis results of the Lattice Estimator are found to be similar, with an error range of less than 1 bit.
- For NCC-Sign, the proposal document presents security analysis results without using the Core-SVP model, and it is confirmed that the measured results using the Lattice Estimator were consistent. However, when measured using the Core-SVP model, it is determined that for parameters I, III, and V, the classical security levels were 123.2 bits, 190.1 bits, and 273.3 bits, respectively. This shows a difference of 18 to 24.5 bits compared to the results without the Core-SVP model in the NCC-Sign proposal document.

Table 2. Claimed vs. Estimated Security for the Round 1 Lattice-based Submissions. For NTRU+, the estimated results for the specification document version are reported in parentheses. For NCC-Sign, the estimated results without the Core-SVP model are reported in parentheses.

	Security Level	Claimed	Estimated
NTRU+	I ($n = 576$)	116	115.9 **(108.9)**
	I ($n = 768$)	161	**164.7 (156.5)**
	III	188	**189.2 (175.4)**
	V	264	263.4 **(243.5)**
SMAUG	I	120.0	120.0
	III	180.2	180.2
	V	260.3	**259.2**
TiGER	I	130	130.5
	III	200	**206.1**
	V	263	**262.0**
HAETAE	I	125	125.5
	III	236	236.1
	V	288	287.1
NCC-Sign	I	147.7	123.2 (147.7)
	III	211.5	190.1 (211.5)
	V	291.3	273.3 (291.3)

Based on the results, the additional attacks that each scheme needs to further consider through the Lattice Estimator are as follows:

- For SMAUG, it is confirmed that the SMAUG512 and SMAUG768 parameters achieve the claimed security levels. However, in the case of SMAUG1280, the claimed values and the estimated values differ for all attacks (`usvp`, `bdd`, `bdd_hybrid`, `dual`, `dual_hybrid`), which are displayed in Table 3. We remark that the displayed measurements are for the LWR instances.
- For TiGER, it is confirmed that the TiGER128 and TiGER192 parameters achieved the claimed security levels. However, for the TiGER256 parameters, the security level against `dual_hybrid` attacks differs between the claimed and the estimated values, which are displayed in Table 4. The displayed measurements are for the LWR instances when the `dual_hybrid` attack is applied.

Paper Organization. This paper is structured as follows: In Chapter II, we introduce lattice-based hard problems, LWE and LWR, and provide definitions for KEM and digital signatures. In Chapter III, we briefly describe the key features of the KpqC 1st round candidates, including three KEM schemes and two digital signature schemes. In Chapter IV, we present the time complexity computation

Table 3. Claimed vs. Estimated Classical Security for the SMAUG1280 parameter set

	claimed	estimated
usvp	317.1	316.2
bdd	319.5	318.4
bdd_hybrid	290.0	288.5
dual	329.1	328.2
dual_hybrid	260.3	259.2

Table 4. Claimed vs. Estimated Classical Security for the TiGER256 parameter set

	claimed	estimated
dual_hybrid	≥ 263	262.0

methods for the BKZ algorithm used in the security analysis of LWE/LWR-based algorithms and discuss the attacks covered in the Lattice Estimator. In Chapter V, we present the security analysis results obtained from the Lattice Estimator for each scheme's proposed parameters and compare them with the claimed security. Finally, in Chapter VI, we summarize the main results and conclude the paper.

2 Preliminaries

2.1 The LWE and LWR Problem

In this section, we introduce lattice-based hard problems, Learning with Errors (LWE) [31] and Learning with Rounding (LWR) [30].

2.1.1 LWE

Let m, n, q be positive integers, $s \in \mathbb{Z}_q^n$ be a secret vector and χ be an error distribution on $\mathbb{Z}$. The LWE distribution $A_{m,n,q,\chi}^{LWE}(s)$ consisting of m samples is obtained as follows: For each $i \in \{1, 2, \ldots, m\}$, compute

$$b_i = \langle \vec{a}_i, \vec{s} \rangle + e_i \mod q$$

by choosing a vector $\vec{a}_i \in \mathbb{Z}_q^n$ uniformly and a small error $e_i \in \mathbb{Z}$ from the distribution χ, and then output $\{(\vec{a}_i, b_i)\}_{i=1}^m$ as the result.

The decision LWE problem is to distinguish either given samples $\{(\vec{a}_i, b_i)\}_{i=1}^m$ is from the distribution $A_{m,n,q,\chi}^{LWE}$ or from the uniform distribution. The search LWE problem is to find $s \in \mathbb{Z}_q^n$, given independent samples $\{(\vec{a}_i, b_i)\}_{i=1}^m$ from $A_{m,n,q,\chi}^{LWE}(s)$.

Variants of LWE. Let n and q be positive integers and $f(x) \in \mathbb{Z}[x]$ an irreducible polynomial of degree n. We define a polynomial ring $\mathcal{R} = \mathbb{Z}[x]/f(x)$ and its quotient ring $\mathcal{R}_q = \mathbb{Z}_q[x]/(f(x))$ modulo q. The Module LWE (MLWE) problem [8] is a variant of the LWE problem defined over a module $\mathcal{R}_q^k$ for positive integers k. The distribution $A_{m,n,q,k,\chi}^{MLWE}(\vec{s})$ for the secret value $\vec{s} \in \mathcal{R}_q^k$ is defined as follows: For $i \in \{1, 2, \ldots, m\}$, sample uniform random $\vec{a}_i \in \mathcal{R}_q^k$ and $e_i \in \mathcal{R} \leftarrow \chi^n$, calculate $b_i = \langle \vec{a}_i, \vec{s} \rangle + e_i \mod q \in \mathcal{R}_q$ and return the set of pairs $\{(\vec{a}_i, b_i)\}_{i=1}^m$ as results. It is also classified into the decision MLWE and search MLWE problems as in the LWE problem. For the specific case of MLWE when the dimension of module k is 1, we call it as Ring-LWE (RLWE) problem [25].

2.1.2 LWR

The LWR problem introduced by Banerjee et al. [6] obfuscates the secret by applying a deterministic rounding procedure ($\lfloor \cdot \rceil$) to linear equations instead of adding errors sampled from discrete Gaussian distributions. Given positive integers m, n, q, p, let $\vec{s} \in \mathbb{Z}_q^n$ be an n-dimensional secret vector. The LWR distribution $A_{m,n,q,p}^{LWR}(\vec{s})$ over $\mathbb{Z}_q^{m \times n} \times \mathbb{Z}_p^m$ consisting of m samples is obtained as follows: For $i \in \{1, 2, \ldots, m\}$, compute $b_i = \lfloor (p/q) \cdot (\langle \vec{a}_i, \vec{s} \rangle \mod q) \rceil$ where $\vec{a}_i \in \mathbb{Z}_q^n$ is uniformly sampled, and return the set of pairs $\{(\vec{a}_i, b_i)\}_{i=1}^m$. The decision LWR problem is to distinguish either given samples $\{(\vec{a}_i, b_i)\}_{i=1}^m$ is from the distribution $A_{m,n,q,\chi}^{LWR}$ or from the uniform distribution. The search LWR problem is to find $\vec{s} \in \mathbb{Z}_q^n$, given independent samples $\{(\vec{a}_i, b_i)\}_{i=1}^m$ from $A_{m,n,q,p}^{LWR}(\vec{s})$. This definition can be extended to Ring-LWR (RLWR) and Module-LWR (MLWR) by using vectors of polynomials as in the LWE problem.

2.2 The Round 1 LWE/LWR-Based Candidates

2.2.1 KEM

A Key Encapsulation Mechanism (KEM) is a triple of algorithms, $\Pi = (\mathsf{KeyGen}, \mathsf{Encaps}, \mathsf{Decaps})$, where

- $(pk, sk) \leftarrow \mathsf{KeyGen}(1^\lambda)$: The key generation algorithm takes security parameter $\lambda > 0$ as an input and then outputs the pair of public key and private key (pk, sk).
- $(c, K) \leftarrow \mathsf{Encaps}(pk)$: The encapsulation algorithm takes the public key pk as an input and then outputs a pair of secret key K and ciphertext c.
- $(K \text{ or } \perp) \leftarrow \mathsf{Decaps}(sk, c)$: The decapsulation algorithm takes the private key sk and the ciphertext c as input, and then outputs the shared key K or $\perp$.

For correctness, it is required that, for all $(pk, sk) \leftarrow \mathsf{KeyGen}(1^\lambda)$ and for all $(c, K) \leftarrow \mathsf{Encaps}(pk)$, $\mathsf{Decaps}(sk, c) = K$ holds. In this section, we review the distinguished features of the KpqC Round 1 lattice-based KEMs NTRU+, SMAUG, and TiGER.

NTRU+. NTRU+ is an algorithm that improves the efficiency of the existing NTRU scheme [19]. It follows the strategy to construct NTT (Number Theory Transform)-friendly settings for NTRU which has been introduced in NTTRU [26] and NTRU-B [17]. The security of NTRU+ is based on the NTRU and RLWE problems. The main features are as follows:

- NTRU+ utilizes the NTT-friendly polynomial rings $\mathcal{R}_q = \mathbb{Z}_q[x]/(f(x))$, where $f(x) = x^n - x^{n/2} + 1$ is a cyclotomic trinomial of degree $n = 2^i 3^j$, and adapt NTT in all computations.
- In the encapsulation and decapsulation, new methods for secret key encoding (SOTP) and decoding (Inv) were proposed. The SOTP and Inv operations for $m \in \{0, 1\}^n$, $u = (u_1, u_2) \in \{0, 1\}^{2n}$, and $y \in \{-1, 0, 1\}^n$ are designed as follows.

$$\mathsf{SOTP}(m, u) = (m \oplus u_1) - u_2 \in \{-1, 0, 1\}^n \tag{1}$$

$$\mathsf{Inv}(y, u) = (y + u_2) \oplus u_1 \tag{2}$$

  One can easily check $\mathsf{Inv}(\mathsf{SOTP}(m, u), u) = m$.
- To satisfy IND-CCA (Indistinguishability against adaptive Chosen-Ciphertext Attacks) security, NTRU+ applies a modified transform of the conventional Fujisaki-Okamoto (FO) transform [18]. The difference is that the decapsulation procedures require re-encryption when applying the FO transform, while NTRU+ removes the re-encryption in the decapsulation by recovering the random polynomial (denoted by r in their scheme) used in the encapsulation twice and then comparing between them.

SMAUG. SMAUG is designed based on the hardness of MLWE and MLWR problems, both of which utilize the sparse ternary secrets following the approaches in Lizard [14] and RLizard [21]. The main features are as follows.

- SMAUG KEM is obtained by first constructing an IND-CPA (Indistinguishability against Chosen-Plaintext Attacks) secure public-key encryption (PKE) scheme and then applying the FO transform [18] on it to achieve the IND-CCA security.
- The secret keys for MLWE and MLWR are sampled as sparse ternary vectors with fixed Hamming weights, respectively.
- The moduli q and p are set to powers of 2 in order to replace the rounding operations in the encapsulation with bit-wise shift operations.

TiGER. TiGER is designed based on the RLWE and RLWR problems with sparse secrets. The main features are as follows.

- TiGER consists of an IND-CPA PKE scheme, and an IND-CCA KEM obtained by applying the FO transform to it.
- All integer modulus in the scheme are set to be power of 2 for the same reason as in SMAUG, in order to replace the rounding operations with bit-wise shifts.
- TiGER pre-defines the Hamming weight of the secrets of RLWE and RLWR and generates sparse vectors. Additionally, the errors for RLWE are also sampled as sparse vectors.
- The sizes of ciphertexts and public keys are relatively small because of using a small modulus of 1 byte ($q = 256$) for all suggested parameters.
- When encoding the secret key in TiGER KEM, they employ an Error Correcting Code (ECC) to reduce decryption failure rates. Therefore, it is possible to adjust the decryption failure rate to be negligible in the security parameter, despite using the small modulus q. They utilize XEf [5], D2 [4] for the ECC methods.

2.2.2   Digital Signatures

Digital signatures is a triple of algorithms $\Pi = $ (KeyGen, Sign, Verify). The key generation (KeyGen) algorithm generates a pair of a public key and a private key. The signing (Sign) algorithm takes the private key and a message as inputs to generate a signature. The verification (Verify) algorithm takes the public key, message, and signature value as inputs to verify the validity of the signatures. These can be summarized as follows:

- $(pk, sk) \leftarrow$ KeyGen(1^λ): The key generation algorithm takes security parameter λ as an input and then outputs a pair of public key and private key (pk, sk).
- $\sigma \leftarrow$ Sign(sk, m): The signature algorithm takes the private key sk and a message m as inputs and then outputs a signature σ.
- 1 or 0 $\leftarrow$ Verify(pk, m, σ): The verification algorithm takes the public key pk, a message m, and a signature σ as inputs. It outputs 1 if the signature is valid, and 0 otherwise.

In this section, we summarize the distinguished features of the KpqC Round 1 lattice-based signature schemes HAETAE and NCC-Sign.

HAETAE. HAETAE utilizes the Fiat-Shamir with Aborts paradigm [23,24] as in the CRYSTALS-Dilithium [16], one of the standards selected in the NIST PQC standardization project. HAETAE uses a bimodal distribution proposed in the rejection sampling of BLISS signatures [15]. The main features are as follows:

- In lattice-based digital signature algorithms, the distribution used for rejection sampling has a significant impact on the signature size. HAETAE uses a hyperball uniform distribution to reduce the signature size, albeit at the cost of speed compared to Dilithium.

- HAETAE leverages a module structure and uses a predefined polynomial ring $\mathcal{R}_q = \mathbb{Z}_q[x]/(x^{256} + 1)$ for all parameter sets, making it easy to adjust parameters according to the required security level.

NCC-Sign. NCC-Sign is a digital signature algorithm that combines the design rationale of CRYSTALS-Dilithium and NTRU prime [7], which were also round 3, 4 candidates for NIST PQC standardization project KEM algorithms. NCC-Sign also adopts Fiat-Shamir with Aborts paradigm as in HAETAE and Dilithium, but instead of using a cyclotomic polynomial ring of $\mathcal{R}_q = \mathbb{Z}_q[x]/(x^n + 1)$, it uses the non-cyclotomic polynomial ring of the form $\mathcal{R}_q = \mathbb{Z}_q[x]/(x^p + x + 1)$, where p is a prime. The main features are as follows:

- Due to the use of a non-cyclotomic ring, NTT cannot be applied to polynomial multiplications. In NCC-Sign, polynomial multiplication is computed using the Toom-Cook method, one of the divide-and-conquer techniques. For a prime p such that $p \leq 4n, n \in \mathbb{Z}$, the algorithm computes polynomial multiplication of degree $4n$ and exploits Toom-Cook-4-way and Karatsuba multiplication.

3   Security Analysis Methods

3.1   Time Complexity Estimation of the BKZ Algorithm

The BKZ algorithm [12] is a state-of-the-art lattice basis reduction algorithm used to find short bases within a given lattice, and it exhibits exponential time complexity. To analyze the security of the LWE/LWR-based algorithms, the instances of LWE/LWR used in the algorithms are induced to the problems to find short vectors in lattices which are given by the choices of attack strategies such as Dual and Primal attacks. Hence, it can be solved by using the BKZ algorithm.

The core idea behind the BKZ algorithm is to iteratively apply a Shortest Vector Problem (SVP) solver to sub-lattices of dimension smaller than the original lattice. When the dimension of the sub-lattice to which the SVP solver is applied is $\beta > 0$, it is referred to as β-BKZ, and this sub-lattice is called a 'block'.

The Core-SVP model [4] is a measurement model used to estimate the time complexity of the BKZ algorithm from a conservative perspective. When calculating the time complexity of the BKZ algorithm using the Core-SVP model, the time complexity of β-BKZ is estimated to be $2^{c \cdot \beta}$, which is a lower bound of the time complexity of a single application of the SVP solver $\left(2^{c \cdot \beta + o(\beta)}\right)$, where $c \in [0, 1]$ is constant. This conservative model is designed to ensure that the security predictions of the BKZ algorithm remain unaffected by improvements in the efficiency of either the number of iterations of applying the SVP solver or the efficiency of the SVP solver itself, thus preserving the algorithm's security guarantees.

In the Core-SVP model, the constant $c \in [0, 1]$ used for calculating the BKZ time complexity is determined based on the efficiency of the SVP solver. In [4], it was employed as shown in Table 5. For quantum SVP solvers, continuous improvements in efficiency have led to the existence of algorithms with $c_Q = 0.257$ [11]. In this paper, we calculate the BKZ time complexity using $c = 0.292$ for classical security. When using the Core-SVP model, quantum security (in bits) can be simply estimated by multiplying classical security (in bits) with $c_Q/0.292$.

Table 5. The BKZ time complexity (T) for classical security and quantum security in the Core-SVP model

	classical	quantum
c	0.292	0.265
T	$2^{0.292\beta}$	$2^{0.265\beta}$

3.2   Dual Attack

The dual attack identifies a short vector v that is orthogonal to matrix A. Given $(A, \vec{b}) \in \mathbb{Z}_q^{k \times l} \times \mathbb{Z}_q^k$ either from the LWE distribution or the uniform distribution, a lattice Λ_m^{dual} can be defined as follow. Let $A_{[m]}$ be the upmost $m \times l$ sub-matrix of A for $m \leq k$.

$$\Lambda_m^{\text{dual}} := \left\{ (\vec{u}, \vec{v}) \in \mathbb{Z}^m \times \mathbb{Z}^l : A_{[m]}^\top \vec{u} + \vec{v} = 0 \bmod q \right\}$$

If it is the case $\vec{b} = A\vec{s} + \vec{e}$, with a short non-zero element $(\vec{u}, \vec{v})$, an attacker can compute $\langle \vec{u}, \vec{b}_{[m]} \rangle = -\langle \vec{v}, \vec{s} \rangle + \langle \vec{u}, \vec{e}_{[m]} \rangle$, where $\vec{b}_{[m]}$ and $\vec{e}_{[m]}$ are the upmost m-dimensional sub-vector of $\vec{b}$. Hence, the attacker can determine it is an LWE instance if $\langle \vec{u}, \vec{b}_{[m]} \rangle$ is short enough. Therefore, finding a sufficiently short non-zero vector in the lattice Λ_m^{dual} implies solving the decision-LWE problem. To find a short lattice element of Λ_m^{dual}, the attack employs the β-BKZ lattice basis reduction algorithm.

3.3   Primal Attack

The primal attack on LWE addresses the bounded distance decoding (BDD) problem directly. In other words, when provided with LWE samples (A, b), it seeks a vector $w = As$ such that $\|b - w\|$ is unusually small. There are two main strategies to solve BDD: the first strategy is to utilize Babai's nearest algorithm with lattice basis reduction [22], and the second is to reduce BDD problem into unique-SVP (uSVP) problem and solve it using the lattice basis reduction algorithms [2,4]. Here, we will elaborate on the second method, which is more widely considered.

Given an LWE instance $(A, b = As + e) \in \mathbb{Z}_q^{m \times n} \times \mathbb{Z}_q^m$, a lattice Λ_m can be defined as follow. $B = \left(A_{[m]} \,|\, I_m \,|\, b_{[m]}\right) \in \mathbb{Z}_q^{m \times (n+m+1)}$.

$$\Lambda_m = \left\{ v \in \mathbb{Z}_q^{n+m+1} : Bv \bmod q \right\}$$

Therefore, a short non-zero vector in the lattice Λ_m can be transformed into the non-trivial solutions for the LWE equation. This attack utilizes the β-BKZ algorithm to find the sufficiently short vector in the lattice Λ_m.

3.4 Hybrid Attack

An attack that combines techniques, such as meet-in-the-middle, with either Primal or Dual attacks is known as a hybrid attack. Hybrid attacks are generally not as efficient as Primal or Dual attacks, but they can be effective in cases where the secret key in LWE follows a specialized distribution. In [20], by incorporating lattice reduction techniques and implementing a meet-in-the-middle (MITM) strategy, it is possible to diminish the complexity of the attack on the NTRUEncrypt private key from $2^{84.2}$ to $2^{60.3}$ for the parameter set for 80-bit security. Also, Jung Hee Cheon et al. [13] introduced a hybrid attack strategy that integrates dual lattice attacks with the MITM approach. This approach involves increasing the error size while simultaneously reducing the dimension and Hamming weights of the secret vector. As the MITM attack cost is strongly correlated with the dimension of the secret vector but less affected by error size, this trade-off significantly reduces the overall cost of the MITM attack when applying it to the LWE with sparse secrets.

4 KpqC Round 1 LWE/LWR-Based Algorithms Security Analysis

4.1 Parameters

In this section, we summarize the proposed parameters used in the underlying LWE/LWR instances in the respective schemes. For simplicity, we use the same notations as in the original specification documents.

NTRU+ Parameters. NTRU+ is based on NTRU and RLWE, and the proposed parameters used to analyze attack complexities of RLWE are as shown in Table 6. They use the quotient ring $\mathcal{R}_q = \mathbb{Z}[X]/(X^n - X^{n/2} + 1)$ for dimension $n = 2^i 3^j$ and fixed modulus $q = 3457$ for all parameters. For the RLWE secret distribution and error distribution, they utilize the uniform distribution on $(0,1)$ and the centered binomial distribution in their specification document and reference implementation, respectively.

Table 6. NTRU+ Proposed parameter sets

	576	768	864	1152
n	576	768	864	1152
q	3457	3457	3457	3457
security level	I	I	III	V

SMAUG Parameters. SMAUG is based on MLWE/MLWR, and the parameters used for the attack on MLWE/MLWR are as shown in Table 7. They use the quotient ring $\mathcal{R}_q = \mathbb{Z}_q[X]/(X^n + 1)$ for power of 2 integer n and positive integer q. The secret keys for each LWE and LWR instance, denoted as s and r are sampled as sparse vectors with fixed Hamming weights, where the Hamming weights are denoted as h_s, h_r, respectively. σ is the standard deviation of the discrete Gaussian distribution to sample the errors in LWE.

Table 7. SMAUG Proposed parameter sets

	SMAUG128	SMAUG192	SMAUG256
n	512	768	1280
m	512	768	1280
q	1024	1024	1024
p	256	256	256
h_r	132	147	140
h_s	140	150	145
σ	1.0625	1.0625	1.0625
security level	I	III	V

TiGER Parameters. TiGER is based on RLWR/RLWE and the parameters used for the attack are as shown in Table 8. They use the quotient ring $\mathcal{R}_q = \mathbb{Z}_q[X]/(X^n + 1)$ for a power of 2 integer n and a positive integer q. k_1 and k_2 are power of 2's and represents the modulus used for ciphertext compression. h_s and h_r are the Hamming weights of the secret key and the ephemeral secret used for encapsulation. h_e is the Hamming weight of the LWE error.

Table 8. TiGER Proposed parameter sets

	TiGER128	TiGER192	TiGER256
n	512	1024	1024
m	512	1024	1024
q	256	256	256
p	128	64	128
h_r	128	84	198
h_s	160	84	198
h_e	32	84	32
k_1	64	64	128
k_2	64	4	4
security level	I	III	V

HAETAE Parameters. HAETAE is based on MLWE/MSIS and the parameters used for the attack are as shown in Table 9. They use the quotient ring $\mathcal{R}_q = \mathbb{Z}_q[X]/(X^n + 1)$ for positive integers n and q which are set to 256 and 64513, respectively, for all parameter sets. (k, ℓ) denotes the matrix size of the module structure. They select the private key from the uniform distribution over $[-\eta, \eta]$, and τ refers to the Hamming weight of the binary challenge.

Table 9. HAETAE Proposed parameter sets

	HAETAE120	HAETAE180	HAETAE260
n	256	256	256
q	64513	64513	64513
(k, ℓ)	$(2, 4)$	$(3, 6)$	$(4, 7)$
η	1	1	1
τ	39	49	60
security level	I	III	V

NCC-Sign Parameters. NCC-Sign is based on RLWE/RSIS and the parameters used for the attack are shown in Table 10. They use the ring $\mathcal{R}_q = \mathbb{Z}_q[X]/(X^p - X - 1)$ for prime numbers p and q. Also, they select the private key from the distribution over $[-\eta, \eta]$, and τ refers to the number of nonzero coefficients in $\{-1, 0, 1\}$.

Table 10. NCC-Sign Proposed parameter sets

	I	III	V
p	1021	1429	1913
q	8339581	8376649	8343469
η	2	2	2
τ	25	29	32
security level	I	III	V

4.2   Analysis Using the Lattice Estimator

In this section, we report our estimated results for the lattice attacks in [3] outlined in Sect. 3. The results of security analysis using the Lattice Estimator for NTRU+, SMAUG, TiGER, HAETAE, and NCC-Sign schemes are shown in Table 11, Table 12, Table 13, Table 14, Table 15, Table 16, and Table 17.

The column names in each table, "sec" and "β" represent classical security in bits and BKZ block size respectively. For the BKZ time complexity estimation, we use the Core-SVP model except Table 17. Among the row names in each table, "usvp" refers to the attack complexity for the Primal attack described in Sect. 3.3, and bdd, bdd_hybrid, bdd_mitm_hybrid attacks are variations of the Primal attack. Also, "dual" means the attack complexity for the Dual attack explained in Sect. 3.2, and dual_hybrid, dual_mitm_hybrid are variations of the Dual attack. For more details about the attacks, we recommend to see [3]. We remark that when analyzing the security of SMAUG and TiGER, we measured attack complexities for both LWE and LWR instances, and reported the minimum value. In the case of NTRU+, since it does not use a sparse secret key in the LWE instance, during the security analysis, we did not measure the attack complexities for bdd_mitm_hybrid and dual_mitm_hybrid, which are expected to be less efficient compared to other attacks.

In the case of NTRU+, Table 11 shows dual_hybrid has the smallest attack complexity. In Table 12, overall attack complexities have increased, and usvp has the smallest complexity. In the case of SMAUG, according to Table 13, the most effective attack differs for each parameter set: the most effective attack for SMAUG128 is usvp, dual_hybrid for SMAUG192, and dual_hybrid for SMAUG256. In the case of TiGER, as listed in Table 14, TiGER128 exhibits the smallest complexity for Primal attack usvp. For TiGER192 and TiGER256, dual_hybrid is the most effective method.

In the case of HAETAE, in Table 15, for the claimed security of 120 bits and 260 bits, the most effective attack method is dual_hybrid followed by usvp. For the security of 180 bits, usvp has the smallest attack complexity. In the case of NCC-Sign, Table 16 and Table 17 show similar results. In Table 16, usvp is confirmed to have the smallest attack complexity, while in Table 17, bdd exhibits the smallest attack complexity.

Table 11. NTRU+ Security Estimation

	576		768		864		1152	
	sec	β	sec	β	sec	β	sec	β
usvp	109.8	376	156.5	536	180.2	617	252.9	866
bdd	110.8	375	157.4	535	181.0	617	253.7	865
bdd_hybrid	111.0	375	157.4	535	181.2	617	316.1	864
dual	114.8	393	162.4	556	186.9	640	261.3	895
dual_hybrid	108.9	372	153.0	523	175.4	599	243.5	833

Table 12. NTRU+ Security Estimation _ rev

	576		768		864		1152	
	sec	β	sec	β	sec	β	sec	β
usvp	115.9	397	164.7	564	189.8	650	266.0	911
bdd	116.9	397	165.7	563	190.7	649	266.9	911
bdd_hybrid	193.2	397	264.1	563	300.0	649	408.9	911
dual	120.9	414	171.1	586	196.5	673	274.8	941
dual_hybrid	117.2	400	164.9	564	189.2	647	263.4	901

Table 13. SMAUG Security Estimation

	128		192		256	
	sec	β	sec	β	sec	β
usvp	120.0	411	187.2	641	316.2	1083
bdd	120.9	411	188.5	642	318.4	1090
bdd_hybrid	121.3	411	189.0	642	288.5	674
bdd_mitm_hybrid	166.5	410	221.0	496	277.8	680
dual	125.9	431	195.3	669	328.2	1124
dual_hybrid	122.7	399	180.2	575	259.2	749

Table 14. TiGER Security Estimation

	128		192		256	
	sec	β	sec	β	sec	β
usvp	130.5	447	277.4	950	279.7	958
bdd	131.4	445	281.5	964	280.7	958
bdd_hybrid	131.4	445	220.2	472	280.7	958
bdd_mitm_hybrid	173.8	419	212.7	503	316.5	730
dual	137.5	471	290.5	995	291.7	999
dual_hybrid	131.9	428	206.1	535	262.0	835

Table 15. HAETAE Security Estimation

	120		180		260	
	sec	β	sec	β	sec	β
usvp	125.6	430	238.0	815	290.2	994
bdd	126.6	429	238.8	815	291.1	993
bdd_hybrid	126.6	429	238.8	815	291.1	993
bdd_mitm_hybrid	219.3	429	390.9	815	472.7	993
dual	130.5	447	245.6	841	298.4	1022
dual_hybrid	126.4	432	236.1	808	287.1	982

Table 16. NCC-Sign Security Estimation with the Core-SVP model

	1		3		5	
	sec	β	sec	β	sec	β
usvp	123.2	422	190.1	651	273.3	936
bdd	124.6	421	191.0	651	274.3	935
bdd_hybrid	124.6	421	191.0	651	274.3	935
bdd_mitm_hybrid	270.0	421	406.1	651	588.6	935
dual	126.4	433	194.2	665	278.6	954
dual_hybrid	124.8	427	191.1	654	273.6	937

Table 17. NCC-Sign Security Estimation without the Core-SVP model as they evaluated in the Round 1 Proposal (less conservative)

	1		3		5	
	sec	β	sec	β	sec	β
usvp	149.7	422	213.9	651	294,0	936
bdd	147.7	413	211.5	641	291.3	924
bdd_hybrid	147.7	413	211.5	641	291.3	924
bdd_mitm_hybrid	261.8	421	394.9	651	574.2	935
dual	153.8	433	219.6	668	302.4	962
dual_hybrid	150.5	421	214.9	651	295.5	937

4.3   Comparisons with the Claimed Security

We present the comparison of the claimed vs. estimated (classical) security in bits for each scheme in Fig. 1a, Fig. 1b, Fig. 1c, Fig. 1d, and Fig. 1e.

For NTRU+, we measured the security based on both the specification document and the implementation. The result from the implementation was similar to the claimed security in the proposal document. However, the result based on the specification document indicated lower security than the implementa-

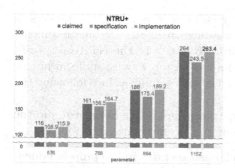

(a) Comparison of the claimed security and estimated results in which estimated results are measured for the versions of specification and implementation for NTRU+, respectively

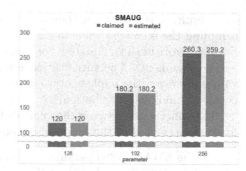

(b) Comparson of the claimed security and estimated results for SMAUG parameters

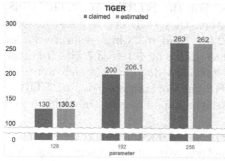

(c) Comparison of the claimed security and estimated results for TiGER parameters

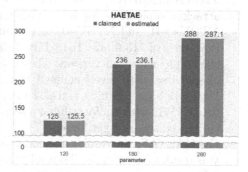

(d) Comparison of the claimed security and estimated results for HAETAE parameters

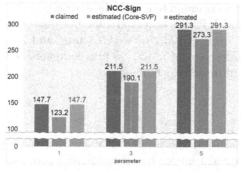

(e) Comparison of the claimed security and estimated results with Core-SVP and without Core-SVP for NCC-Sign parameters

Fig. 1. Comparisons of Claimed and Estimated Security for the Respective Algorithms

tion result. The reason for these different results occurred from the process of sampling the secret 'r' value in the LWE instances using the H function in the Encaps algorithm in NTRU+ (See Algorithm 6 and 9 in the NTRU+ specification document). The specification samples the secret 'r' with uniform binary values, however, the implementation samples it with ternary values following the centered binomial distribution.

The differences between the analysis by using the Lattice Estimator and the analysis presented in the proposal document can be summarized as follows.

- For the SMAUG1280 parameters, the claimed security in the proposal document is of 260.3 bits, but the estimated result using Lattice Estimator resulted in an attack amount of 259.2 bits.
- In the case of TiGER256(Security level V), the classical security of 263 bits was claimed, but the estimated result was 262.0 bits.
- The estimated results of NTRU+ were found different from the claimed attack complexities for all parameters. For the NTRU+576, NTRU+768, NTRU+864, and NTRU+1152 parameters, they each satisfy classical security levels of 115.9 bits, 164.7 bits, 189.2 bits, and 263.4 bits, respectively, for the implementation version. These values differ by 0.1 to 3.7 bits from the classical security levels claimed in the proposal document, which were 116 bits, 161 bits, 188 bits, and 264 bits. For the document version of NTRU+ using LWE with uniform binary secrets, the gaps between the claimed and estimated security get larger.
- For HAETAE, the result claimed in the proposal document and security analysis results were similar about all parameters, with an error range of less than 1 bit.
- In the case of NCC-Sign, the proposal document provided results of security analysis without using the Core-SVP model and the estimations using the Lattice Estimator were found to match these results. When we measured using the Core-SVP model, it was observed that parameters I, III, and V achieve classical security levels of 123.2 bits, 190.1 bits, and 273.3 bits, respectively. This represents differences of 18 to 24.5 bits compared to the results presented in the NCC-Sign proposal document.

5   Conclusion

In this paper, we discussed the results of a security analysis using the Lattice Estimator for five Round 1 lattice-based candidates proposed in the KpqC Competition. It was found that NTRU+ had differences of approximately 0.1 to 3.7 bit compared to the claimed results of security analysis for all parameters when using the centered binomial distribution as a secret distribution in LWE. For SMAUG and TiGER, the classical security of parameters in the security level V was observed to differ by approximately 1 bit from the estimated results. In the case of HAETAE and NCC-Sign, we confirmed that the claimed parameters are closely similar to the security analysis results. We also remark that the Lattice Estimator does not exhaustively cover all recent attacks for LWE including [27].

We will analyze the KpqC Round 1 lattice-based schemes further by applying various recent LWE attacks for future works.

Acknowledgement. This work is the result of commissioned research project supported by the affiliated institute of ETRI [2023-080].

References

1. Ajtai, M.: Generating hard instances of lattice problems (extended abstract). In: Proceedings of the Twenty-Eighth Annual ACM Symposium on Theory of Computing, pp. 99–108. STOC '96, Association for Computing Machinery, New York, NY, USA (1996). https://doi.org/10.1145/237814.237838
2. Albrecht, M.R., Göpfert, F., Virdia, F., Wunderer, T.: Revisiting the expected cost of solving uSVP and applications to LWE. In: Takagi, T., Peyrin, T. (eds.) Advances in Cryptology – ASIACRYPT 2017. ASIACRYPT 2017. LNCS, vol. 10624, pp. 297–322. Springer, Cham (2017). https://doi.org/10.1007/978-3-319-70694-8_11
3. Albrecht, M.R., Player, R., Scott, S.: On the concrete hardness of learning with errors. Cryptology ePrint Archive, Paper 2015/046 (2015). https://eprint.iacr.org/2015/046
4. Alkim, E., Ducas, L., Pöppelmann, T., Schwabe, P.: Post-quantum key exchange— a new hope. In: 25th USENIX Security Symposium (USENIX Security 16), pp. 327–343. USENIX Association, Austin, TX, August 2016. https://www.usenix.org/conference/usenixsecurity16/technical-sessions/presentation/alkim
5. Baan, H., et al.: Round5: Compact and Fast Post-quantum Public-Key Encryption, pp. 83–102, July 2019. https://doi.org/10.1007/978-3-030-25510-7_5
6. Banerjee, A., Peikert, C., Rosen, A.: Pseudorandom functions and lattices. In: Pointcheval, D., Johansson, T. (eds.) Advances in Cryptology – EUROCRYPT 2012. EUROCRYPT 2012. LNCS, vol. 7237, pp. 719–737. Springer, Berlin, Heidelberg (2012). https://doi.org/10.1007/978-3-642-29011-4_42
7. Bernstein, D.J., Chuengsatiansup, C., Lange, T., van Vredendaal, C.: NTRU prime: reducing attack surface at low cost. Cryptology ePrint Archive, Paper 2016/461 (2016). https://eprint.iacr.org/2016/461
8. Boudgoust, K., Jeudy, C., Roux-Langlois, A., Wen, W.: On the hardness of module-LWE with binary secret. In: Paterson, K.G. (eds.) Topics in Cryptology – CT-RSA 2021. CT-RSA 2021. LNCS, vol. 12704, pp. 503–526. Springer, Cham (2021). https://doi.org/10.1007/978-3-030-75539-3_21
9. Brakerski, Z., Langlois, A., Peikert, C., Regev, O., Stehlé, D.: Classical hardness of learning with errors (2013)
10. Center, K.R.: KPQC competition round 1. https://www.kpqc.or.kr/competition.html. Accessed June 2023
11. Chailloux, A., Loyer, J.: Lattice sieving via quantum random walks (2021)
12. Chen, Y., Nguyen, P.Q.: Bkz 2.0: Better lattice security estimates. In: Lee, D.H., Wang, X. (eds.) Advances in Cryptology – ASIACRYPT 2011. ASIACRYPT 2011. LNCS, vol. 7073, pp. 1–20. Springer, Berlin, Heidelberg (2011). https://doi.org/10.1007/978-3-642-25385-0_1
13. Cheon, J.H., Hhan, M., Hong, S., Son, Y.: A hybrid of dual and meet-in-the-middle attack on sparse and ternary secret LWE. IEEE Access **7**, 89497–89506 (2019). https://doi.org/10.1109/ACCESS.2019.2925425

14. Cheon, J.H., Kim, D., Lee, J., Song, Y.: Lizard: cut off the tail! A practical post-quantum public-key encryption from LWE and LWR. In: Catalano, D., De Prisco, R. (eds.) Security and Cryptography for Networks. SCN 2018. LNCS, vol. 11035, pp. 160–177. Springer, Cham (2018). https://doi.org/10.1007/978-3-319-98113-0_9
15. Ducas, L., Durmus, A., Lepoint, T., Lyubashevsky, V.: Lattice signatures and bimodal gaussians.. In: Canetti, R., Garay, J.A. (eds.) Advances in Cryptology – CRYPTO 2013. CRYPTO 2013. LNCS, vol. 8042, pp. 40–56. Springer, Berlin, Heidelberg (2013). https://doi.org/10.1007/978-3-642-40041-4_3
16. Ducas, L., et al.: Crystals-dilithium: a lattice-based digital signature scheme. IACR Transactions on Cryptographic Hardware and Embedded Systems, pp. 238–268 (2018)
17. Duman, J., Hövelmanns, K., Kiltz, E., Lyubashevsky, V., Seiler, G., Unruh, D.: A thorough treatment of highly-efficient NTRU instantiations. In: Boldyreva, A., Kolesnikov, V. (eds.) Public-Key Cryptography – PKC 2023. PKC 2023. LNCS, vol. 13940, pp. 65–94. Springer, Cham (2023). https://doi.org/10.1007/978-3-031-31368-4_3
18. Fujisaki, E., Okamoto, T.: Secure integration of asymmetric and symmetric encryption schemes. In: Wiener, M. (eds.) Advances in Cryptology – CRYPTO' 99. CRYPTO 1999. LNCS, vol. 1666, pp. 537–554. Springer, Berlin, Heidelberg (1999). https://doi.org/10.1007/3-540-48405-1_34
19. Hoffstein, J., Pipher, J., Silverman, J.H.: NTRU: a ring-based public key cryptosystem. In: Buhler, J.P. (eds.) Algorithmic Number Theory. ANTS 1998. LNCS, vol. 1423, pp. 267–288. Springer, Berlin, Heidelberg (1998). https://doi.org/10.1007/BFb0054868
20. Howgrave-Graham, N.: A hybrid lattice-reduction and meet-in-the-middle attack against NTRU. In: Menezes, A. (eds.) Advances in Cryptology – CRYPTO 2007. CRYPTO 2007. LNCS, vol. 4622, pp. 150–169. Springer, Berlin, Heidelberg (2007). https://doi.org/10.1007/978-3-540-74143-5_9
21. Lee, J., Kim, D., Lee, H., Lee, Y., Cheon, J.H.: Rlizard: post-quantum key encapsulation mechanism for IoT devices. IEEE Access 7, 2080–2091 (2018)
22. Lindner, R., Peikert, C.: Better key sizes (and attacks) for lwe-based encryption. Cryptology ePrint Archive, Paper 2010/613 (2010). https://eprint.iacr.org/2010/613
23. Lyubashevsky, V.: Fiat-shamir with aborts: applications to lattice and factoring-based signatures. In: Matsui, M. (eds.) Advances in Cryptology – ASIACRYPT 2009. ASIACRYPT 2009. LNCS, vol. 5912, pp. 598–616. Springer, Berlin, Heidelberg (2009). https://doi.org/10.1007/978-3-642-10366-7_35
24. Lyubashevsky, V.: Lattice signatures without trapdoors. In: Pointcheval, D., Johansson, T. (eds.) Advances in Cryptology – EUROCRYPT 2012. EUROCRYPT 2012. LNCS, vol. 7237, pp. 738–755. Springer, Berlin, Heidelberg (2012). https://doi.org/10.1007/978-3-642-29011-4_43
25. Lyubashevsky, V., Peikert, C., Regev, O.: On ideal lattices and learning with errors over rings. J. ACM (JACM) 60(6), 1–35 (2013)
26. Lyubashevsky, V., Seiler, G.: NTTRU: truly fast NTRU using NTT. Cryptology ePrint Archive (2019)
27. May, A.: How to meet ternary LWE keys. Cryptology ePrint Archive, Paper 2021/216 (2021). https://eprint.iacr.org/2021/216
28. NIST: Post-quantum cryptography. https://csrc.nist.gov/projects/post-quantum-cryptography. Accessed June 2023
29. NIST: Standardization of additional digital signature schemes. https://csrc.nist.gov/projects/pqc-dig-sig/standardization. Accessed August 2023

30. Pointcheval, D., Johansson, T.: Advances in cryptology - EUROCRYPT 2012 : 31st Annual International Conference on the Theory and Applications of Cryptographic Techniques, Cambridge, UK, 15–19 April 2012, Proceedings. LNCS, vol. 7237, EUROCRYPT (31st : 2012 : Cambridge, England), Springer, Berlin (2012). https://doi.org/10.1007/978-3-642-29011-4

31. Regev, O.: On lattices, learning with errors, random linear codes, and cryptography. J. ACM **56**(6) (2009). https://doi.org/10.1145/1568318.1568324

32. Shor, P.W.: Polynomial-time algorithms for prime factorization and discrete logarithms on a quantum computer. SIAM J. Comput. **26**(5), 1484–1509 (1997). https://doi.org/10.1137/s0097539795293172

On the security of REDOG

Tanja Lange[(✉)], Alex Pellegrini[(✉)], and Alberto Ravagnani[(✉)]

Eindhoven University of Technology, Eindhoven, The Netherlands
tanja@hyperelliptic.org, alex.pellegrini@live.com, a.ravagnani@tue.nl

Abstract. We analyze REDOG, a public-key encryption system submitted to the Korean competition on post-quantum cryptography. REDOG is based on rank-metric codes. We prove its incorrectness and attack its implementation, providing an efficient message recovery attack. Furthermore, we show that the security of REDOG is much lower than claimed. We then proceed to mitigate these issues and provide two approaches to fix the decryption issue, one of which also leads to better security.

Keywords: post-quantum crypto · code-based- crypto · rank-metric codes

1 Introduction

This paper analyzes the security of the REinforced modified Dual-Ouroboros based on Gabidulin codes, REDOG [KHL+22a], a public-key encryption system submitted to KpqC, the Korean competition on post-quantum cryptography. REDOG is a code-based cryptosystem using rank-metric codes, aiming at providing a rank-metric alternative to Hamming-metric code-based cryptosystems.

Rank-metric codes were introduced by Delsarte [Del78] and independently rediscovered by Gabidulin [Gab85] in 1985, who focused on those that are linear over a field extension. Gabidulin, Paramonov, and Tretjakov [GPT91] proposed their use for cryptography in 1991. The GPT system was attacked by Overbeck [Ove05, Ove08] who showed *structural* attacks, permitting recovery of the private key from the public key.

During the mid 2010s new cryptosystems using rank-metric codes were developed such as Ouroboros [DGZ17] and the first round of the NIST competition on post-quantum cryptography saw 5 systems based on rank-metric codes: LAKE [ABD+17a], LOCKER [ABD+17b], McNie [GKK+17], Ouroboros-R [AAB+17a], RQC [AAB+17b]. For further information about all these systems

---

Author list in alphabetical order; see https://www.ams.org/profession/leaders/culture/CultureStatement04.pdf. This work was funded in part by the Deutsche Forschungsgemeinschaft (DFG, German Research Foundation) under Germany's Excellence Strategy—EXC 2092 CASA—390781972 "Cyber Security in the Age of Large-Scale Adversaries" and by the Netherlands Organisation for Scientific Research (NWO) under grants OCENW.KLEIN.539 and VI.Vidi.203.045. Date: 2023.11.15. For the full version see [LPR23].

H. Seo and S. Kim (Eds.): ICISC 2023, LNCS 14562, pp. 282–305, 2024.
https://doi.org/10.1007/978-981-97-1238-0_15

see NIST's Round-1 Submissions page. Gaborit announced an attack weakening McNie and the McNie authors adjusted their parameters. A further attack was published in [LT18] and NIST did not advance McNie into the second round of the competition.

ROLLO, a merger of LAKE, LOCKER and Ouroboros-R, and RQC made it into the the second round but got broken near the end of it by significant advances in the cryptanalysis of rank-metric codes and the MinRank problem in general, see [BBB+20] and [BBC+20]. In their report at the end of round 2 [AASA+20], NIST wrote an encouraging note on rank-metric codes: "Despite the development of algebraic attacks, NIST believes rank-based cryptography should continue to be researched. The rank metric cryptosystems offer a nice alternative to traditional hamming metric codes with comparable bandwidth." (capitalization as in the original).

Kim, Kim, Galvez, and Kim [KKGK21] proposed a new rank-metric system in 2021 which was then analyzed by Lau, Tan, and Prabowo in [LTP21] who also proposed some modifications to the issues they found. REDOG closely resembles the system in [LTP21] and uses the same parameters.

Our contribution In this paper we expose weaknesses of REDOG and show that the system, as described in the documentation, is incorrect. To start with, we prove that REDOG does not decrypt correctly. The documentation and [LTP21] contain an incorrect estimate of the rank of an element which causes the input to the decoding step to have too large rank. The system uses Gabidulin codes [Gab85] which are MRD (Maximum Rank Distance) codes, meaning that vectors with errors of rank larger than half the minimum distance will decode to a different codeword, thus causing incorrect decryption in the REDOG system.

As a second contribution we attack ciphertexts produced by REDOG's reference implementation. We show that we can use techniques from the Hamming metric to obtain a message-recovery attack. This stems from a choice in the implementation which avoids the above-mentioned decryption problem. However, the errors introduced in the ciphertext have a specific shape which allows us to apply basic techniques of Information Set Decoding (ISD) over the Hamming metric to recover the message in seconds.

As a third contribution, we show that, independently of the special choice of error vectors in the implementation, the security of the cryptosystem is lower than the claimed security level. The main effect comes from a group of attacks published in [BBC+20] which the REDOG designers had not taken into account. A smaller effect comes from a systematic scan through all attack parameters.

Finally, we provide two ways to make REDOG's decryption correct. The first is a minimal change to fix the system by changing the space from which some matrix P^{-1} is chosen in a way that differs from the choice in REDOG and avoids the issue mentioned above. However, this still requires choosing much larger parameters to deal with our third contribution. The second way makes a different change to REDOG which improves the resistance to attacks while also fixing the decryption issue. We show that, using this strategy, not only are

REDOG's parameters sufficient to reach any claimed security level, but they provide security abundantly beyond each level, allowing room for an eventual optimization. Note, however, that these estimates are obtained from big-$\mathcal{O}$ complexity estimates, putting all constants to 1 and lower-order terms to 0, and thus underestimate the security.

2   Preliminaries and background notions

This section gives the necessary background on rank-metric codes for the rest of the paper. Let $\{\alpha_1, \ldots, \alpha_m\}$ be a basis of $\mathbb{F}_{q^m}$ over $\mathbb{F}_q$. Write $x \in \mathbb{F}_{q^m}$ uniquely as $x = \sum_{i=1}^{m} X_i \alpha_i$, $X_i \in \mathbb{F}_q$ for all i. So x can be represented as $(X_1, \ldots, X_m) \in \mathbb{F}_q^m$. We will call this the *vector representation* of x. Extend this process to $\mathbf{v} = (v_1, \ldots, v_n) \in \mathbb{F}_{q^m}^n$ defining a map $\mathsf{Mat} : \mathbb{F}_{q^m}^n \to \mathbb{F}_q^{m \times n}$ by:

$$\mathbf{v} \mapsto \begin{bmatrix} V_{11} & V_{21} & \ldots & V_{n1} \\ V_{12} & V_{22} & \ldots & V_{n2} \\ \vdots & \vdots & \ddots & \vdots \\ V_{1m} & V_{2m} & \ldots & V_{nm} \end{bmatrix}.$$

Definition 2.1. *The rank weight of* $\mathbf{v} \in \mathbb{F}_{q^m}^n$ *is defined as* $\mathsf{wt}_R(\mathbf{v}) := \mathsf{rk}_q(\mathsf{Mat}(\mathbf{v}))$ *and the rank distance between* $\mathbf{v}, \mathbf{w} \in \mathbb{F}_{q^m}^n$ *is* $d_R(\mathbf{v}, \mathbf{w}) := \mathsf{wt}_R(\mathbf{v} - \mathbf{w})$.

Remark 2.2. It can be shown that the rank distance does not depend on the choice of the basis of $\mathbb{F}_{q^m}$ over $\mathbb{F}_q$. In particular, the choice of the basis is irrelevant for the results in this document.

When talking about the space spanned by $\mathbf{v} \in \mathbb{F}_{q^m}^n$, denoted as $\langle \mathbf{v} \rangle$, we mean the $\mathbb{F}_q$-subspace of $\mathbb{F}_q^m$ spanned by the columns of $\mathsf{Mat}(\mathbf{v})$.

For completeness, we introduce the Hamming weight and the Hamming distance. These notions will be used in our message recovery attack against REDOG's implementation.

The *Hamming weight* of a vector $\mathbf{v} \in \mathbb{F}_{q^m}^n$ is defined as $\mathsf{wt}_H(\mathbf{v}) := \#\{i \in \{1, \ldots, n\} \mid v_i \neq 0\}$ and the Hamming distance between vectors $\mathbf{v}, \mathbf{w} \in \mathbb{F}_{q^m}^n$ is defined as $d_H(\mathbf{v}, \mathbf{w}) := \mathsf{wt}_H(\mathbf{v} - \mathbf{w})$.

Let $D = d_R$ or $D = d_H$. Then an $[n, k, d]$-code C with respect to D over $\mathbb{F}_{q^m}$ is a k-dimensional $\mathbb{F}_{q^m}$-linear subspace of $\mathbb{F}_{q^m}^n$ with *minimum distance*

$$d := \min_{\mathbf{a}, \mathbf{b} \in C, \, \mathbf{a} \neq \mathbf{b}} D(\mathbf{a}, \mathbf{b})$$

and *correction capability* $\lfloor (d - 1)/2 \rfloor$. If $D = d_R$ (resp. $D = d_H$) then the code C is also called a *rank-metric* (resp. *Hamming-metric*) code. All codes in this document are linear over the field extension $\mathbb{F}_{q^m}$.

We say that G is a *generator matrix* of C if its rows span C. We say that H is a *parity check matrix* of C if C is the right-kernel of H.

A very well-known family of rank metric codes are *Gabidulin codes* [Gab85], which have $d = n - k + 1$.

In this paper we can mostly use these codes as a black box, knowing that there is an efficient decoding algorithm using the parity-check matrix of the code and decoding vectors with errors of rank up to $\lfloor (d-1)/2 \rfloor$.

A final definition necessary to understand REDOG is that of isometries.

Definition 2.3. *Consider vectors in $\mathbb{F}_{q^m}^n$. An* isometry *with respect to the rank metric is a matrix $P \in \mathsf{GL}_n(\mathbb{F}_{q^m})$ satisfying that $\mathsf{wt}_R(\mathbf{v}P) = \mathsf{wt}_R(\mathbf{v})$ for any $\mathbf{v} \in \mathbb{F}_{q^m}^n$.*

Obviously matrices $P \in \mathsf{GL}_n(\mathbb{F}_q)$ are isometries as $\mathbb{F}_q$-linear combinations of the coordinates of $\mathbf{v}$ do not increase the rank and the rank does not decrease as P is invertible. The rank does also not change under scalar multiplication by some $\alpha \in \mathbb{F}_{q^m}^*$: $\mathsf{wt}_R(\alpha\mathbf{v}) = \mathsf{wt}_R(\mathbf{v})$. Note that the latter corresponds to multiplication by $P = \alpha I_n$.

Berger [Ber03] showed that any isometry is obtained by composing these two options.

Theorem 2.4. *[Ber03, Theorem 1] The isometry group of $\mathbb{F}_{q^m}^n$ for the rank metric is generated by scalar multiplications by elements in $\mathbb{F}_{q^m}^*$ and elements of $\mathsf{GL}_n(\mathbb{F}_q)$. This group is isomorphic to the product group $\left(\mathbb{F}_{q^m}^* / \mathbb{F}_q^* \right) \times \mathsf{GL}_n(\mathbb{F}_q)$.*

3   System specification

This section introduces the specification of REDOG. We follow the notation of [LTP21], with minor changes.

The system parameters are positive integers $(n, k, \ell, q, m, r, \lambda, t)$, with $\ell < n$ and $\lambda t \leq r \leq \lfloor (n-k)/2 \rfloor$, as well as a hash function $\mathsf{hash} : \mathbb{F}_{q^m}^{2n-k} \to \mathbb{F}_{q^m}^\ell$.

KeyGen:
1. Select $H = (H_1 \mid H_2)$, $H_2 \in \mathsf{GL}_{n-k}(\mathbb{F}_{q^m})$, a parity check matrix of a $[2n-k, n]$ Gabidulin code, with syndrome decoder Φ correcting r errors.
2. Select a full rank matrix $M \in \mathbb{F}_{q^m}^{\ell \times n}$ and isometry $P \in \mathbb{F}_{q^m}^{n \times n}$ (w.r.t. the rank metric).
3. Select a λ-dimensional subspace $\Lambda \subset \mathbb{F}_{q^m}$, seen as $\mathbb{F}_q$-linear space, containing 1 and select $S^{-1} \in \mathsf{GL}_{n-k}(\Lambda)$; see Section 4 for the definition.
4. Compute $F = MP^{-1}H_1^T \left(H_2^T \right)^{-1} S$ and publish the public key $\mathsf{pk} = (M, F)$. Store the secret key $\mathsf{sk} = (P, H, S, \Phi)$.

Encrypt $(\mathbf{m} \in \mathbb{F}_{q^m}^\ell, \mathsf{pk})$
1. Generate uniformly random $\mathbf{e} = (\mathbf{e}_1, \mathbf{e}_2) \in \mathbb{F}_{q^m}^{2n-k}$ with $\mathsf{wt}_R(\mathbf{e}) = t$, $\mathbf{e}_1 \in \mathbb{F}_{q^m}^n$ and $\mathbf{e}_2 \in \mathbb{F}_{q^m}^{n-k}$.
2. Compute $\mathbf{m}' = \mathbf{m} + \mathsf{hash}(\mathbf{e})$.
3. Compute $\mathbf{c}_1 = \mathbf{m}'M + \mathbf{e}_1$ and $\mathbf{c}_2 = \mathbf{m}'F + \mathbf{e}_2$ and send $(\mathbf{c}_1, \mathbf{c}_2)$.

Decrypt $((\mathbf{c}_1, \mathbf{c}_2), \mathsf{sk})$
1. Compute $\mathbf{c}' = \mathbf{c}_1 P^{-1} H_1^T - \mathbf{c}_2 S^{-1} H_2^T = \mathbf{e}' H^T$ where the vector $\mathbf{e}' := (\mathbf{e}_1 P^{-1}, -\mathbf{e}_2 S^{-1})$.
2. Decode $\mathbf{c}'$ using Φ to obtain $\mathbf{e}'$, recover $\mathbf{e} = (\mathbf{e}_1, \mathbf{e}_2)$ using P and S.
3. Solve $\mathbf{m}'M = \mathbf{c}_1 - \mathbf{e}_1$. Output $\mathbf{m} = \mathbf{m}' - \mathsf{hash}(\mathbf{e})$.

Suggested parameters We list the suggested parameters of REDOG for 128,192 and 256 bits of security, following [KHL+22a] submitted to KpqC.

Table 1. Suggested parameters; see [KHL+22a].

Security parameter	$(n, k, \ell, q, m, r, \lambda, t)$
128	$(44, 8, 37, 2, 83, 18, 3, 6)$
192	$(58, 10, 49, 2, 109, 24, 3, 8)$
256	$(72, 12, 61, 2, 135, 30, 3, 10)$

4   Incorrectness of decryption

This section shows that decryption typically fails for the version of REDOG specified in [KHL+22a,LTP21]. The novelty of this specification, compared to that introduced in [KKGK21], lies in the selection of the invertible matrix S^{-1} in Step 3, which is selected with the property that $S^{-1} \in \mathsf{GL}_{n-k}(\Lambda)$, where Λ is a λ-dimensional $\mathbb{F}_q$-subspace of $\mathbb{F}_{q^m}$. This method has been first proposed by Loidreau in [Loi17], but it appears to be incorrectly applied in REDOG. Before providing more details about this claim and proving the incorrectness of REDOG's decryption process, we will shed some light on the object $\mathsf{GL}_{n-k}(\Lambda)$. Unlike the notation suggests, this is not a group, but a potentially unstructured subset of $\mathsf{GL}_{n-k}(\mathbb{F}_{q^m})$ defined as in the next paragraph.

Let $\{1, \alpha_2, \ldots, \alpha_\lambda\} \subset \mathbb{F}_{q^m}$ be a set of elements that are $\mathbb{F}_q$-linearly independent. Let $\Lambda \subset \mathbb{F}_{q^m}$ be the set of $\mathbb{F}_q$-linear combinations of these α_i's. This set forms an $\mathbb{F}_q$-linear vectorspace. Now, $S^{-1} \in \mathsf{GL}_{n-k}(\Lambda)$ is defined to mean that S is an invertible $(n-k) \times (n-k)$ matrix with the property that the entries of S^{-1} are elements of Λ. Note that such an S exists because $\lambda \geq 1$ by assumption. The REDOG documentation [KHL+22a] points out that this does not imply that $S \in \mathsf{GL}_{n-k}(\Lambda)$, hence, despite what the notation may suggest, $\mathsf{GL}_{n-k}(\Lambda)$ is not a group in general.

We continue by giving a proof, and an easy generalization for any q, of [Loi17, Proposition 1].

Proposition 4.1. *Let λ, t, n be positive integers such that $\lambda t \leq n$, $A \in \mathsf{GL}_n(\Lambda)$ where $\Lambda \subset \mathbb{F}_{q^m}$ is a λ-dimensional subspace of $\mathbb{F}_{q^m}$, and $\mathbf{x} \in \mathbb{F}_{q^m}^n$ with $\mathsf{wt}_R(\mathbf{x}) = t$. Then*

$$\mathsf{wt}_R(\mathbf{x}A) \leq \lambda t.$$

Proof. Let Γ be the subspace of $\mathbb{F}_{q^m}$ generated by the entries of $\mathbf{x} = (x_1, \ldots, x_n)$. Since Γ has dimension t, we can write $\Gamma = \langle y_1, \ldots, y_t \rangle$ with $y_i \in \mathbb{F}_{q^m}$. Similarly for Λ, we can write $\Lambda = \langle \alpha_1, \ldots, \alpha_\lambda \rangle$ with $\alpha_i \in \mathbb{F}_{q^m}$. Express $\mathbf{x}A$ as

$$\mathbf{x}A = \left(\sum_{i=1}^{n} x_i A_{i,1}, \ldots, \sum_{i=1}^{n} x_i A_{i,n} \right).$$

Fix $j \in \{1, \ldots, n\}$. Then

$$(\mathbf{x}A)_j = \sum_{i=1}^{n} x_i A_{i,j} = \sum_{i=1}^{n} \left(\left(\sum_{h=1}^{t} x_{i,h} y_h \right) \left(\sum_{k=1}^{\lambda} A_{i,j,k} \alpha_k \right) \right),$$

with $x_{i,h}, A_{i,j,k} \in \mathbb{F}_q$. By rearranging the terms we obtain

$$(\mathbf{x}A)_j = \sum_{h=1}^{t} \sum_{k=1}^{\lambda} \left(\sum_{i=1}^{n} x_{i,h} A_{i,j,k} \right) y_h \alpha_k. \qquad (1)$$

Therefore each entry of $\mathbf{x}A$ can be expressed as an $\mathbb{F}_q$-linear combination of the λt elements of the form $y_h \alpha_k$. $\qquad \square$

We will now show that REDOG typically does not decrypt correctly. In order to do so, we need some preliminary results and tools. The proof of the next lemma uses some tools from combinatorics. It computes the probability that a randomly selected t-tuple of elements of a t-dimensional vector space spans the entire space.

Lemma 4.2. *Let V be a t-dimensional subspace $V \subseteq \mathbb{F}_q^m$ and let $S \in V^s$ be a uniformly random s-tuple of elements of V. The probability $p(q, s, t)$ that $\langle S_i \mid i \in \{1, \ldots, s\} \rangle = V$ is 0 if $0 \le s < t$ and*

$$p(q, s, t) = \sum_{i=0}^{t} \begin{bmatrix} t \\ i \end{bmatrix}_q (-1)^{t-i} q^{s(i-t) + \binom{t-i}{2}} \qquad (2)$$

otherwise, where $\begin{bmatrix} t \\ i \end{bmatrix}_q$ is the q-binomial coefficient, counting the number of subspaces of dimension i of $\mathbb{F}_q^t$, and $\binom{a}{b} = 0$ for $a < b$. In particular, this probability does not depend on m or on the choice of V, but only on its dimension.

Proof. Let $(\mathcal{P}, \subseteq)$ be the poset (partially ordered set) of subspaces of $\mathbb{F}_q^m$ ordered by inclusion. Recall that the Möbius function of $\mathcal{P}$, and of any finite poset, is defined, for $A, B \in \mathcal{P}$, as

$$\mu(B, A) = \begin{cases} 1 & \text{if } B = A, \\ -\sum_{C \mid B \subseteq C \subset A} \mu(B, C) & \text{if } B \subset A, \\ 0 & \text{otherwise.} \end{cases}$$

For the poset of subspaces, the Möbius function is computed e.g. in [Sta11, Example 3.10.2] as

$$\mu(B, A) = \begin{cases} (-1)^k q^{\binom{k}{2}} & \text{if } B \subseteq A \text{ and } \dim(A) - \dim(B) = k, \\ 0 & \text{otherwise.} \end{cases} \qquad (3)$$

We want to compute the function $f : \mathcal{P} \to \mathbb{N}$ defined as

$$f(A) = \# \left\{ S \in (\mathbb{F}_q^m)^s \mid \langle S \rangle = A \right\}.$$

Clearly, if $s < \dim A$, there does not exist any s-tuple S spanning A, hence $f(A) = 0$, which gives the first case of (2). We can therefore restrict ourselves to the case $s \geq \dim A$. Define the auxiliary function $g : \mathcal{P} \to \mathbb{N}$ as

$$g(A) = \sum_{B \subseteq A} f(B)$$
$$= \#\left\{S \in \left(\mathbb{F}_q^m\right)^s \mid \langle S \rangle \subseteq A\right\}$$
$$= |A|^s = q^{s \dim A}.$$

Then by Möbius inversion we can compute:

$$f(A) = \sum_{B \subseteq A} g(B)\mu(B, A). \tag{4}$$

Splitting the sum over the dimensions, and substituting the values in Equation 3, we can obtain

$$f(V) = \sum_{i=0}^{t} \sum_{U \subseteq V, \dim U = i} g(U)\mu(U, V)$$
$$= \sum_{i=0}^{t} q^{si}(-1)^{t-i}q^{\binom{t-i}{2}} \sum_{U \subseteq V, \dim U = i} 1$$
$$= \sum_{i=0}^{t} \begin{bmatrix} t \\ i \end{bmatrix}_q (-1)^{t-i}q^{si+\binom{t-i}{2}}.$$

The probability can be computed by dividing $f(V)$ by the number of s-tuples of elements of V, that is, q^{st}. □

Remark 4.3. The probability given in Lemma 4.2 can be interpreted as the ratio of the number of surjective linear maps from $\mathbb{F}_q^s$ onto $\mathbb{F}_q^t$ over the total number of linear maps.

We next compute the probability that by truncating a rank t vector, the rank stays the same.

Theorem 4.4. *Let* $\mathbf{e} = (\mathbf{e}_1, \mathbf{e}_2) \in \mathbb{F}_{q^m}^{2n-k}$, *with* $\mathbf{e}_1 \in \mathbb{F}_{q^m}^n$ *and* $\mathbf{e}_2 \in \mathbb{F}_{q^m}^{n-k}$, *be a uniformly random error with* $\mathrm{wt}_R(\mathbf{e}) = t$. *Then* $\mathrm{wt}_R(\mathbf{e}_1) = t$ *and* $\mathrm{wt}_R(\mathbf{e}_2) = t$ *with probability* $p(q, n, t)/p(q, 2n-k, t)$ *and* $p(q, n-k, t)/p(q, 2n-k, t)$ *respectively.*

Proof. By definition, the probability that $\mathrm{wt}_R(\mathbf{e}_1) = t$ is the ratio

$$\pi = \frac{\#\{\mathbf{e} \in \mathbb{F}_{q^m}^{2n-k} \mid \mathrm{wt}_R(\mathbf{e}) = t \text{ and } \mathrm{wt}_R(\mathbf{e}_1) = t\}}{\#\{\mathbf{e} \in \mathbb{F}_{q^m}^{2n-k} \mid \mathrm{wt}_R(\mathbf{e}) = t\}}. \tag{5}$$

We can split the cardinalities above over all the subspaces of $\mathbb{F}_q^m$ of dimension t as follows:

$$\pi = \frac{\sum_{V \subset \mathbb{F}_q^m, \dim V = t} \#\{\mathbf{e} \in \mathbb{F}_{q^m}^{2n-k} \mid \langle \mathbf{e} \rangle = \langle \mathbf{e}_1 \rangle = V\}}{\sum_{V \subset \mathbb{F}_q^m, \dim V = t} \#\{\mathbf{e} \in \mathbb{F}_{q^m}^{2n-k} \mid \langle \mathbf{e} \rangle = V\}}. \tag{6}$$

It is not hard to prove that the summands in (6) are independent of the space V. Therefore

$$\pi = \frac{\#\{\mathbf{e} \in \mathbb{F}_{q^m}^{2n-k} \mid \langle \mathbf{e} \rangle = \langle \mathbf{e}_1 \rangle = V\}}{\#\{\mathbf{e} \in \mathbb{F}_{q^m}^{2n-k} \mid \langle \mathbf{e} \rangle = V\}} = \frac{\#\{\mathbf{e}_1 \in \mathbb{F}_{q^m}^n \mid \langle \mathbf{e}_1 \rangle = V\} q^{t(n-k)}}{\#\{\mathbf{e} \in \mathbb{F}_{q^m}^{2n-k} \mid \langle \mathbf{e} \rangle = V\}},$$

where V is any subspace of $\mathbb{F}_q^m$ of dimension t. By applying Lemma 4.2 we then get

$$\pi = \frac{p(q, n, t)\, q^{nt} q^{t(n-k)}}{p(q, 2n-k, t)\, q^{(2n-k)t}} = \frac{p(q, n, t)}{p(q, 2n-k, t)},$$

as claimed. The probability for $\mathbf{e}_2$ can be computed with the same arguments as for $\mathbf{e}_1$. $\square$

Remark 4.5. In the context of a REDOG instance, the data q, n and t is fixed, hence, for the sake of reading simplicity, we denote the probability given in Theorem 4.4 by

$$\bar{p}(r, t) = \frac{p(q, r, t)}{p(q, 2n-k, t)}.$$

Example 4.6. Consider the suggested parameters of REDOG for 128 bits of security from Table 1. Using SageMath [S+21] we computed the probability that $\mathsf{wt}_R(\mathbf{e}_1) = t$, that is $\bar{p}(44, 6) = 0.999999999996419$, and the probability that $\mathsf{wt}_R(\mathbf{e}_2) = t$, that is $\bar{p}(36, 6) = 0.999999999083229$.

We are ready to state the following theorem, which directly implies that REDOG's decryption process fails with extremely high probability.

Theorem 4.7. *Let (n, k, q, m, λ, t) be integers with $k < n < m$ and $\lambda t \leq m$. Let $\Lambda \subset \mathbb{F}_{q^m}$ be a λ-dimensional subspace of $\mathbb{F}_{q^m}$ and $\mathbf{e} = (\mathbf{e}_1, \mathbf{e}_2)$ as in Theorem 4.4. Let $P \in \mathbb{F}_{q^m}^{n \times n}$ be a random isometry matrix (w.r.t. the rank metric) and $S^{-1} \in \mathsf{GL}_{n-k}(\Lambda)$. Then $\mathbf{e}' := (\mathbf{e}_1 P^{-1}, -\mathbf{e}_2 S^{-1})$ has rank weight $\mathsf{wt}_R(\mathbf{e}') \geq \lambda t + 1$ with probability bounded from below by*

$$p_{\mathsf{fail}}(n, k, q, m, \lambda, t) := \bar{p}(n, t)\, \bar{p}(n-k, \lambda t)\, \bar{p}(n-k, t) \left(1 - \begin{bmatrix} \lambda t \\ t \end{bmatrix}_q \Big/ \begin{bmatrix} m \\ t \end{bmatrix}_q \right).$$

Proof. By Theorem 2.4, the isometry P is of the form $\alpha \bar{P}$ for $\alpha \in \mathbb{F}_{q^m}^*$ and $\bar{P} \in \mathsf{GL}_n(\mathbb{F}_q)$, where $q^m \gg q$ and thus typically $\alpha \notin \mathbb{F}_q$. Because of the multiplication by α^{-1}, we can assume that the linear transformation induced by P^{-1} takes a t-dimensional subvectorspace of $\mathbb{F}_q^m$ to a random t-dimensional subspace. Similarly we assume that S^{-1} sends a t-dimensional subspace of $\mathbb{F}_q^m$ to a random subspace of dimension at most λt, by Proposition 4.1. We get the lower bound on the failure probability by showing the following:

1. $\text{wt}_R(\mathbf{e}_1 P^{-1}) = t$ with probability $\bar{p}(n, t)$;
2. $\text{wt}_R(-\mathbf{e}_2 S^{-1}) = \lambda t$ with probability $\bar{p}(n - k, t)\bar{p}(n - k, \lambda t)$;
3. under the conditions in (1) and (2), $\langle \mathbf{e}_1 P^{-1} \rangle \not\subset \langle -\mathbf{e}_2 S^{-1} \rangle$ with probability

$$1 - \begin{bmatrix} \lambda t \\ t \end{bmatrix}_q / \begin{bmatrix} m \\ t \end{bmatrix}_q.$$

Note that (1) follows directly from Theorem 4.4 and the fact that P is an isometry of the space w.r.t the rank metric.

Likewise, $\text{wt}_R(-\mathbf{e}_2) = t$ with probability $\bar{p}(n - k, t)$. The proof of Proposition 4.1 shows that for $\mathbf{e}_2$ with $\text{wt}_R(-\mathbf{e}_2) = t$ we have that $-\mathbf{e}_2 S^{-1}$ is contained in a λt dimensional subspace of $\mathbb{F}_q^m$. Again by Theorem 4.4 we obtain that $\langle -\mathbf{e}_2 S^{-1} \rangle$ spans the entire space with probability $\bar{p}(n - k, \lambda t)$, proving (2).

To prove (3) we will compute the opposite, i.e. the probability that $\langle \mathbf{e}_1 P^{-1} \rangle$ is a subspace of $\langle -\mathbf{e}_2 S^{-1} \rangle$. As mentioned at the beginning of the proof, we treat $\langle \mathbf{e}_1 P^{-1} \rangle$ as a random t-dimensional subspace of $\mathbb{F}_{q^m}$. Thus we can compute this probability as the ratio between the number of t-dimensional subspaces of $\langle -\mathbf{e}_2 S^{-1} \rangle$ and of $\mathbb{F}_q^m$, that is, $\begin{bmatrix} \lambda t \\ t \end{bmatrix}_q / \begin{bmatrix} m \\ t \end{bmatrix}_q$.

Combining the probabilities and observing that (1 – 3) imply $\text{wt}_R(\mathbf{e}') \geq \lambda t + 1$ gives the result. □

Remark 4.8. There are more ways to get $\text{wt}_R(\mathbf{e}') \geq \lambda t + 1$ by relaxing the first two requirements in the proof of Theorem 4.7 and studying the dimension of the union in the third, but p_{fail} is large enough for the parameters in REDOG to prove the point.

Remark 4.9. The proof of property (3) relies on $\mathbf{e}_1 P^{-1}$ being a random subspace of dimension t. We note that for $\alpha \in \mathbb{F}_q$ we have $\langle \mathbf{e}_1 \rangle = \langle \mathbf{e}_1 P^{-1} \rangle \subset \langle \mathbf{e}_2 S^{-1} \rangle$ for $S^{-1} \in \mathsf{GL}_{n-k}(\Lambda)$ and $1 \in \Lambda$. The latter constraint is stated in [KHL+22a] and [LTP21] and it is possible that the authors were not aware of the full generality of isometries. See also the full version [LPR23] for further observations on [LTP21] which are consistent with this misconception.

Recall that the decoder Φ can only correct errors up to rank weight $r = \lambda t$. By Theorem 4.7 we have that $\mathbf{e}'$ has rank weight $\geq \lambda t + 1$, hence the following corollary.

Corollary 4.10. *Let* $(n, k, \ell, q, m, r, \lambda, t)$ *be the parameters of a instance of REDOG with* $r = \lambda t$. *Then REDOG will produce decryption failures with probability at least* $p_{\text{fail}}(n, k, q, m, \lambda, t)$.

Note that a $[2n - k, n]$ Gabidulin code has minimum distance $d_R = 2n - k - n + 1 = n - k + 1$ and can thus correct at most $\lfloor (n - k)/2 \rfloor$ errors and that all instances of REDOG in Table 1 satisfy $\lfloor (n - k)/2 \rfloor = r = \lambda t$.

Example 4.11. As in Example 4.6, consider the suggested parameters for 128 bits of security. Then Theorem 4.7 states that $\text{wt}_R(\mathbf{e}') \geq 19$ with probability at least $p_{\text{fail}}(44, 8, 2, 83, 3, 6) = \bar{p}(44, 8)\bar{p}(36, 6)\bar{p}(36, 18) \left(1 - \begin{bmatrix} 18 \\ 6 \end{bmatrix}_2 / \begin{bmatrix} 83 \\ 6 \end{bmatrix}_2\right) = 0.999996184401789$.

Table 2 reports the value of p_{fail} for each set of security parameters given in Table 1. This shows that REDOG's decryption process fails almost always.

Table 2. Value of decryption failure probability p_{fail} per suggested parameters.

Security parameter	p_{fail}
128	0.999996184401789
192	0.999999940394453
256	0.999999999068677

5   Message recovery attack on REDOG's implementation

Theorem 4.7 and the numerical examples show that, with probability almost 1, REDOG will fail decrypting. However, the probability is not exactly 1 and there exist some choices of $\mathbf{e}$ for which decryption still succeeds. One extreme way to avoid decryption failures, chosen in the reference implementation of REDOG, is to build errors as follows:

Algorithm 5.1 *(REDOG's error generator)*

1. *Pick $\beta_1, \ldots, \beta_t \in \mathbb{F}_{q^m}$ being $\mathbb{F}_q$-linearly independent.*
2. *Pick random permutation π on $2n - k$ symbols.*
3. *Set $\mathbf{e}_{\text{init}} = (\beta_1, \ldots, \beta_t, 0, \ldots, 0) \in \mathbb{F}_{q^m}^{2n-k}$. Output $\mathbf{e} = \pi(\mathbf{e}_{\text{init}})$.*

Error vectors in REDOG's reference implementation[1], whose performance is analyzed in [KHL+22b], are generated in an equivalent way to Algorithm 5.1. Indeed, $\mathbf{e}'$ has rank weight $\text{wt}_R(\mathbf{e}') = (\mathbf{e}_1 P^{-1}, -\mathbf{e}_2 S^{-1}) \leq \lambda t$ and can therefore be decoded using Φ.

Remark 5.2. Algorithm 5.1 produces an error vector $\mathbf{e}$ such that $\text{wt}_H(\mathbf{e}) = \text{wt}_R(\mathbf{e}) = t$ as only t coordinates of $\mathbf{e}$ are nonzero.

We are ready to give the description of an efficient message recovery algorithm.

Algorithm 5.3 *(Message recovery attack)*
Input: *REDOG's public key* pk *and a REDOG's ciphertext* $\mathbf{c} = (\mathbf{c}_1, \mathbf{c}_2) = Encrypt(\mathbf{m}, \text{pk})$ *generated by the reference implementation.*
Output: m

1. *Let C' be the linear $[2n - k, \ell]$-code in the Hamming metric generated by $G = (\text{pk}_1 \mid \text{pk}_2)$. Put $f = 0$.*
2. *While $f = 0$:*
   (a) Randomly select ℓ columns of G to form the matrix A. Let $\mathbf{c}_A$ be the matching positions in $\mathbf{c}$.

---
[1] https://www.kpqc.or.kr/images/zip/REDOG.zip

(b) If A is invertible

    i. Compute $B = A^{-1}$ and $\bar{\mathbf{m}} = \mathbf{c}_A B$.

    ii. Compute $\bar{\mathbf{c}}_1 = \bar{\mathbf{m}}\mathsf{pk}_1$.

    iii. If $\mathsf{wt}_H(\mathbf{c}_1 - \bar{\mathbf{c}}_1) = t_1 \leq t$

        A. Compute $\bar{\mathbf{c}}_2 = \bar{\mathbf{m}}\mathsf{pk}_2$.

        B. If $\mathsf{wt}_H(\mathbf{c}_2 - \bar{\mathbf{c}}_2) = t - t_1$

           Put $\mathbf{m}' = \bar{\mathbf{m}}, \mathbf{e} = (\mathbf{c}_1, \mathbf{c}_2) - (\bar{\mathbf{c}}_1, \bar{\mathbf{c}}_2)$ and $f = 1$.

3. Compute $\mathbf{m} = \mathbf{m}' - \mathsf{hash}(\mathbf{e})$.

The inner loop is Prange's information-set decoding algorithm [Pra62] in the generator-matrix form with early aborts. If the chosen ℓ positions are not all error free then $\bar{\mathbf{m}}$ equals $\mathbf{m}$ with one or more rows of B added to it. Then $\bar{\mathbf{m}}\mathsf{pk}_1$ will be random vector and thus differ from $\mathbf{c}_1$ in more than t positions. If the initial check succeeds there is a high chance of the second condition succeeding as well leading to $\mathbf{e}$ with $\mathsf{wt}_H(\mathbf{e}) = t$.

We now analyze the success probability of each iteration of the inner loop of Algorithm 5.3. The field $\mathbb{F}_{q^m}$ is large, hence A very likely to be invertible. The algorithm succeeds if the ℓ positions forming A are chosen outside the positions where $\mathbf{e}$ has non-zero entries. This happens with probability $\binom{2n-k-t}{\ell}\binom{2n-k}{\ell}$.

Each trial costs the inversion of an $\ell \times \ell$ matrix and up to three matrix-vector products, where the vector has length ℓ and the matrices have ℓ, n, and $n - k$ columns respectively, in addition to minor costs of two vector differences and two weight computations.

We implemented the attack in Algorithm 5.3 in Sagemath 9.5; see online for the code. We perform faster early aborts, testing $\bar{\mathbf{m}}$ on only $t + 3$ columns of pk_1. The probability that a coordinate matches between $\mathbf{c}_1$ and $\bar{\mathbf{c}}_1$ for $\bar{\mathbf{m}} \neq \mathbf{m}$ is q^{-m} and thus negligible for large m. Hence, most candidate vectors $\bar{\mathbf{m}}$ are discard after $(t + 3)\ell^2$ multiplications in $\mathbb{F}_{q^m}$. Running the attack on a Linux Mint virtual machine we broke the KAT ciphertexts included in the submission package for all the proposed parameters. We also generated a bunch of ciphertexts corresponding to randomly chosen public keys and messages and measured the average running time of our algorithm.

As can be seen from Table 3, the attack on the reference implementation succeeds in few steps and is very fast to execute for all parameter sets.

Table 3. Prob is the probability of success of one iteration of the inner loop of Algorithm 5.3. Time$_{KAT}$ is the average timing of message recovery attack over entries in the KAT file (30 for 128 bits, 15 for 192 bits, 13 for 256 bits). Time$_{100}$ is the average timing of message recovery attack over 100 ciphertext generated by REDOG's encryption.

Security parameter	$\log_2(\mathsf{Prob})$	Time$_{KAT}$ (sec.)	Time$_{100}(sec.)$
128	-5.62325179726894	~ 8.01	~ 9.17
192	-7.51182199577027	~ 108.13	~ 112
256	-9.40052710879827	~ 167.91	~ 133.43

6   Recomputing attacks costs

In this section we deal with the computation of complexities of general attacks against cryptosystems relying on the rank decoding problem. We noticed that the official REDOG submission [KHL+22a], as well as [LTP21] do not consider attack algorithms proposed in [BBC+20] and [BBB+23]

Our computations are reported in Table 4 which shows that parameters suggested for REDOG provide significantly less security than expected. The tables also confirm that the parameters do provide the claimed security under attacks prior to [BBC+20] when using a realistic exponent for matrix multiplication. Note that the computations in these tables ignore all constants and lower-order terms in the big-$\mathcal{O}$ complexities. This is in line with how the authors of the attack algorithms use their results to determine the security of other systems, but typically constants are positive and large. We apply the same to [BBB+23] although their magma code makes different choices.

Overview of rank decoding attacks Recall that the public code is generated by the $\ell \times 2n - k$ matrix $(M \mid F)$ over $\mathbb{F}_{q^m}$. The error vector added to the ciphertext is chosen to have rank t. In the description of the attacks we will give formulas for the costs using the notation of this paper, i.e., the dimension is ℓ and the error has rank t; we denote the length by N for reasons that will become clear later. The complexity of algorithms also depends on the matrix multiplication exponent ω.

The GRS [GRS16] algorithm is a combinatorial attack on the rank decoding problem. The idea behind this algorithm is to guess a vectorspace containing the space spanned by the error vector. In this way the received vector can be expressed in terms of the basis of the guessed space. The last step is to solve the linear system associated to the syndrome equations. This has complexity

$$\mathcal{O}\left((N - \ell)^{\omega} m^{\omega} q^{\min\{t\lfloor \ell m/N \rfloor, (t-1)\lfloor (\ell+1)m/N \rfloor\}}\right). \tag{7}$$

Note that we use ω here while the result originally was stated with exponent 3. These matrices are not expected to be particularly sparse but should be large enough for fast matrix multiplication algorithms to apply. The same applies to the next formulas.

The second attack, introduced in [GRS16], which we denote GRS-alg, is an algebraic attack. Under the condition that $\ell > \lceil ((t + 1)(\ell + 1) - N - 1)/t \rceil$ the decoding problem can be solved in

$$\mathcal{O}\left(t^{\omega} \ell^{\omega} q^{t(\lceil ((t+1)(\ell+1)-N-1)/t \rceil)}\right). \tag{8}$$

The attack AGHT [AGHT18] is an improvement over the GRS combinatorial attack. The underlying idea is to guess the space containing the error in a specific way that provides higher chance of guessing a suitable space. It has complexity

$$\mathcal{O}\left((N - \ell)^{\omega} m^{\omega} q^{t(\ell+1)m/N - m}\right). \tag{9}$$

The BBB+ attack [BBB+20] translates the rank metric decoding problem into a system of multivariate equations and then uses Gröbner-basis methods to find solutions. Much of the analysis is spent on determining the degree of regularity, depending on the length, dimension, and rank of the code and error. If $m\binom{N-\ell-1}{t} + 1 \geq \binom{N}{t}$ then the problem can be solved in

$$\mathcal{O}\left(\left(\frac{((m+N)t)^t}{t!}\right)^\omega\right). \tag{10}$$

If the condition is not satisfied then the complexity of solving the decoding problem becomes

$$\mathcal{O}\left(\left(\frac{((m+N)t)^{t+1}}{(t+1)!}\right)^\omega\right) \tag{11}$$

or the same for $t+2$ in place of $t+1$. The authors of [BBB+20] use (11) in their calculations and thus we include that as well.

The BBC+-Overdetermined, BBC+-Hybrid and BBC+-SupportMinors improvements that will follow are all introduced in [BBC+20]. They make explicit the use of extended linearization as a technique to compute Gröbner bases. For solving the rank-decoding problem it is not necessary to determine the full Gröbner basis but to find a solution to this system of equations. Extended linearization introduces new variables to turn a multivariate quadratic system into a linear system. The algorithms and complexity estimates differ in how large the resulting systems are and whether they are overdetermined or not, dependent on the system parameters.

BBC+-Overdetermined applies to the overdetermined case, which matches $m\binom{N-\ell-1}{t} + 1 \geq \binom{N}{t}$, and permits to solve the system in

$$\mathcal{O}\left(m\binom{N-\ell-1}{t}\binom{N}{t}^{\omega-1}\right). \tag{12}$$

In case of an undetermined system, BBC+-Hybrid fixes some of the unknowns in a brute-force manner to produce to an overdetermined system in the remaining variables. The costs are testing all possible values for j positions, where j is the smallest non-negative integer such that $m\binom{N-\ell-1}{t} + 1 \geq \binom{N-j}{t}$, and for each performing the same matrix computations as in BBC on j columns less. This leads to a total complexity of

$$\mathcal{O}\left(q^{jt}m\binom{N-\ell-1}{t}\binom{N-j}{t}^{\omega-1}\right). \tag{13}$$

The brute-force part in BBC+-Hybrid quickly becomes the dominating factor. The BBC+-SupportMinors algorithm introduces terms of larger degrees first and then linearizes the system. This consists in multiplying the equations by some homogeneous monomials of degree b so as to obtain a system of homogeneous equations. However, for the special case of $q = 2$ the equations in the system might not be homogeneous. In this case, homogeneous equations coming from smaller values of b are considered. Let $A_b = \sum_{j=1}^{b} \binom{N}{t}\binom{m\ell+1}{j}$. The degree of the equations formed in BBC+-SupportMinors depends on b, where $0 < b < 2+t$ is minimal such that $a_b - 1 \leq \sum_{j=1}^{b}\sum_{s=1}^{j}\left((-1)^{s+1}\binom{N}{t+s}\binom{m+s-1}{s}\binom{m\ell+1}{j-s}\right)$ if such a b exists. In this case the problem can be solved with complexity

$$\mathcal{O}\left((m\ell+1)(t+1)A_b^2\right). \tag{14}$$

We do not report the last two attacks presented in [BBC+20] as the underlying approach has been pointed out to be incorrect in [BBB+23]. More precisely, [BBB+23] show that the independence assumptions made in [BBC+20] are incorrect. The SupportMinors and MaxMinors modelings in [BBC+20] are not as independent as claimed, and [BBB+23] introduces a new approach that combines them while keeping independence, at least conjecturally and matched by experiments. They again multiply by monomials of degree up to $b-1$ but a relevant difference is that the equations from the SupportMinors system are kept over $\mathbb{F}_{q^m}$. They introduce the following notation:

$$\mathcal{N}_b^{\mathbb{F}_{q^m}} = \sum_{s=1}^{\ell}\binom{N-s}{t}\binom{\ell+b-1-s}{b-1} - \binom{N-\ell-1}{t}\binom{\ell-b-1}{b},$$

$$\mathcal{N}_{b,syz}^{\mathbb{F}_q} = (m-1)\sum_{s=1}^{b}(-1)^{(s+1)}\binom{\ell+b-s-1}{b-s}\binom{N-\ell-1}{t+s}, \text{ and}$$

$$\mathcal{M}_b^{\mathbb{F}_q} = \binom{\ell+b-1}{b}\left(\binom{N}{t} - m\binom{N-\ell-1}{t}\right)$$

and put $\mathcal{N}_b^{\mathbb{F}_q} = \mathcal{N}_b^{\mathbb{F}_{q^m}} - \mathcal{N}_{b,syz}^{\mathbb{F}_q}$.

The problem can then be solved by linearization whenever $\mathcal{N}_b^{\mathbb{F}_q} \geq \mathcal{M}_b^{\mathbb{F}_q} - 1$. The complexity of solving the system is $T(m, N, \ell, t) = \mathcal{O}\left(\mathcal{N}_b^{\mathbb{F}_q}\left(\mathcal{M}_b^{\mathbb{F}_q}\right)^{\omega-1}\right)$.

Moreover, [BBB+23] introduce a hybrid strategy. Compared to BBC+-Hybrid it randomly picks matrices from $\mathsf{GL}_N(\mathbb{F}_q)$ to randomly compute $\mathbb{F}_q$-linear combinations of the entries of the error vector and applies the same transformation to the generator matrix, hoping to achieve that the last a positions of the error vector are all 0 and then shortening the code while also reducing the dimension. This technique has complexity

$$\min_{a\geq0}\left(q^{ta}\cdot T(m, N-a, \ell-a, t)\right). \tag{15}$$

6.1   Lowering the attack costs beyond the formulas stated

The combinatorial attacks GRS and AGHT perform best for longer codes, however, algebraic attacks that turn each column into a new variable perform best with fewer variables. For each attack strategy we search for the best number of columns that we should consider in order to obtain the cheapest cost of a successful break of REDOG. This is why we presented the above formulas using N rather than the full code length $2n - k$. The conditions given above determine the minimum length required relative to dimension and rank of the error.

We then evaluate the costs for each algorithm for each choice of length $N = \ell + t + i$, for every value of $i = 0, 1, \ldots, 2n - k - \ell - t$ satisfying the conditions of the attacks. Figure 1 shows the different behaviour of the algorithms for fixed ℓ and t and increasing i. The jump in the BBB+ plot is at the transition between the two formulas.

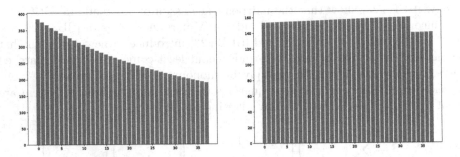

Fig. 1. Plots showing the $\log_2$ of the costs for AGHT and BBB+ for the parameters at the 128–bit security level for different choices of code length.

We point out that [BBC+20] also considered decreasing the length of the code for the case of overdetermined systems, see [BBC+20, Section 4.2] on puncturing the code in the case of "super"-overdetermined systems. We perform a systematic scan for all algorithms as an attacker will use the best possible attack.

The recomputed values We computed complexity costs for all the attacks introduced in the previous subsection, taking into consideration two values of matrix multiplication exponent, namely $\omega = 2.807$ and $\omega = 2.37$. For each possible length $N + i$ for $N = \ell + t$ and $i = 0, 1, \ldots, 2n - k - \ell - t$ we computed the costs for each attack strategy, keeping the lowest value per strategy. For the two cases of BBB+ and the three strategies described for the BBC+-* algorithms, we selected the best complexity among them. For the sake of completeness, we report the value of i in Table 4 as well and the value of a for [BBB+23]. All the values are stated as the $\log_2$ of the costs resulting from the complexity formulas. The lowest costs of the best algorithm are stated in blue. Note the above-mentioned caveats regarding evaluating big-$\mathcal{O}$ estimates for concrete parameters.

As shown in the tables, suggested parameters of REDOG for 128 and 192 levels of security do not resist BBC+ attack and Mixed-attack for any choice of ω, and BBB+ for $\omega = 2.37$. Suggested parameters for level 256 resist all

Table 4. Values of the $\log_2$ of attack costs for REDOG's suggested parameters for all security level (see Table 1).

Algorithm	Formula	128 level			192 level			256 level		
		$\omega = 2.807$	$\omega = 2.37$	i	$\omega = 2.807$	$\omega = 2.37$	i	$\omega = 2.807$	$\omega = 2.37$	i
GRS [GRS16]	7	228.03	-	36	392.30	-	48	604.07	-	60
GRS-alg [GRS16]	8	207.88	-	36	368.18	-	48	595.97	-	60
AGHT [AGHT18]	9	186.68	-	37	337.69	-	49	536.22	-	61
BBB+ [BBB+20]	10 & 11	140.06	118.25	33	210.26	150	0	269.03	227.15	0
BBC+ [BBC+20]	12 – 14	77.83	65.73	33	175.72	159.57	48	337.92	318.01	61
Mixed [BBB+23]	15	80.94	68.61	32	166.67	149.49	49	347.38	311.77	61

attacks except BBB+ for $\omega = 2.37$. In Section 8 we propose a solution to the decryption failures that also boosts the security of REDOG.

7   Solving decryption failures

The core of REDOG's decryption failures is given by point (3) of the proof of Theorem 4.7. Indeed, the crucial step for showing decoding failure of the decoder Φ, is that $\langle \mathbf{e}_1 P^{-1} \rangle \not\subset \langle -\mathbf{e}_2 S^{-1} \rangle$.

In order to solve the issue of decryption failures in REDOG, we propose an alternative that keeps the random choice of an error vector $\mathbf{e}$ with $\mathsf{wt}_R(\mathbf{e}) = t$ and changes the public key. The idea is to retain the method introduced in [Loi17], but also to make sure that $\mathsf{wt}_R(\mathbf{e}') \leq \lambda t$. We suggest to pick $P^{-1} \in \mathsf{GL}_n(\Lambda)$ randomly instead of it being an isometry of the space $\mathbb{F}_{q^m}^n$.

The proof of the next result is an adaptation of the proof of Proposition 4.1.

Proposition 7.1. *Let* $\Lambda \subset \mathbb{F}_{q^m}$ *be a* λ*-dimensional subspace of* $\mathbb{F}_{q^m}$ *and* $\mathbf{e} = (\mathbf{e}_1, \mathbf{e}_2)$ *a random vector with* $\mathsf{wt}_R(\mathbf{e}) = t$ *with* $\mathbf{e}_1 \in \mathbb{F}_{q^m}^n$ *and* $\mathbf{e}_2 \in \mathbb{F}_{q^m}^{n-k}$. *Let* $S^{-1} \in \mathsf{GL}_{n-k}(\Lambda)$ *and* $P^{-1} \in \mathsf{GL}_n(\Lambda)$. *Then* $\langle \mathbf{e}_1 P^{-1}, -\mathbf{e}_2 S^{-1} \rangle \subseteq V$ *for some* λt*-dimensional* $\mathbb{F}_q$*-linear vectorspace* V.

Proof. Let $\Gamma = \langle \mathbf{e} \rangle$ be the $\mathbb{F}_q$-linear subspace of $\mathbb{F}_{q^m}$ generated by $\mathbf{e}$. As before we can write $\Gamma = \langle y_1, \ldots, y_t \rangle$. Write also $\Lambda = \langle \alpha_1, \ldots, \alpha_\lambda \rangle$. As in the proof of Proposition 4.1 we can express the j-th coordinate of $\mathbf{e}_1 P^{-1}$ as a linear combination of the λt elements $y_h \alpha_k$ for $h = 1, \ldots, t$ and $k = 1, \ldots, \lambda$ as $(\mathbf{e}_1 P^{-1})_j = \sum_{h=1}^{t} \sum_{k=1}^{\lambda} c_{h,k} y_h \alpha_k$. The same can be done for each coordinate of $-\mathbf{e}_2 S^{-1}$. Hence both subspaces are contained in the space $V = \langle y_h \alpha_k \rangle$ generated by these λt elements. $\square$

Corollary 7.2. *Let* $\mathbf{e}' = (\mathbf{e}_1 P^{-1}, -\mathbf{e}_2 S^{-1})$ *with* $\mathbf{e}, P^{-1}$ *and* S^{-1} *as in Proposition 7.1. Then* $\mathsf{wt}_R(\mathbf{e}') \leq \lambda t$.

The only change to the specification of REDOG is in the KeyGen algorithm in Step 3; encryption and decryption remain unchanged as in Section 3. Here is KeyGen for the updated version of REDOG with no decryption failures.

1. Select $H = (H_1 \mid H_2)$, $H_2 \in \mathsf{GL}_{n-k}(\mathbb{F}_{q^m})$, a parity check matrix of a $[2n - k, n]$ Gabidulin code, with syndrome decoder Φ correcting r errors.
2. Select a full rank matrix $M \in \mathbb{F}_{q^m}^{\ell \times n}$.
3. Select a λ-dimensional subspace $\Lambda \subset \mathbb{F}_{q^m}$, seen as $\mathbb{F}_q$-linear space, and select $S^{-1} \in \mathsf{GL}_{n-k}(\Lambda)$ and $P^{-1} \in \mathsf{GL}_n(\Lambda)$.
4. Compute $F = MP^{-1}H_1^T \left(H_2^T\right)^{-1} S$ and publish the public key $\mathsf{pk} = (M, F)$. Store the secret key $\mathsf{sk} = (P, H, S, \Phi)$.

Theorem 7.3. *The updated version of REDOG is correct.*

Proof. The correctness of the updated version of REDOG follows from the correctness of the original version, except for decryption correctness, which is proven by Corollary 7.2. $\qquad\square$

8 Solving decryption failures and boosting security

Our second idea of how to deal with REDOG not decrypting correctly is to change how $\mathbf{e}$ is sampled. While the approach in Section 7 works and preserves all considerations regarding parameter sizes, in Section 6 we have shown that these are too small to offer security against the best known attacks. The approach in this section provides a functioning system and increases the security offered by the parameters.

Recall that the public key is $(M \mid F)$, where M has dimension $\ell \times n$ and F has dimension $\ell \times (n - k)$ and both, M and F, have full rank. The relative sizes in REDOG are such that $n - k = \ell - 1$, so F is just one column short of being square, and $n = \ell + t + 1$. The parameters are chosen so that the decryption step can decode errors of rank up to r, while encryption in REDOG adds only an error vector of rank t with $r \geq t\lambda$. All parameter sets have $\lambda = 3$ and $r = \lambda t = (n-k)/2$.

Encryption is computed as $\mathbf{c} = \mathbf{m}'(M \mid F) + \mathbf{e}$, for $\mathbf{m}' \in \mathbb{F}_{q^m}^\ell$. Decryption requires decoding in the Gabidulin code for error $(\mathbf{e}_1 P^{-1}, -\mathbf{e}_2 S^{-1})$, where P is an isometry and $S^{-1} \in \mathsf{GL}_{n-k}(\Lambda)$. We have shown in Theorem 4.7 that this $\mathbf{e}'$ typically has rank larger than r, which causes incorrect decoding, for REDOG's choice of $\mathbf{e}$ with $\mathsf{wt}_R(\mathbf{e}) = t$. Where we proposed changing the definition of P in the previous section to reach a system which has minimal changes compared to REDOG, we now suggest changing the way that $\mathbf{e}$ is chosen.

In particular, we redefine $\mathbf{e}$ to have different rank on the first n positions and the last $n - k$ positions. Let $\mathbf{e} = (\mathbf{e}_1, \mathbf{e}_2)$ with $\mathsf{wt}_R(\mathbf{e}_1) = t_1$ and $\mathsf{wt}_R(\mathbf{e}_2) = t_2$. This can be achieved by sampling t_1 random elements from $\mathbb{F}_{q^m}$, testing that this achieves rank t_1 and taking the n positions in $\mathbf{e}_1$ as random $\mathbb{F}_q$-linear combinations of these t_1 elements. Because m is significantly larger than t_1, this finds an $\mathbf{e}_1$ of rank t_1 on first try with high probability. Similarly, we pick t_2 random elements from $\mathbb{F}_{q^m}$ and use their $\mathbb{F}_q$-linear combinations for $\mathbf{e}_2$.

We keep P being an isometry and $S^{-1} \in \mathsf{GL}_{n-k}(\Lambda)$ as in REDOG. Then the decoding step needs to find an error of rank $t_1 + \lambda t_2$, namely $\mathbf{e}_1 P^{-1}$ on the first

n positions and $\mathbf{e}_2 S^{-1}$ on the last $n - k$ positions. This will succeed if

$$r \geq t_1 + \lambda t_2. \tag{16}$$

Hence, we can consider different splits of r to maximize security.

Considerations for extreme choices of t_1 and t_2 As already explained in Section 6.1, the attacker can consider parts of $\mathbf{c}_1$ and $\mathbf{c}_2$, for example, the extreme choice of $t_1 = 0$ would mean that $\mathbf{c}_1$ is a codeword in the code generated by M and thus $\mathbf{m}'$ would be trivially recoverable from $\mathbf{c}_1 = \mathbf{m}'M$ by computing the inverse of an $\ell \times \ell$ submatrix of M. Because $\mathbb{F}_{q^m}$ is large, almost any choice of submatrix will be invertible.

The other extreme choice, $t_2 = 0$, does not cause such an obvious attack as for the REDOG parameters F has one column fewer than it has rows, meaning that $\mathbf{c}_2 = \mathbf{m}'F$ cannot be solved for $\mathbf{m}'$. Hence, at least one position of $\mathbf{c}_1$ needs to be included, but that means that we do not have a codeword in the code generated by that column of M and F but a codeword plus an error of rank 1. However, a brute-force attack on this system still succeeds with cost q^m as follows:

Let $\bar{F} = (M_i | F)$ be the square matrix obtained from taking M_i, the i-th column of M, for a choice of i that makes $\bar{F}$ invertible. Most choices of i will succeed. Let $\bar{\mathbf{c}} = (c_{1i}, \mathbf{c}_2)$, the i-th coordinate of $\mathbf{c}_1$ followed by $\mathbf{c}_2$.

For each $a \in \mathbb{F}_{q^m}$ compute $\bar{\mathbf{m}} = (\bar{\mathbf{c}} - (a, 0, 0, \ldots, 0))\bar{F}^{-1}$. Then compute $\bar{\mathbf{e}} = \mathbf{c} - \bar{\mathbf{m}}(M \mid F)$ and check if $\mathrm{wt}_R(\bar{\mathbf{e}}_1) = t_1$. If so put $\mathbf{m}' = \bar{\mathbf{m}}$ and $\mathbf{e} = \bar{\mathbf{e}}$.

The matrix operations in this attack are cheap and can be made even cheaper by observing that $\bar{\mathbf{m}} = \bar{\mathbf{c}}\bar{F}^{-1} - a\mathbf{f}$, for $\mathbf{f}$ the first *row* of $\bar{F}^{-1}$, and $\bar{\mathbf{e}} = \mathbf{c} - (\bar{\mathbf{c}}\bar{F}^{-1})(M \mid F) + a\mathbf{f}(M \mid F)$, where everything including $\mathbf{f}(M \mid F) \in \mathbb{F}_{q^m}^{2n-k}$ is fixed and can be computed once per target $\mathbf{c}$. Note also that only the $\mathbf{c}_1$ and $\mathbf{e}_1$ parts need to be computed as by construction $\mathbf{e}_2 = 0$. This leaves just n multiplications and additions in $\mathbb{F}_{q^m}$ and the rank computation for each choice of a. The search over $a \in \mathbb{F}_{q^m}$ is thus the main cost for a complexity of q^m. For all parameters of REDOG this is less than the desired security.

Generalizations of the brute-force attack For $t_1 = 1$, a brute-force attack needs to search over all $a \in \mathbb{F}_{q^m}$, up to scaling by $\mathbb{F}_q$-elements, and over all choices of error patterns, where each position of the error is a random $\mathbb{F}_q$-multiple of a. We need ℓ positions from $\mathbf{c}_1 = \mathbf{m}'M + \mathbf{e}_1$ to compute a candidate $\bar{\mathbf{m}}'$ as in the attack on $t_1 = 0$. Hence, for each $a \in \mathbb{F}_{q^m}$ we need to try at most the q^ℓ patterns for those ℓ positions of $\mathbf{e}_1$ for a cost of $(q^m - 1)q^\ell/(q-1)$. For the REDOG parameters, $q = 2$ and $m + \ell$ is significantly smaller than the security level. Hence, $t_1 = 1$ is also a bad choice.

Starting at $t_1 = 2$, when there are two elements $a, b \in \mathbb{F}_{q^m}$ and error patterns need to consider random $\mathbb{F}_q$-linear combinations of these two elements, the attack costs of $(q^m - 1)(q^m - 2)q^{2\ell}/(2(q-1)^2)$ grow beyond the more advanced attacks considered in Section 6.1.

Lemma 8.1. *In general, the brute-force attack on the left side takes*

$$\binom{q^m - 1}{t_1} q^{t_1 \ell} / (q - 1)^{t_1}$$

steps.

Proof. The error vector on the left, e_1, has rank t_1, this means that there are t_1 elements $a_1, a_2, \ldots, a_{t_1} \in \mathbb{F}_{q^m}$ which are $\mathbb{F}_q$-linearly independent. There are $\binom{q^m-1}{t_1}/(q-1)^{t_1}$ such choices up to $\mathbb{F}_q$ factors.

Each of the ℓ positions takes a random $\mathbb{F}_q$ linear combination. For a fixed choice of the a_i there are $q^{t_1 \ell}$ choices for these linear combinations. Combining these quantities gives the result.   □

Similarly, for $t_2 = 1$ the brute-force attack is no longer competitive, yet less clearly so than for $t_1 = 2$ because a and b appear in separate parts. There are q^m candidate choices for e_{1i} and $(q^m - 1)q^{\ell-1}/(q - 1)$ candidates for e_2. For $q = 2$ this amounts to roughly $2^{2m+\ell-1}$ and $2m + \ell - 1$ is larger than the security level for all parameters in REDOG.

Lemma 8.2. *In general, the brute-force attack on the right side takes*

$$q^m \binom{q^m - 1}{t_2} q^{t_2(\ell-1)} / (q - 1)^{t_2}$$

steps.

Proof. There are q^m choices for e_{1i}. The result follows by the same arguments as for Lemma 8.1, and taking into account that e_2 has length $\ell - 1$.   □

We do not consider other combinations of columns from the left and right as those would lead to higher ranks than these two options. Depending on the sizes of t_1 and t_2, Lemma 8.1 or 8.2 gives the better result, but apart from extreme choices these costs are very high.

Finding good choices of t_1 and t_2 We now turn to the more sophisticated attacks and try to find optimal splits of the decoding budget r between t_1 and t_2 satisfying (16), to $r \geq t_1 + \lambda t_2$. to make the best attacks as hard as possible. For any such choice, we consider attacks starting from the left with (parts of) c_1 and M or from the right with c_2, F, and parts of c_1 and M. The attacks and sub-attacks differ in how many columns they require, depending on the dimension and rank, and we scan the whole range of possible lengths from both sides.

Since $n = \ell + t + 1$, for the t parameter in REDOG, for small choices of $t_1 \leq t$ the attack may take a punctured system on c_1 and M to recover m', similar to the attacks considered in Section 6, or include part of c_2 and F, while accepting an error of larger rank including part of t_2. Hence, the search from the left may start with puncturing of c_1. Once parts of c_2 are included, the rank typically

Table 5. Best parameter choices and achieved security for $\omega = 2.807$, using the original values for ℓ, k, m, and n and splitting the decoding capacity r according to $r \geq t_1 + \lambda t_2$.

parameter set	best attack	$\log_2(\text{cost})$	$N + i$	t_1	t_2	m	n	k	ℓ
128-bit	brute-force	320.00	-	12	2	83	44	8	37
192-bit	BBB+	458.25	61	15	3	109	58	10	49
256-bit	BBB+	628.20	75	21	3	135	72	12	61

increases by one for each extra position, again because m is much larger than t_1 and t_2, until reaching $t_1 + t_2$, after which the rank does not increase with increasing length.

If $t_1 > t + 1$ parts of c_2 need to be considered in any case, with the corresponding increases in the rank of the error, in turn requiring more positions to deal with the increased rank, typically reaching $t_1 + t_2$ before enough positions are available.

Starting from the right, the attacker will always need to include parts from c_1 to even have an invertible system. Hence, the attack is hardest for t_1 maximal in (16) provided that the brute-force attack is excluded. This suggests choosing $t_2 = 1, t_1 = r - \lambda$, as then the attacker is forced to decode an unstructured code with an error of rank $t_1 + t_2 = r - \lambda + 1$.

A computer search, evaluating all attacks considered in Section 6 for all choices of $t_2 \in \{1, 2, \ldots, r/\lambda - 1\}$ and considering both directions as starting points for the attacker confirms that $t_2 = 1$ is optimal. See online for the Sage code used for the search. The original parameters choices for REDOG then provide the attack costs in Table 5.

This means that this second idea solves decryption failures and takes the parameters of REDOG to a safe level of strength. Actually our optimized choice of t_1 and t_2 allows enough margin to shrink the other system parameters.

Note that, as pointed out before, these computations use big-$\mathcal{O}$ complexity estimates and put all constants to 1 and lower-order terms to 0. This is in line with how estimates are presented in the papers introducing BBB+ [BBB+20] and BBC+ [BBC+20] but typically underestimates the security.

Remark 8.3. After we developed this idea but before posting it, the REDOG authors informed us that they fixed the decryption issue in a manner similar to the approach in this section, namely by having different ranks for e_1 and e_2. Their choice of $t_1 = r/2$ and $t_2 = r/(2\lambda)$ satisfies $r \geq t_1 + \lambda t_2$. but provides less security against attacks. The Sage script gives the results in Table 6 as a byproduct of computing the costs for all values of t_2.

9   Conclusions and further considerations

In this paper we showed several issues with the REDOG proposal but also some ways to repair it. One other issue is that REDOG has rather large keys for a rank-metric-based system. A strategy used by many systems in the NIST post-quantum competition, is to generate parts of the secret and public keys from seeds and storing or transmitting those seeds instead of the matrices they generated. Implementations written in C always need to define ways to take the output of a random-number generator and this strategy includes the use of a fixed such generator into the KeyGen, encryption, and decryption steps. For REDOG, this approach permits to reduce the size of the secret key sk and, at the same time, moderately shrink the size of the public key pk.

Let $f : \{0,1\}^{256} \to \{0,1\}^*$ be such a generator, where $\{0,1\}^*$ indicates that the output length is arbitrary, in a use of f the output length N must be specified. Most recent proposals use SHAKE-256 or SHAKE-512. The idea is to pick a random 256-bit seed s and initialize f with this seed, the output bits of $f(s)$ are then used in place of the regular outputs of the random-number generator to construct elements of the public or secret key. This method is beneficial if s is much smaller than the key element it replaces. The downside is that any use of that key element then incurs the costs of recomputing that element from s.

As one of the more interesting cases, we show how to build the isometry P form $f(s)$ for some seed s. Let $(n, k, \ell, q, m, \lambda)$ denote the same quantities as in REDOG.

Example 9.1. Let $N = (n^2 + m)\lceil \log_2(q) \rceil + 256$ and let $\{\alpha_1, \ldots, \alpha_m\}$ be a basis of $\mathbb{F}_{q^m}$ over $\mathbb{F}_q$. Choose a random seed s and produce the N-bit string $f(s)$. Use the first $n^2\lceil \log_2(q) \rceil$ bits of $f(s)$ to determine n^2 elements in $\mathbb{F}_q$ and build an $n \times n$ matrix Q with these elements. The matrix Q is invertible with probability roughly 0.29. If this is not the case, use the last 256 bits of the output as a new seed s', discard s, and repeat the above with $f(s')$ (an average of 3 trials produces an invertible matrix).

Once an invertible Q has been constructed, use the middle $m\lceil \log_2 q \rceil$ bits of $f(s)$ to define m coefficients in $\mathbb{F}_q$ and to determine an element $\gamma \in \mathbb{F}_{q^m}$ as the $\mathbb{F}_q$-linear combination of the α_i. Then compute $P = \gamma Q$ which, by Theorem 2.4 is an isometry for the rank metric.

As a second example we show how to select S.

Example 9.2. We first observe that $\mathbb{F}_{q^m}$ is a large finite field, so any choice of λ elements for $\lambda \ll m$ will be $\mathbb{F}_q$-linearly independent with overwhelming probability. Using $N = (m + (n - k)^2)\lambda\lceil \log_2(q) \rceil$ we can determine λ random

Table 6. Results for the modified parameter for REDOG using $t_1 = r/2$ and $t_2 = r/(2\lambda)$. The stated costs are achieved by BBB+ at length $N + i$.

Intended security in bits	128	192	256
Achieved security in bits ($\omega = 2.807$)	271.75	384.03	500.50
Number of columns ($N + i$) ($\omega = 2.807$)	46	61	76
Achieved security in bits ($\omega = 2.37$)	229.45	324.24	422.58
Number of columns ($N + i$) ($\omega = 2.37$)	46	61	76

elements from $\mathbb{F}_{q^m}$ which define the subspace $\Lambda \subset \mathbb{F}_{q^m}$. We then define the $(n-k)^2$ entries of $S^{-1} \in \mathsf{GL}_{n-k}(\Lambda)$ as $\mathbb{F}_q$-linear combinations over those λ elements, using the next $(n-k)^2 \lambda \lceil \log_2 q \rceil$ bits. The resulting matrix is almost certainly invertible and permits computing $S = (S^{-1})^{-1}$.

Similar strategies can be applied to compute the matrices M, H_1 and H_2. Let $s_P, s_S, s_M, s_{H_1}, s_{H_2}$ be the seeds corresponding to the matrices P, S, M, H_1 and H_2, respectively. Then we can set $\mathsf{sk} = (s_P, s_S, s_{H_1}, s_{H_2})$ and $\mathsf{pk} = (s_M, F)$ where $F = MP^{-1}H_1^T (H_2^T)^{-1} S$. This approach cannot be used to compress F as it depends on the other matrices. In this way we reduced the private key size of REDOG to 1024 bits and public key of size of REDOG to $256 + \ell(n-k)m \lceil \log_2(q) \rceil$. For the 128-bit-security level, we obtain a secret key size of 0.13 KB compared to the original 1.45 KB and a public key size of 13, 85 KB, compared to the original 14, 25KB (which was obtained by choosing M to be a circulant matrix) at the expense of having to recompute the matrices from their seeds when needed. Given that matrix inversion over $\mathbb{F}_{q^m}$ is not fast, implementations may prefer to include S and S^{-1} in sk and use seeds for the other matrices. To save even more space, it is possible to replace $s_P, s_S, s_M, s_{H_1}, s_{H_2}$ by a single seed s and generating those five seeds as a call to $f(s)$. The public key then includes the derived value s_M but the secret key consists only of s. Note that in that case each non-invertible Q will be generated for each run expanding the secret seed, before finding the Q and P that were used in computing pk. In summary, this strategy provides a tradeoff between size and computing time.

References

AAB+17a. Carlos Aguilar Melchor, Nicolas Aragon, Slim Bettaieb, Loic Bidoux, Olivier Blazy, Jean-Christophe Deneuville, Phillipe Gaborit, Adrien Hauteville, and Gilles Zémor. Ouroboros-R. Technical report, National Institute of Standards and Technology, 2017. available at https://csrc.nist. gov/projects/post-quantum-cryptography/post-quantum-cryptography-standardization/round-1-submissions

AAB+17b. Carlos Aguilar Melchor, Nicolas Aragon, Slim Bettaieb, Loic Bidoux, Olivier Blazy, Jean-Christophe Deneuville, Phillippe Gaborit, and Gilles Zémor. RQC. Technical report, National Institute of Standards and Technology, 2017. available at https://csrc.nist.gov/projects/post-quantum-cryptography/post-quantum-cryptography-standardization/round-1-submissions

AASA+20. Gorjan Alagic, Jacob Alperin-Sheriff, Daniel Apon, David Cooper, Quynh Dang, John Kelsey, Yi-Kai Liu, Carl Miller, Dustin Moody, Rene Peralta, Ray Perlner, Angela Robinson, and Daniel Smith-Tone. Status report on the second round of the NIST post-quantum cryptography standardization process. NIST IR 8309, 2020. https://doi.org/10.6028/NIST.IR.8309

ABD+17a. Nicolas Aragon, Olivier Blazy, Jean-Christophe Deneuville, Philippe Gaborit, Adrien Hauteville, Olivier Ruatta, Jean-Pierre Tillich, and Gilles Zémor. LAKE. Technical report, National Institute of Standards and Technology, 2017. available at https://csrc.nist.gov/projects/post-quantum-cryptography/post-quantum-cryptography-standardization/round-1-submissions

ABD+17b. Nicolas Aragon, Olivier Blazy, Jean-Christophe Deneuville, Philippe Gaborit, Adrien Hauteville, Olivier Ruatta, Jean-Pierre Tillich, and Gilles Zémor. LOCKER. Technical report, National Institute of Standards and Technology, 2017. available at https://csrc.nist.gov/projects/post-quantum-cryptography/post-quantum-cryptography-standardization/round-1-submissions

AGHT18. Nicolas Aragon, Philippe Gaborit, Adrien Hauteville, and Jean-Pierre Tillich. A new algorithm for solving the rank syndrome decoding problem. In *ISIT*, pages 2421–2425. IEEE, 2018

BBB+20. Magali Bardet, Pierre Briaud, Maxime Bros, Philippe Gaborit, Vincent Neiger, Olivier Ruatta, and Jean-Pierre Tillich. An algebraic attack on rank metric code-based cryptosystems. In Anne Canteaut and Yuval Ishai, editors, *EUROCRYPT 2020, Part III*, volume 12107 of *LNCS*, pages 64–93, Zagreb, Croatia, May 10–14, 2020. Springer, Heidelberg, Germany

BBB+23. Magali Bardet, Pierre Briaud, Maxime Bros, Philippe Gaborit, and Jean-Pierre Tillich. Revisiting algebraic attacks on minrank and on the rank decoding problem. *Designs, Codes and Cryptography*, pages 1–37, 07 2023

BBC+20. Magali Bardet, Maxime Bros, Daniel Cabarcas, Philippe Gaborit, Ray A. Perlner, Daniel Smith-Tone, Jean-Pierre Tillich, and Javier A. Verbel. Improvements of algebraic attacks for solving the rank decoding and MinRank problems. In Shiho Moriai and Huaxiong Wang, editors, *ASIACRYPT 2020, Part I*, volume 12491 of *LNCS*, pages 507–536, Daejeon, South Korea, December 7–11, 2020. Springer, Heidelberg, Germany

Ber03. Thierry P. Berger. Isometries for rank distance and permutation group of Gabidulin codes. *IEEE Trans. Inf. Theory*, 49(11):3016–3019, 2003

Del78. Philippe Delsarte. Bilinear forms over a finite field, with applications to coding theory. *Journal of Combinatorial Theory, Series A*, 25(3):226–241, 1978

DGZ17. Jean-Christophe Deneuville, Philippe Gaborit, and Gilles Zémor. Ouroboros: A simple, secure and efficient key exchange protocol based on coding theory. In Tanja Lange and Tsuyoshi Takagi, editors, *Post-Quantum Cryptography - 8th International Workshop, PQCrypto 2017*, pages 18–34, Utrecht, The Netherlands, June 26–28, 2017. Springer, Heidelberg, Germany

Gab85. Ernst M. Gabidulin. Theory of codes with maximum rank distance. *Problems of Information Transmission*, 21(1):1–12, 1985

GKK+17. Lucky Galvez, Jon-Lark Kim, Myeong Jae Kim, Young-Sik Kim, and Nari Lee. McNie. Technical report, National Institute of Standards and Technology, 2017. available at https://csrc.nist.gov/projects/post-quantum-cryptography/post-quantum-cryptography-standardization/round-1-submissions

GPT91. Ernst M. Gabidulin, A. V. Paramonov, and O. V. Tretjakov. Ideals over a non-commutative ring and thier applications in cryptology. In Donald W. Davies, editor, *EUROCRYPT'91*, volume 547 of *LNCS*, pages 482–489, Brighton, UK, April 8–11, 1991. Springer, Heidelberg, Germany

GRS16.   Philippe Gaborit, Olivier Ruatta, and Julien Schrek. On the complexity of the rank syndrome decoding problem. *IEEE Transactions on Information Theory*, 62(2):1006–1019, 2016

KHL+22a.   Jon-Lark Kim, Jihoon Hong, Terry Shue Chien Lau, YounJae Lim, Chik How Tan, Theo Fanuela Prabowo, and Byung-Sun Won. REDOG. Submission to KpqC Round 1, 2022

KHL+22b.   Jon-Lark Kim, Jihoon Hong, Terry Shue Chien Lau, YounJae Lim, Chik How Tan, Theo Fanuela Prabowo, and Byung-Sun Won. REDOG and its performance analysis. Cryptology ePrint Archive, Report 2022/1663, 2022. https://eprint.iacr.org/2022/1663

KKGK21.   Jon-Lark Kim, Young-Sik Kim, Lucky Erap Galvez, and Myeong Jae Kim. A modified Dual-Ouroboros public-key encryption using Gabidulin codes. *Appl. Algebra Eng. Commun. Comput.*, 32(2):147–156, 2021

Loi17.   Pierre Loidreau. A new rank metric codes based encryption scheme. In Tanja Lange and Tsuyoshi Takagi, editors, *Post-Quantum Cryptography - 8th International Workshop, PQCrypto 2017*, pages 3–17, Utrecht, The Netherlands, June 26–28, 2017. Springer, Heidelberg, Germany

LPR23.   Tanja Lange, Alex Pellegrini, and Alberto Ravagnani. On the security of REDOG. Cryptology ePrint Archive, Paper 2023/1205, 2023. https://eprint.iacr.org/2023/1205

LT18.   Terry Shue Chien Lau and Chik How Tan. Key recovery attack on McNie based on low rank parity check codes and its reparation. In Atsuo Inomata and Kan Yasuda, editors, *IWSEC 18*, volume 11049 of *LNCS*, pages 19–34, Sendai, Japan, September 3–5, 2018. Springer, Heidelberg, Germany

LTP21.   Terry Shue Chien Lau, Chik How Tan, and Theo Fanuela Prabowo. On the security of the modified Dual-Ouroboros PKE using Gabidulin codes. *Appl. Algebra Eng. Commun. Comput.*, 32(6):681–699, 2021

Ove05.   Raphael Overbeck. A new structural attack for GPT and variants. In *Mycrypt*, volume 3715 of *Lecture Notes in Computer Science*, pages 50–63. Springer, 2005

Ove08.   Raphael Overbeck. Structural attacks for public key cryptosystems based on Gabidulin codes. *Journal of Cryptology*, 21(2):280–301, April 2008

Pra62.   Eugene Prange. The use of information sets in decoding cyclic codes. *IRE Transactions on Information Theory*, 8(5):5–9, 1962

S+21.   William A. Stein et al. *Sage Mathematics Software (Version (9.3))*. The Sage Development Team, 2021. https://www.sagemath.org

Sta11.   Richard P. Stanley. *Enumerative Combinatorics*, volume 1 of *Cambridge Studies in Advanced Mathematics*. Cambridge University Press, 2 edition, 2011

Author Index

H. Seo and S. Kim (Eds.): ICISC 2023, LNCS 14562, pp. 307–308, 2024.
https://doi.org/10.1007/978-981-97-1238-0

Printed in the United States
by Baker & Taylor Publisher Services